4 GROUP BOMBER COMMAND
An Operational Record

4 GROUP BOMBER COMMAND

An Operational Record

Chris Ward

Pen & Sword

AVIATION

First published in Great Britain in 2012 by
Pen & Sword Aviation
an imprint of
Pen & Sword Books Ltd
47 Church Street
Barnsley
South Yorkshire
S70 2AS

ISBN 978 1 84884 884 9

A CIP catalogue record for this book is
available from the British Library

Typeset in Times by
Phoenix Typesetting, Auldgirth, Dumfriesshire

Printed and bound in England by
CPI Group (UK) Ltd, Croydon, CR0 4YY

Pen & Sword Books Ltd incorporates the Imprints of Pen & Sword Aviation, Pen &
Sword Family History, Pen & Sword Maritime, Pen & Sword Military, Pen &
Sword Discovery, Wharncliffe Local History, Wharncliffe True Crime, Wharncliffe
Transport, Pen & Sword Select, Pen & Sword Military Classics, Leo Cooper, The
Praetorian Press, Remember When, Seaforth Publishing and Frontline Publishing

For a complete list of Pen & Sword titles please contact
PEN & SWORD BOOKS LIMITED
47 Church Street, Barnsley, South Yorkshire, S70 2AS, England
E-mail: enquiries@pen-and-sword.co.uk
Website: www.pen-and-sword.co.uk

Foreword and Acknowledgements

As always in my books I have attempted to provide as much detail as possible in the narrative section. There is insufficient space to make mention of every loss of an aircraft and/or crew, and I have, therefore, featured particular squadrons as being representative of the fortunes of all within the Group operating the same aircraft type at the same time.

I would like to register my gratitude to the archivists in the collections department at the Yorkshire Air Museum at Elvington, Bill and Mark Napier and John Larder, for selecting and processing photographs for this publication and for answering queries. Unless otherwise stated the photographs are from this source.

As always I am indebted to my good friend, Andreas Wachtel, for providing photographs of some of the Bomber Command crewmen whose remains rest in Den Burg Cemetery on Texel. The background information on these and the *Luftwaffe* pilots involved in their demise results from Andreas's exhaustive research. Andreas is also responsible for bringing together the information on the crew of John Wilson to whom this book is dedicated. The details of their final flight are described in the appropriate section of this publication.

Chris Ward. Lutterworth, May 2012.

This book is dedicated to James Hopkins and the other seven occupants of 77 Squadron Halifax JD413 KN-G, which crashed in Germany on the way home from Berlin in the early hours of 1 September 1943.

Flight Lieutenant J.L. Wilson	pilot	KIA
Flight Sergeant R.W. Barlow	second pilot	KIA
Sergeant J.F. Hopkins	flight engineer	PoW
Flight Sergeant J.J. Leicester	navigator	PoW
Sergeant R.A. Sims	bomb-aimer	KIA
Sergeant E.J. Wilson	wireless operator	DoI
Sergeant J.A. Baxter	mid-upper gunner	KIA
Pilot Officer K.G. Sheward	rear gunner	KIA

Contents

General Notes

This profile is a reference work on the activities of the squadron during World War II. Bomber Command operated exclusively from stations in the UK, and used overseas bases purely for shuttle operations, or as advanced staging posts for specific purposes. For this reason, periods spent on detachment or permanent postings to overseas Commands do not fall within the scope of this work.

This profile is not intended to serve as a comprehensive squadron history, but to provide as much information as possible in a non-anecdotal form. The brief history narrative is basically an account of Bomber Command's war, with the individual squadrons' involvement interwoven into it. The publications listed in the Bibliography are not only recommended reading, but represent the best available sources of information for serious students of the subject. The operational record is based almost entirely on the figures provided in the *Bomber Command War Diaries* by Martin Middlebrook and Chris Everitt, and I am indebted to Martin Middlebrook for allowing me to use them.

An aircraft is included in Chapter 3 if a) it spent time on squadron charge, no matter how briefly, and irrespectively of whether or not it operated; or b) the type was used operationally by the squadron. Information is restricted in most cases to where from and where to, unless it completed its service with the squadron, in which case some detail of its demise appears. Aircraft which failed to return have the date and target recorded. Where no information follows the serial number of a type still in use when the squadron departed Bomber Command or at war's end, it can be assumed that the aircraft was still on squadron strength. However, where there is a blank space following the serial number of a type which has been withdrawn from service with Bomber Command, it signifies that I don't know its ultimate fate. An absence of information does not imply that the aircraft flew no operations during its time with the squadron.

Finally, information has been drawn from a variety of sources, ranging from Records Branch to individuals with squadron connections, and I am grateful for their contributions. There will inevitably be errors and omissions when dealing with a subject as vast as Bomber Command, and I am happy to be corrected and/or updated by readers.

CHAPTER ONE

A World War II Operational Record

4 Group Bomber Command was born out of the expansion programme prompted by events in Europe during the 'thirties. It was formed at Mildenhall on 1 April 1937 as the offspring of 3 Group, and the future Bomber Command chief, Air Commodore A.T. Harris, was installed as its first Air-Officer-Commanding on 12 June. By the end of the month the Group Headquarters had moved from Suffolk to take up residence at Linton-on-Ouse in Yorkshire, the county with which the Group would forever after be associated. The stations at Leconfield, Driffield, Dishforth and Finningley were brought into the fold along with their resident units, respectively, 97 & 166 Squadrons, 75 & 215 Squadrons, 10 & 78 Squadrons, 7 & 76 Squadrons and 51 & 58 Squadrons, the last two mentioned actually located at Boscombe Down while construction work was in progress at Linton-on-Ouse. The Group inherited a variety of aircraft, Heyfords, Whitleys, Virginias, Wellesleys and Ansons, which reflected the operational and training roles of the squadrons. Apart from the Whitley Mk I, which equipped 10 Squadron only, the remaining types were obsolete. 78 and 58 Squadrons were next to re-equip, and thus accounted for the full meagre production run of a little over thirty machines of the Mk I.

When war came on 3 September 1939, the squadrons of 4 Group alone had the necessary training and experience in night-flying to venture deep into hostile territory, the rest of the Command having been trained for daylight operations in line with the theory of the inviolability of the self-defending bomber formation. Five squadrons, 10, 51, 58, 77 and 102 were declared operational immediately, while 78 Squadron was held in reserve as a Group pool training unit to feed fresh crews into the line. 10 Squadron, known as 'Shiny Ten', was still stationed at Dishforth and was under the command of W/C Staton, a World War I pilot in his early forties. 51 Squadron was commanded by W/C Silvester and resided at Linton-on-Ouse, a station which it shared with 58 Squadron under W/C Potter. 77 and 102 Squadrons, meanwhile, occupied Driffield under the command of W/Cs Bradbury and Toogood respectively. 78 Squadron was the first to receive the Whitley Mk V, and did so during September 1939. Under the command of W/C Harrison, who had been in post since March 1937, 78 Squadron moved to Ternhill on 1

September as part of the 'scatter' arrangement, but returned temporarily to Dishforth on the 15th, where it shared the facilities with 10 Squadron. On the first night of hostilities, the 3/4th, three 51 Squadron Whitleys and seven from 58 Squadron were loaded with more than 5 million propaganda leaflets which were to be dispensed over Hamburg and Bremen in Germany's north, and nine cities in the Ruhr. There were no losses to the enemy defences, but three of the Whitleys landed in France, among them 58 Squadron's K8969 with the crew of F/O O'Neill, which was written off in a forced landing after seven and a half hours in the air. Two 102 Squadron aircraft failed to return from operations on the night of the 8/9th, K8950 coming down east of the Ruhr to deliver the entire crew of S/L Murray into enemy hands, while K8985 strayed into neutral Belgian airspace and was forced to land. Its crew became interned, and although they soon returned to the UK, the Whitley remained and was ultimately destroyed during the German invasion. 58 Squadron sustained its second casualty on the night of the 10/11th, when K8965 crashed on take-off from Rheims-Champagne airfield when bound for a leafleting sortie. The Whitley caught fire, but not before Sgt Dixon and his crew had scrambled clear with nothing more than a few cuts and bruises between them.

The requirements of what the Americans would dub the 'Phoney War' dictated that only paper weapons could be dropped on German soil for fear of reprisals and damage to civilian property. Consequently leaflet operations, known as 'nickels', continued, and despite the ineffectiveness of such efforts in persuading the Germans to capitulate, they provided much useful experience and training in night-flying and navigation over enemy territory. There would be twenty-two nights of such operations between 3 September and Christmas involving 113 sorties, some, as in the case cited above, launched from advanced airfields in France. On the night of 1/2 October, three 10 Squadron Whitleys became the first Allied aircraft to overfly Berlin, and a fourth, K9018 piloted by Flight Lieutenant Allsop, had the doubtful distinction of being the first from the squadron to fail to return, when it disappeared into the North Sea somewhere off Scotland on the way back from Denmark. On 6 October 58 Squadron departed Linton-on-Ouse temporarily for Boscombe Down, and 78 Squadron moved in on the 15th to join 51 Squadron. That arrangement would last only until 9 December when 51 Squadron took up residence at Dishforth, by which time Mk IV Whitleys had largely replaced the unit's Mk IIs and IIIs. 4 Group lost a total of six Whitleys to enemy action or crashes during October, but just one in November. On 1 November W/C Appleton succeeded W/C Bradbury at the helm of 77 Squadron. During December some Whitley crews found themselves assigned to reconnaissance operations, day and night shipping sweeps and security patrols, completing almost eighty sorties without loss. The winter of 1939/40 was harsh, and Whitley crews suffered unbelievable discomfort from the extreme cold inside their unheated aircraft. It speaks great volumes for the courage and determination of the crews, who pressed on deep into enemy territory, and often spent ten hours or more in the air.

1940

For the purpose of this book 58 Squadron's experiences will represent those of 4 Group during the year.

There was very little operational activity to occupy the crews of Bomber Command during January and February as the winter deepened, and it was not until towards the end of February that the freezing conditions loosened their grip. W/C Harrison concluded his time as commanding officer of 78 Squadron on 9 January, and he was succeeded by W/C Wiblin. 4 Group continued with its patrols as conditions allowed, and on the 12th sent aircraft as far as Prague and Vienna for leafleting and reconnaissance. Thereafter, the weather closed in for six weeks, and aircraft were literally frozen to the ground. W/C Burton took over from W/C Toogood at 102 Squadron in the midst of the big freeze on 5 February, and on Valentine's Day 58 Squadron left Boscombe Down and headed back north to take up residence at Linton-on-Ouse alongside 78 Squadron. W/C Silvester relinquished command of 51 Squadron on 5 March and handed the reins to W/C Owen. It was only in March that the first opportunity arose to drop bombs on a German land target, and this came in retaliation for a *Luftwaffe* attack on elements of the Royal Navy at Scapa Flow on the 16th, during which a stray bomb inadvertently killed a civilian on the island of Hoy. The target selected was the seaplane base at Hörnum on the island of Sylt, and the operation by thirty Whitleys and twenty Hampdens was mounted on the 19/20th. The plan allowed the 4 Group force a four-hour window to carry out its attacks, which would be followed up by the Hampdens of 5 Group. 10 Squadron contributed eight aircraft led by W/C Staton, and all returned safely amid wild claims of an outstanding success, which was duly splashed across the front pages of the national press. The reality was that reconnaissance on 6 April could detect little if any damage to the base, but the propaganda value to the folks at home was massive. It is believed that W/C Burton of 102 Squadron undertook his first operation with the squadron on this night, probably flying as a second pilot. Reconnaissance sorties occupied the crews thereafter, and returning from one on 6/7 April, 10 Squadron's K9032 crashed in Lincolnshire after nearly nine hours in the air, although happily without injury to the crew of F/O Pryor, who were able to walk away. During the course of March Mk V Whitleys finally replaced the IVs at 10 and 58 Squadrons, and 51 Squadron would receive its allotment in May. The other 4 Group units had been operating the newer type since the back end of 1939.

On 7 April 4 Group Headquarters swapped Linton-on-Ouse for Heslington Hall, an Elizabethan mansion in a village close to York. Two days later the German invasion of Norway and Denmark brought an end to the shadow-boxing which had characterized events since September, and it was the signal for the bombing war to begin hesitantly, but in earnest. While the Navy tried to do its best after the horse had bolted, and was unable because of the distance to directly support the British and French response at Narvik in the north, Bomber Command targeted airfields in the south which were being used by the enemy to bring in troops and supplies. Elements of 10, 77 and 102

Squadrons detached to a forward base at Kinloss, and on the 15/16th raided the airfield at Stavanger without loss. The operation was repeated on the 20/21st, 10 Squadron this time in company with 51 and 58 Squadrons, and again all returned. On the 21st, the long term of office as 10 Squadron's leader came to an end for W/C Staton, and W/C Singer began a short period of tenure as commanding officer. On the last night of the month 4 Group returned to Sola airfield at Stavanger and Oslo's Fornebu airfield with twelve Whitleys each, but the Battle of Norway had been lost before it even began, and the efforts of Bomber Command could not prevent the inevitable. 58 Squadron experienced its first loss of a crew on this night when N1465 failed to return from Stavanger, and news eventually came through that Sgt Heayes and his crew had lost their lives.

This campaign, however, was only a dress rehearsal for the storm which was about to break. 77 Squadron moved back to Driffield on 4 May in time for the end of the 'Phoney War', which came with the German advance across the Low Countries at first light on the 10th. While the Battle and Blenheim squadrons of the Advanced Air Striking Force and 2 Group were being massacred at Maastricht and Sedan, Bomber Command was sent to attack communications and industry in the Ruhr and west of the Rhine. 10 Squadron sent twelve Whitleys to oil plants and marshalling yards on the 15/16th and succeeding nights, including Bremen on the 17/18th, during which a number of the squadron's crews fired Verey lights to attract the rest of the force, thus employing perhaps the earliest and most rudimentary form of target-marking. It was a time when, for the period, quite large forces were being committed to delay the enemy's progress; over ninety aircraft to northern France on the 20/21st, and 120 on the following night to attack railways in Germany. Even so, such was the need to slow the German advance that the Command was forced to divert a goodly proportion of its resources towards the end of the month to tactical strikes against concentrations of troops and armoured vehicles. A number of 4 Group airmen would survive the early days to go on to greater things, and one of these was P/O Womersley of 102 Squadron. On the 21/22nd, he and his crew were forced to abandon N1528 over France during the course of a raid on a target at Euskirchen, and all arrived safely on the ground to return home. In 1944 Womersley's distinguished career would see him command 139 Squadron, a Mosquito unit in the Pathfinder Light Night Striking Force, and he was destined to finish the war as station commander at Gransden Lodge, home of the Pathfinders' 142 and 405 Squadrons. During the course of the month W/C Sutton succeeded W/C Potter as commanding officer of 58 Squadron, and W/C Groom took over from W/C Burton at 102 Squadron on the 16th. Between 26 May and 3 June the evacuation from Dunkerque occupied substantial elements of Bomber Command, but 4 Group played only a minor role, supplying a handful of Whitleys to make night attacks on German positions around the perimeter. The month of June had started for 77 Squadron with the arrival of W/C MacDonald as the new commanding officer in place of W/C Appleton. He had previously served as a flight commander with 102 Squadron, and had led the earlier mentioned attack on the seaplane base at Hörnum in March.

The largest commitment of aircraft to date saw a mixed force of over 140 attack multiple targets in Germany, including Homberg, on the 3/4th of June. The arrival at Driffield on the 5th of a certain Pilot Officer G.L. Cheshire to join the ranks of 102 Squadron was probably barely noticed. Who could have guessed the extent of his future achievements? He would begin his operational career as second pilot to New Zealander F/O Frank 'Lofty' Long, and they flew their first sortie together on the night of the 9/10th against a bridge at Abbeville. On the following night their target was a bridge at Poix, but poor visibility forced them to bring their bombs home. A few days after Cheshire's arrival on the squadron, he was joined by a friend from his Trinity College Oxford days. P/O Henry Melvin Young, later known as 'Dinghy', would also write his own page in history three years hence as a member of 617 Squadron. On the 11/12th, 4 Group contributed to attacks against wide-ranging targets in Italy, Germany and France. Ten Whitley crews were briefed for communications targets in support of the land battle, and a single 10 Squadron aircraft failed to return. Meanwhile, thirty-six crews were briefed to attack the Fiat works at Turin, in commemoration of that country's entry into the war on the 10th. The 10, 51 and 58 Squadron contingents arrived at Guernsey in the afternoon to top up their fuel tanks, while 77 and 102 Squadrons staged at Jersey airport. Electrical storms and severe icing on the route to the target persuaded many of the participants to abort their sorties, and only ten bombed in the target area, causing little damage to the factory complex. One 77 Squadron aircraft failed to return. The 13/14th was devoted to communications targets in France and the occupied countries, and on the following night the Whitley brigade provided support for the ground forces in a futile effort to save France from imminent collapse. On the 15th W/C Singer was posted to command 101 Squadron, and he was replaced at 10 Squadron by W/C 'Sid' Bufton. Over the ensuing war years he and his brother 'Hal' would make major contributions to the bomber war, although mostly from behind a desk. For five consecutive nights from the 17/18th Whitleys were over Germany, and it was on that first night that 58 Squadron's N1463 suffered engine failure and crashed in Holland during a sortie to the oil town of Gelsenkirchen. F/S Ford and one member of his crew lost their lives, while their three colleagues became the first from the squadron to fall into enemy hands. On the following night the squadron's N1460 crashed in Germany during a sortie to another oil town, Castrop-Rauxel, and there were no survivors from the crew of F/O MacInnes. For the third time in four nights 58 Squadron posted missing another crew to a Ruhr target, this time Essen on the 20/21st, but at least this time F/O Walker and his crew all survived the demise of N1442 to become PoWs. France finally fell on the 22nd, and most of the effort for the remainder of the month was directed at targets in Germany.

It was at this point that the Battle of Britain began, and Bomber Command would play its part by continuing the offensive against communications and industrial targets in Germany and airfields in the occupied countries. On the first night of July five Whitleys were sent to Kiel to attack the German cruiser *Scharnhorst*, and 58 Squadron's N1461 crashed in the target area, killing P/O Jones and all but one of his crew. On the 8th 10 Squadron moved to Leeming, which would be home to the squadron for the next two years. That night over sixty aircraft were despatched to, among other destinations, north German ports and airfields in Holland. Twelve of them were Whitleys, of which one from 10 Squadron failed to return from Kiel. It was back to the Ruhr for eight Whitleys on the night of the 11/12th, when Leverkusen was the target for 58 Squadron's N1424. It failed to return, having crashed in Belgium, and there were no survivors from the crew of Sgt Young. On the 15th 78 Squadron took up residence at Dishforth and was declared operational. It operated for the first time four nights later when four of its Whitleys set out to raid marshalling yards in the Ruhr, led by A Flight commander S/L Wildey. He alone bombed his primary target, railway installations at Recklinghausen at the eastern end of the Ruhr, while the others attacked alternative targets. 78 Squadron's B Flight commander during its operational baptism was S/L 'Charles' J.N.H. Whitworth. He was a short, squat man with the cut-glass accent of the English aristocracy. It was, in fact, Whitworth who led 78 Squadron's second foray on the night of the 20/21st, when aircraft assembly plants at Wenzendorf and Wismar were among the objectives for 4 Group. Assigned to Wenzendorf, Whitworth returned safely in P5001, only to discover that an electrical fault had prevented his bombs from releasing. We will meet up with Whitworth again in due course. Two nights later 58 Squadron lost N1472 to flak over Germany during a sortie to Paderborn, and there were no survivors from the crew of Sgt Jones. Happily, this would be the squadron's last loss for more than a month.

The policy of small-scale raids on multiple targets continued into August, while the Battle of Britain was raging overhead. One of the weird and wonderful devices put forward as a weapon was 'Razzle', incendiary pellets designed to set fire to crops and wooded areas, and on the 11th some Whitley crews were given an opportunity to dispense some of these near Cologne. It was quickly decided that Razzle did not possess war-winning potential, and was consigned to the 'It was worth a try' file. The 'Whitley Boys' were out in force on the night of the 13/14th, twenty returning to the Fiat works at Turin, while seventeen others targeted Milan. One 10 Squadron aircraft lost an engine to a night fighter, and made it back as far as the Kent coast before crashing into the sea with the loss of the pilot and co-pilot. On the 14th W/C MacDonald concluded his tour as commanding officer of 77 Squadron. He was replaced by W/C Jarman, who had arrived from 10 OTU as the new B Flight commander on the 2nd, and would remain at the helm for a considerable time. W/C MacDonald took over at 82 Squadron in 2 Group, where he remained for four months before being screened. In January 1942 he was appointed to command XV Squadron in 3 Group, a position he occupied until the start of June. A month later, and now a Group Captain and station commander at Horsham St Faith, he borrowed a Mosquito from 139 Squadron, as did W/C Oakshott, commanding officer of 105 Squadron, and the pair headed in broad daylight for the port of Flensburg in Northern Germany. Both aircraft were shot down, and while Oakshott and his navigator failed to survive, MacDonald and his crewman spent the remainder of the war as guests of the *Reich*. Whether by design or in error, Driffield found itself the objective for a raid by the *Luftwaffe* on the 15th, which left five 102 Squadron Whitleys in ruins, N1378, N1413, N1420, P4945 and P5022, in addition to a number belonging to 77 Squadron. Damage to the airfield was such that it would be necessary for both squadrons to move out while repairs were undertaken, but until the move took place to Leeming on the 25th, operations continued from battle-scarred Driffield. On the following night forty-eight Whitleys joined 100 other aircraft undertaking wide-ranging operations to German targets, among them the Karl Zeiss optical works at Jena in the east of the country and the M.A.N. factory in Augsburg in the south. Just a week after being forced out of Driffield, 102 Squadron left Leeming and headed up to Prestwick. This was occasioned by a temporary detachment to 15 Group Coastal Command, under whose auspices it would carry out convoy escort duties. One Flight was kept at Aldergrove in Northern Ireland to increase operational range, and the crews settled into a routine of long, tedious and generally uneventful patrols. *(Such operations do not fall within the scope of this work. However, on 7 October Melvin Young would be forced to ditch in the Irish Sea after engine failure, and he and his crew would spend twenty-two hours afloat in their dinghy before rescue came.)* Distant targets in Italy and Germany continued to occupy the Whitley force for the remainder of the month. 77 Squadron changed address again on the 28th with a move to Linton-on-Ouse, but this would also prove to be a temporary home. Returning from Berlin on the night of the 30/31st, 58 Squadron's P5002 ran out of fuel and was abandoned over the Yorkshire coast. P/O Clements and three of his crew were picked up, but the other crew member failed to survive. This proved to be the first of three fuel-related incidents to afflict the squadron.

September brought with it the climax of the Battle of Britain, and for small elements of the Whitley brigade, the long slog to Italy or Berlin on each of the first six nights of the month, with other long-range targets at Munich, Magdeburg and Regensburg thrown in for good measure. Returning from Genoa on the night of the 2/3rd, two 58 Squadron Whitleys ran out of fuel and were forced to ditch. N1427 came down off the Kent coast, and S/L Bartlett and his crew paddled ashore in their dinghy. Meanwhile F/S Moore and his crew were rescued from the cold North Sea, leaving N1459 to its watery fate. 4 Group Whitleys joined forces with types from the other Groups to raid industrial targets in Berlin and other German locations on the 3/4th, to mark the first anniversary of the outbreak of war. The campaign against invasion craft in the occupied ports was still in full swing, and would remain so well into October, even after the threat had diminished with the defeat of the *Luftwaffe* in mid-month. On the 7/8th, a number of Whitleys were employed on flare-dropping over Boulogne to light up the assembled barges for the rest of the force. On three consecutive nights, from the 9/10th to the 11/12th, Whitleys attacked Berlin and Bremen. During the second of these operations 58 Squadron posted missing the crew of P/O Thompson in T4134, who, it was later learned, had survived and were PoWs. Then it was back to the anti-invasion campaign at Dunkerque and Calais on the 13/14th, and Antwerp on the 14/15th. The Battle of Britain reached a crescendo on the 15th, when the *Luftwaffe* suffered its heaviest losses to date, but it would be some time before invasion fever diminished, and consequently, the ports of Zeebrugge and Ostend were attacked on the 17/18th, and Zeebrugge and Antwerp on the following night. Also on the 18/19th a handful of Whitleys targeted Hamm, during which 58 Squadron's P5008 succumbed to a night fighter attack which killed Sgt Crossland and his crew. During the remainder of the month, Whitleys trekked to Berlin a further four times and Magdeburg once, and in-between, supported the attacks on the occupied ports. The Berlin operation on the 23/24th involved 129 aircraft, whose crews were optimistically briefed for eighteen precision targets within the city. It would take the infamous Butt Report eleven months hence for the futility of such requirements to be fully realized. Twenty-four hours later 58 Squadron's N1470 crashed almost immediately after take-off for the capital, and Sgt Cornish and two of his crew were killed when the bomb-load went up. An indication of the endurance and reliability of the Whitley was made manifest on the last night of the month, when 10 Squadron's N1483 ditched in the Irish Sea on return from Berlin after twelve hours forty minutes aloft. Having completely over-flown England, F/O Wood and all of his crew were picked up by a trawler, safe and sound, if a little shaken by their ordeal.

On 2 October W/C Owen concluded his period in command of 51 Squadron and was replaced by W/C Brescon. That night seven Whitleys were sent to Frankfurt am Oder, close to Germany's eastern frontier with Poland, and 58 Squadron's N1434 crashed in Germany without survivors from the crew of F/O Esply. On the 5th Sir Charles Portal relinquished his post as A-O-C Bomber Command after a short term of office, and was appointed Chief-of-the-Air-Staff. He was replaced by Air Marshal Sir Richard Peirse, who was to undergo a torrid time at the hands of the Air Ministry with frequently shifting priorities and an ever-increasing workload of targets. Also on the 5th 77 Squadron changed address yet again with a move to Topcliffe, and 102 Squadron returned to Bomber Command from its maritime duties on the 10th, taking up temporary residence at Linton-on-Ouse. That night 58 Squadron's T4137 suffered engine trouble on the way home from Gelsenkirchen, and crashed while trying to land at Bircham Newton, killing P/O Hadley and his crew. On the 14th a 4 Group element was briefed for an operation that night on the distant port of Stettin on the Baltic coast. They were to attack the synthetic oil plant and, happily, all aircraft returned to home airspace, which was when the problems arose for a number of them, particularly those of 10 Squadron. Flight commander S/L Ferguson and his colleagues had to abandon P4952 over Northumberland when they ran out of fuel after eleven hours in the air. Fortunately they all arrived safely on the ground, but it would prove to be but a temporary reprieve. F/L Tomlinson experienced his second major incident within six weeks, after a similar fuel shortage forced him to give the order to abandon aircraft. Unlike the total survival of the Ferguson crew, however, when the wreckage of T4143 was picked over on the following morning, the bodies of two crew members were found still inside. Perhaps even more poignant for 10 Squadron was the loss of Sgt Wright and his crew earlier in the evening, which had occurred after

P4993 collided with a barrage-balloon cable over Surrey on return from Le Havre. 58 Squadron's T4150 also ran low on fuel on return from Stettin, and was successfully crash-landed in Yorkshire by F/O Brooke. The same crew was on the order of battle for the night of the 20/21st, when another distant location was selected for attention. The Skoda works at Pilsen in Czechoslovakia would occupy the minds of Bomber Command planners for some time to come, and it would prove to be elusive. The night turned into something of a trial for 58 Squadron as its crews returned to home airspace, and F/O Brooke was once more to feature. He was forced to ditch P5058 in the River Humber and survived the experience, as did the other members of his crew, two of whom had been with him six nights earlier. P5089 ditched off the Norfolk coast, and P/O Wilding and his crew were picked up none the worse for their adventure. Finally, T4170 was caught by an intruder over Yorkshire and shot down, killing P/O Brown and two of his crew. Two others survived with injuries, but one of them succumbed two days later.

November 5 was a momentous day in Bomber Command. It brought with it the reformation of 35 Squadron at Boscombe Down, where it was attached to the A&AEE with the specific purpose of introducing the Handley Page Halifax into operational service. Under the command of the portly figure of W/C R.W.P. Collings, the squadron received its first example of the type, L9486, on the 13th. A week later it would move north to Leeming and become 4 Group's latest recruit. Elsewhere the nightly grind continued and men continued to die. It was always tragic when death came to a crew as home and safety were at hand, but it was a frequent occurrence for the crews of Bomber Command, particularly in the early days. Returning from Milan on the 5/6th of November, and after almost twelve hours in the air, 10 Squadron's P/O Jones and his crew ditched in the sea in P5001 and disappeared without trace. On the following night 58 Squadron's P4943 was lost without trace during a sortie to Hamburg, and the names of Sgt Elton and his crew were added to the ever-expanding squadron Roll of Honour. On the 7th, 58 Squadron welcomed a new commanding officer as W/C Smith succeeded W/C Sutton. On the night of the 12/13th, Len Cheshire provided evidence of the press-on spirit that was to characterize his wartime career when piloting P5005 to an oil refinery at Wesseling near Cologne. In an aircraft severely damaged by enemy action, fire and an exploding fire extinguisher, and compounded by injuries to his crew, he took the bomb-load to an alternative target in the form of marshalling yards at Cologne and returned home. For this exploit he was awarded the DSO, the first of his many decorations in a career which would take him to the command of 76 and 617 Squadrons, and culminate in the award of the Victoria Cross after completing 100 operations. A major blow to 10 Squadron on the 13/14th was the loss of the long-serving W/C Ferguson, now the stand-in commanding officer, while W/C Bufton was temporarily absent. Ferguson was last heard from four hours after taking off for the distant town of Merseburg. T4230 failed to return to Leeming and was presumed lost in the sea. On the following night the Whitleys took a beating as the result of an operation to Berlin, when four failed to return, one ditched and one crashed at home. This amounted to six aircraft out of twenty-two despatched, or more than 25 per cent, and 58 Squadron was the hardest hit with three failures to return. Flight Commander S/L Webb was killed with three of his crew when T4174 crashed in Germany, and the sole survivor was taken into captivity. He was joined by Sgt Kerr and his entire crew from T4239. Flak accounted for T4170 over Germany, and there were no survivors from the crew of F/O Champness. 102 Squadron completed its move from Linton-on-Ouse to Topcliffe on the 15th where it joined 77 Squadron, and this time it could look forward to putting down roots for a year. 78 Squadron welcomed a new commanding officer during the course of the month in the form of W/C 'Charles' Whitworth, who was promoted from within to succeed W/C Wiblin. He was to enjoy a long and impressive career, particularly once his operational days were behind him, but that was still a short time in the future. Sixty-eight crews were involved in operations on the 20/21st, forty-three of them briefed for Duisburg. 102 Squadron's commanding officer W/C Groom joined the crew of F/O Selby in P5072, and they all lost their lives when the Whitley crashed into the North Sea on the way home, almost four and a half hours after take-off. A new commanding officer would not be appointed until the New Year, but in the meantime operations continued, and the Royal Arsenal at Turin was selected for attention on the 23/24th. 102 Squadron's T4216 didn't quite make it back to terra firma because of a shortage of fuel, and this forced F/O H.M. Young to ditch the Whitley in the Channel off the coast of Devon. Thereafter, he and his crew were required to paddle around in their dinghy until rescue came, the second such experience for Young in a matter of six weeks. Almost inevitably, Young acquired the nickname that he carried to his untimely death in the sea off Holland in May 1943, on return from 617 Squadron's epic Operation *Chastise*. His contribution to the success of the operation was acknowledged by Gibson, particularly with regard to his role in overseeing the training of the crews. It should also be remembered that Young's bomb was the first to be delivered accurately against the Möhne Dam, and almost certainly sealed the structure's fate.

The pattern of operations remained more or less the same for the remainder of the year, and 58 Squadron registered its first incident in December on the night of the 2/3rd. T4207 crashed in Yorkshire on return from Lorient, but Sgt Gosling and his crew emerged unscathed from the wreckage. In retaliation for recent heavy *Luftwaffe* attacks on British cities, including the devastating one on Coventry in mid-November, Sir Richard Peirse launched 134 aircraft against Mannheim on 16/17 December, the largest force yet to a single target. The operation was led by experienced crews who were to start fires in the city centre to act as a beacon to those following behind. Despite clear conditions, the initial bombing was not accurate and the raid became scattered. Nevertheless, 240 buildings were destroyed or damaged and only three aircraft failed to return. Earlier on the 16th W/C Brescon was posted from 51 Squadron to be replaced by W/C James Tait, an officer who would become something of a legend as the war progressed, and who, in November 1944, would lead 617 Squadron to success against the mighty battleship *Tirpitz*. Returning early from Boulogne with technical problems, 58 Squadron's P5098 collided with a parked Lysander of 4 Squadron and both aircraft burst into flames. F/O Clements and all but one of his crew escaped unhurt, but the rear gunner lost his life. On that same night the squadron's T4159 crashed into the sea somewhere off the Devon coast, and no trace of it or the crew of Sgt Smith was ever found.

The Bordeaux operation of the 27/28th was directed at an aircraft factory, and involved nine Whitleys as part of a force of seventy-five aircraft. It proved to be a testing time for two participating pilots from 77 Squadron who were examples of officers who would go on to distinguished careers, although sadly, neither of them would survive the war. F/L Gomm was trying to land P5111 at Abingdon after eleven hours in the air, but the Whitley crashed, happily without injury to those on board. F/L Gomm, whose life and career in many ways paralleled that of Dambuster W/C Guy Gibson, was from an expatriate family resident in Brazil, although he was educated in England. *(Gibson's parents were in India.)* Following his tour with 77 Squadron, he would undergo a tour on night fighters, *(as did Gibson)* and eventually be the first commander of 467 Squadron RAAF in 1942/43, a 5 Group Lancaster unit, which would gain a fine reputation for efficiency and performance under his leadership. His personal reputation was based on leading his squadron from the front, and it was while doing this in August 1943 that he lost his life during an operation to Milan. Flight commander S/L Robinson was also experiencing difficulties while returning from Bordeaux in T4335, and this Whitley eventually crashed in South Wales, again without injury to the crew. This officer's future career would see him command 78 Squadron early in the coming year, and twice command 35 Squadron, the first Halifax unit in the Command, and attain the status of Group Captain and Station Commander at Graveley, from where he would fly to Berlin in August 1943 after his operational service had officially ended, and fail to return.

It had been a curious year in a number of ways, although without a precedent to go on, the crews had probably not noticed. The unreality of the 'Phoney War' had been shattered in May, and from then on it had been a backs-to-the-wall struggle to present a defiant face to an, as yet, all-conquering enemy. Worryingly, the coming year was to produce little in the way of improvements to encourage optimism. This was despite the fact that three new bomber types had been put into the hands of a squadron, each in preparation for their introduction to operational service early in the New Year. Leonard Cheshire was to be part of this. He flew his last operation for 102 Squadron against Merignac airfield in the south of France on 27/28 December, and before long he would join 35 Squadron, a newly-reformed unit selected to blood the Halifax. The fact that Britain was still in the war at the end of 1940 was a surprise to many looking on from the outside, but if the conflict was eventually to be won, the fight had to be taken to Germany itself and Bomber Command was the only offensive arm which could do this. For the crews in general, the coming year promised more of the same, and as events were to prove, much of it would be spent treading water.

1941

First quarter

The year began in harsh weather conditions and with operations directed mainly against ports in Germany and along the occupied coast, principally Bremen and Wilhelmshaven. The former was the destination for the year's first major operation on New Year's Night, and the Focke-Wulf aircraft factory received some hits. Earlier in the day 102 Squadron had welcomed W/C Cole as its new commanding officer some six weeks after the loss in action of W/C Groom. A return to Bremen on the following night was much less effective, and it resulted in the loss of 102 Squadron's T4227 which was shot down into the sea off the Yorkshire coast by an intruder. Sadly there were no survivors, and the loss of this crew, captained by F/O Desmond Coutts, was a bitter blow to Leonard Cheshire. Coutts had served his apprenticeship as second pilot to Cheshire, and had been on the trip to Wesseling which had not only almost cost Cheshire his life but had also resulted in the award of his DSO. 35 Squadron doubled its complement of production Halifaxes on the 4th with the arrival of L9487, and this was followed on the 12th by L9489. Tragedy struck on the following day when L9487 crashed in Yorkshire during a fuel consumption test, and F/O Henry DFC and his five passengers were killed. Also on that day W/C Wilson was appointed to replace W/C Tait at 51 Squadron, and he would preside over a loss-free period that would take the squadron through to the second week of February. Meanwhile, W/C Tait and three other 51 Squadron crews were attached to Ringway on the 15th, along with four crews selected from 78 Squadron. They were to train in the art of delivering airborne troops of the recently-formed X Troop No 11 SAS Battalion for Operation *Colossus*, a specially conceived attack on the Tragino aqueduct in Italy, which if successful would become the forerunner of future airborne operations. Wilhelmshaven was the destination for eighty aircraft on the night of the 16/17th, following up the previous night's successful operation. This time, however, the raid failed to produce more than light damage, and 10 Squadron registered its first loss of the year when T4220 failed to return and was lost without trace with the crew of F/O Skyrme. On the previous day a new Air Ministry directive had pointed to a critical period ahead for the German oil industry, and a list of seventeen production sites was drawn up for attention, the top nine of which represented around 80 per cent of total output. It would be February before the directive was put into effect but even then, French and German ports would continue to feature along with other urban targets in Germany.

The beginning of February saw operations directed largely against French ports, but a reaffirming of the Oil Plan in January meant that the crews would be going to industrial Germany until the next Air Ministry directive was issued. On 3 February the Whitleys bound for Operation *Colossus* under W/C Tait flew from Ringway to Mildenhall, where they remained until departing for Malta on the evening of the 7th. They arrived at Luqa airfield at dawn on the 8th after an eleven-hour flight, and had to land on a strip pitted with craters from the constant *Luftwaffe* bombardment. The plan was for six of the Whitleys to carry members of X Troop, while two others were detailed to deliver a diversionary attack on the marshalling yards at Foggia some 30 miles away. The operation took place on the night of the 10/11th, all but one of the aircraft delivering its parachutists into the correct location. Unfortunately one crew got lost and dropped its troops into the wrong valley along with a large amount of explosives and that left insufficient available to destroy the viaduct, although it was severely damaged. The 78 Squadron Whitley T4167, which had been assigned to the diversionary bombing of Foggia, developed engine problems and had to be abandoned south of Naples by P/O Wotherspoon and his crew and, once on the ground, they were quickly rounded up by the Italian military. As a result of this, the night's only loss, the planned rendezvous between X Troop and a Royal Navy submarine which was to take them home was cancelled and the entire commando force joined the Whitley crew in captivity.

The Command's big effort for the month was directed at industrial targets in the city of Hanover and took place while Operation *Colossus* was in progress hundreds of miles away on the other side of the Alps. The 222 aircraft despatched represented the largest number to date to a single target, and 183 crews claimed to have reached and bombed their primaries. Inhospitable weather conditions continued to affect the number of aircraft reaching targets, however, and only twenty-seven from seventy-nine got as far as Bremen on the following night. Although no aircraft were lost to the defences, twenty-two crashed while trying to land after fog shrouded their bases. 51 Squadron was particularly hard hit and suffered the loss of four aircraft. Sgts Fenton, Bowyer and Beddow and crews abandoned P4974, P4981 and P5013 respectively over Yorkshire, sustaining a number of injuries in the process, and P/O Sharp and crew left T4217 to its fate over Norfolk and also picked up a number of knocks. Operations at this time were mostly low-key, employing small numbers of aircraft against multiple targets and were consequently rarely effective. W/C Whitworth departed 78 Squadron on the 14th to be replaced by W/C Toland, whose period in command would be brief indeed. That night became the first to be devoted to the German oil industry under the new directive, when Gelsenkirchen and Homberg were attacked. Whitleys were not called into action on this night, but twenty-seven of the type participated in a raid on the Holten plant at Sterkrade twenty-four hours later. The final week of the month saw Whitleys raiding Düsseldorf on the 21/22nd and 24/25th, Calais on the 23/24th and Cologne on the 26/27th; the 78 Squadron element on the last mentioned occasion led by the new commanding officer. On return, and apparently off track, P4996 crashed into high ground in Scotland, killing W/C Toland and all the others on board.

It was Cologne that opened the March account on the 1/2nd, and in contrast to the raid of a few days previously this was reasonably effective, and left some useful damage in the docks area on both sides of the Rhine. Two more 51 Squadron Whitleys failed to return, however, and the crews of Sgt Beddow and Sgt Bruce were posted missing. The former's N1481 disappeared into the sea with no survivors, while the latter's P5108 was crash-landed on a sandbank off the German coast, from where they were rescued by the enemy. Sadly, the rescue aircraft crashed on landing and three of the captives were killed, leaving Sgt Bruce and one other to continue their journey to a PoW camp. (*Bomber Command Losses* Vol 2, W.R. Chorley.) The same operation brought the end for 10 Squadron's Sgt Hoare and his crew, who disappeared into the North Sea in T4265. This attack was followed up on the night of the 3/4th, but this time only the fringes of the city were hit. 78 Squadron's new commanding officer was appointed on the 6th to fill the gap created by the loss of W/C Toland. The already mentioned Basil Vernon 'Robbie' Robinson was a pre-war pilot from the North-East who was promoted from within to take up the reins. On the 9th yet another new Air Ministry directive was received, which changed the emphasis of the Command's operations from oil to maritime matters. Unacceptably high shipping losses to U-boats in the Atlantic forced the War Cabinet to order an all-out assault on this menace and its partner in crime, the long-range reconnaissance bomber, the Focke-Wulf Condor. They were to be hunted down at sea, in their bases and at the point of their manufacture, and the new campaign would begin at Hamburg in three days' time. Meanwhile, the supply of Halifaxes to 35 Squadron had been little more than a trickle, but fifteen crews were by this time under instruction, and seven were declared operational to enable the squadron to venture into battle for the first time. In the event six crews took off on the evening of the 10th, led by W/C Collings in L9486. It was intended to be a gentle introduction to operations with an attack on the docks at Le Havre. Four crews did actually locate and bomb the target, while another attacked an alternative objective and the sixth was forced to abort with flak damage. On return L9489 was intercepted by an RAF fighter over the Surrey/ Hampshire border, and shot down. S/L Gilchrist and one of his crew managed to parachute to safety as the only survivors. Gilchrist would become the first official commanding officer of 405 Squadron later in the year.

   The first salvoes of the maritime campaign were delivered upon Hamburg on the night of the 12/13th. Twenty-five Whitleys joined fifty-three other aircraft and inflicted some damage on the Blohm & Voss U-boat yards, while a second force raided Bremen, the home, as already stated, of a Focke-Wulf aircraft factory which also took a number of hits. A third contingent went to Berlin with poor results, and 102 Squadron's T4326 fell victim to flak over Holland and crashed. F/L 'Lofty' Long, Len Cheshire's guide and mentor in the earliest days of his operational career, lost his life with three of his crew, while the sole survivor was marched off into captivity. Even greater success was gained at Hamburg on the following night, when two 35 Squadron Halifaxes took part in what would be the squadron's last operation for a month. Other elements of the Command inflicted some useful damage at Gelsenkirchen twenty-four hours later as part of the oil campaign. Attacks followed on Bremen and Kiel on the 17/18th and 18/19th respectively. The latter was the most effective raid on this target to date, but it was on return from here that 10 Squadron's T4202 was partially abandoned over Yorkshire after a fire developed. When the wreckage was examined on the following morning the body of the pilot, Sgt Watson, was found still at the controls.

Lorient was the target for Whitleys and Manchesters on the 20/21st, and then apart from an inconclusive raid on Berlin by a force which included twenty-eight Whitleys on the 23/24th, minor operations saw out the remainder of the month. A similar incident to that of the 18/19th saw another 10 Squadron aircraft, Z6477, abandoned by its crew in the early hours of the 28th, this time near Grantham on 5 Group's patch. It occurred on return from a small-scale raid on Düsseldorf, and happily it was resolved without loss of life among the crew of S/L Holford. On the 29th the German cruisers *Scharnhorst* and *Gneisenau* were reported to be off Brest, and by the following day they had taken up residence, thus beginning an eleven-month saga which would be taxing in the extreme for Bomber Command. A total of 109 assorted aircraft took off that night to attack them, in the event scoring no hits.

Second quarter

The presence of the *Scharnhorst* and *Gneisenau* at Brest would occupy much of the Command's attention during the month of April, and would continue to do so until the infamous 'Channel Dash' episode in February 1942 finally resolved the matter. On the 1st of the month 4 Group was boosted by the addition of the first of two new squadrons. Up to this point 104 Squadron had been a training unit, absorbed into 13 OTU in April 1940. Now it was being reformed as a front-line Wellington squadron at Driffield, and had actually received the first examples of its Merlin-powered Mk IIs, W5417 and W5417 on 20 March. By the end of April this number would have risen to sixteen aircraft. The advantage of the Mk II was its ability to carry the new 4,000lb 'cookie' light case blast bomb, the so-called blockbuster. The first operation would be mounted in May, and until then working-up proceeded under the initial supervision of S/L Tomlinson. On the night of the 3/4th ninety aircraft tried again to hit the German lodgers at Brest and fared no better, and 51 Squadron registered the loss of two aircraft, one of them to the sort of unfortunate 'friendly fire' incident which are all too common in war. Z6556 fell victim to the defences and crashed in France, killing F/L Harrington and his crew, but T4299 was shot down by a Hurricane over Dorset, and although P/O Sharpe and three of his crew survived intact, one man lost his life. Two 77 Squadron crews also encountered difficulties on their return home on this night, and the outcome for both was unfortunate. P4947 stalled and crashed while Sgt Kyle was trying to land at Topcliffe and he died with all but one of his crew, and Sgt Dowling was diverted to Tangmere where he and two others of his crew were killed in the attempt to land Z6583. Two more attacks went in at Brest on the 4/5th and 6/7th, with just two Whitleys participating in the latter. It was after the former, however, that one crew claimed a hit on one of the ships, which could not be confirmed. What was confirmed, however, was that an unexploded bomb had lodged in the dry dock occupied by the *Gneisenau*, and her captain decided to move her out into the harbour on the following day while it was dealt with. Despite being moored in comparatively open water, the *Gneisenau* was protected on all sides by dozens of flak guns, and her position made an attack by torpedo almost impossible. Nevertheless, a lone Coastal Command Beaufort delivered a near-perfect attack into the teeth of the most ferocious flak barrage and caused severe damage to the vessel, which would take six months to repair. F/O Campbell and his crew can have had no illusions about their chances of survival, and all died in the wreckage of their aircraft immediately after the attack. In recognition of his gallantry, the pilot was posthumously awarded the Victoria Cross.

78 Squadron moved from Dishforth to Middleton-St-George on the 7th. It was a new station, opened in January, and for the time being at least, 78 Squadron would be its only resident unit. Forty-nine Whitleys joined forces with 180 other aircraft to deliver an unusually telling blow on Kiel that night, inflicting particular damage in the docks area where two U-boat yards were put out of action for a number of days. Just four aircraft failed to return, and one of the two missing Whitleys was 102 Squadron's Z6468, captained on this night by W/C Cole; he and his crew were killed when it crashed into the sea. His replacement would not be appointed until the 21st, but in the meantime the squadron would continue to operate under one of its flight commanders. A follow-up at Kiel on the following night was also accurate for the loss of just four aircraft, but a further nine crashed in the UK on their return. Brest remained the principal target throughout the month, receiving in all another six raids, while Kiel, Cologne, Bremen, Berlin and Mannheim also featured. On the 12th W/C Bufton and one complete flight departed 10 Squadron to convert onto Halifaxes with 35 Squadron at Linton-on-Ouse, in preparation for the reformation of 76 Squadron as the second Halifax unit. He was replaced as commanding officer by W/C V.B. Bennett, not to be confused with W/C D.C.T. Bennett whose period of command lay in the future. Training of the 76 Squadron crews began on the 15th, and that night 35 Squadron returned to the fray when sending five Halifaxes to Kiel. Kiel continued to be a popular target throughout the month, receiving further visits from forces containing Whitleys on the 15/16th, 24/25th, 25/26th and on the last night of the month. It was an operation to Bremen that resulted in 10 Squadron's only loss of the month. Z6557 crashed off the Dutch coast on return on the 16/17th, and took with it Sgt Salway and his crew. Whitleys were also present at Berlin, Düsseldorf, Cologne and Mannheim during the course of the month, but the attacks continued to be more of a nuisance value than to have any meaningful effect on Germany's war effort. W/C Howes was appointed to the command of 102 Squadron on the 21st, and two days later 4 Group's second new Wellington unit was formed at Driffield.

405 Squadron had the honour of becoming the very first RCAF bomber unit to be formed overseas under Article XV of the BACTP agreement. To avoid confusion with other dominion air force units, all Canadian squadrons were to be numbered within the 400–450 range. 405 Squadron came into existence on 23 April 1941 under the temporary command of S/L Tomlinson DFC who, for the previous three weeks, had been in command of fellow new boys and Driffield residents, 104 Squadron. It is not certain that he transferred immediately to 405, but S/L Beare stepped into his shoes at 104 on the 23rd. Just like 104, 405 Squadron was to operate the Merlin-powered Mk II Wellington, and these would, in fact, be the only two units in Bomber

Command to be entirely equipped with the variant. A few examples of the type had by this time found their way into a number of radial-powered Wellington squadrons, but they were additional to the standard equipment. The first four aircraft, W5487, W5489, W5490 and W5491 were taken on 405 Squadron charge on 6 May, and within a month a further ten would be added.

The first three weeks of May brought a hectic round of operations, beginning at Hamburg on the 2/3rd. No major damage occurred, and it was a similar story at Cologne on the 3/4th. Unconfirmed hits were claimed on the German cruisers at Brest on the 4/5th, and on the following night Mannheim escaped with superficial damage despite the claims by 120 crews to have bombed the target. Eighty crews made similar claims after raiding Hamburg on the 6/7th, but the fact that only thirty-three people were bombed out tells its own story. It was better news on the 8/9th, however, when 180 aircraft returned there and left dozens of large fires burning. A simultaneous attack by 133 aircraft on Bremen included seventy-eight Whitleys, two of which failed to return. One of them was 10 Squadron's P4946, which ditched off the Dutch coast on return, and the crew of P/O Guest all fell into enemy hands. Later on the 9th, W/C Burnett was appointed as the new commanding officer of 51 Squadron, arriving in time to despatch a squadron contingent to the twin towns of Mannheim and Ludwigshafen that night. Moderate damage was inflicted at both locations for the loss of one Wellington and a single Whitley, the latter P5106 of 51 Squadron which was shot down by a night fighter over Holland on the way home with no survivors from the crew of P/O Myers. This was the night on which 104 Squadron opened its account, and all of its participants returned home safely. The busy period continued at Hamburg on the 10/11th, when P/O Gough, who had survived a training crash shortly before Christmas, died with his crew after P5048 disappeared into the sea on the way home. S/L Beare relinquished his temporary command of 104 Squadron on the 11th to make way for W/C Simonds, but he would return to the hot seat in time. The night of the 11/12th was the second occasion on which simultaneous raids took place against Hamburg and Bremen, the latter with a strong Whitley presence. Each operation was rewarded with a respectable degree of success, but a return to Mannheim and Ludwigshafen on the 12/13th was disappointing.

S/L Tomlinson undertook 405 Squadron's very first flight on the 15th, with a round trip from base to Linton-on-Ouse and Dishforth, and was accompanied by among others F/O Wigham, the squadron gunnery leader. Meanwhile, Whitleys formed part of forces sent to Hanover on the 15/16th, Cologne on the 16/17th and 17/18th, and Kiel on the following night, none of which produced anything outstanding. On the 20th W/C Gilchrist, a Canadian, was posted from 35 Squadron at Linton-on-Ouse where he had been a flight commander, and was installed as 405 Squadron's first official commanding officer. It will be recalled that he had survived being shot down by an RAF fighter on return from the first Halifax operation in March. Over the succeeding three weeks he would oversee the training of the crews as they worked up to operational status, but even when this was achieved, the squadron's initial contribution to the offensive would be modest. It was also going to take time to build up a strong Canadian presence, and in the meantime the squadron was a polyglot of nationalities, just like any other in the Command. S/L Bisset would be appointed A Flight commander on the 28th, and S/L Keddy B Flight commander on the 30th. By the end of its first full month, 405 Squadron would boast nine officers, 238 airmen and twelve aircraft, the last mentioned all grounded with a nacelle bearing weakness.

Meanwhile, W/C Jarman completed his tour as commanding officer of 77 Squadron on the 21st, and a week later he was appointed to the command of 76 Squadron as successor to W/C Bufton who was promoted to Group Captain and appointed Station Commander at the newly-completed station at Pocklington. Jarman was replaced at 77 Squadron by W/C Hanafin, who had previously served as a flight commander with 10 Squadron. Following Kiel on the 18/19th the Whitley brigade had not been committed in numbers again until the 27/28th, when forming the bulk of a force briefed for Cologne. A few high-explosive bombs were scattered around the city, and over 150 buildings were damaged to some extent. Fourteen Whitleys attempted to bomb the *Tirpitz* at Kiel on the following night, but thick cloud and storms dissuaded all but three crews from pressing on to the target. The *Tirpitz* remained undamaged, and 78 Squadron's Z6484 was the single Bomber Command casualty, falling victim either to the defences or the conditions and crashing in Germany with fatal consequences for Sgt Copley and his crew.

Düsseldorf received the first of its eight raids of varying sizes during June on the night of the 2/3rd, and reported only scattered superficial damage. On the 4th 76 Squadron completed its move from Linton-on-Ouse to Middleton-St-George, where it now shared the facilities with 78 Squadron. Results by an all-Whitley force at Dortmund on the 8/9th were equally as disappointing as those at Düsseldorf, and 51 Squadron's Z6663 crashed in Yorkshire on return, killing Sgt Stubbs and his crew. The well-trodden route to Brest was rejoined by Hampdens, Wellingtons and Whitleys on the 10/11th, but again no hits were scored on the German lodgers, which had now been joined by the *Prinz Eugen*. Over 200 aircraft were in action on the night of the 11/12th of June to a variety of targets, the principal ones Düsseldorf and Duisburg. It was a record night for 35 Squadron, which put up nine Halifaxes for the latter. On the following night the squadron sent eight Halifaxes to Hüls in company with three from 76 Squadron on its first operation. This was a busy night on which briefings took place for three other targets. Eighty Whitley crews were assigned to railway yards at Schwerte, but in the presence of ground haze only half the force bombed. This was also the operational debut for 405 Squadron, which had eight Mk II Wellingtons and five crews fit and ready to go. Four took off, and although W5484 turned back with mechanical failure, the others completed the operation and returned home safely. The Reaper nearly claimed another 10 Squadron crew on this night when Z6721 was forced to ditch following an early return. Fortunately, P/O Littlewood and crew survived the experience, and were picked up some hours later after receiving unexpected help from the crew of a Heinkel 111, which had seen them struggling with their upturned dinghy and directed an ASR launch to their rescue. (W.R. Chorley, *Bomber Command Losses* Vol 2.) For the remainder of the month, Cologne and Düsseldorf featured prominently, and were attacked simultaneously on no fewer than nine occasions by forces of varying sizes between the nights of the 15th and the 30th. Whitleys were involved at the former on the 16/17th, 17/18th, 23/24th, 24/25th, 25/26th and 26/27th, and at the latter on the 15/16th, 19/20th, 21/22nd and 25/26th.

W/C Smith was posted from 58 Squadron on the 15th after a seven-month tour as commanding officer. In March 1943 he would be appointed to command 5 Group's 9 Squadron, only to be killed in action a few weeks later. His successor at 58 Squadron was W/C Clarke, who was to enjoy a lengthy spell at the helm. 35 Squadron set another record when sending ten Halifaxes to Hanover in company with other aircraft for a small-scale raid on the 15/16th that started a large fire. Cologne and Düsseldorf were the main targets on the night of the 16/17th, and it was to the former that a 405 Squadron contingent operated in company with 100 other aircraft of four types. The raid was disappointing, scattering a few bombs across the city, and 405 Squadron's Sgt MacGregor and his crew were last heard transmitting on w/t at 03.03, four hours after take-off. W5522 never arrived back, and presumably crashed into the sea on the way home, taking its crew to an unknown grave and endowing them with the dubious privilege of being the first names on the squadron's Roll of Honour. Unlike their squadron colleagues a few nights earlier, the 10 Squadron crew of Sgt Bradford had no guardian angel in the form of an enemy crew to save them when they crashed into the sea off the North Frisians on return from Bremen in Z6671 on the 18/19th, and all lost their lives. On the 20th 405 Squadron moved to Pocklington, the station which, as already mentioned, had opened as recently as April under the command of G/C Sid Bufton. The battleship *Tirpitz* became a target in its berth at Kiel, and the Halifax squadrons were given an opportunity to attack it. Over 100 aircraft took part on the 20/21st, including six Halifaxes from 35 Squadron and five from 76, but the target was not identified and the town became the focus of attention. 405 Squadron now had sixteen Wellingtons on charge, but only half were fit for operations, along with eight crews. As the only residents of Pocklington for the time being, the squadron had the honour of launching the station's first offensive foray late on the evening of the 22nd. W5476 was first away with Sgt Richard at the controls, and it was followed by six others after technical problems grounded a seventh. Two returned early, and a third crew jettisoned its bombs after failing to locate the target of Wilhelmshaven. This was not an unusual occurrence, and not one of the twenty-five other participating crews managed to land a bomb within 4 kilometres of the town. Further attempts were made on the *Tirpitz* on the 23/24th and 26/27th and by daylight on the 30th. This last occasion involved six Halifaxes from 35 Squadron in two vics led by James Tait, who had reverted to the rank of Squadron Leader following his posting from the command of 51 Squadron. Heavy and accurate flak greeted the small force, but an effective attack was delivered before fighters arrived on the scene and shot down L9499. This was the first 35 Squadron aircraft to fail to return from operations, and it was later learned that F/L Robison had died with five of his crew. Following this operation Tait was awarded the first of his record number of DSOs.

The month ended with operations to Bremen on the 27/28th and 29/30th, each employing over 100 aircraft, and a general attack on the Ruhr area on the night of the 30th for which Cologne, Duisburg and Düsseldorf were designated the primary objectives. The first of the Bremen operations was a disaster for 4 Group, 10, 77 and 102 Squadrons losing between them eleven of the thirty-five Whitleys despatched, and together with three missing Wellingtons this amounted to a new record casualty rate for a single night. Some of the more than 100 participating crews bombed Hamburg in error, and the night fighters enjoyed a major success. It was certainly 10 Squadron's worst experience to date with four missing aircraft and crews. P5016 crashed in the general target area, killing Sgt Knape and three of his crew but Sgt Lewis, who survived, was later reported shot by the SS after escaping from a PoW camp. P5055 also came down in north Germany, with no survivors from the crew of Sgt Rickcord. Sgt Shaw was killed with his crew in T4179, and Z6561 was hit by flak and abandoned over Kiel Bay, Sgt Gregory and three of his crew surviving as PoWs. An expensive end to 10 Squadron's month was complete when P5018 failed to return from Duisburg on the last night of June and P/O Barrett and one other were killed, and Z6584 fell victim to an intruder over Norfolk on return, resulting in the deaths of Sgt Beveridge and one of his crew.

Third quarter

After four months of maritime-related operations, July would bring a new focus for the Command in general. There was little change in the pattern of operations at the start of the month, however, and the situation at Brest continued to divert the Command's resources from more useful targets in Germany. After a blank night on the 1/2nd, the month began with Whitleys involved in operations in reasonable numbers on the following eight nights. Chronologically, the first objectives were Cologne on the 2/3rd, Essen on the 3/4th, Brest on the 4/5th, Münster on the 5/6th and Dortmund on the 6/7th. It was during the Münster operation that 10 Squadron's Z6793 fell victim to a night fighter over Holland, and P/O Goulding and his crew were killed. Dortmund accounted for two 77 Squadron crews after both Z6642 and Z6652 were brought down onto Dutch soil. The latter certainly fell victim to flak, but happily both crews, those of Sgt Bizley and P/O Simmonds survived intact to be taken prisoner. On the following night Z6799 was shot down by a night fighter also over Holland during the course of an operation to Osnabrück, and just one man survived as a PoW from the crew of the experienced F/L Petley DFC. Two nights later, an operation to Aachen claimed the lives of Sgt McLean and his crew when Z6743 crashed in Belgium, and this concluded an expensive first quarter of the new month for 77 Squadron.

The month had begun for 35 Squadron with the departure of W/C Collings to pastures new on the 3rd. His career would continue to flourish, and he was destined to return to the operational scene in June 1943 as a Group Captain and commanding officer of 8 Group's 156 Squadron at Warboys, a role which he was to combine with that of Station Commander. In February 1944 he would be appointed Station Commander at another 8 Group station at Bourn before moving to a similar post at Little Staughton in March. His successor at 35 Squadron was W/C Robinson, who had just completed a four-month tour as commanding officer of 78 Squadron. 78 Squadron's new commanding officer was W/C Sawyer, who had completed over twenty operations with 10 Squadron in 1940/41 before becoming a founder member and flight commander of 76 Squadron, the second unit to receive the Halifax and now a fellow resident of Middleton-St-George. Another new Air Ministry directive issued on the 9th indicated the enemy's transport system and the morale of the civilian population as the weak points, and attacks on these would form the basis of the latest campaign now that the maritime diversion was over. The major railway centres ringing the Ruhr were the primary targets, to restrict the import of raw materials and the export of finished war-related products. Railways were precision targets requiring clear conditions and they were to be attacked on any night offering good visibility, while on moonless nights area raids were to take place on Cologne, Duisburg and Düsseldorf. On dark, dirty nights, the bomber force would roam further afield into central and southern Germany, but some effort would continue to be directed at the German warships at Brest. A predominantly Whitley force claimed good results at Osnabrück on the 7/8th but 10 Squadron again lost a crew, that of Sgt Black in Z6816 which crashed into the sea off Yorkshire with no survivors. A similar fate presumably befell F/S Lewis and his crew, who disappeared without trace in Z6627 on the following night when Hamm was the target. Also on this night 78 Squadron's T4209 was damaged by flak, and had to be ditched off the east coast. The observer, Sgt Hafferden, swam 9 miles to the shore to raise the alarm, but the effort took him many hours and by the time the search was initiated, no sign of Sgt McQuitty and the remaining members of his crew could be found. A change of leadership at 104 Squadron saw S/L Beare promoted from his flight commander post to replace W/C Simonds on the 20th. A few days earlier the squadron had suffered its first loss since being reformed. On the night of the 14/15th W5513 was shot down by a night fighter over Holland while bound for Hanover, and there were no survivors from the crew of P/O Rowse.

Sporadic losses now belonged to the past, as the enemy defences became more organized and adept in the face of greater Bomber Command activity. A steady rate of attrition would afflict all front-line squadrons from now on, and multiple losses from a single operation would become a regular feature. A hangover from the maritime campaign, the German capital ships at Brest remained a target, and a complicated major daylight operation was drawn up for the 24th. The plan was for three high-flying Fortress Is from 2 Group's 90 Squadron to attract the enemy fighters, while eighteen 5 Group Hampdens performed a similar role at a less rarefied altitude under the umbrella of three squadrons of Spitfires. This, it was intended, would allow a force of seventy-nine Wellingtons from 1, 3 and 4 Groups and a force of Halifaxes to sneak in and carry out the attack. On the eve of the operation reconnaissance revealed that the *Scharnhorst* had slipped out of Brest and was now at La Pallice, some 200 miles further south. Consequently, it was decided to send the Halifaxes to attack the *Scharnhorst*, while the remainder of the original plan went ahead against *Prinz Eugen* and *Gneisenau* at Brest. A forward base was used for the Halifax element at Stanton Harcourt from where they took off at around 10:30 hours. Without the comfort of an escort the fifteen Halifaxes, nine of which were from 35 Squadron, were met by intense flak and fighter opposition, despite which sufficient damage was inflicted upon *Scharnhorst* to necessitate her return to Brest where better repair facilities were on hand. This success cost 35 Squadron two Halifaxes and 76 Squadron three, and not one of the surviving ten aircraft escaped damage entirely. A combination of flak and a fighter accounted for L9512, which was successfully abandoned by F/S Greaves and his crew who were taken into captivity. F/S Godwin and four of his crew perished when L9527 went down.

405 Squadron contributed nine Wellingtons to the attack at Brest, led by W/C Gilchrist in W5551. Despite the Fortress and Hampden distractions, the Wellington force met a stronger than expected fighter response, and the flak defence from the ships and batteries around the port was always spirited. Six hits were claimed on the *Gneisenau* but these were unconfirmed, and ten Wellingtons were shot down. It became a bad day for 405 Squadron when three of its aircraft failed to make it home. The fate of Sgt Craig's crew was quickly established, after they ditched 300 yards off the coast of Devon and were picked up by a motor boat. They were able to describe how W5581 had undergone four attacks by BF109s, during which the rear gunner was wounded. He remained at his post, however, and claimed to have shot down at least one of the assailants. The heavily-damaged Wellington was coaxed back across the Channel at low level before landing on the water, and a number of the crew sustained slight injuries. W5530 was also attacked by two fighters, and the rear gunner was seriously wounded in the engagement. Sgt Scott brought the Wellington home to a crash-landing at Roborough near Plymouth but the gunner, Sgt Darnley, died later in hospital. Even so, this crew was more fortunate than that of P/O Trueman in W5537 which was lost without trace, presumably in the Channel. Finally, W/C Gilchrist was shot down for the second time in four months, the only consolation on this occasion being, perhaps, that it was at least by the enemy. He and all but one of his crew baled out over France, while the rear gunner, F/O Wigham, the squadron gunnery leader, alone lost his life. W/C Gilchrist was initially captured, but somehow managed to escape later and made his way back home via Switzerland. Two other members of the crew also evaded capture, and ultimately reached Gibraltar for passage home. S/L Keddy assumed temporary command of the squadron pending the arrival of a new commanding officer. The same operation accounted for 104 Squadron's second loss since its re-formation. P/O Nicholls was observed to make two passes over the target to ensure the accurate delivery of his bombs, but he also had at least four enemy fighters for company and they won the day, sending W5438 crashing into the sea without survivors.

A mixed force of Whitleys and Hampdens raided Hanover on the 25/26th, and 10 Squadron lost two crews. P/O Spiers and crew died in T4231 when it crashed in Belgium, and Z6624 went into the North Sea, taking with it S/L Landale and his crew. In his Abschuss report Oblt zur Lippe-Weissenfeld described patrolling in the Den Helder area, and being vectored onto a target which was difficult to find because of the poor visibility. He eventually came upon it at 2,200 metres and was then able to identify it as a Whitley V. It was flying so slowly that he had to deploy his landing flaps to remain in contact, and carried out his attack from below. His fire hit home between the left engine and the fuselage, and the engine burst into flames. With the entire wing on fire the aircraft went down vertically, and the wing broke away just before impact with the sea some 15 kilometres south-west of Den Helder. The body of observer Sgt George Wells, a New Zealander, was washed ashore on Texel on 15 August and was buried in Den Burg Cemetery with full military honours on the following day. The body of his crew mate Sgt Christie was recovered from the sea on the 23rd and he was buried on Sylt two days later. The brother of Sgt Wells was destined to lose his life also, when the 1651CU Stirling in which he was the rear gunner was lost during an operation to Hamburg on 29 July. 102 Squadron also posted missing a notable member of its ranks after Z6576 was shot down into the North Sea by a night fighter. The pilot was S/L Verdon-Roe, a member of the founding family of the Avro Aircraft Company, who died alongside his crew. Another member of this family was to lose his life with 156 Squadron later in the war. 35 Squadron sustained another loss when L9507 failed to return from Berlin on the same night, and it was later learned that P/O Cooper and his crew had perished. Twelve Whitleys were recalled when bound for Boulogne on the 30/31st, but the order did not affect T4212 which had crashed immediately after take-off. Happily, P/O Iveson and his crew were unhurt, and in just over two years' time he would be appointed to the command of 76 Squadron, a post which he would hold throughout the main Battle of Berlin and the pre- and post-invasion periods.

August began for the heavy brigade with operations against Hamburg, Berlin and Kiel on the 2/3rd. Eight Halifaxes were assigned to the 'Big City', and although weather conditions and the paucity of the attacking force rendered the mission ineffective, they all made it home. Sadly, that was not the case for 104 Squadron's W5580 and the crew of P/O McGlashan who were forced to ditch in the North Sea, presumably on the way home from their briefed objective of Berlin. A week later and following stormy weather, a dinghy was washed ashore on the Dutch coast containing the bodies of two of the crew. The body of another member of the crew came ashore some seventeen days later. This was the first missing crew in what would become a very expensive month for 104 Squadron. Three nights later Mannheim, Karlsruhe and Frankfurt were raided, with a 4 Group contribution at the last two mentioned. Eleven Halifaxes contributed to a force of almost 100 assorted aircraft sent to attack railway targets at Karlsruhe, half of which were 5 Group Hampdens. A 76 Squadron Halifax was among the three failures to return, and another was 104 Squadron's W5485 in which P/O Jones and his crew lost their lives. Damaged by flak, W5517 was also written off that night after crash-landing at Horsham-St-Faith on return from Saarbrücken. Sgt Stephenson and his crew emerged unscathed from the wreckage, but it would be only a temporary reprieve. Essen escaped with only slight, superficial damage when attacked on the 7/8th by a force including twelve Halifaxes, all of which returned. Only four Whitleys accompanied fifty Hampdens to Kiel on the 8/9th, but one of these, 10 Squadron's Z6815, was lost in the target area with no survivors from the crew of P/O Littlewood. Another tilt at Berlin was launched on the night of the 12/13th using a larger force than that employed at the start of the month. In the event only thirty-two of the seventy-strong force reached the target, and nine aircraft failed to return, a massive 12.9 per cent. 35 Squadron's contingent all made it home, but L9497 had lost an engine to flak and crash-landed in Norfolk with just one member of P/O McGregor-Cheers' crew sustaining injury. 76 Squadron posted missing two crews, one of them captained by F/L Christopher Cheshire, younger brother of Leonard, whose Halifax, L9530, was shot down by flak near Germany's north-western coast. He and the crew members up front survived to fall into enemy hands, but both gunners lost their lives. 76 Squadron lost a third aircraft and entire crew when L9562 stalled and crashed on approach to land and burst into flames. It proved to be a bad night for 104 Squadron, which posted missing the crews of flight commander S/L Budden and Sgt Holyman in W5461 and W5443 respectively. There were no survivors from the latter, but S/L Budden and his crew all became PoWs. S/L Budden was a pre-war pilot, who had completed his first tour of operations with 51 Squadron in 1940. Another long-range operation took seven 35 Squadron Halifaxes and two from 76 Squadron to Magdeburg on the 14/15th to attack railway installations. Results couldn't be determined because of the cloud cover, and L9500 failed to return home having crashed in Germany with the loss of P/O Lisle and crew. 104 Squadron's W5486 was taking part in a simultaneous operation to Hanover when it was brought down over Germany with the loss of P/O Drewson and his crew. The vulnerability of the Whitley was becoming apparent, and this was confirmed at Cologne on the 16/17th when seven of the twenty-nine despatched with thirty-seven Wellingtons failed to return. Three of them came from 10 Squadron: Z6586 which crashed in Belgium, killing P/O Spiers and all his crew; Z6794, in which Sgt Lager and one of his crew died; and Z6805, from which Sgt Craske and three of his crew survived as PoWs, one later being shot following a mass escape from a PoW camp. The new commanding officer of 405 Squadron, W/C Fenwick-Wilson AFC who, like W/C Gilchrist, was a Canadian serving in the RAF, arrived at Driffield on the 17th. Late that evening aircraft began taking off from Driffield for Cologne, among them 104 Squadron's W5532. Just thirty-five minutes later the Wellington crashed in Lincolnshire killing all on board. The crew was that of Sgt Stephenson, who had crash-landed their flak-damaged aircraft at Horsham-St-Faith just eleven days earlier.

It was on the 18th that Mr D.M. Butt published his report on the Command's effectiveness, and the contents were to send shock waves reverberating around the corridors of Whitehall. Having pored over 4,000 photographs taken during 100 night operations in June and July, he concluded that only a tiny fraction of bombs were falling within miles of their intended targets. It was a massive blow to morale, and demonstrated that thus far, the efforts of the crews had been totally ineffective in reducing Germany's capacity to wage war. The claims of the crews were shown to be wildly optimistic, as were those of the Command who were using them as propaganda on the front pages of the press. Sir Richard Peirse's tenure as C-in-C Bomber Command would be forever unjustly blighted by the report's revelations.

On the night of the Butt study's release, five out of seventeen Whitleys were lost, again during an operation to Cologne, and 10 Squadron posted missing the crews of P/O Evill, all killed in Z6564, and S/L Kane, who survived as a PoW with one other when Z6672 crashed near the Dutch/German border. It turned into an even worse night for 51 Squadron which posted missing three crews and lost another in England. Z6566 was hit by flak over the target, and it became necessary for the crew to bale out over Holland. The pilot, Sgt James, gave up his parachute after one of his crew found his to be unusable, a gesture for which he was later awarded the DFM, and he then crash-landed the Whitley and was captured along with the rest of his crew. While in captivity he developed tuberculosis and was repatriated, only to succumb to the illness in 1944. (*Bomber Command Losses* Vol 2, W.R. Chorley.) Z6569 was attacked by a night fighter over Belgium, during which one of the crew was killed and P/O Robertshaw and the others baled out to fall into enemy hands. Z6811 went down over Holland, killing Sgt Jamieson and three of his crew, and finally, Z6731 crashed in Suffolk on return and none survived from the crew of P/O Loney. The next target for the Halifax brigade was Kiel on the 19/20th, when six accompanied 100 other aircraft to attack railway installations. Thick cloud and icing conditions over north-western Germany discouraged almost half of the force from pressing on, and hardly any bombs fell on the town. 104 Squadron contributed to this operation also, and posted missing the crew of F/L Burton in W5461, which disappeared into the sea. Further 10 Squadron fatalities occurred on the 22/23rd, when T4234 crashed in Westmoreland on return from Le Havre, and only three of P/O Liebeck's crew survived, albeit with injuries.

It was odd how an accident of some sort, perhaps a forced landing, frequently seemed to presage a greater disaster for the crew in the near future, like that of 104 Squadron's Sgt Stephenson already mentioned. Another 104 Squadron aircraft, W5477, crashed while trying to land at Driffield after a transit flight from Martlesham Heath where it had landed on return from the previous night's operations. Sgt Richardson and his crew were all admitted to hospital, but he and three others would be declared fit to fly again before long with fatal consequences. Just twelve days after the 35 Squadron crew of McGregor-Cheers had successfully crash-landed in Norfolk with a defunct engine, they failed to return from Düsseldorf in L9572, having died on Belgian soil during an ineffective modestly-scaled operation on the night of the 24/25th. The first Australian Wellington squadron to join 4 Group was formed at Holme-on-Spalding-Moor on the 25th. Its commanding officer was W/C Mulholland, an Australian of long service in the RAF. The Squadron's first two Wellingtons, R1490 and R1695, would arrive on the 30th, followed by Z1272 and Z1273 on the following day. A further fifteen would be taken on charge during September to bring the squadron up to full strength. More than 100 aircraft set off for Duisburg on the night of the 28/29th, and another only marginally useful result cost 35 Squadron the crew of P/O Adkins in

L9501 which came down in Germany without survivors. It also cost 104 Squadron yet another crew in what was becoming an unsustainable attrition rate. W5595 failed to make it home for reasons that were never established, and there were no survivors from the crew of Sgt Spickett. Taking this night's loss into account, the squadron had lost ten aircraft and eight crews during August, the equivalent of one complete flight or half the squadron.

September began for 35 and 76 Squadrons with the contribution of five and two Halifaxes respectively to a raid on Berlin on the 2/3rd, while a larger force went to Frankfurt. It was an expensive night that resulted in two empty dispersals to contemplate at Linton-on-Ouse, the home of 35 Squadron, on the following morning, those that should have been occupied by L9508 and L9560. F/O James and one of his crew died in the former, while P/O Fraser and four of his crew lost their lives in the latter after it came down in Germany. 104 Squadron's bad run continued with the crash in Yorkshire of W5435 during an operation to Frankfurt. P/O Doherty and his crew all survived, but they sustained injuries to some extent. W/C Jarman was posted to HQ 4 Group on the 4th, and W/C Sutton succeeded him at 76 Squadron. He, it will be recalled, had commanded 58 Squadron for six months in 1940. After eleven months at Topcliffe 77 Squadron moved to Leeming on the 5th, and would carry out its first operation from its new home on the night of the 6/7th. The crews conducted air-tests in preparation, and in poor weather, 10 Squadron's Sgt Stuart landed Z6932 at Acklington to get his bearings. On take-off for base the aircraft struck high-tension cables, crashed and caught fire, killing the pilot and two others. Eighty-six Whitleys, Wellingtons and Hampdens took off for the target, a chemicals factory at Hüls, and returning crews claimed good results. Seven aircraft failed to return, however, and five of them were Whitleys, of which two were from 77 Squadron. Z6668 crashed in Germany with no survivors from the crew of Sgt Mercer, and a night fighter accounted for Z6824 over Holland, killing flight commander S/L Hannigan and all but one of his crew, while the survivor was captured. To compound these losses, Z6654 crash-landed on the shore at Cromer with battle damage sustained in a brush with a night fighter, but P/O Havelock and his crew emerged unscathed. Sadly, time was also running out for this crew, and only one member would survive to see the New Year. 10 Squadron's Z6478 fell victim to a night fighter over Holland, and Sgt Poupard and crew were killed. Z6942 also failed to return to complete a bad night for the 'Shiny Tens', but happily F/S Holder and all of his crew survived as PoWs. Almost 200 aircraft, including thirty-one Whitleys, took off for Berlin on the following night and some damage was created, although nothing of a serious nature. 104 Squadron's W5362 was lost without trace with the crew of Sgt Richardson and three of the crew who had survived the landing crash at Driffield two weeks earlier.

The 8th was the day on which 10 Squadron bade farewell to W/C V.B. Bennett and welcomed in his stead W/C Tuck, who would preside over the squadron's impending conversion from Whitleys to Halifaxes. On the 9th W/C Hanafin was posted away from 77 Squadron at the conclusion of his tour, and he was replaced by W/C David Young. Berlin was the main target on the 7/8th for which almost 200 aircraft set off. Only six Halifaxes took part, five of them from 35 Squadron, and although a third of the force turned back before reaching the target, those that pressed on produced a reasonably effective attack and bombed out almost 3,000 people. A Halifax contingent crossed the Alps to raid Turin on the 10/11th, and good results were claimed by returning crews. Not among them was that of F/O Williams, who were beginning a new career as PoWs after L9566 was brought down. In the meantime, a Whitley force was sent to attack the docks at Warnemünde on the Baltic coast on the 11/12th, and it began a series of 10 Squadron losses involving the sea, some ending happily, others not. P5109 took the crew of P/O Purvis to a watery grave in the North Sea, possibly as the result of fuel shortage, and that was definitely the cause of Z6867's ditching off Bridlington, following which P/O Hacking and crew were picked up safely. Also grateful to the rescue services were the crew of Sgt Rochford, following the ditching off the Yorkshire coast of Z6802 on the 20/21st. This was again through fuel shortage on return from Wismar, which they had bombed as an alternative to the primary target of Berlin. In-between these incidents, on the 15/16th, an unusually effective attack for the period fell on Hamburg and inflicted much property damage. The eight missing aircraft included 35 Squadron's L9503, in which P/O Brown was killed, while his crew survived to fall into enemy hands.

Fourth quarter

A small force of Whitleys and Wellingtons delivered an ineffective raid on Stuttgart on the 1/2nd of October, and a lack of fuel forced 10 Squadron's P/O Godfrey to ditch Z6941 in the Bristol Channel on return, from where he and his crew were picked up safe and sound. It would be a full two months before the squadron's next casualty occurred, despite operations to some well-defended targets in the meantime. The first destination of the month for the Halifax brigade was Brest on the 2/3rd, from which all six participants returned safely with claims of witnessing bomb bursts close to the warships. On the 5th W/C Howard was appointed as the new commanding officer of 102 Squadron, and he had a week to settle in before presiding over his and the month's first large-scale operation. This would be the first concerted effort to target the birth place of Nazism, the southern German city of Nuremberg. Some 152 crews attended briefings on the 12th, including fifty-four from 4 Group Whitley squadrons and nine from the Halifax units. Most got away between 19.00 and 20.00, but it seems that few actually arrived over the target city and many outlying communities found themselves under the bombs. Nuremberg reported few bombs falling and only slight damage, and it would prove to be an elusive objective for some years to come. W/C Sawyer led the 78 Squadron contingent on this night, and it would be his last operation as commanding officer. On the way home, his aircraft was subjected to thirty minutes of accurate predicted flak, which came up through the clouds at 14,000 feet, relentlessly pursuing the lone aircraft until it was out of range. A follow-up raid two nights later was equally ineffective, but the Halifax contingent returned without incident.

Earlier in the month 40 Squadron of 3 Group and 4 Group's 104 Squadron had been ordered to prepare for what was initially intended to be a two-month tour of duty on Malta. Accordingly, W/C Beare led fifteen aircraft to a forward base in mid-month before setting out for Luqa. They took up residence there on the 18th, leaving behind a skeleton home echelon at Driffield under the command of S/L Protheroe, whose brief was to rebuild the squadron. On the 20th 78 Squadron moved to Croft, a newly-opened satellite of Middleton-St-George a few miles to the south-west. Conditions, as at all of the hastily constructed new airfields springing up in bomber country, were spartan and a snap inspection by the AOC, AVM Roddy Carr, produced some embarrassment for W/C Sawyer and his base commander G/C Traill. The move was not allowed to interfere with operational requirements, however, and 78 Squadron was expected to be on top line throughout the upheavals. 458 Squadron went to war for the first time on the night of the 20/21st, when ten of its Wellingtons were involved in operations against Emden and docks at Antwerp and Rotterdam. Z1218 failed to return from the Antwerp contingent, and Sgt Hamilton died with all but one of his crew. A few days after the move to Croft, W/C Sawyer was notified of his impending screening from operations at the end of the month, and that he was to be succeeded at 78 Squadron by one of the flight commanders, S/L Mercer. A period of relative inactivity had ensued after the Nuremberg operations, which was broken for six of the Halifax brigade when they joined forces with Wellingtons and Whitleys to attack Mannheim on the 22/23rd. Less than half the force arrived in the target area after icing conditions were encountered and the operation failed. The Halifax was still very much a junior partner in operational terms, but the new Mk II examples were beginning to roll out of the factories and 35 Squadron received its first two examples, R9364 and V9979, on the 25th. On the last night of the month 123 aircraft set off for Hamburg, and following a relatively useful attack four Whitleys failed to return, two each from 51 and 77 squadrons with not a single survivor among them. 51 Squadron's Z9141 crashed into the Waddenzee off Texel after encountering the Do215 of Ofw Paul Gildner of II/NJG1 out of Leeuwarden. The bodies of S/L Barsby and his crew were recovered over the ensuing days and buried in Den Burg Cemetery with full military honours.

An operation to Kiel on the night of the 1/2nd of November wrecked W/C Sawyer's intended departure from 78 Squadron. S/L Mercer failed to return, and Sawyer's posting would have to be postponed until a new candidate could be found. As a result W/C Sawyer would remain in command for the rest of the year, although not participating in operations. Possibly frustrated by the recent run of bad weather, Peirse planned a major night of operations for the night of 7/8 November, and despite a further unfavourable weather forecast, they were allowed to go ahead. Berlin was to be the main target, and the original plan called for more than 200 aircraft to be involved. However, doubts about the weather prompted the 5 Group A-O-C, AVM Slessor, to object, and he was allowed to withdraw his contribution of seventy-five aircraft and send them instead to Cologne. A third force of Wellingtons drawn from 1 and 3 Groups was assigned to Mannheim, and a number of minor operations were also laid on. A new record number of 392 sorties were involved in all the night's activities, and 169 of them set course for Berlin over a period of a few hours throughout the evening. 10 Squadron contributed five Whitleys to a force of forty-two of the type heading for the capital, while 35 Squadron put up four Halifaxes and 76 Squadron five. It was destined to be a night of disappointment and losses, as demonstrated by 51 Squadron's experiences. S/L Dickenson led eight Whitleys to the capital, and five crews, those of P/O Monro in Z9133, P/O Potter in Z6554, and Sgts Brown, Abercassis and Pohe in Z6879, Z9146 and Z9165 respectively all claimed to have reached their destination and bombed as briefed, while Sgt Edwards in Z9164 attacked an alternative target. 77 Squadron's contribution was eight aircraft, led by Z6943 with W/C Young at the controls. He and three other crews, those of P/O Ogier in Z6628, F/L Parkin in Z6952 and P/O Havelock in Z9225, reached and bombed the primary target before returning safely home after more than ten hours in the air. P/O Scott-Martin and his crew attacked Sylt as an alternative target in Z6822, and the three remaining sorties were abandoned altogether. All of the 35 Squadron aircraft bombed the primary target and returned safely, but less than half the total force made it to Berlin, and damage was consequently scattered and light. The 5 Group attack on Cologne was also totally ineffective and according to the Mannheim authorities no bombs fell there. The Berlin failure cost the Command twenty-one aircraft, and seven Wellingtons failed to return from Mannheim. There were no losses from Cologne but a further nine aircraft were lost from the minor operations, bringing the missing total to thirty-seven, more than twice the previous highest for a single night. Of these, one was a 35 Squadron Halifax which was shot down by a night fighter over Holland during a 'Rover' patrol to Essen. P/O Whitaker was killed along with two of his crew, and the remainder fell into enemy hands. This disastrous night was the final straw for the Air Ministry, and Sir Richard Peirse was summoned to an uncomfortable meeting with Churchill to make his explanations. W/C Sutton was posted to HQ Bomber Command on the 9th, leaving 76 Squadron temporarily without a commanding officer. S/L Bouwens stepped into the breach until the appointment of a new commanding officer in mid-December. On the 13th C-in-C Peirse was ordered to restrict operations while the future of the Command was considered at the highest level, leaving the very existence of Bomber Command in the balance.

On the 15th the charismatic, pipe-smoking W/C 'Pick' Pickard succeeded W/C Burnett as the new commanding officer of 51 Squadron, fresh from his starring role in the propaganda feature film *Target for Tonight*, in which he played the captain of Wellington F for Freddie. This paralleled his actual career to date, having served a first tour with 99 Squadron before being posted to the command of 311 Czech Squadron in July 1940 and then serving as a flight commander with 9 Squadron. On the very same day, and exactly a year since its arrival at Topcliffe, 102 Squadron departed for Dalton, a new airfield which had just opened. Operations would continue from here, but the end was in sight for the venerable and highly reliable Whitley, as the squadron was earmarked to become the fourth to receive the Halifax. On the 24th 458

Squadron gave birth to a new Australian unit, 460 Squadron, when donating four officers and more than 100 NCOs. 460 would serve with 1 Group and become one of the most prolific squadrons in the Command. German ports and those along the occupied coast dominated the second half of the month, but the Halifaxes were not heavily committed until the 25/26th when eleven of them were joined by seven Stirlings for another attempt on the German cruisers at Brest. A further eleven were contributed to a force of 180 aircraft sent to Hamburg on the last night of the month, and those reaching the target produced a reasonable degree of damage, including twenty-two fires, for the loss of thirteen of their number. Only one Halifax failed to return, 35 Squadron's L9582, from which F/S Hamilton and five of his crew parachuted into captivity. 405 Squadron's highly experienced flight commander, S/L Bissett DFC*, sent a signal saying he was abandoning his sortie, but W5476 never arrived home and presumably crashed into the sea. A sea search was mounted on the following day, but no trace of the aircraft or its crew was found. It was also on this last night of November that the Reaper returned to 10 Squadron after a lengthy absence. Z9166 was swallowed up by the cold North Sea on the way home from Emden, and took with it the crew of P/O Nelson. The squadron's long association with the trusty old Whitley was coming to an end and just two more would be lost before they gave way to the Halifax.

December began for 77 Squadron with another change of leadership. The very popular and respected W/C Young was posted away on the 2nd, shortly to assume command of 76 Squadron, a post in which he was to remain for the next nine months. In September 1942 he would be posted to the Middle East to take command of the newly-forming 462 Squadron of the Royal Australian Air Force, a unit which would eventually find itself posted to 4 Group for a short spell in 1944 before completing its wartime service as one of 100 Group's heavy squadrons. The new commanding officer at 77 Squadron was W/C Don Bennett, who had been readmitted to the RAF after a civilian career as an airline pilot, and having most recently pioneered the Atlantic Ferry service. As an airman Bennett undoubtedly ranked among the best, and as a navigator he was unrivalled. He was somewhat disappointed at finding 77 Squadron still equipped with Whitleys, but he would make the best of the situation and bring the benefits of his vast experience to his crews. It was during December that Halifaxes began to arrive at Dalton to allow 102 Squadron to begin the conversion process. The first, R9390, turned up on the 3rd, and working up to operational status began immediately under the likes of P/O Wally Lashbrook, formerly of 35 Squadron. A Conversion Flight would be formed, but that wouldn't happen until early January. The evolution to operational status was to prove a very slow process, largely because of the constant modifications to the type, and in the meantime, the squadron would soldier on with the Whitley.

The month would follow a similar pattern of operations, with ports receiving the bulk of the attention. 10 Squadron's penultimate loss of a Whitley occurred when Z9162 crashed on landing on return from an abortive sortie to Dunkerque on the 7/8th, and despite having retained its bomb load and catching fire, the crew of Sgt Barber scrambled away unhurt. Cologne was raided by a small force on the 11/12th and 35 Squadron posted missing the crew of P/O Buckley in L9600, which went down off the Belgian coast without survivors. Returning from the same operation 10 Squadron's Z9188 crashed in Yorkshire, injuring P/O Kenny and three of his crew, and killing one other. With that incident 'Shiny Ten' bade farewell to the Whitley era. Halifaxes had begun arriving at Leeming during December, and working-up began under the watchful eye of W/C Tuck. The squadron was the third in the Command to receive the type after 35 and 76 Squadrons, and operational status would be achieved in time to participate in Operation *Veracity* on the 18th. In the meantime W/C Young was appointed to command 76 Squadron on the 15th in place of S/L Bouwens, who was posted to HQ 6 Group. Operation *Veracity* was a daylight attack on the German cruisers *Scharnhorst* and *Gneisenau* at Brest to be carried out by Halifaxes, Stirlings and Manchesters. The operation called for six aircraft each from the Halifax squadrons, with eighteen Stirlings and eleven Manchesters. Taking off shortly after 10:00 hours, W/C Tuck was forced to abandon his sortie in L9619 with technical problems, but the remaining 10 Squadron crews maintained their tight formation with the other Halifaxes and pressed on. W/C Robinson led the 35 Squadron contingent and W/C Young those from 76 Squadron, one of which was forced to pull out of the formation with an engine problem, reducing the Halifax numbers to sixteen. A fighter escort was provided, and this was already in action when first sighted by the approaching bombers. The murky conditions of the early part of the flight were replaced by clear visibility, and the attack took place in the face of spirited opposition. Flak damaged both port engines of W/C Robinson's V9979, and one burst into flames. The fire was extinguished, but it proved impossible to feather the propellers and maintain height, and consequently W/C Robinson was forced to ditch some 60 miles off the English coast. The Halifax remained afloat for a considerable time, and a rescue was successfully carried out later in the day. All the other Halifaxes returned home, and the crews were optimistic about the results of their efforts.

After enjoying a previously loss-free month and a relatively kind final quarter of the year, the Düsseldorf operation on the 27/28th provided 77 Squadron with a sharp reminder of the hazards of serving with Bomber Command. Three of its aircraft failed to return: Z6956, from which W/O Grace and three of his crew escaped with their lives to become PoWs; Z9226, with total loss of life among the crew of P/O Scott-Martin; and Z9306, which was shot down by a night fighter over Holland, killing P/O Havelock and all but one of his crew. 458 Squadron was also involved in this operation, and after delivering his bombs F/L Saville allowed his front gunner to open up at a Heinkel 111 as it landed and watched with satisfaction as it careered off the runway. Saville was a courageous and inspirational officer, who became commanding officer of 3 Group's 218 Squadron at the end of March 1943. Sadly, he was to lose his life when his Stirling was shot down on the first of the four Hamburg raids in July of that year. As far as the German warships at Brest were concerned, only slight damage had been caused to the *Gneisenau* on the 18th, but encouraged by the apparent success, it was decided to mount

Operation *Veracity* II by sixteen Halifaxes with Stirlings and Manchesters from 3 and 5 Groups on the 30th. In the event the 3 and 5 Group contribution was withdrawn, apparently because of concerns over the weather, and the Halifaxes would make the trip alone with a fighter escort. On the night before, 10 Squadron suffered its first Halifax loss as the result of an unfortunate night-training incident. During the take-off, W/C Tuck's V9981 and L9614, piloted by Sgt Tripp, collided and came to grief, both being written off. There were no casualties among the CO's crew, but Sgt Tripp and one of his crew were killed. Again fierce flak and fighter opposition greeted the Halifaxes over Brest, and 35 Squadron's V9979 succumbed to the former before crashing in the target area with fatal consequences for S/L Middleton and his crew. 10 Squadron's R9374 was badly damaged by flak, and then had to survive the attentions of a fighter, before eventually ditching well out to sea off Cornwall. One of the crew was killed during the engagement, but F/S Whyte and the rest of his crew were picked up safely. 76 Squadron's L9615 was brought down by flak off the French coast, and there were no survivors from the crew of P/O King. All the returning Halifaxes displayed the scars of battle, but the attack was inconclusive and probably caused no further damage to the warships.

Thus ended a forgettable year for the Command. It had begun promisingly, with the operational debuts of the new generation of heavy bombers, but all three types had failed to meet expectations, and had been grounded for lengthy periods while essential modifications were carried out. There was little to show in the way of advancement on the previous year's performance, and the year turned with a dark cloud settling over the Command. There was one bright light, however, emanating from a corner of Lincolnshire, where the first production Lancasters had been delivered to 5 Group's 44 Squadron. Early in the coming year a new Commander-in-Chief would be appointed, into whose hands the Lancaster would be placed as the 'shining sword'.

1942

First quarter

The year began with the pre-occupation with the German cruisers at Brest, and no fewer than eleven operations of varying sizes were directed at the port during January alone. First, though, 78 Squadron exchanged commanding officers on the 1st with the departure, finally, of W/C Sawyer to 4 Group HQ and the arrival of W/C Corbally. 102 Squadron's Z9289 took off for Brest in the early hours of the 6th, but was forced by engine problems to head back to Dalton, reaching the Barnsley area of Yorkshire before crashing with just the pilot still on board. Sgt Hollingworth was killed, one of his crew failed to survive his descent by parachute, and another man sustained injuries. As events turned out, this was to be the squadron's penultimate Whitley casualty. Later in the day the 102 Squadron Conversion Flight was formed under the command of S/L Robinson. On the 8th AM Sir Richard Peirse left Bomber Command to take up an appointment as C-in-C India and South-East Asia, and the vacant seat was taken temporarily by AVM Baldwin, the AOC 3 Group. Two raids were also sent against Hamburg in mid-month and returning from the second of these on the 15/16th, 10 Squadron's L9622 crashed in Yorkshire, killing six of the crew, although the pilot, Sgt Schneider survived with severe injuries. Two nights later Bremen was the objective for eighty-three aircraft, eight of them participating in what was 405 Squadron's fifty-fifth operation of the war. This was the occasion selected to deliver the RCAF's first 4,000lb 'cookie', which was carried in S/L Fauquier's Z8431. Only eight aircraft reached the primary target, most of them ultimately bombing at Hamburg, or joining in a small-scale raid on Emden. S/L Fauquier was among the latter, and he reported his bomb falling into the middle of the town with 'terrific' results. Z8329 failed to arrive back at Pocklington with the crew of the B Flight commander, S/L Keddy, and it was only when two of the crew were rescued from their dinghy by a Royal Navy destroyer some fourteen hours later that the story of its demise emerged. The starboard engine had begun to falter over the target, and had caught fire on the way home. S/L Keddy carried out a ditching some 20 miles off the Yorkshire coast, but he and three others failed to survive. He was replaced as flight commander by S/L McCormack.

On the 22nd S/L Cheshire relinquished his post as flight commander of 35 Squadron on his posting to the Halifax Conversion Flight at Marston Moor. W/C Robinson was also posted away on the 26th at the conclusion of his tour as commanding officer of the squadron, but he would return. His successor was W/C 'Charles' Whitworth, who had commanded 78 Squadron early in 1941. 102 Squadron's final loss of a Whitley occurred on the 26/27th when Z9283 failed to return from Emden, and was lost without trace with the crew of Sgt White. Later that day W/C Bintley was appointed as the Squadron's new commanding officer and he would preside over the squadron's final Whitley operation, to Le Havre on the last night of the month. Also at the end of the month 10 and 76 Squadrons despatched four and five Halifaxes respectively to Lossiemouth for an attempt against the *Tirpitz*, which was moored near Trondheim in Norway. The operation was carried out on the night of the 29/30th, but none of the 10 Squadron crews were able to locate the ship's position and returned home. On the 29th a flight of 104 Squadron Wellingtons moved into Pocklington on a temporary basis, as Driffield had become unserviceable. As already described, most of the squadron had been posted to the Middle East in October for a short period of duty, leaving a small home echelon to continue operating under Bomber Command. This had been building up gradually to squadron strength, and once it was decided in January that the overseas element would remain in the Middle-Eastern theatre, it was assumed that the home echelon would retain the coveted 104 Squadron number plate. In fact, messages were being transmitted back and forth between the powers that be in the UK and W/C Beare and his ally, W/C Stickley of 40 Squadron, now both at Kabrit in Egypt, over entitlement to the numbers. 102 Squadron was now stood down to concentrate fully on the Halifax conversion programme. It would be April before it achieved operational status on the type, and this was partly the result of the lack of

Gee-equipped aircraft because of the inability to install the device retrospectively.

February was to be a significant month for the Command in a number of ways, and there would also be changes at 405 Squadron. The Duke of Kent visited Pocklington on the 1st in his capacity as the principal RAF welfare officer, and he carried out an inspection of crews and aircraft. Sadly he was to be killed in August while flying in a Coastal Command Sunderland. The squadron was on stand-by from the 3rd to the 8th, and took no part in the few operations mounted. During this period on the 6/7th, sixty aircraft were involved in another attack on Brest, but only a third of the crews claimed to have bombed near the warships and the results were inconclusive. Twenty aircraft tried again on the 10/11th and encountered complete cloud cover, while two 405 Squadron freshmen targeted Le Havre. Earlier on the 10th, ACM Sir Arthur Harris had departed Boston, on America's eastern seaboard, in the armed merchant ship *Alcantara*, to return home specifically to be installed as the new Commander-in-Chief of Bomber Command. On the evening of the 11th, eighteen Wellingtons went once more to Brest for what would prove to be the final raid in this long-running saga. Shortly before midnight, the *Scharnhorst*, *Gneisenau* and *Prinz Eugen* slipped anchor, and headed into the Channel under a destroyer escort in an audacious bid for freedom. The War Cabinet had prepared a plan for precisely this eventuality, under the code name Operation *Fuller*. Sadly, it appears that its full requirements had not filtered down to those who would be charged with its implementation, and the 12th was to become something of a disaster for Bomber Command and a humiliation for the nation. The German fleet commander had chosen appalling weather conditions for the breakout, characterized by squalls and low cloud. It was late morning on the 12th before the warships were spotted making their way eastwards along the Channel, and only 5 Group was standing by at four hours' readiness. The first aircraft were not launched until 13.30 hours, and from then until darkness fell, a record number of 242 daylight sorties were thrown against the enemy fleet. Pocklington despatched a first wave of six aircraft, which came below the cloud base to search at 300 feet, and only one crew claimed a fleeting sight of the quarry. A second wave of three aircraft made contact through a gap in the clouds, and one bomb load straddled a ship, but scored no hits. This was the experience of all those who made attacks in the impossible conditions, and fifteen Bomber Command aircraft and crews were lost in the sea. The enemy fleet passed through the Straits of Dover making good its escape into more open sea, and although *Scharnhorst* and *Gneisenau* struck mines laid in recent weeks around the Frisians by 5 Group aircraft, their progress was only marginally inhibited and all arrived in home ports on the following morning. The episode almost brought down the government, but as far as Bomber Command was concerned this annoying itch had been scratched for the last time, and it could now concentrate more on the kind of strategic operations to which it was better suited.

A new Air Ministry directive was issued on the 14th which decreed that the morale of the enemy population, particularly its workers, would be the new priority, thus opening the way for the blatant area bombing of German urban areas without the pretence of aiming for industrial and military targets. In eight days time a new C-in-C would arrive at the helm, who would pursue this policy with a will and gradually develop the force and the strategies to put this into effect. Also on this day 104 Squadron ceased to exist in Bomber Command. The long-running dispute over the number had been resolved in favour of the overseas element, as was the case with 3 Group's 40 Squadron. 104 Squadron became 158 Squadron, whose proud history would continue with 4 Group for the remainder of the war, and 40 Squadron became 156 Squadron, which, later in the year, would become a founder member of the new target-finding and marking force known as the Pathfinders. W/C Stevens was installed as the first commanding officer of 158 Squadron, while S/Ls Protheroe and Lane, who had been with the home echelon during its rebuilding process, remained as the flight commanders. That night the squadron contributed seven Wellingtons to a force of almost 100 targeting Mannheim, and all returned safely. W/C Fenwick-Wilson relinquished his command of 405 Squadron, and took up his new appointment as Station Commander at Pocklington on the 21st. He was succeeded by W/C MacAllister, whose period of tenure would be brief in the extreme. ACM Sir Arthur Harris took up his appointment as Commander-in-Chief on the 22nd, and set about the task of putting Bomber Command in order. He arrived with firm ideas already in place about how to destroy urban areas, recognizing the need to overwhelm the defences by pushing the maximum number of aircraft through the target in the shortest possible time. He also recognized that built-up areas are destroyed by fire, not blast, and it would not be long before bomb loads reflected this thinking. This day also signalled the end in Bomber Command service for 458 Squadron. It had been told during the previous month to prepare to be sent overseas, and on the 22nd W/C Mulholland led two other aircraft on the 1,400-mile journey to Malta. The other pair arrived safely, but W/C Mulholland was shot down into the Mediterranean and died with all but one of his crew. The remainder of the squadron was ferried out over the ensuing days, but other units borrowed and stole 458's aircraft and it would be September before it regained its identity and November before operations began from North African landing-grounds.

During his first week Harris contented himself with a continuation of the small-scale raids on German ports, and it was during such an operation to Kiel on the 26/27th that the war threw up one of its ironies. While attacking the floating dock, one of forty-nine participating aircraft landed a high-explosive bomb on the bows of the *Gneisenau*, now supposedly in safe haven after enduring eleven months of constant bombardment at Brest. Such was the damage inflicted that the vessel's sea-going career was ended, and her main armament was ultimately removed for coastal defence work. Nine aircraft from 405 and 158 Squadrons took part in the operation, but only four crews claimed to have bombed the target. This was W/C MacAllister's first operation with 405 Squadron, and he was flying as second dickey to F/L Robson in W5516. Also on board was F/S Robson, whom fate had spared on 5 January when the rest of his crew died in an air-test accident. This time there was to be no reprieve and the entire crew was lost without trace, presumably in the sea. The tough and highly-experienced former bush pilot S/L 'Johnny' Fauquier was thrust into the hot seat from flight commander, to begin the first of his two spells as 405 Squadron's commanding officer. He would quickly stamp his personality on the squadron, and by the war's end would be a legendary figure in the history of both the RAF and RCAF, seeing the bombing war out as the commanding officer of the famed 617 Squadron. On the following night 51 Squadron was involved in a quietly spectacular success, when W/C Pickard led a force of twelve commando-carrying Whitleys to Bruneval on the French coast, along with a radar technician, to dismantle and return with a Würzburg installation. The operation proceeded almost without a hitch, and the ground party returned home by sea with all the vital components and a captured German operator.

At the beginning of March, the Halifax squadrons were screened from operations to allow installation of the navigation device 'Gee' or TR1335. As a result, only a few Halifaxes were available for a special operation to be launched on the night of the 3/4th. This was the first tangible sign of a new hand on the Command's tiller as Harris put into practice some of his ideas. In response to an Air Ministry request, an operation was prepared against the Renault lorry factory at Billancourt near Paris, where 18,000 vehicles a year were being added to the enemy inventory. The three-wave attack was to be led by the most experienced crews, and there would be extensive use of flares to illuminate the target. In the face of what was expected to be a scant anti-aircraft defence, the crews were to bomb from as low as possible, both to ensure accuracy and to avoid as far as possible casualties among French civilians. A new record force to a single target of 235 aircraft included nine from 405 Squadron, and they got away in the early evening. The prediction of only light defence was accurate, providing the crews with a clear run, and despite the unprecedented concentration of aircraft passing through the target there were no collisions. Over 300 bombs fell into the factory and every building sustained damage, halting all production at the plant for four weeks. An added bonus was the loss of just one aircraft, but the night's success was marred by the heavy casualties among civilians in adjacent residential districts, which amounted to 367 killed and a similar number seriously injured. The operation was declared an outstanding success, and it was something of a paradox, therefore, that Harris, as a champion of area bombing, should gain his first major victory by way of a precision attack.

On the following day the newly-numbered 158 Squadron left Pocklington to return to Driffield. As one of Germany's industrial giants and home to Krupp, Essen was to feature prominently in Harris's future plans. Many small-scale raids in the past had barely left scratches, and this was not only because of the insignificant weight of bombs employed. The entire urban sprawl of the Ruhr contained over twenty conurbations from cities to small towns, most of which were spewing industrial pollution into the atmosphere. This formed a layer of haze over the region, which even by day could make the identification of individual built-up areas impossible. Harris would place his faith in the development of electronic eyes which could penetrate the cloud and haze, and the first of these, Gee, a navigation aid, became available for the opening of a series of operations against Essen on the 8/9th. A total of 211 aircraft took off over a three-hour period either side of midnight, the leading aircraft equipped with Gee to guide the first wave to the general target area. The result was a highly disappointing raid which destroyed a few houses and other buildings while missing the Krupp works, and eight aircraft were lost. 405 Squadron sat out the operation, but was called into action on the following night for a return to Essen. Some 187 aircraft took part on this night, including seven from 405 Squadron, and each of the crews returned to claim bombing the target. In fact, bombs had again been liberally distributed around the Ruhr, twenty-four towns reporting being hit. Damage in Essen was negligible, but the failure at least cost the Command only a modest three aircraft and crews. For the third consecutive night, Harris went for Essen on the 10/11th, this time with 126 aircraft. Only half of the crews claimed to have bombed as briefed, while thirty-five others attacked alternative targets and Essen again escaped with barely a scratch. On the 11th S/L Fauquier was promoted to the rank of wing commander, and W/C Fenwick-Wilson was posted to Washington. He would return to the operational scene in March 1944 to take command of 3 Group's 218 Squadron, with which he would complete a seven-month tour. W/C Whitworth concluded his short term of office at the helm of 35 Squadron on the 12th, and he was succeeded by W/C Jimmy Marks, one of the Command's new breed of dynamic young officers whose skills had been tempered in the heat of battle. Whitworth would be base commander when Scampton was selected as the home for the newly-forming 617 Squadron, who would go on to fame as the Dambusters. Two further attempts were made against Essen on the 25/26th and 26/27th with equally disappointing results, while the Halifax squadrons continued to sit out the period on the ground.

If the Command were to become an effective weapon, the problems of navigation and target identification had to be overcome and Harris could not wait for the introduction of new electronic aids already in the pipeline. If his crews could see the ground and were given clearly identifiable pinpoints by which to navigate, he was confident that they could deliver the results. Coastlines offered the clearest navigational references, and would generally be free of industrial haze. With this in mind Harris prepared a major operation against the ancient Baltic port city of Lübeck, which was expected to be only lightly defended. The narrow streets and half-timbered buildings in its old centre would also aid the spread of fire, and the two-thirds incendiary bomb loads carried by the 234 participating aircraft reflected Harris's purpose. The now familiar three-wave raid took place on Palm Sunday, the 28/29th, but did so without a contribution from the Halifax brigade. The city lay beyond the range of Gee but the device helped with preliminary navigation, and the presence of a moon also enabled the force to remain on track and aided the identification of the target. Crews came down to as low as 2,000 feet to carry out their attacks, and the result was the first major success for the area-bombing policy. Fire devastated the city centre, destroying over 1,400 houses and seriously damaging almost 2,000 more, and an estimated 30 per cent of the built-up area was reduced to rubble. Twelve aircraft were lost, but not one of them was from 4 Group. At the end of the month the three Halifax squadrons sent detachments to Lossiemouth and Kinloss in Scotland to renew acquaintance with the *Tirpitz* which was now sheltering in Aasen Fjord in Norway. A total of thirty-four Halifaxes took off between 18:00 and 19:00 hours on the 30th, each carrying four 1,000lb spherical mines which were intended to roll down the hillsides surrounding the ship's mooring and explode underneath its hull. Once again the would-be attackers failed to locate the ship and lost six of their number in the process. 35 Squadron sustained its worst casualties to date, losing R9496 and W1015 to flak in the target area with fatal consequences for the crews of F/Ss Archibold and Steinhauer, and R9438 took the crew of F/S Bushby to their deaths in the sea on the way home. 10 Squadron posted missing two crews and 76 Squadron one to complete a bad night for the Group. The squadrons remained in Scotland for a further five days awaiting favourable weather conditions for another attempt, but as this was not forthcoming they returned to their stations.

Second quarter

April would bring to an end 405 Squadron's association with the Wellington, but the final two weeks of operations with the type were to prove expensive. On the night of the 1/2nd raids took place on Le Havre, Hanau and the Ford motor works at Poissy in Paris. Four of the squadron's aircraft joined thirteen other Wellingtons and twenty-four Whitleys to attack the last mentioned, and the crews returned with enthusiastic claims. Later photographic reconnaissance failed to confirm their optimism, and the target was seen to have escaped damage. One aircraft failed to return and this was 405 Squadron's Z8527, which crashed in France killing F/S Howsan and all but his observer who fell into enemy hands. The Hanau raid resulted in the disastrous loss of twelve of the thirty-five Wellingtons taking part; 57 and 214 Squadrons suffering casualties of five and seven aircraft respectively. On the following night Wellingtons and Stirlings returned to the Ford factory, and this time carried out an accurate attack. On the afternoon of the 4th the Pocklington station Miles Magister crashed near Barmby Moor after failing to recover from a slow roll at low altitude. On board were S/L McCormack and the senior squadron navigation officer, F/L Featherstone, both of whom were killed instantly. The loss of the B Flight commander in this way was an especially sad event, particularly after he had managed to survive twenty-five operations.

April's first major operation involved a new record force of 263 aircraft whose crews were briefed to attack Cologne on the night of the 5/6th, again without the support of the Halifax brigade. The results were disappointing and the record did not endure for long. 4 Group bade farewell to one of its long-serving squadrons on the 8th, when 58 Squadron was posted permanently to Coastal Command and began flying patrols from St Eval on the 19th. The recently-set record was broken when a force of 272 aircraft headed for Hamburg on the night of the 8/9th, and this time twelve Halifaxes took part. Their presence made no difference to the outcome, however, and few bomb loads fell into the city; it was a similar story at Essen on the 10/11th and 12/13th. Harris had now mounted eight major raids against Essen, and the statistics made discouraging reading. A total of 1,555 aircraft had been despatched, around two-thirds of them reaching the target area to bomb. The only resulting industrial damage was a fire in the Krupp works, and apart from that a small amount of housing had been hit. In return the Command had lost sixty-four aircraft, most of them with their crews, and it was clear, for the time being at least, that the destruction of Essen lay beyond the crews' capability. Nevertheless, Harris would try again in June, while in the interim turning his attention elsewhere. Meanwhile, over at Dalton, 102 Squadron had now been declared operational and was about to put a toe tentatively back into the water. The problem arising from the lack of Gee-equipped Halifaxes had been solved by the donation of six aircraft by 35 Squadron and one of these, R9488, became the first to be lost by the squadron. Pilots F/L Williams and Sgt Morris took the Halifax for an air-test in the early afternoon of the 14th, probably in preparation for the squadron's maiden operation that night. During the course of the flight the Halifax entered a spin and crashed near Ripon, killing all eight men on board. While the main operation went ahead at Dortmund, two 102 Squadron Halifaxes joined a small-scale raid on Le Havre to open the squadron's Halifax account. The operation failed to find the mark, but both aircraft returned safely. The attempt to hit Dortmund in the main raid also foundered when bombs were sprayed all over the Ruhr.

On the 15th W/C Don Bennett was posted to 10 Squadron from his command at 77 Squadron to replace W/C Tuck, who would return to the operational scene as the commanding officer of 51 Squadron in a month's time. Bennett, who, as previously mentioned, already had an unparalleled career in civil and military aviation behind him and a glittering future ahead, was a man who led from the front and thought nothing of taking a sprog crew into battle to give them confidence. His successor at 77 Squadron was W/C Embling. 405 Squadron carried out its final Wellington operation on the 17/18th, when Hamburg was the objective for over 170 aircraft, five of them from Pocklington. One returned early, three attacked alternative targets, and just one bombed as briefed. The operation was moderately successful when compared with recent attempts over the Ruhr, and over seventy fires were started, thirty-three of them classed as large. The squadron negotiated its Wellington swan song without casualty and was stood down on the 18th to prepare to convert to Halifaxes, a process which would keep it away from the operational scene for six weeks. Wellingtons were not removed immediately from Pocklington as the first Halifaxes had not yet arrived. Four crews carried out a sea search following the Hamburg raid, in the hope of finding crews missing from Driffield but nothing was found. The first five Halifaxes arrived from Middleton-St-George on the 23rd, to be followed by two more from Croft on the 25th. The actual conversion training was carried out with 1652CU, commanded at that time by S/L Len Cheshire, at Marston Moor.

A number of significant operations took place in the absence of 405 Squadron, the first of them against Cologne on the 22/23rd. A Gee-equipped force, consisting predominantly of Wellingtons, attempted to use the device as a blind bombing aid to overcome the problems of cloud and haze. The result was a marginal improvement on recent performances, but still only a small proportion of the bombs fell within the city. On the following night Harris returned to the formula that had brought him success at Lübeck at the end of March. Rostock was another lightly-defended port on the Baltic coast with narrow streets in its old town, and as an added attraction, a Heinkel aircraft factory situated in its southern outskirts. The series of four raids on consecutive nights was to include a 5 Group contingent directed specifically at the factory, while the main element attacked the town with mostly incendiary bomb loads. The first operation ended disappointingly when the Heinkel works escaped damage altogether, and most of the bombs intended for the town centre fell 2 to 6 miles away. It was on return from this first operation that 51 Squadron registered its final Whitley casualty under Bomber Command. BD190 ran out of fuel over Yorkshire, and was crash-landed by F/L Towsey without injury to himself or his crew.

It was a different story twenty-four hours later, however, when the town centre was heavily bombed although the factory remained unscathed. The town was again pounded on the 25/26th, and on this night, W/C Guy Gibson led a 106 Squadron element in a successful attack on the Heinkel factory. The final raid took place on the 26/27th, when more than 200 aircraft were divided equally between the town and the factory. When the local authorities were able to assess the damage, they recorded over 1,700 buildings totally destroyed, 500 seriously damaged and an estimated 60 per cent of the main built-up area devastated.

102 Squadron's second night of Halifax operations came on the 27/28th, and involved three aircraft. The main target for the night was Cologne which was attacked to moderate effect by over ninety aircraft, of which seven failed to return. The single missing Halifax was 102 Squadron's W7653, which was shot down by a night fighter while outbound over Belgium. Three men were killed and three of the survivors fell into enemy hands, but the pilot, F/S Carr, was picked up by the escape and evasion network on the ground and entered neutral Spain in mid-May. This was actually the squadron's second operational Halifax loss, as shortly before its demise on the same night, R9528 fell to flak in the target area during an attack on the docks at Dunkerque and thus became the squadron's first operational loss. Sgt Barber and two others lost their lives, but three of this crew ultimately evaded capture. Also on this night a mixed force of Halifaxes and Lancasters flew north again for a further attack on the *Tirpitz* which on this occasion was located and bombed, although without the hoped-for result. Defence was, as always, spirited, and W1037 was brought down in Norway and five of the crew, including the pilot, F/L Miller, survived to fall into enemy hands. W1041 was also undone by flak and had to be force-landed by W/C Bennett, which he accomplished without injury to the crew. Four men were captured, but the ever resourceful Bennett and two others managed to evade capture, he returning to the squadron to resume command within a month. 35 Squadron's W1020 fell victim to flak and crashed near Trondheim, as a result of which F/L Pools and his crew lost

their lives. Another victim of the barrage was W1048, which P/O MacIntyre skilfully brought to a crash-landing on the frozen Lake Hocklingen before disappearing into the surrounding countryside with four of his crew to ultimately evade capture. The burning Halifax melted the ice and eventually settled on the bottom of the lake, from where in 1973 it was recovered and now resides in an unrestored state in the Bomber Command Hall at the RAF Museum at Hendon. The *Tirpitz* had again escaped damage at a cost to the Command of a further four Halifaxes and a Lancaster. A smaller force returned on the following night and claimed a number of unconfirmed hits on *Tirpitz*, but two more 35 Squadron Halifaxes failed to return having been shot down by the flak defences. W1053 crashed in Norway and P/O Roe and four of his crew survived to be captured. W7656 went down in the target area, delivering F/L Petley and three of his crew into enemy hands.

May began with a raid by eighty aircraft on Hamburg on the 3/4th, although only fifty-four crews reported bombing through cloud on estimated positions. Despite this, the operation was an outstanding success which belied both the conditions and the numbers involved. Over 100 fires were started, half of them classed as large, and one cookie reputedly destroyed eleven apartment blocks. During Don Bennett's absence, and while he made his way home from Norway, the highly-experienced and previously mentioned W/C James Tait assumed command of 10 Squadron on the 4th, and he too would become associated with the *Tirpitz* when leading 617 Squadron on the three epic and successful attacks against the ship during late 1944. Three raids on Stuttgart on consecutive nights began on the 4/5th, but this would prove to be an elusive target until much later in the war, largely because of its location in a series of valleys. Decoy sites were also employed, and the nett result of the three operations was little significant damage for the loss of eleven aircraft. On the 6th 51 and 77 Squadrons left Bomber Command on a temporary posting to Coastal Command and took up residence at Chivenor. The activities of these squadrons during their Coastal Command service do not fall within the scope of this work, but a record of their quite considerable losses can be found in this book in the Aircraft History section pertaining to each unit. A disastrous attempt was made on the Baltic port of Warnemünde and its nearby Heinkel factory on the 8/9th which cost nineteen aircraft for little return, and thereafter minor operations held sway. On the 18th W/C Pickard was posted away from 51 Squadron to be replaced by W/C Tuck, who had commanded 10 Squadron during its conversion onto Halifaxes. In October Pickard would take command of 161 Squadron at Tempsford, with which he would be involved in many daring operations on behalf of the Special Operations Executive and the Secret Intelligence Service. In February 1944 this inspirational leader of men would lose his life during Operation *Jericho*, the audacious and brilliant attack on the walls of Amiens prison by Mosquitos of the 2nd Tactical Air Force. Also on this day W/C Corbally was replaced as commanding officer at 78 Squadron by W/C Lucas. The temporary lull in major operations came to a halt on the 19/20th when Mannheim was selected as the target. Sadly, the effort of mounting the operation was largely wasted as most of the bombs from the 155 aircraft reaching the target found open country. 405 Squadron was by now sufficiently well advanced in its progress towards operational status with Halifaxes to be ready in time to participate in the next large-scale operation, which would take place at the end of the month.

There now followed another lull in major operations while Harris prepared for his masterstroke, which would probably decide the fate of his Command one way or the other. On taking up his appointment as C-in-C, Harris had asked for 4,000 bombers with which to win the war. While there was never the slightest chance of getting them, Harris needed to ensure that those earmarked for him were not spirited away to what he considered to be less deserving causes. Quite properly for the head of a bomber force, all causes outside of Bomber Command were categorized by him as less deserving at a time when other services and theatres of operation seemed to be constantly demanding bomber aircraft. Despite a number of notable successes, the Command had not yet re-established itself in the minds of many powerful people. Harris needed a major success, and perhaps a dose of symbolism, to demonstrate the war-winning potential of his force. Out of this was born the Thousand Plan, Operation *Millennium*, the commitment of 1,000 aircraft in one night against one of Germany's premier cities, for which Hamburg was pencilled in. Harris did not have 1,000 front-line aircraft, and would require the cooperation of other Commands if he were to reach the magic figure. In a letter to him on the 22nd, the C-in-C Coastal Command pledged a generous contribution of aircraft but following an intervention by the Admiralty, this was withdrawn a few days later. Undaunted, he, or more likely his affable and able deputy, AM Sir Robert Saundby, scraped together every airframe capable of a semblance of controlled flight, and pulled in the screened crews from their instructional duties. Over the succeeding days, from a wide range of training establishments from OTUs to gunnery schools came a motley collection of aged Wellingtons, Whitleys and Hampdens. They assembled on bomber stations the length of the country from Co. Durham to Bedfordshire, giving rise to much speculation about their purpose. In this way, come the night, not only would the symbolic figure of 1,000 aircraft be reached, it would be comfortably surpassed. The only remaining question was the weather, which, as the days ticked inexorably by towards the end of May, was not entering into the spirit of things. Harris was acutely aware that the giant fleet of aircraft was already being talked about. There existed a very real danger that it might draw attention to itself, particularly through enemy reconnaissance flights, and thereby compromise the operation in terms of both security and the element of surprise. There had been no major operations since Mannheim, and this could easily suggest to the enemy that something out of the ordinary was afoot. Harris allowed a raid by seventy-seven aircraft to take place on the 29/30th, against the Gnome & Rhone aero-engine factory at Gennevilliers in Paris, knowing that the time was fast approaching when *Millennium* would either have to take place or be abandoned for the time being. The raid was a failure, and reduced the *Millennium* force by four Wellingtons and a Halifax and their crews.

It was in an atmosphere of frustration, yet hopeful anticipation, that 'morning prayers' began at Harris's High Wycombe HQ on the 30th, all eyes turned upon the chief meteorological adviser, Magnus Spence. The initial weather forecasts were not promising and Spence awaited an update before giving his considered opinion. Finally, he was able to state with some certainty that north-western Germany, including Hamburg, would be concealed beneath a heavy front of cloud, while the Rhineland should have clearing skies after midnight with a chance of moonlight to illuminate the ground. After a moment or two of deliberation, Harris announced that Operation *Millennium* would be mounted that night against Cologne, towards which fate's fickle finger now pointed unerringly. It was a big day at Pocklington as 405 Squadron prepared for its maiden operation with Halifaxes. All crews had been recalled from leave on the 25th, and they were addressed by 4 Group's AOC, AVM Roddy Carr, on the 26th. With the green light for the operation possible at any moment, ground crews and armourers worked into the night on the 27/28th to ensure that all sixteen aircraft were on top line, with ammunition belts for the .303s securely installed. There was to be a late take-off for the squadrons equipped with four engine types which were to form the third and final wave of the attack, and it would be midnight or after before the 405 Squadron contingent left Pocklington. Nineteen Halifaxes were detailed to take part, including three from the Conversion Flight, but five were scratched before take-off through being unserviceable. One of the major worries of pushing large numbers of aircraft across the aiming point in a short period of time was the risk of collision. It had been determined by the statisticians that two aircraft would collide over the target, and legend has it that on one station a wag at the back of the room asked if the statisticians had worked out which two would be involved.

All in all, the 4 Group squadrons responded magnificently to the call for maximum effort and managed to launch 130 Halifaxes, nine Wellingtons and seven Whitleys, the last mentioned from training and HQ Flights. They took off with the rest of the force of 1,047 aircraft between 22.30 and shortly after midnight, some of the older training hacks climbing somewhat reluctantly into the air, lifted more by the enthusiasm of their crews than by engine power and flying characteristics. Some of these, unable to climb to a respectable height, would be among those failing to return from this historic operation. 405 Squadron managed to raise fourteen Halifaxes for its operational debut with the type; 102 Squadron launched nineteen; while 10, 35 and 76 Squadrons each put up twenty-one and 78 Squadron twenty-two. Even 1652 Conversion Unit at Marston Moor contributed twelve, and although a total of fourteen Halifaxes turned back early, the remainder played their part in a resoundingly successful assault. The leading crews of 1 and 3 Groups were again in Gee-equipped aircraft, and this enabled the spearhead of the giant force to locate the target without difficulty in the conditions. Magnus Spence was spot-on with his weather forecast, and Germany's third-largest city lay bathed in moonlight. This was not entirely good news, however, for while the conditions were eminently favourable to the bomber crews, they also assisted the defenders in equal measure and the night would bring anything but a one-sided contest. A total of 868 aircraft reached the target to bomb one of the three aiming points with their predominantly incendiary loads and the result was 2,500 individual fires, 1,700 of which were classed as large. The Cologne defences were completely overwhelmed, and the raid caused the destruction of over 3,000 buildings with damage to 10,000 more. Forty-one aircraft failed to return and this figure included 10 Squadron's W1042, which succumbed to a night fighter over Holland, killing Sgt Moore and two of his crew. The statisticians were correct in their prediction of just one collision over the target, and 405 Squadron's W7707 is believed to have been involved. Sgt Wadman and his crew lost their lives along with the crew of the other aircraft, a 61 Squadron Lancaster. One of the Conversion Unit Halifaxes was also missing, along with three Wellingtons, and a 78 Squadron Halifax was lost after colliding with another aircraft on the way home over Cambridgeshire.

Having expended so much effort to bring the Thousand force together, Harris intended to use it a number of times before it broke up. Buoyed up by the success at Cologne, he turned his attention upon Essen and prepared an operation for the night of 1/2 June. Some 956 aircraft and crews were able to answer the call for maximum effort, but despite extensive use of flares dropped again by the 3 Group raid leaders, Essen once more proved almost impossible to identify through the haze and partial cloud, and bombs were scattered over a wide expanse of the Ruhr. Only eleven houses were destroyed in the city, and less than 200 others were seriously damaged, a highly disappointing return for the massive effort expended and the loss of thirty-one aircraft. Despite the failure at Essen, the success at Cologne guaranteed the future of the Command and Harris could set about the fine-tuning of his strategies. The first of a number of follow-up raids was launched against Essen on the 2/3rd but the city again escaped serious damage. W/C Don Bennett resumed command of 10 Squadron on the 4th following his speedy return from Norway, and W/C Tait departed, soon to take over at 78 Squadron. Essen provided the objective for over 150 aircraft on the 5/6th, another failure, and the operation claimed 10 Squadron's W7696 near Cologne, with four survivors from the crew of F/S Rochford. 158 Squadron completed its move from Driffield to East Moor on the 6th, while 102 Squadron also changed residence on the 7th with a move from Dalton back to Topcliffe whence it had come some seven months earlier.

Essen hosted another raid on the night of the 8/9th, this time by 170 aircraft, more than half of them Wellingtons. The city remained elusive and suffered only minor damage for the loss of nineteen aircraft. It was a bad night for 35 Squadron, which had three Halifaxes brought down on enemy soil and a fourth ditch off Great Yarmouth. The last mentioned crew was picked up safely later on the 9th; one crew survived intact to be taken into captivity; another had two survivors, including the pilot who evaded capture; and one crew was killed to a man. W7699 was caught by Ofw Paul Gildner and sent crashing into the North Sea which swallowed up the pilot, P/O MacKenzie of the RNZAF, and two members of his crew. The others eventually came ashore between 16 July and 12 August, and were initially buried at the Hague, Bergen-op-Zoom and Den Burg, Texel. P/O MacKenzie's brother, a squadron leader and flight commander with 467 Squadron, was killed a year and three days later during an operation to Düsseldorf, and his fiancé was killed in

February 1944 while flying with the Air Transport Auxiliary. 78 Squadron completed its move back to Middleton-St-George from Croft on the 10th, but it would be a relatively short period of residence. Before the final 1,000 bomber raid took place, Emden was subjected to three medium-scale attacks in four nights, none of which was effective, and the first of these, on the 19/20th, cost 10 Squadron W1158. The Halifax crashed near Leeming half an hour after take-off, Sgt Ball having aborted the sortie in the face of technical problems, and there were no crew casualties. The second of the series, on the following night, resulted in BB201 going missing and with it went the crew of P/O Senior who had survived a ditching at the beginning of the month.

4 Group welcomed a newly-constituted French Canadian squadron to its bosom on the 25th in the form of 425 Squadron which took up residence at Dishforth under the command of W/C St Pierre. It would take until early October for the squadron to work up to operational readiness. The Thousand force was employed for the final time against Bremen on the 25/26th, when 960 Bomber Command aircraft were supported by 102 from Coastal Command which had been ordered by Prime Minister Churchill to take part. Officially these were recorded as separate operations, but the numbers converging on Bremen on this night exceeded those going to Cologne at the end of May. 405 Squadron despatched a creditable nineteen aircraft including two from the Conversion Flight, but two returned early with technical problems. While not achieving the success of the Cologne raid, the results far surpassed the debacle of Essen and left 572 houses completely destroyed and more than 6,000 others damaged to some extent, while some important war industry concerns were also hit. Forty-eight aircraft failed to return and this represented a new record high. It turned into a bad night for 102 Squadron, which had four empty dispersals to contemplate next morning. One of the squadron's missing Halifaxes was the Conversion Flight's V9987 in which F/S Duff and one of his crew were killed while the others were captured. These were the only survivors, after R9446, W7654 and W7759 all went into the sea with the crews of P/O Morgan, F/L Wright and F/L Harris respectively. Bremen received three follow-up raids in five nights, each with a degree of success, and culminating in one on 2/3 July which sank one ship in the harbour and damaged others besides inflicting the usual residential destruction.

Third quarter

1 July was celebrated at Pocklington as Canadian Dominion Day and happily no operations were planned for that night. A sports meeting was held during which W/C Fauquier reputedly won the 100-yard sprint, and a dance took place in the officers' mess that evening. Operationally, July began as June had ended, with a raid on Bremen for which over 300 aircraft were detailed. Much of the bombing probably fell on the city's southern fringes and beyond, but damage was caused to around 1,000 houses and seven ships were hit in the port. 405 Squadron's flight commander, S/L Fraser, had an eventful trip which included being flipped upside-down by a close burst of flak. Despite inoperative elevator trim, he went on to attack an alternative target before

returning safely along with the rest of the 405 Squadron contingent. Only one more major operation was mounted during the first half of the month, to Wilhelmshaven on the 8/9th: 285 aircraft took part, but a disappointing performance deposited most of the bombs in open country to the west of the town. On the 10th the much-travelled W/C Tait took over the reins of 78 Squadron from W/C Lucas. Having failed so spectacularly at Essen, Harris turned his attention upon another Ruhr giant, Duisburg, situated right at the western end of the region. He began a five-raid series on the 13/14th, a night beset with cloud and electrical storms. A scattered attack ensued which caused limited damage to residential property for the loss of six aircraft. An all four-engined force of ninety-nine aircraft was despatched to Vegesack on the 19/20th to attack the Vulkan U-boat yards if visibility allowed, or otherwise to bomb the town on Gee. Complete cloud cover enforced the latter but no bombs fell in Vegesack, while a few caused fairly minor damage in nearby Bremen. The next three raids on Duisburg took place over five nights from the 21/22nd. Almost 300 aircraft took part and the operation was modestly effective within the context of the period and the target. Ninety-four houses were destroyed and a further 250 seriously damaged but twelve aircraft were lost, most of them to night fighters operating in the Dutch coastal region. Two nights later 405 Squadron returned to the fray after sitting out the previous raid and contributed nine aircraft to a force of 215. Heavy cloud again led to scattered bombing and a modest amount of housing was destroyed or damaged. On return, W7769 crashed in Pocklington village as F/S Albright was attempting to land and all eight men on board were killed. Mercifully and miraculously, the crash in a narrow part of New Street resulted in no civilian casualties, and only slight damage was sustained by one house. Over 300 aircraft returned to Duisburg on the 25/26th, but visibility was again poor and no assessment was possible from the air. Some damage had been caused but less than in the two earlier raids, and another twelve aircraft failed to make it back.

Reversals in the Middle East campaign resulted in requests for heavy bombers to be sent out to Palestine. 10 and 76 Squadrons were ordered to send a detachment each of sixteen aircraft for what was supposed to be a short-term detachment. The first two from 'Shiny Ten', W1174 and W7756, departed for the staging post at Gibraltar on 4 July. Less than two hours before departure, W/C Bennett was told to hand over command of the detachment to W/C Seymour-Price, and thereafter to report to Bomber Command HQ. Seven more Halifaxes left on the following day, and the final seven on the 6th. Shortly before 04.00 on the 10th the first of 76 Squadron's eight Halifaxes roared down the runway at Middleton-St-George and lifted off for Gibraltar and warmer climes. Four days later W/C Young led off the second flight of eight, which navigated its way down the Welsh coast past the Bay of Biscay, hugging the coast of Portugal and negotiating the Straits of Gibraltar. The activities of this detachment, no longer under Bomber Command control, fall outside the scope of this work. The home echelon would continue to operate at reduced capacity, and the Middle East contingent would eventually be absorbed into 462 Squadron under the command of W/C Young. S/L

'Jock' Calder was put in temporary command of the 76 Squadron's home echelon on the 14th and began the process of rebuilding. A force of ninety-nine four-engined aircraft targeted the Vulkan U-boat yards at Vegesack on the night of the 19/20th, but encountered complete cloud cover and bombed on Gee. No bombs fell within the town and three Halifaxes failed to return. Among them was W1179 of 158 Squadron, which was shot down into the sea off Terschelling at 02.40 local time by Major Alfred Helm of II NJG 2 based at the so-called Wasps Nest aerodrome at Leeuwarden. There were no survivors from the crew of P/O Skelly, whose body was the first to be washed ashore later that day. The sea gave up five other crew members at various locations between then and 8 August, among them navigator Sgt Roland Smith, who was found on 1 August and interred in Den Burg Cemetery, Texel later that day with full military honours.

In each year of the war the Command attacked Hamburg during the final week of July. Over 400 aircraft were assembled for take-off late on the 26th, W/C Fauquier leading the 405 Squadron contingent of thirteen with G/C Brook, the 4 Group SASO, acting as his second pilot. Icing conditions during part of the outward flight caused some difficulties, but the skies were clear over Germany's second city and most of the bomb loads found their way into its residential and commercial districts where over 800 fires were started. It was Hamburg's worst night of the war to date, which left over 800 houses in ruins and a further 5,000 damaged to some extent. Bomber losses were high, however, amounting to twenty-nine. Two nights later Hamburg was raided again, only this time by a force of sixty-eight 3 Group aircraft, after bad weather had intervened. The 1, 4 and 5 Group contribution had been withdrawn altogether, and an OTU contingent had been recalled while outbound over the North Sea. The first large raid of the war on Saarbrücken took place on the 29/30th and involved almost 300 aircraft, including seven 405 Squadron Halifaxes. Opposition was expected to be light, and crews were urged to attack from lower than normal to ensure accuracy. A number of the 405 Squadron crews entered into the spirit of the occasion by attacking from as low as 4,000 feet, and they returned to report fires visible from 75 miles away. The town had indeed been dealt a telling blow, in which almost 400 buildings were destroyed in central and north-western districts. On the last night of the month 630 aircraft were assembled for a raid on Düsseldorf, in which the training units were again to take part. After the obligatory early return, eleven 405 Squadron crews pressed on to the target, and contributed to a highly effective attack which destroyed over 450 buildings in the city and in nearby Neuss. The defenders fought back to claim another twenty-nine bombers, and 405 Squadron was again forced to post missing two of its crews. W1109 crashed in Germany without survivors from the crew of Sgt Hunter, and W7718 went down in flames over Belgium taking with it the rear gunner. Sgt West and four others escaped by parachute to fall into enemy hands, but the severely wounded wireless operator died three days later. This left only the bomb-aimer unaccounted for, and he, Sgt Pearce, ultimately evaded capture to return home.

August would bring changes for 405 Squadron and, indeed, for the

Command as a whole. First, however, W/C Wildey officially took command of 10 Squadron on the 1st, and set about the task of bringing it back up to full strength after the departure of the Middle East echelon some four weeks earlier. 405 Squadron sent two aircraft as part of a force of ten Halifaxes on a daylight cloud-cover operation to Hamburg on the 3rd. These forays rarely if ever resulted in success as cloud invariably disappeared when enemy territory was reached, and the crews would be forced to return early. They were also dangerous operations, and W/C Fauquier, typically, was in one of the 405 Squadron aircraft that cruised up and down the enemy coast in vain for ninety minutes in the hope that cloud might materialize. Late on the 4th, thirty-eight aircraft took off to bomb Essen, but severe icing conditions during the outward flight prevented more than half of the force from reaching the target area. Of the five 405 Squadron participants, one returned early after trying to press on with a dead engine, until overheating in the other three forced the issue. Flak over the Ruhr was fierce, and after bombing on Gee, two of the squadron's aircraft returned with damage. On the 5th, as his highly successful tour as commanding officer was about to end, W/C Fauquier was awarded a well-deserved DFC. Also on the 5th W/C Cheshire was appointed to the command of 76 Squadron in place of S/L Calder. 420 Squadron joined 4 Group from 5 Group on the 6th and moved into Skipton-on-Swale. As a Hampden unit it had taken part in ninety operations since its formation on 19 December 1941. W/C Bradshaw had been in command ever since, and would remain at the helm until well into the coming year. It would take some time to fully re-equip with Wellington IIIs but the first one, BJ644, arrived immediately, to be followed on the 11th by X3808 and X3809. Three more would be taken on charge on the 19th, X3814, Z1724 and BJ717, while X3963 would arrive on the 27th and BJ966 on the 28th. The remainder were to be received in September, chronologically X3800, BK235, BJ915, BK295, BK296, BK297, BJ917 and BK331, but it would be the following month before the squadron could be declared operational.

The last of the five-raid series on Duisburg was undertaken by over 200 aircraft on the 6/7th, but in keeping with the general performance over the Ruhr at the time, most of the bombing fell into open country. Eighteen houses were destroyed, and this brought the tally of destruction to a little over 200 houses from 1,229 sorties over three weeks for the loss of forty-three aircraft. In this, 405 Squadron's final operation from Pocklington, six aircraft took part, one of them returning early to collide with two parked Wellingtons. The others returned safely, although one was displaying the evidence of an encounter with a night fighter. Earlier in the day, W/C Fauquier had handed over command of the squadron to the newly-promoted W/C Fraser, and departed to take up a staff post with the RCAF's Overseas HQ. The next day, the squadron swapped stations with 102 Squadron, and moved to Topcliffe for what would be a short stay. For 102 Squadron, however, Pocklington would provide a home for the next three years. The process of changing residence was never allowed to interfere with operations, and 405 Squadron had barely settled in at its new home before next appearing on the order of battle. The target on the 9/10th was Osnabrück, for which almost 200 aircraft were detailed. The operation took place in good visibility but the flares were not concentrated, and this led to a general scattering of bombs across the town. Some 200 houses were destroyed, while a further 4,000 were damaged to some extent and a number of industrial concerns were hit, as was the docks area which sustained considerable damage. This first operation mounted by 405 Squadron from Topcliffe was soured by a casualty, as W7709 failed to return. It was later established that the Halifax had been shot down by a night fighter over Holland, and that F/L Bain and his crew had lost their lives. Two raids on Mainz followed on the 11/12th and 12/13th, the former providing W/C Cheshire with his first opportunity to lead 76 Squadron into battle. The two operations left extensive damage in central districts, where the railway station was hit, and also in industrial areas. The two operations cost a total of eleven aircraft, including a 405 Squadron Halifax during the earlier one, and this was W7748, which crashed in Germany. F/S Langford-Pudney and three of his crew were killed, while the flight engineer, navigator and rear gunner escaped by parachute to become PoWs. A disproportionately high loss rate among Halifaxes had led to an investigation, which pointed to rudder-overbalance as a major cause of accidents. It was decided to modify all tail units and this took place during August, thus grounding squadrons for periods and reducing the Halifaxes contribution to the offensive. It was during this time, on the 12th, that 419 Squadron arrived at Leeming with its Wellingtons on posting from 3 Group. 419 was the third Canadian unit to be formed in Bomber Command, and that had occurred on 15 December 1941. Since then it had participated in seventy-seven operations, but it had now been earmarked for conversion to the Halifax, and ultimately for a home within the soon-to-be-formed Canadian 6 Group. Its commanding officer was W/C Walsh, who had been in the hot seat for just one week, but it carried in its name, Moose, the memory of its first boss, W/C 'Moose' Fulton, a highly popular and inspirational leader who had disappeared into the North Sea with his crew back on 29 July.

On the 15th, the Pathfinder Force came into existence under the then Group Captain Don Bennett, who proved to be a controversial but inspired choice by Harris. Bennett's pre-war experience as a pilot and navigator was unparalleled, and his grasp of all matters pertaining to engineering and technology left most floundering in his wake. Before embarking on his operational career he had been entrusted with setting up the highly successful Atlantic Ferry Service, which brought much-needed American aircraft to the UK. As already described, his operational experience was current and had been gained as the commanding officer of 77 and 10 Squadrons between December 1941 and July 1942, and his adventures in Norway had ably demonstrated his airmanship and resourcefulness. He would set standards that few could achieve but despite this, and his well-documented humourless personality, he was to attract a fierce loyalty among his crews, who would one day include those of 405 Squadron. The appointment of such a junior officer ruffled a few feathers among the other AOCs, all but one of whom shared Harris's opinion, that the formation of an elitist target-locating and marking force was both unnecessary and ill-advised. Once overruled, of course, Harris, in typical fashion, gave the new organization his unstinting support and was eager to bring it into battle at the first possible opportunity. Each heavy Group provided one squadron as a founder member, and would be responsible for maintaining a steady supply of the best crews from its front-line units. Only 4 Group's AVM Roddy Carr was kindly disposed towards the Pathfinders from the beginning, and he would ensure that his Group 'played the game' with regard to the posting of quality crews to 35 Squadron. He also proved to be a useful ally to Bennett, who had served him well during his time with 4 Group. The new force would fall nominally under the control of 3 Group until being granted Group status in its own right, and would, therefore, lodge somewhat uneasily on the stations of AVM Baldwin, one of those least well-disposed towards it. 1 Group was represented by the former 3 Group unit, 156 Squadron, with its Wellingtons at Warboys, while 3 Group nominated 7 Squadron, which remained with its Stirlings at Oakington. 35 Squadron took up residence at Graveley with its Halifaxes, and 5 Group's 83 Squadron flew its Lancasters into Wyton, where Bennett initially set up his HQ. This all took place between the 15th and the 17th, and 109 Squadron, already at Wyton since the 6th, joined the Pathfinder ranks to continue its pioneering work in marrying the Oboe blind-bombing device to the Mosquito.

Leeming turned out to be only a staging post for 419 Squadron, which departed the station on the 17th after a stay of just five days. Its new home was at Topcliffe, where it would also have little time to settle in before moving on again. A raid on Osnabrück on the night of the 17/18th had been intended as the maiden operation for the new force, but in the event it went ahead as a standard operation by over 100 aircraft, and achieved moderate success. On the following night, the Pathfinders went to war for the first time with thirty-one aircraft ahead of eighty-seven from the main force bound for the port of Flensburg. Situated on the narrow neck of land where Germany and Denmark meet, it should have been relatively easy to locate, but the only bombs to fall on this night were reported by the occupants of Danish towns. It was not a distinguished beginning to what would become an illustrious career for the PFF, and there was little improvement at Frankfurt on the 24/25th, when the city proved difficult to locate in cloudy conditions. Enough bombs found it to cause fires and some property damage, but most fell into open country to the north and west. The third Pathfinder-led operation took place against Kassel on the 27/28th, when sparse cloud allowed the city to be illuminated sufficiently for the main force crews to identify the aiming points, and over 450 buildings were either destroyed or seriously damaged. Thus far, path-finding had amounted to locating the target and illuminating it with flares, but the process evolved somewhat on the 28/29th, when rudimentary target indicators in 250lb bomb casings were used for the first time at Nuremberg. The Pathfinder crews carried out their briefed task accurately, but the main force crews produced scattered bombing and damage was fairly modest. Meanwhile, an experimental raid was in progress at Saarbrücken, employing Wellingtons, Hampdens and twenty-four Halifaxes from 4 Group, which were still being rested from main force operations while undergoing modifications. No Pathfinder aircraft were present, and the operation was an almost complete failure. 10 Squadron had by this time undertaken its final wartime change of address, when moving on the 19th to Melbourne. Between 28 August and 23 October, however, 10 Squadron would conduct its operations from Pocklington, the home of 102 Squadron since its move from Topcliffe on the 7th, while the runways at Melbourne were brought up to standard.

4 Group returned fully to operations at the start of September, and contributed aircraft to a raid intended for Saarbrücken on the night of the 1/2nd. In an ignominious beginning to the month's operations, the Pathfinders posted a 'black' by marking the nearby non-industrial town of Saarlouis in error. For once, the main force bombing was accurate and dealt a severe blow to the town. It was spared the bombs of one 405 Squadron Halifax, however, which suffered an engine fire over the English coast while outbound. Structural failure of the wing followed, and BB216 plunged earthwards to crash in Lincolnshire, a few miles north of Skegness. Sgt MacKenzie and three of his crew were killed, at least two of them through parachuting into the sea and drowning, but three others survived with injuries. The Pathfinder blunder might have been seen as an ill omen for the remainder of the month, but in the event, it heralded an almost unprecedented series of effective operations over the ensuing two weeks. On the 2/3rd, Karlsruhe was rocked by an accurate attack which left 200 fires burning for the loss of twelve aircraft. The single missing Halifax was 405 Squadron's DT487, in which the eight-man crew of F/L Hillier were killed following an encounter with a night fighter over Belgium. Two nights later, over 200 aircraft destroyed 480 buildings in Bremen, and seriously damaged a further 1,400. This was the occasion on which the Pathfinders introduced the three-phase technique of illumination, visual marking and backing-up, which was to form the basis of all future operations. On the 6/7th, over 100 buildings were destroyed in a scattered raid on Duisburg and although this was a relatively modest haul, it still represented something of a victory at this elusive target. The run of successes was temporarily halted at Frankfurt on the 8/9th, another notoriously difficult target to locate, when most of the bomb loads fell miles away. The force of 479 aircraft bound for Düsseldorf on the 10/11th included a contribution from the Training Groups, and the Pathfinders employed 'Pink Pansies' in 4,000lb bomb casings for the first time. Accurate marking and bombing resulted in the destruction of over 900 houses in the city and nearby Neuss, and many thousands more were damaged to some extent. Bomber losses were high, however, amounting to thirty-three aircraft missing, although the 405 Squadron casualty occurred at home. Problems began for Sgt Webb and his crew when BB212 was hit by flak over enemy territory and began to lose height. Both gunners were ordered to bale out, but sadly failed to survive their descent, and the others remained with the aircraft as it struggled back to Topcliffe. On landing the Halifax collided with a parked 419 Squadron Wellington before coming to a halt, and the wireless operator was found to be dead at the scene. Whether he was killed by the flak or in the crash is uncertain, but Sgt Webb and the two remaining crew members survived with minor injuries to earn a very short-lived reprieve.

The advanced party of a new recruit to 4 Group began moving from Balderton in Nottinghamshire into Leeming on the 13th. 408 Squadron was the second RCAF unit to be formed in Bomber Command, and came into existence in 5 Group on 24 June 1941. It took part in 191 operations, all but one of them in Hampdens, and a single operation, in fact just a single sortie was undertaken in a Manchester. That was to Cologne in the first of the 'Thousand' raids at the end of May, and technical problems had forced it to return home early anyway. This was the start of a new era in a new Group with new aircraft. Meanwhile, 446 aircraft began taking off either side of midnight on the 13/14th for a return to Bremen, the numbers again bolstered by an element from the training units. Almost 850 houses were destroyed, and a number of highly important war industry factories were damaged sufficiently to cause a loss of production. This impressive success for the Command exceeded that gained by the Thousand force back in June, yet employed a force only half as large. On the 14/15th Wilhelmshaven recorded its heaviest and most destructive raid to date, during which 408 Squadron carried out the final bombing sorties of the war by the venerable old Hampden. Even Essen was hit harder than ever before when attacked by over 300 aircraft on the 16/17th, and fifteen high-explosive bombs fell into the Krupp complex, along with a crashing bomber. Despite the improvement in accuracy, however, many bombs were sprayed onto other Ruhr towns, and the answer to pinpoint accuracy over the region had still not been found. The burgeoning effectiveness of the Ruhr defensive screen was also apparent from the loss of a massive thirty-nine aircraft, one of which was a 405 Squadron Halifax. W7770 had begun to display technical problems during the outward flight, but F/S Murray and his crew pressed on to the target to bomb. On the way home, the ailing aircraft was picked up by a night fighter and shot down over France, killing the pilot and four others. The flight engineer, the only non-Canadian member of the crew, and the wireless operator escaped by parachute, the latter ultimately evading capture.

It can be no coincidence that this period of more effective operations had come at a time when the fledgling Pathfinder Force was coming to terms with the complex and demanding requirements of its role. The crews had been pitched into the offensive without dedicated training, and had to learn their trade during the heat of battle. If any period can be identified as the turning point in the long metamorphosis to becoming a war-winning weapon, then perhaps these two weeks in September was it. There would be no overnight transformation, and failures would continue to outnumber successes for some time to come, but the signs were there, and it boded ill for German towns and cities in the future. 78 Squadron was on the move again, and completed its move from Middleton-St-George to Linton-on-Ouse on the 16th. 408 Squadron was stood down from operations on the 17th, the day on which it completed its move to Leeming, and a conversion flight was set up to begin the training of crews on the Halifax. Air crews were detached to 1652 HCU at Marston Moor, while ground crews were sent to other Halifax units to begin their training. The larger crew complement of the type demanded an increase in personnel, and these were forthcoming from the OTUs. W/C 'Tiny' Ferris had been in command since the start of the month, and would remain at the helm for another year. The 17th was also the day on which 76 Squadron completed its move from Middleton-St-George to join 78 Squadron at Linton-on-Ouse. The weather during the second half of September was not helpful to bombing operations, and a number of nights were devoted to small-scale raids conducted without a Pathfinder presence. 425 Squadron suffered its first casualties on the 22nd through a training accident. F/S Kuzyk and his crew were engaged in a fighter affiliation exercise when BJ695 collided with a Spitfire over Yorkshire and crashed, killing all on board. The Spitfire, flown by an American, Sgt Norman, also crashed, and he too lost his life. Flensburg was to feature prominently for the Halifax brigade, and twenty-eight of them set out for the port on the night of the 23/24th. Only sixteen crews reported bombing as briefed, and five aircraft failed to return. The sole 405 Squadron casualty involved the previously mentioned Sgt Webb, who had four new crewmen with him to replace those lost two weeks earlier. Their Halifax, W1274, crashed in Denmark, and all on board were killed. Another attempt was made on this target on the 26/27th, but all but one crew responded to a recall signal and abandoned their sorties. 419 Squadron was on the road again, completing its move to Croft on the 30th having taken part in three operations while at Topcliffe.

Fourth quarter

October began with yet another operation to Flensburg on the night of the 1/2nd, this time by twenty-seven Halifaxes of which eight were from 405 Squadron, although two of these came back early. Twelve returning crews claimed good results, but by the time they had completed their debriefing, it was evident that 4 Group had suffered a disastrous night. Twelve Halifaxes failed to return home, and 25 per cent of them were from 405 Squadron. W7780 went down over the target with a 425 Squadron crew on board and none survived, and W7802 also crashed in the target area, killing the eight-man crew of P/O Duncan. W7710 was shot down close to Germany's frontier with Denmark, and took with it to their deaths the crew of F/O Olsen. On the very next night, DG228 failed to return from a disappointing raid on Krefeld, and it was later established that the Halifax had been brought down by flak over Holland with no survivors from the crew of Sgt Murphy. 419 Squadron launched its first nine sorties from Croft on the night of the 2/3rd when Krefeld was the target. The operation did not reflect the successes of the previous month, and the squadron registered the loss of its first crew from its new home. BK269 failed to survive an encounter with a night fighter over Holland, and just one man survived as a PoW from the crew of F/S Stowe. On the 5th 77 Squadron returned from Coastal Command to reclaim its rightful place in Bomber Command. Still under the command of W/C Embling, it took up residence at the newly-opened station at Elvington. The Whitleys were exchanged for Mk II Halifaxes, but these were withdrawn temporarily and replaced with Mk Vs. Working up to operational status was to prove a lengthy process, and would not be achieved until well into the coming year. That night over 250 aircraft took off in bad weather conditions, which persisted all the way to Aachen. The attack was only modestly effective, and many of the bombs fell

17 miles away onto the Dutch town of Lutterade. *(This was not appreciated at Bomber Command HQ, which would select a power station in the town for the first Mosquito Oboe bombing operation in December, believing it to be free of bomb craters and therefore suitable for use as a calibration check on the device's margin of error.)* 405 Squadron's W7703 was low on fuel as it returned across the south coast, and Sgt Hudema opted to land at West Malling. He aborted his first attempt, and while going round again, the Halifax stalled and plunged towards the Kent countryside north-east of Sevenoaks. The bomb-aimer and rear gunner managed to escape by parachute before the impact, but the pilot and four others were killed. This was the first operation for 425 Squadron, which despatched eight Wellingtons, but it became an unhappy debut after X3943 crashed in Essex on return, killing the crew of Sgt O'Driscoll. This operation also marked the return of 420 Squadron to operational duties. The squadron's move from Skipton-on-Swale to Middleton-St-George occurred at this time, although the next few operations would be launched from Leeming.

405 Squadron's harrowing start to the month continued two nights later, when W7763 was shot down over Holland by a night fighter during a raid on Osnabrück. P/O Stewart and his crew all abandoned the stricken Halifax, but one of the gunners was killed when his parachute failed to deploy. The survivors were all taken into captivity. W/C Stevens relinquished his command of 158 squadron on the 7th on posting to 10 OTU at Abingdon, and he was replaced by flight commander W/C Robinson who was recalled from leave. On the 8th W/C Tuck handed over the command of 51 Squadron, still in Coastal Command, to W/C Sawyer, who had been the commanding officer of 78 Squadron between July 1941 and the end of the year, and had also served with 76 Squadron. It was he who presided over 51 Squadron's return to Bomber Command on 27 October, and oversaw its conversion onto the Halifax at Snaith, a station at which the squadron would remain almost until the end of hostilities. The first Mk II Halifaxes arrived on squadron charge during November, but it would not be until the first day of the New Year that the squadron would be declared operational.

There were no major operations during the following week, and it was during this period, on the 10th, that 466 Squadron RAAF was formed on paper at Driffield under the command of S/L Bailey, who would soon be promoted in keeping with his status. It seems that the physical formation probably occurred on the 15th, but the first Wellingtons, X3790 and Z1692, did not arrive until the 29th. By the end of November a further twenty-four would be on charge, but it seems likely that some of these found their way to another new unit forming in early November. On the 11th 408 Squadron began to take delivery of its first Halifaxes. They were Mk Vs, which differed from Mk IIs only in the manufacture of the undercarriage. Training would occupy the squadron for the remainder of the year, and as events turned out, the squadron would be posted from 4 Group before conducting any operations under its banner. The next major operation took place on the night of the 13/14th when the target for almost 300 aircraft was Kiel, where a nearby decoy fire site had been prepared. This was highly effective in attracting at least half of the bomb loads, while the remainder inflicted moderate damage within the town. This was the last time that 420 Squadron operated out of Leeming, and all of its participants returned safely to home airspace before problems arose for two of them. P/O Adilman overshot the approach when trying to put X3963 down at Docking in Norfolk, and the Wellington ultimately crashed near the airfield, although fortunately without serious injury to the crew. F/S Croft and his crew, on the other hand, had no luck and all were killed when DF636 crashed during an attempted landing at Leeming.

Two new Canadian squadrons came into existence in 4 Group on 15 October, 424 at Topcliffe under the command of W/C Carscallen, and 426 at Dishforth under W/C Blanchard. Both were to begin life on Wellingtons, although neither would carry out operations with the type before their transfer to 6 Group. BJ658 was the first example to be taken on 424 Squadron charge six days after formation, and twelve more were added by 8 November. This allowed the process of working-up to operational status to begin in earnest, and no aircraft or crews were lost during the training period. 426 Squadron received its first four Wellingtons, BJ888, DF617, DF619 and DF620 on the 23rd. Meanwhile, on the night of their formation, the 15/16th, a force of over 280 aircraft was prepared for a raid on Cologne where another decoy site was equally successful in luring the crews away from the real objective. Only a handful of high-explosive bombs landed in the city, and damage was consequently minor. This failure was achieved at a cost of eighteen aircraft, among them 10 Squadron's W1058 which crashed near Bonn killing W/C Wildey and two of his crew. 420 Squadron suffered again, when X3808 was lost without trace with the crew of F/S White on what was the squadron's first operation launched from Middleton-St-George. This operation also brought about 405 Squadron's seventh loss in the space of two weeks. W7854 fell victim to a night fighter over Belgium, and F/S Longley and his crew were all killed. As events turned out, this was to be the last of the squadron's crews to go missing under Bomber Command for five months. New surroundings and a new role beckoned with Coastal Command, and preparations were put in hand to move the squadron from Yorkshire to Beaulieu, on the edge of the New Forest in Hampshire. W/C Carter was installed as the new commanding officer of 10 Squadron on the 16th. On the 24th, fifteen 405 Squadron Halifaxes and crews took part in the move to Beaulieu, along with five from 158 Squadron at East Moor, and they would consequently miss the next phase of the bomber offensive which now switched to Italian targets in support of Operation *Torch*, the Allied landings in North Africa. 405 Squadron would return to Bomber Command in March 1943 to serve briefly with the Canadian 6 Group. After around five weeks, however, it would be posted to 8 Group, as the Pathfinder Force had by then become, as the only RCAF representative.

The above-mentioned campaign in support of Operation *Torch* had opened with a 5 Group attack on Genoa on the 22/23rd, with 3 and 4 Groups following up twenty-four hours later, although actually bombing the coastal town of Savona in error. A tragic event in the early hours of the 24th on return from this operation cost 102 Squadron its commanding officer. Having landed at Holme-on-Spalding-Moor, W/C Bintley's DT512 was unable to clear the runway because of a burst tyre, and it was hit by the squadron's W1181 which was captained by F/S Berry. The latter crew was unhurt, but W/C Bintley was killed, and his wireless operator later succumbed to his injuries. Also on board W/C Bintley's aircraft but escaping injury, was the Pocklington Station Commander G/C Corbally. Later on the 24th, 5 Group raided Milan to good effect in daylight, to be followed by elements of 1 and 3 Groups after dark, and this effectively ended the month's operations.

W/C Holden was posted in as 102 Squadron's new commanding officer on the 26th, having on the previous day relinquished his command of 158 Squadron's Conversion Flight. His career to this point had been distinguished, and he had been involved in some unusual and spectacular operations. He had also rubbed shoulders with some of the Command's finest young bloods, many of whom were gathered within the squadrons of 4 Group, and were themselves seen as shining lights. Holden began basic training, presumably part-time as a reservist, in May 1937. On 1 September 1939, the day German forces began their assault on Poland, he joined 9 FTS at Hullavington, moved on to Benson between January and early May 1940, and thence to 10 OTU at Abingdon, where he learned to fly Whitleys. He passed out as a first pilot, day only, with an average rating on 18 September, and immediately joined 78 Squadron at Dishforth. Here he began working up to operational status, and undertook his first sortie as second pilot to a F/L Pattison in a raid on Antwerp on the night of 26/27 September. His second sortie was flown to Amsterdam with his flight commander, S/L Wildey, and it was not until 11 November that Holden was signed out as a fully qualified Whitley captain by his newly-appointed commanding officer, W/C 'Charles' Whitworth. Two nights later he undertook his first operation as crew captain, his eighth sortie in all, but like many others operating in poor weather conditions that night, he was forced to abandon his sortie and return home. He put matters right on the 15/16th, however, when participating in an unusually effective raid on Hamburg.

Among the pilots from 78 Squadron selected for the previously mentioned SAS attack on the aqueduct at Tragino in 1941 was P/O Holden, who flew with Tait on a container-dropping test as part of the run-up on 2 February. This operation was Holden's twentieth, and his last with 78 Squadron, which he left with an above average rating to join 35 Squadron at Linton-on-Ouse. Holden arrived on 25 February 1941, and met up again with Tait. Holden flew his first Halifax sortie against Duisburg on 11/12 June, and over the ensuing five weeks managed ten more. He flew against the German cruiser *Scharnhorst* at La Pallice in daylight on 24 July, when he was forced to bring his bombs home after flak shot away the electrical release gear. One of his crew was killed while two others were wounded, one seriously. Holden concluded his tour on a total of thirty-two operations, and was posted to the Heavy Conversion Flight at Linton-on-Ouse on 18 August. Here he remained until December, when he was detached to Upavon before progressing to Marston Moor, Leeming and Pocklington progressively in the role of instructor. At Pocklington, and now in the rank of Squadron Leader, he was put in charge of the Conversion Flight of 405 Squadron, and while there flew on the second thousand-bomber raid against Essen on 1/2 June and the third and final one on Bremen on the 25/26th, his thirty-third and thirty-fourth sorties. In July he was posted to 158 Squadron's Conversion Flight at East Moor, where he remained until called to fill the vacancy at the helm of 102 Squadron.

51 Squadron returned to Bomber Command on the 27th and settled in at Snaith, the station that would be its home almost until the end of hostilities. The first Mk II Halifaxes arrived on squadron charge during November, but it would not be until the first day of the New Year that the squadron would be declared operational. On 1 November W/C Tait relinquished command of 78 Squadron on posting to 4 Group HQ, and he was succeeded by W/C Warner. Tait was to finish the war with one of the finest records of service in the entire Command, and perhaps his 'finest hour' came after he succeeded Cheshire as commanding officer of 617 Squadron in July 1944. It took an outstanding leader of men to follow in the steps of Gibson and Cheshire and to command a group of men who believed themselves to be a special and privileged breed. Tait would lead the squadron from the front and end his operational career in December 1944 with a deserved and unprecedented three DSOs. Back to November 1942 and 158 Squadron settled into its new home at Rufforth following the move from East Moor. 427 Squadron was formed on the 7th, on the same day that 428 and 429 Squadrons also came into existence as the eighth, ninth and tenth Canadian units in Bomber Command. 427 Squadron's first home was at Croft, and its nucleus was provided by ten crews from 419 Squadron, who remained on the station while their colleagues moved to the Heavy Conversion Unit at Topcliffe and ultimately Middleton-St-George to take on Halifaxes. Three more crews were added from elsewhere, and sixteen Wellington IIIs were made available on the 9th, so that training could begin under the watchful eye of the commanding officer, W/C Burnside. 428 Squadron's first home was at Dalton, where it took on Wellingtons, the first two, X3545 and X3546, arriving from 466 RAAF Squadron on 26 November. Eleven more aircraft would be taken on charge by 8 December so that training could begin in earnest under the supervision of the commanding officer, W/C Earle. Unlike the other two new units, 429 Squadron was destined to remain in 4 Group until the end of March 1943, when its home station of East Moor would also be transferred to Canadian control. Commanded by W/C Owen, the squadron's first four Wellingtons, BJ798, BJ799, BJ908 and DF625 arrived on 24 November, and a total of twenty-six aircraft were on strength by 10 December. Yet another new Wellington unit was formed in 4 Group on this day, 196 Squadron at Driffield, although it would have to wait until 1 December before receiving its first aircraft. Presumably it would borrow whatever it could lay its hands on in the meantime, and possibly called upon fellow Driffieldites, 466 Squadron. X3357 finally arrived on 1 December, and within a week there would be fifteen on charge, by which time W/C Waterhouse had been installed as the commanding officer. He got down to the business of training up his crews, who would not be called upon to operate until the following February.

A low-key start to operations in November meant that the Halifax contingent remained on the ground until the night of the 7/8th, when forty-five of the type joined Lancasters and Stirlings at Genoa. Training on a new type rarely proceeded without incident, and almost inevitably, 408 suffered a serious accident which cost it a Halifax and the greater part of a crew. It occurred on the 9th, when DG238 stalled near Croft while engaged in a fighter affiliation exercise, and F/S Bell and four of his crew died in the ensuing crash. This was the first Mk V Halifax to be written off in Bomber Command service. Also on the 9th 419 Squadron completed its move from Croft, having flown eight operations from the station. Its new home was Middleton-St-George, where it would begin a conversion programme onto the Halifax, and examples of the less-than-popular Mk II variant began to arrive on squadron charge during the course of the month. That night over 200 aircraft were sent to Hamburg, where a disappointing attack ensued for the loss of fifteen aircraft, an unhealthy 7 per cent of the force. 102 Squadron's DT539 was on its way home when it was hit by flak from a number of batteries, and crashed onto the island of Texel at 22.05 local time. There was a mixed RCAF/RAF crew on board plus a second pilot, and F/S Marler and his colleagues all lost their lives. They were buried with full military honours in Den Burg Cemetery on the 13th. Yet another new Canadian squadron, 431, was formed in 4 Group on the 11th. Its first home was at Burn, where W/C Coverdale would be installed as commanding officer on 1 December. The squadron was equipped with Wellington Mk Xs, and it would be one of those units remaining and operating in 4 Group until well after the majority had congregated in 6 Group. Other operations involving the Group included Genoa on the 15/16th, Turin on the 18/19th and 20/21st and Stuttgart on the 22/23rd, the last-mentioned a disappointing raid. The month ended for 4 Group with participation in another attack on Turin on the 28/29th, which proceeded according to plan after initial difficulties. 419 Squadron registered its almost inevitable training accident during the conversion stage on the 30th, when DT540 crash-landed at Middleton-St-George while in the hands of F/S Frederick and crew, but no injuries were reported. The Moosemen would not be declared operational until after their transfer to 6 Group on the first day of the coming year.

The Lions, 427 Squadron, were declared operational on 1 December, remarkably soon after formation, and now had eighteen Wellingtons on charge. December would turn out to be a less hectic month, beginning with a trip to Frankfurt on the 2/3rd which produced nothing of note. While on attachment to 102 Squadron to gain operational experience on Halifaxes, 77 Squadron's W/C Embling took part in this operation in W7916, captained by S/L Walkington. This was one of three 102 Squadron aircraft to fail to return on this night, but W/C Embling survived and ultimately evaded capture. Two 427 Squadron crews flew their Wellingtons to Middleton-St-George on the 4th to take on mines for the squadron's maiden operation, but poor weather conditions forced it to be called off. Mannheim was the target for a mixed force on the night of the 6/7th, but heavy cloud led to an ineffective attack. Later on the 7th, Mk II Halifaxes began to arrive at Leeming to replace the Mk Vs, and these would now form 408 Squadron's equipment for the next nine months. It was back to Turin on the 9/10th and 11/12th, neither of which operations was successful, and half of the force turned back early from the latter because of severe icing conditions. A week after W/C Embling's failure to return from Frankfurt, W/C 'Lofty' Lowe was installed as 77 Squadron's new commanding officer. Arthur Lowe had joined the RAF as a 'Halton Brat' in 1930, and learned the trade of wireless operator/air gunner. He was a good athlete, displayed leadership qualities, and was named 'Lofty' by his peers. While a corporal with 77 Squadron at Driffield in 1940, he was promoted to sergeant and selected for training as a gunnery leader. On his return to Driffield he was commissioned and began his rise through the ranks. As a gunner, Lowe's appointment to the command of 77 Squadron was not popular among the pilots, particularly his two flight commanders who considered themselves to have been overlooked, and it took time for the resentment to subside. In time, however, his characteristic firmness, fairness and friendliness to all ranks would win over the detractors, and he became a popular and well-respected leader. 427 Squadron eventually opened its account on the night of the 14/15th, when three of the former 419 Squadron crews, those of Sgts Gagnon, Higgins and Fellner, took off from Middleton-St-George in Z1626, BK364 and Z1676 respectively as part of a mining operation around the Frisians. Only the first-mentioned found his pinpoint and delivered his mines, while the others had to bring their loads home. Sadly, and by coincidence, all three of these pilots would be taken from the squadron in June 1943, two fatally on the same night, and the other as a seriously wounded PoW. The Group ended the year at Duisburg on the 20/21st, when contributing to over 200 aircraft whose crews claimed a successful operation. 429 Squadron suffered its first aircraft loss on the 21st, when DF624 had to be abandoned over Yorkshire by Sgt Black and his crew after engine problems developed. They floated safely to earth with just one injury between them, but next time Sgt Black found himself in trouble with a new crew, he would not be so lucky. 196 Squadron was posted out of Driffield on the 22nd and moved into Leconfield, where it would stay for the remaining seven months of its service with 4 Group. 466 Squadron registered its first casualty on that day, after HE391 crashed into the North Sea during a training exercise, and there were no survivors from the crew of Sgt Egerton. The squadron followed in 196's wake on the 27th and took up residence at Leconfield, a station it would call home for the next eighteen months. It had been another tough year for the crews of 4 Group, and the Halifax was still not delivering to its full potential. An even tougher year lay ahead, but at least the effect of their efforts against the enemy would be clear for all to see.

1943

The New Year began with the official formation of a new Group. On 31 October 1939, negotiations had begun between representatives of the British and Canadian governments on the subject of the British Commonwealth Air Training Plan (BCATP). Both sides approached the talks with entirely different perceptions and goals, and this would lead to protracted discussions and acrimonious relations over the following three years. The

'Canadianization' of Royal Canadian Air Force personnel serving with the Royal Air Force was enshrined in Article XV of the BCATP agreement, which originally called for the formation of twenty-five RCAF squadrons overseas. These were to be financed by Canada's contribution to the Plan, still known to this day in the UK as the Empire Air Training Scheme, which was agreed at $350 million. From the outset the talks were dogged by the questions of control of the RCAF contingent and finance, and the Canadian negotiators found themselves being constantly out-manoeuvred by their British counterparts. Canada envisaged an independent air force operating alongside the RAF, much as the American 8th Air Force would from 1942. Britain, however, saw Canada as a source of manpower, and intended to integrate Canadian personnel into existing RAF Squadrons, or at least, to place the RCAF squadrons within RAF Groups. Canada expressed itself unwilling to finance RCAF personnel over whom it had no control, and after much wrangling, a compromise was eventually reached, which would allow all RCAF squadrons to operate from stations within close proximity to one another and under the same RAF Group. Once sufficient squadrons had been formed, an RCAF Group would come into existence. By the time that negotiations had reached this stage it was already 1942, and only four RCAF squadrons had thus far been formed, all in 1941. In the event, outside influences caused the programme to be cut back, allowing for just seven new squadrons in 1942, making a total of eleven. However, the number was considered acceptable to constitute an effective Group, and this compromise became a cherished dream in itself, achieving realization on 1 January 1943 as 6 Group. This was the best that Canada could achieve, having been backed into a corner by its own negotiators, and thus the RAF acquired the manpower and the control while Canada footed the bill. 4 Group immediately surrendered the stations at Croft, Dalton, Dishforth, Leeming, Linton-on-Ouse, Middleton-St-George, Skipton-on-Swale, Tholthorpe and Topcliffe, along with 408, 419, 420, 424, 425, 426, 427 and 428 Squadrons. This meant that just two Canadian units remained with 4 Group, 429 and 431 Squadrons, and in time they too would find a home with 6 Group.

It was going to be a hectic year for the squadrons of Bomber Command with major campaigns throughout, but it was the Lancasters of 1 and 5 Groups which were most active during the first two weeks of January, relatively small numbers of them acting as the main force in seven raids on Essen and one on Duisburg as part of the Oboe trials programme. Since joining the Pathfinders in the previous August, 109 Squadron had conducted development work with the device in Mosquitos under Hal Bufton, brother of 10 Squadron's former commanding officer Sid, and the hard work of the crews would bear fruit magnificently in the months ahead. Outstanding successes would be punctuated by expensive failures in the coming year and by the end of it, the Stirlings and older Halifaxes would have demonstrated their vulnerability to the highly efficient German defences. 77 Squadron welcomed in the New Year by writing off one of its Halifaxes on the 4th, but Sgt Ellis and crew emerged unscathed from the wreckage of DT555 following their take-off crash. The Pathfinders officially became 8 Group on the 8th, and that night the freshly-converted 51 Squadron returned to the battle with eight crews participating in a sizeable mining effort off the Danish coast.

On the following night, 120 aircraft took off for similar duties off the Frisians and North Germany, and 51 Squadron registered the first of what would become a harrowingly long list of losses during the year. DT483 failed to return to Snaith, and no trace of it or the crew of Sgt Banks-Martin was ever found. 466 Squadron went to war for the first time on the 13th when sending five of its Wellingtons to lay mines off the Frisians. On the 14th, a new Air Ministry directive opened the way for the area bombing of those French ports which housed U-boat bases and support facilities. A list of four such targets was drawn up accordingly, and that night Lorient received the first of its nine raids over the succeeding month. 4 Group Halifaxes made up almost half of the 120-strong force, but bombing was scattered and relatively ineffective. This was 51 Squadron's first bombing operation with its new equipment, and on return DT506 crash-landed at Pocklington, although without injury to Sgt Brett and crew. A smaller force was sent mining on the same night, and 466 Squadron suffered its first loss when German naval flak accounted for HE152 off the Frisians and Sgt Babington and his crew lost their lives. A return was made to Lorient on the following night, when an improvement in accuracy led to the destruction of 800 houses. Main force Halifaxes sat out two operations to Berlin on the 16/17th and 17/18th, and neither raid produced any useful damage, although the first one destroyed the 10,000-seater Deutschlandhalle, the largest covered venue in Europe. 429 Squadron eased itself gently into operational mode with a sea search by six aircraft on the 21st, and all returned safely to East Moor, although without having sighted any downed airmen. The Bisons' first offensive operation took place that night, when they contributed aircraft to a force sent to the Frisians for a mining operation. BK432 was shot down by flak over the Waddenzee, and F/O Johnson and his crew were all killed. The crew of 51 Squadron's DT581 became lost while returning from the same operation, and eventually crashed into high ground in Yorkshire, killing two of those on board and injuring P/O Getliffe and the others. It was back to Lorient on the 23/24th, the Halifaxes again predominant, and a successful attack was claimed by returning crews. Two more raids were directed at the town before the end of the month, but both were inconclusive. 51 Squadron provided a contingent of four Halifaxes for a predominantly Lancaster attack on Düsseldorf on the 27/28th, on the occasion of the first use of Oboe ground-marking, and extensive damage was caused to the city's southern districts. Two of the three missing Halifaxes were from Snaith, however, and both DT705 and DT721 were despatched by night fighters over Holland. Sgt Barrett and three of his crew were killed in the former, and W/O Weakley died with two of his crew in the latter, all of the seven survivors falling into enemy hands. It had been an expensive first month of Halifax operations for 51 Squadron, and to compound this, W1185 crashed on the airfield at Burn during an air-test while in the hands of F/S Whitworth on the 29th, and although the crew scrambled clear unhurt, a workman was killed on the ground.

February

February opened with an experimental raid on Cologne on the 2/3rd, during which both Oboe and H2s were employed by the marker force, sadly with disappointing results. Hamburg followed twenty-four hours later when a much larger 4 Group contribution failed to improve the outcome, but Turin was hit hard on the following night by the 156 aircraft that reached the target area, while Lorient hosted a simultaneous all-incendiary attack by more than 100 aircraft. Most of these were Wellingtons, and among them were eight from 196 Squadron participating on their maiden operation. By this time 10 Squadron had a new commanding officer, W/C Carter having relinquished his position through ill health. W/C Edmonds, an Irishman with strong tendencies towards a disciplinarian style, was posted in from 102 Squadron earlier on the 4th, and quickly became known as 'The Sheriff'. A further raid on Lorient on the 7/8th preceded an attack on Wilhelmshaven on the 11/12th, during which an explosion in a naval ammunition depot laid waste to 120 acres, and left substantial damage in the town and the docks area. During bombing-up on the 13th for the night's attack on Lorient, incendiaries fell from 51 Squadron's DT722's bomb bay at Snaith and ignited, and the Halifax was destroyed in the ensuing inferno along with DT724. 196 Squadron sustained its first casualty since beginning operations, when HE169 was lost without trace with the crew of F/L Milne during an operation to Cologne on the night of the 14/15th. Lorient was raided for the final time on the 16/17th, after which it was nothing more than a deserted ruin. Wilhelmshaven was attacked three more times, on the 18/19th, 19/20th and the 24/25th, but each raid failed to produce anything other than superficial scattered damage. Within minutes of taking off for the first of these, 51 Squadron's W7818 suffered engine failure and was safely crash-landed by Sgt Haly. There was some improvement at Nuremberg on the 25/26th, when 300 buildings were damaged by a force of over 300 Lancasters, Stirlings and Halifaxes, which included a contribution of thirteen from 51 Squadron. However, the majority of bombs still found only the fringes or fell outside of the city altogether. Earlier in the day, 51 Squadron's W7855 had been crash-landed at Snaith by F/S Johnsen and crew at the end of a training flight, and although all on board escaped unhurt on this occasion, their reprieve would be short-lived. It was a similar story of a missed opportunity at Cologne on the 26/27th, in what was the largest force despatched to a German target during the month. Again only perhaps a quarter of the bomb loads fell within the city boundaries, enough to leave over 6,000 residents bombed out of their homes, but the remainder of the effort was wasted south-west of the city. 158 Squadron completed its final wartime change of address on the 28th with its move to Lissett. Having disposed of Lorient, the Command now turned its attention upon St Nazaire, which wilted under a devastating attack on the last night of the month. On return 51 Squadron's DT648 crashed on landing, and for the second time in the space of a month, Sgt Whitworth and crew emerged unscathed.

March

March was about to bring the first major campaign of the year against mainland Germany, and the first campaign of the war for which the Command was adequately equipped and prepared. First, however, there were two other operations for the crews to negotiate, beginning at Berlin on the 1/2nd. Despite the attack being scattered over a wide area, it was the most effective to date at this target, destroying over 800 houses and seriously damaging many industrial buildings. It was a relatively expensive night which cost seventeen aircraft, and among them was 51 Squadron's BB223, which fell victim to a night fighter over Holland without survivors from the crew of F/S Stenhouse. A number of 429 Squadron Wellingtons were sent mining around the Frisians on the following night in company with others from 6 Group, and HZ260 failed to return. The previously mentioned Sgt Black had managed to put it down in the North Sea, and he and Sgt Rothena, the only member of his original crew, made it into the dinghy. They alone survived the ditching, but when rescue came on the 5th it was an hour or two too late for Sgt Black, who had by then died of exposure. 431 Squadron began its 4 Group operational career on this night, when sending a handful of Wellingtons to join the others on mining duties. Hamburg was the target for over 400 aircraft on the 3/4th, when the operation did not go according to plan. The small town of Wedel, 13 miles downstream of the Elbe, received many of the bombs intended for Germany's second city, again largely through misinterpretation of the H2s returns. Hamburg did not escape entirely, however, and the fire department had to deal with 100 fires before going to the aid of its neighbour. Again 51 Squadron was represented among the missing, this time by W7861 which was lost without trace with the previously mentioned crew of F/S Johnsen. While this operation was in progress, 431 Squadron despatched seven Wellingtons for further mine-laying duties around the Frisians. Sgt Morton's aircraft was attacked by a JU88, which left a fire burning behind the cockpit and damaged the undercarriage, but he managed to carry out a belly-landing at Burn and there were no crew casualties.

After a night's rest, Harris embarked on the campaign which was to demonstrate that the Command had evolved into something resembling a war-winning weapon, and for the next five months the vast industrial Ruhr, the arsenal of Germany's war effort, would undergo a pounding unprecedented in history. No longer would the region's blanket of industrial haze conceal its towns and cities from the bomb-aimers high above, as the electronic age took over in the form of Oboe, a device now close to full operational reliability. It began at Essen on the night of the 5/6th, for which a force of 442 aircraft took off. 51 Squadron provided eleven Halifaxes and crews for this momentous occasion, and they were as follows: DT738 F/L Hay, DT513 F/L Pexton, DT686 F/O Johnstone, W7772 P/O Garforth, DT690 P/O Harris, BB241 W/O Clayton, who would later serve with 617 Squadron, BB244 F/S Collins, DT645 F/S Stewart, DT729 F/S Locksmith, W1212 Sgt Haly and DT567 Sgt Rawcliffe. These were assigned to the first of three waves, and all reached and bombed the target as briefed on a night when an unusually large number of early returns reduced those doing so to around 360. The attack was an outstanding success, nevertheless, which destroyed over 3,000 houses and damaged fifty-three buildings within the giant munitions works of Dr Gustav Krupp. All of the 51 Squadron crews returned safely, but by the end of the campaign, five of the above-mentioned would have been posted missing. 431 Squadron contributed just three aircraft to the main operation, while sending four others back to the Frisians, but as in each of its first two operations there were two early returns. It was at this time that 77 Squadron was once more declared operational, having been away from the front line for almost twelve months, and it contributed two crews to this night's mining operation off the Frisians. 4 Group sent twenty Wellingtons and Halifaxes to lay mines off the Frisians on the 7/8th, and 51 Squadron's DT567 failed to return having crashed into the sea without survivors from the crew of P/O Holmes. 431 Squadron registered three early returns on this night after joining forces with 429 Squadron, and also recorded its first failure to return in the form of HE202 which was brought down by flak in the target area, delivering Sgt Pitts and his crew into enemy hands.

It would be a week before the next Ruhr operation, and in the meantime Harris switched his forces to southern Germany, attacking Nuremberg, Munich and Stuttgart on the 8/9th, 9/10th and 11/12th respectively. Beyond the range of Oboe, neither of the first two mentioned achieved anything like the success at Essen, but over 600 buildings were destroyed at the former and 300 at the latter. 51 Squadron contributed thirteen and five Halifaxes respectively, and all returned safely to Snaith. It was from Munich that the first of what would ultimately be many 77 Squadron Halifax casualties failed to return. DT734 was forced to turn back early and was heading westwards over Belgium when a night fighter shot it down, killing one of the crew. The rest of those on board managed to escape by parachute, S/L Sage and two others falling into enemy hands, while three men evaded capture. JB795 went down over southern Germany and there were no survivors from the crew of F/O Huggard. Following this operation, 419 and 431 Squadrons took part in an unsuccessful sea search for downed crews. Later on the 10th W/C Robinson was posted from his command of 158 squadron to be succeeded by W/C Hope. In order to remain on operations, Robinson dropped a rank and joined 138 Squadron at Tempsford to fly secret operations on behalf of SOE and SIS. In mid-May his Halifax would be crippled by light flak, forcing him to bale out some of his crew before carrying out a forced landing in France. All on board would survive, but Robinson was among those taken into captivity. Most of the bombing at Stuttgart fell into open country, but a torrid time lay ahead for this city later in the year and in 1944. The second Ruhr operation was launched against Essen on the 12/13th, and on this occasion the bombing was centred on the Krupp works where 30 per cent more damage was inflicted than in the attack a week earlier. Four 431 Squadron aircraft returned early and another, HE205, was badly damaged by a night fighter and the navigator killed. F/S Hamby and his crew brought the Wellington home to a safe landing at East Wretham, and there were no further casualties. Minor operations took the Command through to the 22/23rd, when a return to the U-boat campaign saw a concentrated attack fall on St Nazaire. The importance of Oboe to success at the Ruhr was highlighted by a dismal failure at Duisburg on the 26/27th, when technical malfunctions among five of the 109 Squadron Mosquitos forced them to return early and a sixth was lost in the sea. Two heavy raids were directed at Berlin at the end of the month; the first, on the 27/28th, producing only superficial damage; and the second, two nights later, destroying around 150 buildings while wasting the bulk of the effort in open country. The cost in bombers over the two nights amounted to thirty. 51 Squadron's BB244 was caught by a night fighter over Holland during the latter operation, and the sole survivor from the crew of F/O Harris became a PoW. The month ended for 196 Squadron with the departure of W/C Waterhouse for pastures new on the 31st. He was succeeded by W/C Duguid, a pre-war veteran who had been serving as a flight commander with 3 Group's 149 Squadron when the war began.

April

April began for 429 Squadron with a posting to 6 Group on the 1st to join its fellow Canadian units. The transfer did not require of the squadron a physical move, as East Moor was also donated to the Canadian Group. April would prove to be the least rewarding month of the Ruhr offensive, but largely because of the number of operations conducted outside of the region, beyond the range of Oboe. It began promisingly, however, with another successful assault on Essen on the 3/4th in which over 600 buildings were destroyed, but from which 51 Squadron's DT738 failed to return. It had been shot down in the target area, and there were no survivors from the crew of Sgt Rawcliffe. DT666 made it back to the Snaith circuit, but then crashed and Sgt Pheloung and two of his crew lost their lives. On the following night the largest non-1,000 force to date, 577 aircraft, took off for Kiel and almost entirely wasted their effort. Twelve aircraft paid the price for this failure, and 51 Squadron posted missing the crew of F/L Emery who were all killed when DT686 crashed in Germany. W/C Cheshire concluded his time in command of 76 Squadron on the 7th and was posted to command the training station at Marston Moor. While here he famously had a railway carriage hauled onto the site as his residence, into which he installed himself and his American wife, the former actress, Constance Binney. Cheshire's successor at 76 Squadron was W/C Don Smith, who would have to see the squadron through a tough period of operations. Duisburg escaped all but very minor damage on the 8/9th, as did Frankfurt on the 10/11th, and it was largely the despised 'creep-back' phenomenon that seemed to be a part of all Bomber Command raids which saved an attack on Stuttgart on the 14/15th, when it fell across an important industrial area containing war industry factories. The route to and from Stuttgart required a long flight across France, and night fighters were waiting on the return leg to catch the unwary and tired crews. A number of 431 Squadron aircraft were involved in encounters with the enemy. Sgt Morton's HE201 was attacked by two BF110s, one of which was seen to explode in the face of return fire from the Wellington, while the second one went down with a wing and engine on fire. HE374 was damaged by flak before being set upon by a night fighter, and was abandoned over Switzerland by Sgt Avery and his crew. After a period of internment they were repatriated on 29 June. HZ357 was a night-fighter victim over Germany on the way home, and Sgt Denby died with all but one of his crew, the survivor becoming a PoW.

The 16/17th was a night of major activity, on which the Lancaster and Halifax squadrons slogged their way to distant Pilsen in Czechoslovakia to bomb the Skoda armaments works. A diversionary raid on Mannheim by a predominantly Wellington and Stirling force was designed to split the enemy defences, but as events were to prove, this ploy was not entirely successful. On what was forecast to be a moonlit night, the main force element was briefed to identify the Skoda factory visually, and use the Pathfinder markers as a rough guide. However, confusion over the appearance of Pathfinder route markers led to much of the bombing falling onto an asylum some 7 miles from the target. No bombs fell within miles of the main raid's intended aiming point, and a massive thirty-six bombers, divided evenly between the two types, were brought down by the defences. Although the results at Mannheim were infinitely better, that force too lost eighteen aircraft. It was the most expensive single night to date for the Command, but the percentage loss among the Halifax brigade was disproportionately high, and amounted to almost 14 per cent of those despatched. It turned into a particularly bad night for 51 Squadron which had contributed a creditable seventeen Halifaxes. There were no survivors from the crew of Sgt Cox in DT561, and Sgt Inch and four of his crew were killed when flak brought down DT670 over France, although one of the two survivors ultimately evaded capture. DT690 was damaged by a night fighter while outbound, and an alternative target was bombed before further damage was inflicted by flak. This forced Sgt McCrea and his crew to take to their parachutes over France, and he and two others also managed to evade capture. Another of the squadron's Halifaxes to fall on French soil was HR784 in which F/S Stewart and five of his crew were killed, and finally, there was just one survivor from the eight-man crew of W/O Edwards in HR729. Including the crash at the start of the month, April had now claimed eight 51 Squadron aircraft and crews, and it was by no means done yet. Another notable casualty from this operation was 102 Squadron's HR663, which was shot down by a night fighter on the way home over France. It contained the crew of the highly-experienced S/L 'Wally' Lashbrook, who had been a member of 35 Squadron as a sergeant pilot during the type's introduction to operational service in the early days of 1941. In December 1941 he was posted in to help with the 102 Squadron Halifax conversion programme; since then he had served with 51 Squadron, and had only a week earlier begun his second tour after being appointed 102 Squadron's C Flight commander. He evaded capture along with three of his crew, and they arrived back home during May and June. Two other members of this crew fell into enemy hands, and one man was killed.

On the 20th W/C George Holden was posted away from 102 Squadron, and eventually arrived at Scampton in early July to join 617 Squadron as commanding officer elect. On 3 August he would be officially appointed to replace W/C Gibson VC at 617 Squadron, only to lose his life with four members of Gibson's Dams crew when bound for the Dortmund-Ems Canal in September. He was succeeded at 102 Squadron by W/C Coventry, whose own period in command would sadly be brought to a premature end. That night he presided over his first operation, when sending fifteen crews to another distant target. Stettin, which in the modern world is part of Poland's Baltic coast, was perhaps the only regularly-visited target never to escape lightly at the hands of Bomber Command. Excellent Pathfinder marking on this night was exploited by the main force, and around 100 acres in the centre of the city were reduced to rubble, with industry and housing suffering alike. Twenty-one aircraft failed to return from the 300 Lancasters and Halifaxes despatched, and 51 Squadron posted missing the eight-man crew of Sgt Brett, who were lost without trace in DT628. A force of over 500 aircraft, including 119 Halifaxes, set course for Duisburg on the 26/27th, and this time managed to deliver one of the more successful attacks to date on this important industrial centre. Some 300 buildings were destroyed, but bombs were also scattered onto other Ruhr towns. Among the seventeen missing aircraft were two from 51 Squadron, HR778 and HR787, both of which crashed in Germany without survivors from the crews of Sgt Fisher and Sgt Brigden. 102 Squadron's JB918 was set upon by the BF110 of Unteroffizier Georg Kraft of IV/NJG 1 out of Leeuwarden, which shot it down into the North Sea north of Texel. F/S Grainger and his crew were all killed, and three of them were washed ashore on Texel, Sgts Foley and Beck on the 28th and Sgt Oatridge on the 29th, where they were buried with full military honours. Two very large mining efforts took place on the 27/28th and 28/29th, employing 160 and 207 aircraft respectively, and 4 Group Halifaxes were strongly represented on both occasions. On the 28th W/C Sawyer's period in command of 51 Squadron came to an end, and W/C Franks was installed as his successor in time to preside over the final operation of the month, to Essen on the night of the 30th. Less than 240 of 300 crews reported bombing as briefed, but these managed to produce fresh damage in return for the loss of twelve aircraft. 51 Squadron registered its final casualty of the month on this night, when HR733 crashed in Germany, killing Sgt Wilson and four of his crew. It had been an extremely testing four weeks for the crews at Snaith, who had seen twelve of their number go missing, and it was perhaps fortunate that the survivors were unaware that it had been but a prelude to the events of the month ahead.

May

May brought a return to winning ways with some outstanding successes. First, however, the now Group Captain Sawyer was appointed as Station Commander at the newly-opened 4 Group airfield at Burn on the 2nd, moving later in the war to occupy similar posts at Driffield and Lissett. The month began badly for 51 Squadron, when DT729 crashed in Yorkshire through engine failure during a training flight on the 3rd and Sgt Greenhorn and his crew were killed. The new month's bombing onslaught began at Dortmund on the 4/5th, when a new record non-1,000 force of 596 aircraft inflicted extensive damage in central and northern districts. But for a decoy site luring away a proportion of the bombs, the damage would have been even more severe, but it was never a one-sided contest and the defences claimed thirty-one bombers. Twelve of the casualties were Halifaxes, although all ten from 51 Squadron returned safely. Sadly, high losses would become a feature of the campaign from now on. For the following week the heavy squadrons stayed at home, and it was not until the 12/13th that they were called into action again, to carry out the fourth raid of the campaign on Duisburg. Thus far, Germany's largest inland port had been spared the worst ravages of a Bomber Command attack, but on this night it succumbed to a highly accurate and concentrated assault delivered by over 500 aircraft. Almost 16,000 buildings were destroyed and 60,000 tons of shipping was sunk or damaged, but thirty-four aircraft failed to return home, and it was another disastrous night for 51 Squadron. DT645 crashed in Holland with no survivors from the crew of Sgt Smith, and a similar outcome attended the destruction by a night fighter of P/O Locksmith's HR786 over the same country. DT685 went down in the target area killing all but one of the crew of Sgt Jones, and a combination of flak and a night fighter accounted for JB806 over Belgium, forcing Sgt Brown and his crew to parachute into captivity. Finally, DT637 force-landed in Yorkshire on return and happily, Sgt Thompson and crew were able to walk away from the wreckage unscathed. On the following night 442 aircraft set off for Bochum, while a predominantly 5 Group force unsuccessfully attempted to rectify the previous month's failure at Pilsen. The former operation was moderately effective, destroying almost 400 buildings for the loss of twenty-four aircraft, among which were two more from Snaith. DT526 was damaged by flak before being finished off by a night fighter, but F/L Johnstone and four of his crew escaped with their lives to fall into enemy hands. A night fighter alone was responsible for the demise of HR790 over Holland, and P/O Byres and three of his crew likewise survived to become guests of the *Reich*. Another long rest from main force operations allowed the crews to draw breath, and it was during this period that 617 Squadron ensured its place in bomber folk-lore with its epic attack on the dams on the 16/17th.

It was not until the 23/24th that the Command ventured forth once more in numbers. It was another record non-1,000 force, this time of 826 aircraft, which was sent back to Dortmund on this night, and they destroyed around 2,000 buildings predominantly in central, northern and eastern districts, while causing damage to some important war industry factories. The defences again fought back, and this time downed a hefty thirty-eight aircraft. Nineteen Halifaxes had departed Snaith, and on the following morning, five empty dispersals told their own sorry story of 51 Squadron's fortunes. HR835 crashed at Essen, killing Sgt Wright and his crew, while HR836 was shot down by a night fighter over Holland with no survivors from the crew of F/O Rigby. The pilot of HR842, Sgt Parker, alone of his crew was killed, and the six survivors were soon joined in captivity by Sgt Mascall and his crew, who all survived the destruction of HR844. JB792 made it back to Woolfox Lodge in Rutland, where P/O Andrew carried out a safe crash-landing, and no injuries were reported. 431 Squadron's HE198 was coned twice by searchlights, and

F/L Hall put the Wellington into a steep dive on each occasion in a vain attempt to escape. It required the assistance of Sgt Sloan, the bomb-aimer, to pull out of the second dive, and sometime during the incident the aircraft sustained a flak hit. In the belief that a fire had broken out the pilot gave the order to bale out, although some members of the crew failed to hear it. F/L Hall and the rear gunner departed, and it was only then that Sgt Sloan discovered he and two others were alone. He took over the controls, and with the assistance of his crew mates returned to England to pull off a perfect landing at Cranwell. He was awarded the coveted CGM, and the wireless operator and navigator the DFC and DFM respectively. The two latter joined the crew of W/C Coverdale, while Sgt Sloan took a pilot's course and returned to operations with 158 Squadron in January 1945, ultimately to survive the war. The 25/26th brought the month's first real failure, when a force of 700 aircraft could only inflict superficial scattered damage on Düsseldorf at a cost of twenty-seven aircraft. The destruction of Sgt Lewis's JB837 from 77 Squadron was a tragedy for three squadrons. Caught by a night fighter close to Germany's western border, the Halifax exploded in the air with such force that it brought down two Stirlings, one each from 7 and XV Squadrons, and all twenty-one men lost their lives. After a night's rest over 500 aircraft took off for Essen, and delivered an attack which destroyed almost 500 buildings, but as a measure of the advances made by the Command since the bad days of 1941 and early 1942, even this could be considered only a modest success. Almost half of the twenty-three missing aircraft were Halifaxes, and 51 Squadron's disastrous month continued with the failure to return of two more of its crews. HR750 fell to a night fighter over Holland, and the crew of W/O Beeston was grateful to the parachute packers for its survival intact, although all were captured. They were at least more fortunate than most of their colleagues in HR789, which was shot down over the Ruhr with the crew of Sgt Prothero, he and just one other surviving as PoWs. On the 29/30th, the Barmen half of Wuppertal was subjected to the most accurate and concentrated raid of the campaign to date, which left 80 per cent of its built-up area in ruins and over 3,000 of its inhabitants dead. This success cost the Command thirty-three aircraft, but for once there were no absentees from among the thirteen despatched from Snaith. It had been a terrible month for 51 Squadron, and sadly, June would provide little respite.

June

There were no major operations in June until the 11/12th, when the target was Düsseldorf, for which 783 crews were briefed. It was a milestone for the Halifax force, over 200 of them operating to a single target for the first time. Much of the force deposited its bombs into central and southern districts, and destroyed around 130 acres of the city. Had not an errant Oboe-marker fallen well away from the city and attracted a proportion of the bombing, the city might well have suffered even greater damage. Even so, the catalogue of destruction included almost 9,000 separate fires, stoppage of production at forty-two war industry factories, a vast amount of housing, shipping in the inland port, and a large number of military establishments. The defenders, however, were not to be outdone, and fought back to claim thirty-eight bombers, two of which belonged to 51 Squadron. HR788 crashed in the southern coastal region of Holland, killing F/S Anderson and his crew, but all eight men of the crew captained by F/S Harvey survived the destruction by flak of HR852, and all became guests of the *Reich*. The tendency of Allied convoys to fire first and ask questions later resulted in DT742 ditching 10 miles off the Norfolk coast on the way home, and one of F/S Collins's crew failed to survive to be rescued. On the following night 130 acres of Bochum were reduced to ruins by a force approaching 500 aircraft, twenty-four of which failed to return. 51 Squadron posted missing the crew of Sgt Chambers after a night fighter accounted for DT568 over Holland, and the pilot was the sole survivor. 78 Squadron moved out of Linton-on-Ouse on the 16th and settled in at Breighton, where it would remain until the end of the war. On the following day 76 Squadron also changed address for the final time during the war when it too departed Linton-on-Ouse and became resident at Holme-on-Spalding-Moor. Following Bochum 4 Group had been left off the order of battle until the night of the 19/20th, when it was joined by elements of 3, 6 and 8 Groups for an attack on the Schneider armaments works at Le Creusot, the target for an epic daylight raid by 5 Group Lancasters back in October 1942. 51 Squadron contributed twenty Halifaxes to the operation, which failed to produce the desired results, but at least all returned safely to Snaith.

A hectic round of four major operations in the space of five nights began at Krefeld on the 21/22nd. The catalogue of destruction included 5,500 houses, but heavy night-fighter activity contributed to the loss of forty-four aircraft, which represented the highest casualty figure of the campaign to date. 35 Squadron, formerly of 4 Group, lost six Halifaxes, while 77 Squadron posted missing three. 431 Squadron's HF518 failed to return to Burn with W/C Coverdale and his crew, which included the wireless operator and bomb-aimer recently decorated with Sgt Sloan. The Wellington was lost without trace, and the names of the crew are commemorated on the Runnymede Memorial. The single 51 Squadron casualty, JD244, was a victim of flak in the target area, and struggled towards home as far as Belgium before a crash-landing became necessary. The crew of Sgt Heathfield emerged unscathed from the wreckage, but quickly found themselves in captivity. On the following night it was the turn of Mülheim to experience an accurate and concentrated attack, which destroyed 1,100 buildings and damaged 12,000 more. 51 Squadron's JD251 crashed into the target, and Sgt Elliot and all but one of his crew were killed, this just one of thirty-five missing aircraft on the night. 77 Squadron lost two Halifaxes, but one of its returning crews claimed the destruction of a night fighter over the North Sea. After a night's rest, 600 aircraft returned to Wuppertal, and all but erased its Elberfeld half from the map. After the war it was assessed that 94 per cent of the built-up area had been destroyed on this one night, and this had to be added to the 80 per cent destruction of the Barmen half at the end of May. Among the thirty-four aircraft missing from the operation was 51 Squadron's JD250, which became another night-fighter victim over Holland, and there were no survivors from the crew of F/O Mackenzie.

The run of successes came to an end at Gelsenkirchen on the 25/26th, when bombing was scattered all over the Ruhr with little if any falling where intended. The cost to the Command was thirty aircraft, and there were two more empty dispersals to contemplate at Snaith next morning, those belonging to HR731 and JD261. The former was shot down by a night fighter which sent it crashing into the Ijsselmeer, taking with it to their deaths the crew of Sgt Osmond, and F/O Davis and his crew were also all killed when another night fighter brought the latter down onto Dutch soil. Later on the 26th W/C Bill Newson was installed as the new commanding officer of 431 Squadron, and he would see the squadron through its final operations on the trusty Wellington, the transfer to 6 Group and the conversion onto the Halifax. On the same day W/C Duguid relinquished command of 196 Squadron and was succeeded by W/C Alexander. In a little over three weeks he would oversee the squadron's transfer from 4 to 38 Group. A series of three operations against Cologne spanned the turn of the month, and began on the 28/29th. This was the Rheinland city's worst night of the entire war, and by the following morning more than 6,000 buildings had been reduced to rubble and 4,300 people had been killed. It was again night fighters which accounted for the two missing 51 Squadron aircraft; DT513 over Holland and HR839 over Belgium. Sgt Sigournay and crew all lost their lives in the former, while two of the eight-man crew of P/O Tay survived from the latter, one of them ultimately evading capture.

July

Having closed the June account, it fell to Cologne to open that of July on the night of the 3/4th, the occasion on which the *Luftwaffe* employed its Wilde Sau night-fighter system for the first time. Day fighters were used by Hajo Hermann and his pilots to attack bombers over the target when they were silhouetted by the fires raging below. Despite their deployment, a further 2,200 houses were destroyed in return for the loss of thirty aircraft, among which was 51 Squadron's JD262 with the crew of Sgt Garnham. It was later learned that this Halifax had been undone by a night fighter over Belgium, killing the pilot and four others, and that one of the two survivors had managed to retain his freedom. 431 Squadron posted missing a Wellington crew for the last time as a result of this operation. LN284 was despatched by a night fighter in the target area, and only one man survived from the crew of Sgt Apperley. It was left to the Lancaster brigade to complete the series against Cologne on the 8/9th, by which time a total of 11,000 buildings had been destroyed, 5,500 people had been killed, and a further 350,000 had been rendered homeless. A further attempt to hit Gelsenkirchen failed on the 9/10th, although the loss of a more modest twelve aircraft was a small compensation. It was an eventful night for the crew of HR843, after the 51 Squadron Halifax entered a spin while evading flak. Two crewmen baled out in the confusion and both fell into enemy hands, but Sgt Foulston and the other four on board brought the aircraft home to a crash-landing in Surrey and no injuries were reported. Although two more operations to the region would be mounted at the end of the month, the Ruhr campaign had now effectively run its course, and Harris could look back over the past five months with genuine satisfaction at the performance of his squadrons. Certainly, the losses had been grievously high, but the factories had more than kept pace with the rate of attrition, and eager new crews were being fed into the line by the Empire Training Schools overseas. A major blow had been dealt to Germany's industrial heartland, and many of its major towns and cities lay partly or wholly in ruins, forcing production to be dispersed around the country and the considerable slack in the manufacturing capacity to be taken up.

An all-Lancaster force raided Turin to good effect on the 12/13th, the night on which 431 Squadron conducted its final operation both on Wellingtons and as a member of 4 Group. It was another mining operation in French waters in company with elements of 429 Squadron. Halifaxes, Wellingtons and Stirlings made up a force of 370 aircraft for an attack on Aachen on the following night, another highly successful operation which resulted in the destruction of almost 3,000 buildings, and for once, all of the twenty aircraft despatched by 51 Squadron returned safely. Sadly, 102 Squadron posted missing the crew of its commanding officer, W/C Coventry, and news eventually came through that none had survived the crash of JD297 in France. Lost with him were the squadron navigation and gunnery leaders, F/Ls King and Hogg. On the 15th 431 Squadron completed its move to Tholthorpe, which it would share with the recently-formed 434 Squadron, and thus finally joined the other Canadian squadrons in 6 Group. It would now remain off the order of battle until early October, while the crews trained on Halifaxes. W/C Fowle was appointed as the new commanding officer of 102 Squadron on this day. That night an all-Halifax force went to Montbelliard near the French border with Switzerland to try to knock out the Peugeot motor works. Few bombs hit the intended mark, and collateral damage to the town killed over 100 civilians. Five of the force failed to return, but all seventeen participants from 51 Squadron came home safely. On the 19th 196 Squadron completed its move from 4 Group to take up transport duties with 38 Group at Witchford.

With confidence high in the ability of his Command to deliver a knockout blow almost at will, Harris prepared for his next offensive, the destruction by 10,000 tons of bombs of an important city in a short, sharp campaign. For the past three years the Command had visited Hamburg during the final week of July, and it was here that Operation *Gomorrah* would be played out. As Germany's second city, Hamburg had the necessary political status to satisfy Harris's requirements, and its importance to the German war effort as a centre of production, particularly in the area of U-boats, was undeniable. There were, however, other important considerations which made it the ideal target, not least of which was its location close to a coastline, and its proximity sufficiently near the bomber stations to allow an operation to be concluded during the scant hours of darkness afforded by high summer. Finally, beyond the range of Oboe, which had proved so decisive at the Ruhr, Hamburg boasted the wide River Elbe, which would provide excellent H2s returns for the Pathfinder navigators high above. The campaign began on the night of the 24/25th, and was aided by the first operational use of 'Window', the tinfoil-backed strips of paper designed to blind the enemy night fighter, searchlight and gun-laying radar. The device had actually been available for a year, but had been withheld in case the enemy copied it. In fact, Germany had developed its own version called Düppel, which had also been held back for the same reason. Some 791 aircraft set off in the late evening, and few combats took place before the target was reached. The few aircraft that were lost at this stage of the operation had strayed off track and put themselves outside of the protection of the bomber stream. Among these was HR940, one of a record twenty-four Halifaxes put up by 51 Squadron. It contained the crew of Sgt Murray, who were on their maiden operation and were all killed when they fell victim to a night fighter over Denmark. At the appointed time the designated 'windower' in each aircraft began funnelling the strips into the airstream and they drifted in great clouds slowly to earth. Once in the target area the efficacy of Window was immediately made apparent by the absence of the usual efficient coordination between the searchlights and flak batteries, and the anti-aircraft defence was random and largely ineffective.

Despite this, an opportunity was missed when the Pathfinders slightly misplaced their markers and a pronounced creep-back developed. Nevertheless, a swathe of destruction was cut from the city centre along the line of approach across the north-western districts and out into open country, where a proportion of the bombing was wasted. There was extensive damage in those areas afflicted and 1,500 people were killed, while a very modest twelve aircraft failed to return. On the following night Harris switched his force to Essen, to take advantage of the body blow dealt to the enemy's defences by Window. It was another outstandingly accurate attack on this city, where nearly 3,000 houses were destroyed, and the Krupp works suffered particularly severe damage. Among the twenty-six missing aircraft were two more from 51 Squadron, HR749, which was lost without trace with the crew of Sgt Jones, and HR934, which crashed into the sea off the Dutch coast, and took with it the crew of F/O Cole. On the 27/28th a force of 787 aircraft set out for round two of Operation *Gomorrah*, unaware of the horrific events which were to result from their actions. A number of factors conspired on this night to seal the fate of this great city and its hapless inhabitants, in an orgy of destruction which was quite unprecedented in air warfare. An uncharacteristically hot and dry spell of weather had left the city a tinderbox. The spark to ignite it came with another example of misplaced Pathfinder markers, which fell with unusual concentration into the densely populated working-class residential districts of Hamm, Hammerbrook and Borgfeld. To compound this, the main force bombed with rare precision and almost no creep-back, depositing much of their 2,300 tons of bombs into a relatively compact area. The individual fires joined together to form one giant conflagration, which sucked in oxygen from surrounding areas at hurricane speeds to feed its voracious appetite. Trees were uprooted and flung bodily into the inferno, along with debris and people, and temperatures at the seat of the flames exceeded 1,000 degrees Celsius. The defences were overwhelmed, and the fire service was unable to pass through the rubble-strewn streets, but even had they done so, they would not have been able to enter the firestorm area, and only after all the combustible material had been consumed did the flames subside. By this time there was no-one alive to rescue, and an estimated 40,000 people died on this one night alone. The first of what would become an exodus of more than a million people began to file out of the city on the following morning, and this undoubtedly saved many from the ravages of the next raid. A night's rest preceded this next round, which involved a force of 777 aircraft, 707 of which reached and bombed the target as planned. The Pathfinders again missed the intended aiming point, and marked an area just south of that devastated by the firestorm. Many bomb loads stirred up the embers here, before very concentrated bombing hit the residential districts of Wandsbek and Barmbek further north. Another very large area of fire developed, although without ever reaching the intensity of a firestorm. The defenders were beginning to fight back from the body blow of Window, and were in the process of changing their tactics to combat the device. Twenty-eight aircraft failed to return on this night, and after coming through the firestorm raid unscathed, 51 Squadron suffered the loss of JD309, which was shot into the sea by a night fighter with no survivors from the crew of F/S Fletcher. This crew had claimed the destruction of a night fighter during the first round of Operation *Gomorrah* on the 24/25th. A comparatively small force of under 300 aircraft, comprising more or less equal numbers of Halifaxes, Stirlings and Lancasters, raided Remscheid on the 30/31st and left the town 83 per cent destroyed, and it was this operation which brought down the final curtain on the Ruhr offensive.

August

Before Operation *Gomorrah* came to a close, W/C Warner departed 78 Squadron to be replaced by W/C Lawrence on 1 August. The final raid in the series on Hamburg was mounted on the 2/3rd, a night on which violent electrical storms and icing conditions on the route out persuaded many crews to jettison their bombs over the sea or to attack alternative targets. A small number did press on to Hamburg, but their efforts produced little worthwhile new damage. Thirty aircraft failed to return, some of them victims of the conditions although it is believed that a night fighter claimed 51 Squadron's HR859, which disappeared without trace with the crew of Sgt Sklarchuk. During the offensive against Hamburg, 51 Squadron launched eighty-seven sorties of which seventy-one were successful, and three Halifaxes were lost. August was to bring the final Bomber Command operations of the war against Italy, which was now teetering on the brink of capitulation and needed a gentle nudge to push it over, which, it was hoped and expected, would come with a short offensive against its major cities between the 7/8th and the 16/17th. The month would also see the start of a new major offensive against Germany's capital city and, before that, an operation of vital importance to the defence of this country. 51 Squadron lost P/O Lambert and his crew to a training accident on the 6th, after HR783 suffered engine failure and crashed in Yorkshire. The first of the trips to Italy involved an all-Lancaster force on the night of the 7/8th, and then came two attacks on cities in southern Germany,

Mannheim on the 9/10th and Nuremberg on the following night. The former was highly successful if scattered, and all sixteen 51 Squadron Halifaxes returned home safely. The latter produced some useful damage in central and southern districts for the loss of sixteen aircraft, one of which was 51 Squadron's HR838, and this crashed in Germany killing the pilot, W/O Leeper, while his crew escaped by parachute to fall into enemy hands. HR981 was one of twenty Halifaxes despatched from Snaith on this night, and it crashed in Lincolnshire thirty minutes after take-off, killing one man and injuring P/O McPherson and the remainder of his crew. 158 Squadron's HR938 was shot down by a night fighter over Belgium and four of the crew, including the bombing leader, were killed in the ensuing crash. W/C Hope was seriously wounded and spent many months recovering in hospital before moving on to a prison camp. W/C Calder was instructing at Riccall when he received the call to become 158 Squadron's new commanding officer, but he was the ideal man for the job. He had served a tour of operations with 76 Squadron, and had taken command of the home echelon for a period during the summer of 1942. 51 Squadron participated in just one of the Italian raids, that against Milan on the night of the 12/13th, and all nineteen aircraft returned from what was deemed to be a successful night. Thereafter the crews were allowed a break from operations until one of paramount importance was laid on for the night of the 17/18th.

Since the very beginning of the war, intelligence had suggested that Germany was researching into and developing rocket technology, and although scant regard was given to the reports, photographic reconnaissance had confirmed the existence of an establishment at Peenemünde on the island of Usedom on the Baltic coast. Churchill's chief scientific adviser, Professor Lindemann, or Lord Cherwell as he became, steadfastly refused to give credence to the existence and feasibility of rocket weapons, and held stubbornly to his viewpoint even when presented with a photograph of a V-2 taken by a PRU Mosquito in June 1943. It required the combined urgings of Duncan Sandys and the brilliant scientist, Dr R.V. Jones, to persuade Churchill to act, and an operation was planned for the first available opportunity. It was vital that the installation should be destroyed, ideally at the first attempt, and consequently a maximum effort was called for. In the event not all the Stirlings of 3 Group were available after being diverted on their return from Italy the night before, and a somewhat depleted number of 597 aircraft and crews answered the call for a maximum effort. The plan required the attack to be conducted in three waves from low to medium level, each wave assigned to one of the specific targets: the housing estate, where the scientists lived; the factory; and the experimental site, with the Pathfinders responsible for shifting the point of aim accordingly. The operation was to be led by a Master of Ceremonies, who would provide instructions to the crews throughout the raid, much in the manner of Gibson at the Dams, and the man selected was, in fact, his successor at 106 Squadron, and now the commanding officer of 83 Squadron, G/C John Searby. A spoof raid on Berlin by eight Mosquitos of 139 Squadron was incorporated to draw away enemy night fighters, and this was led by the squadron's commanding officer, G/C Slee, who had previously served with 5 Group as commanding officer of 49 Squadron.

Twenty-four 51 Squadron crews were briefed to attack the housing estate in the first wave, along with the rest of 4 Group and 3 Group, and this, with 158 Squadron, equalled the largest effort in the Group. Remarkably, on a night when many squadron and flight commanders were operating, no less than nineteen of the squadron's aircraft were captained by NCOs, and the highest participating officer rank was flight lieutenant. Most of the main force aircraft took off between 21:00 and 21:30 hours for an outward flight of almost three hours for the opening of the raid at 00:15. The attack began inauspiciously when the initial markers fell more than a mile south of the intended aiming point and highlighted the Trassenheide forced workers camp, which contained hundreds of men from the occupied countries, some of whom had been responsible for getting intelligence to London. Trapped inside their wooden barrack buildings, they had no chance of escape and many of them were killed or injured. Once rectified, the attack proceeded more or less according to plan, and the first wave was on its way home before the night fighters began to arrive in the target area. They had been sent to Berlin in response to the 139 Squadron spoof, but the glow of fires was visible well to the north and the crews took the decision to head towards them. Losses among the first and second waves were low compared with those suffered later on, when predominantly 5 and 6 Group aircraft were attacking the experimental site. The night fighters proceeded to take a heavy toll of bombers both in the skies above Peenemünde and on the route home towards Denmark, and in all, forty aircraft failed to return. 4 Group escaped the carnage, and 51 Squadron saw all of its Halifaxes return to Snaith, which in the light of its heavy losses during the year must have been a shot in the arm for morale. While not entirely successful, the attack on Peenemünde left sufficient damage in its wake to set back the development programme by a number of weeks, and ultimately to force the V-2 testing to be withdrawn eastwards into Poland, out of range of Harris's bombers. On the following night, HR951 crashed on landing at Snaith after a training flight and was written off, but Sgt Long and his crew were unhurt.

Harris had long believed that Berlin, as the seat and the symbol of Nazi power, held the key to ultimate victory, and that its destruction would so affect the German people that they might rebel against their masters and sue for peace. First, though, Halifaxes were well represented in a force of more than 400 aircraft on the 22/23rd, which failed when trying to hit the I.G. Farben factory at Leverkusen. (*It was learned after the war that this company, which was developing synthetic oil, made extensive use of slave labour.*) On the following night the first phase of Harris's assault on Berlin took place, when 727 aircraft took off for the 'Big City', a number that included a record contribution for 51 Squadron of twenty-seven Halifaxes. The Pathfinder marking fell well short of the city centre, and it was the southern outskirts that received most of the bombs to actually fall within the city boundaries. Nevertheless, there was extensive residential and industrial damage amounting to 2,600 buildings. Much of the effort was wasted in open country, and numerous outlying communities were afflicted, something which would become a feature of Berlin operations from this point on. The bombers were met by a ferocious defence, and a new record of fifty-six aircraft failed to return home, twenty-three of them Halifaxes. 51 Squadron posted missing the crew of P/O Cribb in HR936, which was brought down over Holland but all on board survived to become guests of the *Reich*.

Among the missing on this night was the former 4 Group stalwart and personality G/C B.V. 'Robbie' Robinson. After relinquishing command of 35 Squadron in favour of W/C Whitworth back in January 1942, Robinson had returned to the hot seat in September 1942 on the loss in action of Whitworth's successor, W/C Jimmy Marks. By this time, of course, 35 Squadron had become a founder member of the Pathfinders and was stationed at Graveley. In February 1943 Robinson was promoted to the rank of Group Captain, and at the start of May he departed 35 Squadron on his appointment as Station Commander at Graveley. Ever the warrior, he joined a highly-decorated 35 Squadron crew for the Berlin operation, and died alongside them when their Halifax was shot down by a night fighter. At the time of his death, he was the holder of the DSO, DFC and Bar, and AFC. He had become something of a legend because of his involvement in a number of well-documented incidents, including the ditching of his flak-damaged Halifax on the way home from attacking the German cruisers at Brest in December 1941. Perhaps his most famous exploit occurred during an operation to Turin on the night of 18/19 November 1942. While over the Alps, a fire broke out in the bomb bay, which appeared to be terminal. He maintained control while his crew baled out, and as he was about to follow them he discovered that the fire had died down. Resuming his seat, he flew the Halifax single-handedly back home to a crash-landing at Colerne, while his crew all fell into enemy hands.

Nuremberg escaped serious damage at the hands of over 600 aircraft on the 27/28th, when most of the bombs fell into open country. The disappointment was compounded by the loss of thirty-three aircraft, one of which was from among the twenty-one despatched by 51 Squadron. HR869 crashed on German soil, and there were no survivors from the crew of F/L Dobson. The twin towns of Mönchengladbach and Rheydt received a highly accurate and concentrated attack on the night of the 30/31st, and the catalogue of destruction included over 2,300 buildings, some of an industrial, military, public and transport nature, along with a vast amount of housing. Twenty-four hours later, a force of 600 aircraft returned to Berlin for round two, and failed to inflict more than relatively minor damage in return for the loss of a hefty forty-seven aircraft. The outcome was a major disappointment, brought about by woefully short marking and a pronounced creep-back, and was in no way commensurate with the effort expended and the heavy losses. 51 Squadron's HR931 crashed in the target area, killing P/O Cates and three of his crew, and Sgt Turner and two others died in JN902, the survivors from both aircraft becoming PoWs. The Stirling contingent suffered disproportionately badly on this night, and the alarm bells began to sound at High Wycombe.

77 Squadron's JD413, KN-G, gathered speed as it lumbered down the long runway at Elvington and lifted heavily into the air, weighed down by its bomb load of one 1,000-pounder, forty x 30lb incendiaries and 450 x 4lb

incendiaries, and sufficient petrol to get it and its crew to Berlin and back. The time was 20.16 and a long and harrowing night lay ahead for the eight occupants, some of whom would never see another dawn. The crew had come together at 1658 Heavy Conversion Unit at Riccal in February, and consisted of pilot John Wilson, a 26-year-old Australian and at that time a pilot officer; Sgt James Hopkins, flight engineer; F/S Jack Leicester, navigator; Sgt Ted Wilson, wireless operator; Sgt Bob Sims, bomb-aimer; Sgt John Baxter, mid-upper gunner; and P/O Ken Sheward, rear gunner. They trained on the Halifax from 1 March until 4 April, getting to know both the aircraft and each other. Training complete, the fledgling crew was posted to 77 Squadron at Elvington, a few miles to the south-east of York, where the two commissioned members found accommodation in officers' quarters on the station, while the others were assigned to Nissen huts in a field by the road to Elvington village. They flew a 77 Squadron aircraft for the first time on 8 April and continued working up to operational status, which came finally on the night of the 14/15th, with a long haul down to Stuttgart in southern Germany. They came safely home, having logged seven hours and fifteen minutes flying time, and operated another five times during the month, to Stettin, Pilsen, Duisburg, mining in the Baltic and finally Essen. Flight engineer Jim Hopkins missed the Pilsen trip, which took a mammoth ten hours and twenty minutes to complete. May brought a more relaxed schedule with just two operations, to Dortmund and Düsseldorf, and more training, and John Wilson was promoted to the rank of flight lieutenant. On the 22nd the crew flew with S/L Bainbridge to carry out a low pass over Lancaster to celebrate Wings for Victory day. June was another quiet month with a second trip to Düsseldorf and one to Cologne, the latter resulting in an early return through engine trouble. July was much busier for the Wilson crew with operations to Cologne, Gelsenkirchen, Aachen, Montbeliard, Essen and the three raids on Hamburg under Operation *Gomorrah*. The series against Hamburg was completed on the night of 2/3 August, and the crew operated against Mönchengladbach just twenty-four hours before the fateful Berlin trip. Jim Hopkins remembers the second Düsseldorf raid as a bit hairy, and handing the Halifax back to the ground crew with numerous holes courtesy of the local flak. The bomb-aimer was hit on the backside by a piece of it, but fortunately it was spent and caused only bruising. The other abiding memory was of the electrical storms on the way to Hamburg for the final raid on the city, and Jim decided he preferred the flak!

Sixty years after the event, Jim Hopkins tried to recall his crew mates. John Wilson was acting A Flight commander at the time of the Berlin operation, and was a conscientious man and first-rate pilot. On the ground he was one of the boys, but in the air everything was done by the book and there was no chit-chat over the intercom. He came from Double Bay, Sydney, Australia, and was the only married member of the crew. He had talked about applying for a posting to the Pathfinders and doing a tour of fifty straight operations, and he wanted his crew to join him. Navigator Jack Leicester had trained as a pilot in Canada under the Empire Training Scheme, but washed out of the course and remustered. Jack was from Warrington and was an excellent footballer who was on the books at Manchester City for a time. He later worked for British Rope, where wire hawsers were manufactured. His best friend on the crew was Ted Wilson, the wireless operator. Ted came from Liverpool, not far from Warrington, so the two of them had much in common. Ted was a typical Liverpudlian, very talkative, and a good wireless operator, and he would fly wearing his girlfriend's scarf. Bob Sims, the bomb-aimer, was from Dorset and was another who failed his pilot's course and decided to remuster. Jim remembers him as the quietest member of the crew and a bit of a loner. Jack Baxter was from Richmond in Surrey, and was another quiet man who took his gunnery seriously and spent a lot of time in the gunnery section when not flying. Ken Sheward, the rear gunner, was the third member of the crew to hail from the North-West, in his case Nantwich in Cheshire. He was the other officer in the crew, and he took his trade seriously, seeming to enjoy flying into battle. He looked forward to having the opportunity to face a night fighter and shoot it down. As for Jim Hopkins himself, he came from Birmingham and is reticent to talk much about himself. In contrast to many stories of heavy drinking and partying on off-duty nights, Jim remembers that his crew had few friends outside of each other, and that there was very little partying. In fact, he recalls only one occasion when the crew went out together for a drink.

The Wilson crew was given a brand new Halifax, JD413, to take to Mönchengladbach on the night of 30/31 August, and although it brought them safely home, it suffered brake problems on landing. It was immediately handed over to the engineering section to diagnose and repair in time for the Berlin operation that night. The entire port undercarriage assembly was removed, repaired and reinstalled, and the Halifax was declared fit and ready for operations. The removal and reinstallation of such a major chunk of metalwork should have been succeeded by a recalibration of the compass to check the degree of deviation, without which accurate navigation would be impossible. However, the need to get the job done and the aircraft ready to operate meant that this did not happen. The hastiness of the procedure possibly also led to the engine problem, but the flight out across the North Sea was initially uneventful and gave no hint of what was to come. On this night the crew had an eighth member, F/S Raymond Barlow, a pilot gaining operational experience before taking his own crew into battle. It seems probable that he had only arrived on the station that day. It was shortly after crossing the enemy coast over Texel that Jim Hopkins noticed a rise in the temperature of the port-inner engine caused by a glycol leak, and it promptly burst into flames. The fire was extinguished and the propeller feathered, and the pilot informed the crew that they would be pressing on to the target. Even though JD413 was a new aircraft, it struggled to maintain altitude and speed on three engines. There was also a tendency to drift off course, which suggested that the compass was indeed giving a faulty reading, and it was down to PFF route markers to keep the Halifax on track. Despite the problems the target was reached late, around midnight, and bombed from 11,000 feet instead of the intended 18,000. Having lost the servo power of the port-inner engine, Hopkins had to pump up the bomb doors by hand afterwards.

The return route was south of the Ruhr, and by the time they had been home-bound for about an hour and a half they had drifted down to 7,000 feet, and unknown to them, they were north of track by some miles. Suddenly they were coned in searchlights and being hammered by accurate flak, which punctured the port wing fuel tank and set it alight. The entire wing from root to tip was ablaze and F/L Wilson gave the order to bale out. Hopkins grabbed his chute and made his way to the rear door, where he plugged back into the intercom system in time to hear his pilot ask the wireless operator to hand him his parachute. Hopkins left the Halifax, and seconds after his canopy deployed he saw a mighty flash on the ground. He landed safely and managed to hide until the evening when he was spotted by a farmer and reported to the authorities. It was only then that he learned where he was, and realized that any chances of evading capture had been slim. The Halifax had come down at Datteln, a small town on the north-eastern edge of the Ruhr, not far from Gelsenkirchen and Dortmund and well north of the track they should have been on. They had been brought down at 02.23 German time by Battery 3 of 524 Flak Division based in the Recklinghausen area, just a short distance from the crash site. Jim discovered then that only he, Jack Leicester and Ted Wilson had survived. Ted Wilson had sustained second-degree burns to his head, both hands, right arm and both legs. He was screaming in agony when the local Nazi doctor, Dr Hagener, arrived on the scene and refused to administer treatment to alleviate his suffering. The doctor further suggested that if those attending the scene wanted to help the man, they should kill him. Wilson was eventually taken to a hospital in Gelsenkirchen where he was treated humanely, but succumbed to his injuries on 4 September. Hopkins was taken to Stalag Luft IVB, where he spent the remainder of the war. It was here that he finally learned of the fate of his crew mates.

The remains of the Halifax were left where they fell once the crew remains had been removed for burial. After the war a swimming pool was built on the site, and JD413 was built into the foundations and lost to the light of day for almost the next sixty years. Early in 2005 work began to excavate the site in preparation for the construction of a new sports hall and swimming pool for the high school. The stench of aviation fuel prompted contractors to call in the services of experts, who could determine whether or not the remains of the Halifax contained unexploded ordnance. In April the author's good friend Andreas Wachtel became involved in the project. He is the chief executive of a children's hospital in Datteln, and was well acquainted with Herr Wenner, the head of the local fire service. Recognizing that Andreas's expertise put him among Germany's leading historians of Bomber Command, Herr Wenner invited him onto the site, and Andreas arrived just as an undercarriage leg and wheel was being raised. Andreas immediately recognized it as belonging to a Halifax, and he was then able to carry out the necessary research to identify it and its crew, principally to ensure that any human remains would be properly dealt with and their relatives kept informed. Once it had been established that the site was safe, Andreas was able to gain close access, and when partial human remains were recovered, he undertook making enquiries to try to establish to which of the crew they belonged. Pieces of dark blue tunic recovered with the bones showed them to belong to an Australian airman, who could only be the pilot, F/L John Wilson, the bulk of whose remains already lay in Reichswald War Graves Cemetery. Andreas contacted the Australian Embassy, but was told that they could not correspond with a private individual, and that they could deal only with an official organization. The Fire Department took over, and eventually the bones were collected by the Australian military and taken for forensic examination to determine a DNA profile. This eventually confirmed that all but one bone did, indeed, belong to F/L Wilson, and because of the location of the unidentified specimen close to his remains, it was assumed that it belonged to the second pilot, F/S Barlow. Andreas was contacted by Derek Hopkins, the son of James Hopkins, the only surviving member of the crew, and plans were put in place for him to attend the interment. It took considerable time for all of the pieces to come together but finally, at the start of March 2006, the author was privileged to join Andreas, James Hopkins and Derek at a moving ceremony at Reichswald.

September

It was left to the Lancaster squadrons to conclude this first series against the capital on 3/4 September, which they did with modest success at a cost of twenty-two aircraft. Whether the heavy losses at Berlin forced Harris's hand is open to debate, but there would now be an autumn break before the Battle of Berlin resumed in November. In the meantime, another set of twins, Mannheim and Ludwigshafen, were targeted on the night of the 5/6th, when the raid planners intentionally built in the creep-back phenomenon to great effect. The initial markers were to be dropped on the eastern side of Mannheim on the Rhine's eastern bank so that, as the main force of more than 500 aircraft approached from the west, the bombing would spread back across Mannheim, over the Rhine and into Ludwigshafen on the west bank. The operation was a major success, which left almost 2,000 fires burning, half of them large. It seemed though, that wherever the Command went, it could not escape heavy losses and the tally on this night was thirty-four. 51 Squadron's JD263 was shot down in the target area, killing F/S King and four of his crew, and the two survivors were captured. After a disappointing raid on Munich on the 6/7th, fairly minor operations dominated the next two weeks, 4 Group participating in attacks on the Dunlop Rubber factory at Montlucon on the 15/16th and railway yards at Modane twenty-four hours later. The former was successful and the latter not, but at least 51 Squadron came through unscathed on both occasions. W/C Fowle's short period in command of 102 Squadron came to an end on the 17th, and he was succeeded on the 21st by W/C Marchbanks, who had been with the squadron for a month to gain operational experience and had carried out a number of sorties.

A series of four raids on Hanover spanning the next four weeks began on the 22/23rd, and the poor results reflected the difficulty which the Command would experience over the following twelve months when carrying out attacks in this region of Germany. A night fighter accounted for 51 Squadron's

JN901, just one of twenty-six missing aircraft, but at least P/O Pohe and his crew escaped with their lives to become PoWs. Sadly, the pilot was to be one of those murdered by the Gestapo following the Great Escape in 1944. 76, 77 and 158 Squadrons each posted missing two crews from this operation, and the treatment of one 76 Squadron survivor contrasted starkly with that of the unfortunate 77 Squadron member cited on the previous page. Sgt Dennis, mid-upper gunner in EB253 was found by German soldiers in the shattered wreckage of the Halifax. They tended to his injuries as best they could before getting him to hospital. Here a German surgeon worked miracles on his shattered legs and ultimately saved them from being amputated. Sgt Dennis would be repatriated a year later. 77 Squadron's LW224 became a victim of coastal flak, and crashed into the Waddenzee off Den Helder. The navigator and flight engineer, Sgts Corlett and Clarke respectively, were washed ashore on Texel on 16 October and buried on the following day after being examined by a pathologist. His report accurately described Sgt Corlett as having been in the water for three to four weeks, and ascribed his death to drowning as there were no external injuries. Sgt Clarke, on the other hand, he estimated had been in the water for twelve to fifteen weeks, and he made mention of the head having the appearance of leather, perhaps as a result of being burned by oil. On the next night Mannheim was subjected to its second heavy blow of the month, and almost 1,000 buildings were destroyed there, while a proportion of the bombing spilled over into Ludwigshafen and a number of nearby small towns. The defenders fought back, however, and the cost to the Command was another thirty-two aircraft. It was back to Hanover on the 27/28th, when 51 Squadron's JN900 was forced to return early with engine failure and crashed while trying to land at Ridgewell, although without injury to the crew of P/O Bishop. The raid itself did not proceed according to plan, the concentrated bombing falling into open country north of the city, and this failure was paid for by thirty-eight missing aircraft. The balance was somewhat redressed at Bochum on the 29/30th, when the force of over 300 Lancasters and Halifaxes benefitted from the use of Oboe, which had now long since overcome its teething problems, and heavy damage was inflicted for the more modest loss of nine aircraft. On the 29th W/C Bailey completed his tour as commanding officer of 466 Squadron after almost a year in office, and he handed over to W/C Forsyth.

October

There was a hectic start to October for the Lancaster squadrons, elements of which were called on to operate six times during the first eight nights. It began at Hagen on the 1/2nd and Munich on the 2/3rd, and while the latter was in progress, a large mining effort took place from Lorient to Heligoland. Just one aircraft was lost from this, the 51 Squadron Halifax LW287, which perished without trace with the crew of Sgt Nixon. JN924 was almost another casualty, but it survived the attentions of a night fighter to return home in the hands of P/O Cheal and crew, only to be declared damaged beyond repair. An attack on Kassel on the 3/4th was the first bombing foray of the month for the Halifax brigade, and the type was the most populous in an overall force of more than 540. The operation was only partially successful, but the bombs that did land in the target area devastated an eastern suburb and inflicted useful damage on two aircraft factories. Among the twenty-four missing aircraft was 51 Squadron's HR728, which crashed in Germany without survivors from the eight-man crew of F/L Irwin. Accurate Pathfinder marking on the 4/5th led to the first really effective raid of the war on Frankfurt, and it was the eastern districts and the inland docks which received the main weight of bombs which created extensive areas of fire. A more acceptable ten aircraft fell to the defences, but 51 Squadron's casualty was the result of bad weather at home. HR727 crashed in Derbyshire on return, killing Sgt Fenning and four of his crew, and injuring the two survivors. Halifaxes were omitted from a successful raid on Stuttgart on the 7/8th, the night on which 101 Squadron operated its ABC communications-jamming Lancasters in numbers for the first time. The third Hanover operation was mounted on the following night, and this time a concentrated attack developed within the city. All but the western districts suffered extensive damage with large areas of fire, and almost 4,000 buildings were classed as totally destroyed. Two 51 Squadron Halifaxes failed to return home, however, JD253 and JN885 both having crashed in Germany without survivors from the crews of Sgt Chislett and F/S James respectively. Earlier in the day, W/C Edmonds had concluded his tour as commanding officer of 10 Squadron and he was replaced by W/C Sutton. 77 Squadron welcomed a new commanding officer on the 12th on the departure of W/C Lowe. W/C Roncoroni was a veteran of the battle for France in the early summer of 1940 when he was serving as a flight commander with 57 Squadron. It seems that he had been away from the operational scene for most if not all of the intervening period, but was destined to remain at the helm of 77 Squadron through the Command's most critical period.

This concluded the feverish start to the month and thereafter, minor operations took the Command through to the 18/19th, when an all-Lancaster force carried out the final one of the four raids on Hanover. It was another ineffective attack which dumped most of the bombs in open country north and north-west of the city. Earlier on the 18th 51 Squadron's HR870 had crashed on take-off from Snaith when bound for a training flight, but happily, P/O Price and his crew were unhurt. An all-Lancaster force went to Leipzig for the first time on the night of the 20/21st, but appalling weather conditions rendered the operation scattered and ineffective. The last major operation of the month took a force of over 500 aircraft back to Kassel on the 22/23rd, and it turned into a night of devastating consequences for this city. Accurate and concentrated marking by the Pathfinders was exploited by the main force, and 3,600 fires were started, some combining to create a firestorm along the lines of that at Hamburg, although to a lesser degree. Nevertheless, over 4,000 apartment blocks were destroyed, which amounted to 53,000 individual dwellings, and half as many again were damaged and over 6,000 people lost their lives. Included among more than 150 industrial scalps was the Henschel aircraft factory, where the V-1 was being built. The carnage was not one-sided, however, and forty-three bombers failed to return home, among them 51

Squadron's JN920 which crashed in Belgium, killing Sgt Hall and his crew. There were no further operations during the month, and as November dawned, there was some good news for the hard-pressed Halifax crews, who could soon look forward to receiving the greatly-improved Hercules-powered Mk III, the first of which would enter service with 466 Squadron on the 3rd.

November

In a memo to Churchill on 3 November Harris stated that, with the assistance of the American 8th Air Force, he could 'wreck Berlin from end to end', and win the war without the need for the kind of bloody and protracted land campaigns that he had personally witnessed during the Great War. The Americans, however, were committed to victory on land, and there was never a chance that Harris could enlist their support. It is only in the light of more recent conflicts that we know that no war can be won by bombing alone without the physical occupation of the land. In Harris's defence, however, it should be pointed out that it was not until the middle of 1943 that this long-held theory could actually be put to the test for the first time. Undaunted as ever, Harris would go to Berlin alone in an offensive that would drag on until the following spring, and in the process try the resolve of the crews to the absolute limit. First, however, Düsseldorf received a heavy blow on the 3/4th from a force of almost 600 aircraft, of which 230 were Halifaxes. There was to be only one more operation for the Halifax brigade before attention was turned towards Berlin, and this was an attack on marshalling yards at Cannes on the 11/12th. 51 Squadron's contribution was scrubbed after briefing had taken place, and in the event the operation managed only to inflict damage on working-class residential districts in the town. On the 14th W/C Wilkerson was posted in from his Inspector of Training role at 41 Base to assume command of 51 Squadron as successor to W/C Franks. David Wilkerson was a popular and well-respected officer of long experience, who had begun his operational career as a second pilot with 58 Squadron back in May 1941. In June he was posted to 35 Squadron, where he continued as a second pilot until the hydraulics problems dogging the Halifax's serviceability forced its temporary grounding. As a result all second pilots were sent across the tarmac to 58 Squadron in July to continue their development towards crew captaincy, and Wilkerson soon gained a reputation as an above-average pilot. He returned to 35 Squadron in September and took part in numerous operations, including the daylight attack on the German warships at Brest on 18 December. Following his promotion to squadron leader he was posted in the summer of 1942 to command 158 Squadron's Conversion Flight during the changeover from Wellingtons to Halifaxes.

On the night of the 18/19th the Lancaster force rejoined the long and rock-strewn road to the 'Big City', while the Halifaxes and Stirlings carried out a diversionary raid on Mannheim and Ludwigshafen. Both operations resulted in scattered bombing, but the diversion seems to have helped in restricting losses at the capital to a modest nine aircraft. The Mannheim force, however, lost twenty-three of its number, although none from the nineteen despatched from Snaith. The Lancasters stayed at home on the following night, while the Halifaxes and Stirlings went to Leverkusen in the Ruhr and scattered bombs everywhere except the target, which reported just a single bomb. Fortunately, only five crews paid the price for this debacle, but one of them was from 51 Squadron. HR950 was hit by flak which killed one crew member, but five others were able to take to their parachutes before the ensuing crash in which the pilot, F/S McCutcheon, and one other were killed. Over 700 aircraft took off for Berlin on the 22/23rd, and those which reached the target delivered upon it its most destructive raid of the war. Devastation stretched from the centre westwards, and large areas disappeared under a sea of flame. The catalogue of destruction included 3,000 houses, numerous industrial premises, and government and public buildings, and around 2,000 people lost their lives. Two 51 Squadron Halifaxes were among the twenty-six failures to return, HR726 and LW286. The former crashed in Germany, killing W/C Wright and four of his crew, and it must be assumed that this officer was gaining operational experience before being given command of his own squadron. The latter Halifax went into the sea, and took with it to their deaths P/O Farley and his crew. Having arrived back over Yorkshire shortly before midnight, LW264 of 77 Squadron collided with LW333 of 102 Squadron in the Pocklington circuit, and both aircraft plunged into the ground without survivors. Because of the disproportionately high casualty rate among the Stirlings during the autumn period, and the loss of 10 per cent on this night, the type was withdrawn from operations over Germany with immediate effect. It was mostly Lancasters that returned to the capital on the following night, and guided by the glow of still-burning fires visible through the cloud, they destroyed another 2,000 houses, some industrial premises and killed a further 1,400 inhabitants. A 4 and 6 Group main force of over 200 Halifaxes carried out a scattered and only marginally effective attack on Frankfurt on the 25/26th, and on the following night, covered a Lancaster raid on Berlin by raiding Stuttgart, again with little useful damage.

December

December began with the operational debut of the new Hercules-powered Mk III Halifax on the night of the 1/2nd, when 466 Squadron despatched twelve to sow mines off the Frisian island of Terschelling. The following night brought the now familiar slog to Berlin by the Lancaster brigade, but they were joined by Halifaxes twenty-four hours later for a tilt at Leipzig. The most successful raid of the war on this eastern city ensued, but Halifaxes made up the bulk of the twenty-four missing aircraft, and two of them belonged to 51 Squadron. HR732 was lost without trace with the crew of P/O Savage, and HR782 was brought down by flak over Germany on the way home and Sgt Ainsworth and one of his crew were killed. This Halifax had already survived a mid-air collision with a Lancaster at the end of August, in which it lost the top half of its port fin. An air-test on the 5th ended for F/L McCreanor and his crew with a crash-landing at Snaith in JN922, but all emerged from the wreckage without injury. There were no further operations for the main force units until the 16/17th when the Lancasters went to Berlin, and many returned home to find their stations fog-bound. It became one of the great tragedies to afflict Bomber Command during the war, as twenty-nine Lancasters either crashed or were abandoned by their crews during the desperate search for somewhere to land, and around 150 airmen lost their lives. It was the 20th before the Halifax crews were called on to operate again, and during that day 51 Squadron's JN923 was struck by practice bombs during training while in the hands of F/L Blyth and crew, and on return to Snaith it was declared beyond economical repair. That night 250 Halifaxes were among a total force of more than 600 aircraft setting off for Frankfurt. Some crews were misled by decoy fires and dummy target indicators but even so, quite extensive damage did result, although at a cost of forty-one aircraft, including twenty-seven Halifaxes. 51 Squadron's HR948 was brought down by flak in the target area, killing F/L Burchett and three of his crew, while four others survived as PoWs. They were more fortunate than their squadron colleagues in JD123, however, as P/O Sherer and his crew all failed to survive their crash in Germany. W/C Smith's tour as commanding officer of 76 Squadron came to an end on the 22nd with a posting to 42 Base, and he was succeeded by W/C 'Hank' Iveson, who would officially take over on Boxing Day.

In the meantime a force of mainly Lancasters continued the assault on Berlin on the 23/24th, before the fifth wartime Christmas was celebrated in relative peace. Then came a round of three trips to the capital in the space of five nights spanning the turn of the year. The first of these took place on the 29/30th for which 700 aircraft took off, and in the face of complete cloud cover, it was the southern and south-eastern districts which received most of the bombs that fell within the city, and only a moderate amount of damage resulted. Twenty aircraft failed to return, and 51 Squadron posted missing the crew of F/S Baird in JD264. This Halifax developed engine trouble over Germany and had to be abandoned, and the entire crew arrived safely on the ground to be rounded up by their captors. It had been an extremely testing year for 51 Squadron, characterized by persistent losses, and the only consolation was that when its crews next went to war, they would do so in an aircraft which was vastly superior to anything they had operated in the past. The new and much improved Mk III Halifaxes were now emerging from the factories and filtering through to some of the squadrons of 4 and 6 Groups. Others, though, would have to soldier on with the older types, and would suffer the consequences. It was perhaps fortunate that the crews of the Command as a whole could not foresee the events of the coming year. Suffice to say, that those beginning their operational careers at this time were doing so when morale would reach its lowest ebb.

1944

Berliners, too, were feeling the strain, but as in London during the Blitz of 1940, the sharing of their trials drew the population together in a bond of unity. A hardy breed, Berliners first and Germans second, they faced their fate with fortitude and humour, and there was as much chance of breaking their spirit as there had been in London. People still somehow got to work through the shattered streets, and the music halls and cinemas put on entertainment at night for those who wished to venture out. The radio was a great source of encouragement, and provided a useful air-raid early warning service, while linking the men at the front with loved ones at home through request programmes featuring the popular songs of the day. Among these was 'Nach jedem Dezember kommt immer ein Mai', 'After every December there's always a May', and the sentiment of the song hinted at a change of fortunes with the onset of spring. Banners were paraded through the streets proclaiming, 'You may break our walls but not our hearts', and this was the rock upon which the early defeat of Nazism through the destruction of Berlin was to founder. The beleaguered residents of Berlin and the hard-pressed bomber crews doubtless shared a common wish as the New Year dawned, that Germany's capital city would cease to be the main objective. This hope was dashed before New Year's Day was over, as a force of Lancasters headed eastwards and arrived over the city in the early hours of the 2nd. It was a disappointing start to the year in the face of complete cloud cover and the consequent use of skymarkers. These soon drifted away from the city, and most of the bombs were wasted in wooded and open country to the south. Damage was negligible at a cost of twenty-eight Lancasters, and the following night brought no improvement for the loss of a further twenty-seven. A worrying feature was the number of Pathfinder aircraft missing with their experienced crews, as these would be impossible to replace. A new squadron was formed in 4 Group on the 7th, when C Flight of 158 Squadron was hived off under the command of S/L Leicester and renumbered A Flight of 640 Squadron. B Flight of the new unit was made up largely of personnel from 466 Squadron, and while A Flight would begin operations from Leconfield within two weeks, equipment shortages would keep B Flight on the ground until the end of the month. While its changeover to the Mk III Halifax took place, 51 Squadron was stood down from operations, and C Flight was hived off on the 14th to form the nucleus of the newly-forming 578 Squadron, which would share the facilities at Snaith for the next three weeks. W/C Wilkerson was posted to command the new unit, but his replacement would not be appointed at 51 Squadron for a further two weeks.

102 Squadron had a much more gentle introduction to the year, and apart from a night of mining on the 6/7th, remained inactive for the next two weeks. By this time, the Lancaster crews had operated successfully against Stettin on the 5/6th, and failed dismally and expensively at Brunswick on the 14/15th. Now on the night of the 20/21st came a maximum effort operation against Berlin involving 769 aircraft, for which 102 Squadron put up sixteen Halifaxes. After one early return, fifteen others pressed on towards the target and headed for disaster. The attack fell mostly into the previously relatively undamaged eastern districts of the capital, and a reasonable amount of damage was inflicted for the loss of thirty-five aircraft, the bulk of which were Halifaxes. It was a sad night indeed for 102 Squadron, and there would be seven empty dispersals to contemplate at Pocklington next morning, two of

which belonged to aircraft lying wrecked in England. HX187 was hit by flak over the target, and was then picked up by a night fighter after the bombs had been dropped. P/O Dean and five of his crew abandoned the stricken Halifax and were captured, but one of them later succumbed to his injuries to join the three who had died in the crash. Sgt Compston and four of his crew survived the destruction over Germany of JD461, and they also fell into enemy hands. F/S Render, the pilot of JN951, was added to the growing list of captured 102 Squadron air crew as the sole survivor of his crew. A night fighter accounted for LW227 during the outward flight over Germany, but the entire crew of W/O Wilding escaped with their lives. LW337 was a victim of flak over Berlin and four men died in its wreckage, but F/O Griffiths and three others survived. It was a remarkable number of survivors in the circumstances, but the night had not yet done with the squadron, and two more crews were in trouble in home airspace. HR716 had been damaged by the flak barrage over Berlin, and had lost fuel steadily on the way home. On arrival over Yorkshire, F/O Hall ordered his crew to bale out and then coolly force-landed the Halifax near Driffield. Just twenty minutes later at half-past midnight an out-of-fuel and flak-damaged JD302 crashed on the outskirts of Norwich, and F/S Proctor survived with all but one of his crew. It is unclear whether they had abandoned their aircraft or carried out a crash-landing. 51 Squadron returned to operations on this night, and it was also the debut for 578 and 640 Squadrons. 51 Squadron put eleven brand-new Mk IIIs into the air, and all returned safely from what was an effective operation.

There was no time to mourn the missing men in the 'business as usual' atmosphere of a bomber station, and that night briefings took place for a raid on Magdeburg, for which over 600 aircraft were detailed. Night fighters picked up the bomber stream before it crossed the German coast, and a running battle ensued all the way to the target. An indeterminate outcome at this eastern city was paid for by a massive fifty-seven bombers and their crews, a new record, and thirty-five of them were Halifaxes. As the type's disproportionately high casualties continued, it was a point not lost on the hierarchy at Bomber Command HQ. 102 Squadron registered its second black night in a row, and posted missing four crews. A night fighter fell upon HX149 as it was leaving the target and three men died in the ensuing crash, while F/S Gregory and three others of his crew joined the now well-trodden path to a PoW camp. Another night fighter accounted for HX150 during its outward flight across Germany, and F/S Ellis and three of his crew died in its wreckage. W/O Headly and four of his crew were killed in JN952, and LW274 went into the sea off the Yorkshire coast, taking with it to their deaths the crew of Sgt Smith. The Halifax element was withdrawn from the Berlin raid on the 27/28th, but took part on the following night when a heavy blow was dealt to western and southern districts, and 180,000 people were rendered homeless. Forty-six aircraft were hacked down by the defences, and the percentage losses among the Halifaxes were again substantially higher than among the Lancasters. 102 Squadron was unable to escape the carnage and lost two more aircraft, LW277 to flak over Berlin, and JD165 to a ditching in the North Sea. P/O Linsell and six of his crew survived from the former, but F/S Pugh and three survivors from the latter had to endure three days in a dinghy before rescue came, by which time it was too late for one of them. The Lancaster crews carried out their third Berlin trip in the unprecedented space of just four nights on the 30/31st, and were accompanied by eighty-two of the new Hercules-powered Mk III Halifaxes. Eight of these were supplied by 51 Squadron, with a further thirteen from 578 Squadron, which would be operating from Snaith for the last time before moving to Burn on 6 February. They helped to set a large area of the city on fire, and 1,000 people on the ground lost their lives. On the debit side thirty-three bombers paid the price and unusually, all but two of them were Lancasters, which suggested that the new Halifaxes had bridged some of the gap between the two types.

February

A more disastrous start to the year for 102 Squadron is hard to imagine, and although things would calm down to an extent, the summer would bring with it an even more distressing month. Although the crews were unaware of the fact, the Berlin campaign had now effectively run its course, the three raids in four nights at the end of January representing the final concerted effort against the city. The two remaining operations to the capital would be in isolation over the next two months and thereafter, no more RAF heavy bombers would be sent to the 'Big City' during what remained of the war. W/C Ayling took up his appointment as the new commanding officer of 51 Squadron on 1 February, and had two weeks to settle in while the main force stayed on the ground, largely because of inhospitable weather. It did at least give the crews a chance to draw breath, and the squadrons an opportunity to replenish with aircraft and fresh manpower. It was during this lull on the 6th that 578 Squadron moved out of Snaith and took up residence at Burn. When the bomber force next took to the air on the night of the 15/16th, it turned out to be the penultimate raid on Berlin, and a record-breaking effort all round. The 891 aircraft despatched represented the largest non-1,000 force to date, and it was the first time that over 300 Halifaxes and 500 Lancasters had operated together. The weight of bombs carried by those aircraft reaching the target area, over 2,600 tons, was also a record. Much of it was put to good use within the city, where extensive damage resulted, although many outlying communities were once again hit. 102 Squadron's ill luck continued with the loss of two more of its own. The eight-man crew of P/O Kularatne was killed to a man in HX155, and there was just one survivor from the crew of F/L Hilton after flak brought down LW339 over Germany. As already stated, the new, much-improved Mk III Halifaxes had been filtering through to the operational scene since November, and the end was in sight for the less efficient Mk II and V variants. However, they still represented the bulk of the Halifax force, but events four nights after Berlin were to hasten their departure from the front line to less demanding tasks. It was on the night of the 19/20th that over 800 aircraft took off either side of midnight and headed for Leipzig in Germany's east. The crews couldn't have known that they were flying towards the biggest disaster to befall the Command thus far in the war.

German night fighters met the bomber stream as it crossed the Dutch coast, and remained in contact all the way to the target. Wrongly-forecast winds led to some aircraft arriving too early in the target area, compelling them to await the arrival of the Pathfinders, and around twenty of these fell victim to the local flak, while four others were lost to collisions. Cloud prevented an assessment of results, but even had the attack been an outstanding success, it could not have compensated for the Command's heaviest defeat of the war to date. When all of the returning aircraft had been accounted for, there was an unbelievable shortfall of seventy-eight, and although numerically speaking the Lancaster casualties were higher, the losses among the Halifaxes was a staggering 15 per cent of those pressing on to the target after the early returns had been taken out of the equation. 102 Squadron's HX185 was shot down by a night fighter over Germany, but the entire crew of F/O Dean escaped by parachute to be taken prisoner. A combination of flak and a night fighter proved too much for JN972 also over Germany, and only the flight engineer and navigator survived from the crew of F/S Cummings. This was the final straw for Harris, who now withdrew the Merlin-powered Halifaxes from operations over Germany with immediate effect, just as he had the Stirlings in November. From now until the arrival of the Mk III, 102 Squadron would occupy itself with mining duties and the bombing of targets in France.

Some of 4 Group's longest-serving squadrons were now out of the main offensive until they got their hands on the Mk III, and in the case of 102 Squadron, it would be May before it returned to the front line. This meant watching from the sidelines as the remainder of the month's major operations ran their course. Despite the huge losses during the Leipzig debacle, almost 600 aircraft were made ready on the following night to attack Stuttgart. This operation was much more satisfactory, and caused considerable damage within the city's central districts for the loss of a modest nine aircraft. Though not able to bomb Germany, 102 Squadron could still play its part in the war, and spent the remainder of the month gardening. On the 21/22nd, while the main force stayed on the ground, five Halifaxes departed Pocklington to plant vegetables in the sea lanes around St Nazaire. A new tactic was introduced for the next two operations over Germany, to Schweinfurt on the 24/25th and Augsburg twenty-four hours later. The forces were split in two and separated by two hours, in the hope of catching the night fighters on the ground refuelling and rearming as the second wave passed through. Although the former operation suffered badly from undershooting and failed, the second wave lost 50 per cent fewer aircraft than the first in an overall casualty figure of thirty-three. In contrast, the latter operation was one of those rare occasions when everything proceeded according to plan, and the beautiful city of Augsburg lost centuries of irreplaceable cultural history as a raging inferno engulfed its central districts. Twenty-one aircraft failed to return, a figure well below the average loss rate since the winter campaign began in November, and this suggested some merit in the new system. Certainly those at Bomber Command HQ were impressed with the results, and a split bomber force would become a regular feature of major operations right up to the end of the war. While these two operations were in progress, 102 Squadron contributed thirteen and ten aircraft respectively to forces of more than 100 aircraft laying mines in Kiel Bay. Such large mining forces registered on German radar and acted as a diversion, and this may have contributed to the relatively low losses from the Augsburg raid. Two 102 Squadron aircraft returned on two engines on the latter occasion, one landing safely at base while the other, LW331, had to be ditched off Flamborough Head near Bridlington. Sadly, no trace of F/S Rogers and his crew was found.

March

March began with another assault by the main force on Stuttgart on the night of the 1/2nd. This operation was equally as effective as the earlier one, and was concluded for the remarkably low loss of just four aircraft. There would be no further operations to Germany by the main force until mid-month, but the Halifaxes of 4 and 6 Groups, both the old and new variants, would be put to work over France throughout the month. The pre-invasion campaign against the French and Belgian railway networks, the Transportation Plan, was about to begin and the, for now at least, inadequately defended marshalling yards were ideal targets for the Halifax force. First, however, on the night of the 2/3rd, 8 Group Mosquitos marked the SNCA aircraft factory at Meulan-les-Meureaux for more than 100 4 and 6 Group Halifaxes, including thirteen from 102 Squadron. There was no opposition, the marking and bombing were accurate, and no aircraft were lost. On the following night, five Pocklington Halifaxes laid mines off St Nazaire, and then on the 6/7th came the first of the interdiction operations designed to pave the way for the invasion of Europe. The first priority was to dismantle the railway system to prevent its use by the enemy to bring up forces to face the landings. The opening salvo was fired against the marshalling yards at Trappes by around 250 Halifaxes from 4 and 6 Groups, of which sixteen were from 102 Squadron, and enormous damage was inflicted upon track, installations and rolling stock. The force was bolstered by Lancasters of 3 Group at Le Mans marshalling yards on the following night, and this too was a successful operation, although there was collateral damage and thirty French civilians were killed. Thirteen 102 Squadron Halifaxes took part, and they all returned safely. Meanwhile, Mk III Halifaxes had begun to arrive at Melbourne for 'Shiny Ten', and their final operations on the older marks were the above-mentioned on the 6/7th and 7/8th. Le Mans was hit again on the 13/14th, when 102 Squadron put up sixteen aircraft without loss.

The main force concluded its three-raid series against Stuttgart on the night of the 15/16th, with a raid by well over 800 aircraft. Clear weather conditions should have led to accurate marking, but strong winds were probably a factor in causing the raid to undershoot, and in the event, the enemy night fighters reaped the benefits of the good visibility. Arriving on the scene shortly before the target was reached, they contributed to the destruction of thirty-seven bombers. Taking off at the same time as the Stuttgart-bound force, and masked by its massive presence as it flew out across France, ninety-four Merlin-powered Halifaxes and thirty-eight Stirlings headed for the marshalling yards at Amiens. Oboe Mosquitos accurately marked the aiming point, and another successful attack ensued. 102 Squadron despatched twenty-two aircraft, and only one was forced back early with a dead engine, the others pressing on to bomb and return safely. Despite the successful outcome, a similar force returned on the following night and carried out another accurate attack without loss, 102 Squadron this time contributing seventeen Halifaxes of which one returned early. On the 18/19th, over 800 Pathfinder and main-force aircraft delivered the first of two devastating blows against Frankfurt. Over 6,000 buildings were destroyed or seriously damaged in central, eastern and western districts, and much of the city's cultural history was lost forever. 102 Squadron contributed to the diversionary measures by sending twelve aircraft to join a mining effort in the Heligoland area. The second Frankfurt operation took place on the 22/23rd, and was even more destructive than the first. Half of the city was left without water, gas and electricity for an extended period, many war industry factories suffered total loss of production and almost 1,000 people were killed on top of 120,000 who were bombed out. 10 Squadron returned to the fray for this operation after full conversion to the Halifax III and two weeks working-up, and contributed thirteen aircraft, eleven of which bombed the primary target. Among this night's diversionary measures was another large mining effort in northern waters, for which 102 Squadron put up eighteen aircraft without loss. Railway yards at Laon provided the objective for over 140 aircraft of 3, 4, 6 and 8 Groups on the 23/24th, while the main force was rested. The Master Bomber called a halt to the proceedings after half had bombed, possibly when the aiming point became obscured by smoke. Even so, some useful damage was inflicted, although civilian housing again found itself in the firing line. This operation brought 102 Squadron's first missing crew for a month, that of F/S Garside, who were lost without trace in HR978.

The time had now arrived for the final assault of the campaign on Berlin, and this would be the nineteenth since its beginning in August, and the sixteenth since the resumption in November. Over 800 aircraft took off in the early evening of the 24th, and once at cruising altitude, they encountered winds of unprecedented strength coming from the north. The windfinder system, whereby selected crews assessed wind strength and direction during the course of the flight and transmitted the data back to Group for broadcasting to the outbound bombers, failed to cope with the situation. The windfinders could not bring themselves to believe the evidence, and so modified their findings. Group also did not believe what they read, and modified the figures further. This resulted in large numbers of aircraft being driven south of their intended track, and the cohesion of the bomber stream was broken. This led to a scattered raid, which produced moderate damage in south-western districts particularly, but afflicted over 100 outlying communities. Crews found it difficult to adhere to their briefed route home, and many aircraft were blown over heavily-defended areas of Germany, giving the flak batteries their best night of the war. Seventy-two aircraft failed to return, two-thirds of them estimated to have fallen victim to predicted flak. 102 Squadron spent this night on the ground, and while the main force licked its wounds at home on the following night, it contributed ten aircraft to a mixed force of Halifaxes, Stirlings and Lancasters which failed to destroy the marshalling yards at Aulnoye after slightly inaccurate marking.

The Berlin offensive was now over, and never again would the city be attacked by RAF heavy bombers. From now on it would be up to the Mosquitos of the Pathfinder Light Night Striking Force to harass the city until the arrival in its suburbs of Russian troops in April 1945. The winter campaign, however, still had a week to run and two more major operations for the crews to negotiate, and the first of these was directed at Essen on the 26/27th. It was another devastating raid, thus continuing the remarkable run of success against this once elusive target since the introduction of Oboe to main-force operations a year earlier. Over 1,700 buildings were reduced to rubble, and industry was severely afflicted as the defences were caught napping by the sudden and unexpected switch to the Ruhr. Only nine aircraft failed to return, and none at all were lost from a simultaneous successful attack on the railway yards at Courtrai to which 102 Squadron contributed sixteen aircraft. Sadly, much of the bombing spilled beyond the confines of the yards and more than 250 French civilians lost their lives. The winter campaign ended on the night of the 30/31st with a standard deep-penetration operation to Nuremberg. A conference of the Group commanders decided to adopt a 5 Group-inspired direct route to the target, which involved a straight leg of some 250 miles across Germany to a point about 50 miles north of the target from where the final approach would be made. Pathfinder chief AVM Bennett protested vehemently and predicted a disaster, but he was overruled. From the moment that a 1409 Met Flight Mosquito crew's warning about the inaccuracy of the forecast conditions went unheeded, the components for a tragedy were in place. W/C Ayling was on leave at the time, prior to being posted from 51 Squadron, and it was S/L Hill who presided over the proceedings, he unaware that ahead lay one of the squadron's unhappiest nights of the war, and his own death.

Taking off either side of 22.00 hours it was not long before the almost 800 crews began to notice some unusual and disquieting features in the conditions. The fairly new moon cast an unusually bright light, and there was a rare crystal clear quality to the visibility. It was possible to observe the other aircraft in the stream, and this was in complete contrast to the norm of feeling completely alone until the target was reached. The forecast cloud at cruising altitude did not materialize, as the Met Flight crew had predicted, but formed instead well below the bomber stream, silhouetting the aircraft like flies on a tablecloth. Condensation trails began to form in the cold clear air to further advertise the bombers' presence, and as the final insult the jetstream winds, which had so adversely affected the Berlin raid a week earlier, were also present, only this time from the south. The carnage began over Charleroi in Belgium, and continued all the way to the target, the route marked out on the ground by the burning wreckage of RAF bombers. The bomber stream was scattered by the wind, and many crews were unaware that they had been pushed up to 50 miles north of their intended track. As a result, they turned onto the final leg towards Nuremberg from a false position, and around 120 bombed

Schweinfurt in error. More than eighty aircraft were lost before the target was reached, and by the time the battered remnant arrived home, ninety-five were missing and others would be written off in crashes or with battle damage too severe to repair. 4 Group contributed 119 Halifaxes, of which twenty failed to return and three others were wrecked in crashes at home. The hardest-hit unit was 51 Squadron with five missing and one wrecked from seventeen despatched. Meanwhile, ten 102 Squadron aircraft had spent the night mining in the Heligoland area and all returned safely.

It had been a gruelling winter campaign and represented the Command's lowest point, and it was the only time when the morale of the bomber boys was in question. That now facing the crews of Bomber Command was in marked contrast to what had been endured during the past four and a half months. In place of the arduous slog to Germany on dark, often dirty nights there would be generally shorter-range trips to France and Belgium in improving weather conditions. Also no longer would it be necessary to traverse the 40-mile-deep searchlight and flak defence zones surrounding the Ruhr and Berlin. Even so, these new targets would be equally demanding in their way and would require of the crews a greater commitment to accuracy to avoid civilian casualties. The main fly in the ointment for the crews was a dictate from on high dating from the first week of March, which decreed that most operations to the nearby occupied countries were to count as just one-third of a sortie towards the completion of a tour. This was an unpopular move, and until the flawed policy was rescinded, an air of discontent pervaded the bomber stations. Despite the horrendous losses over the winter, the Command was in remarkably fine fettle to face its new challenge. Harris was in the enviable position of being able to achieve what had eluded his predecessor, namely, to attack multiple targets simultaneously with forces large enough to make an impact. He could now assign targets to individual Groups, to Groups in tandem or to the Command as a whole, as dictated by operational requirements, and although invasion considerations would now have priority, he would never entirely shelve his favoured policy of city-busting.

April

10 Squadron began the spring offensive under a new commanding officer, as W/C Radford replaced W/C Sutton on 1 April. W/C Ling took up his appointment as the new commanding officer of 51 Squadron on the same day. The pre-invasion campaign against the French and Belgian railway systems had begun in March, as already mentioned, by the Halifax and Stirling squadrons withdrawn from the main battle, and now the rest of the Command was about to join in. As far as 102 Squadron was concerned, the new phase of operations effectively returned it to the front line. Only a few isolated operations would take place against Germany from which it was exempt, while the vast majority would be in line with the Transportation Plan. 102 Squadron's first activity of the month involved mining operations to the Frisians on the nights of the 1/2nd and 7/8th, for which a total of twenty-one sorties were launched. The

new campaign began in earnest on the night of the 9/10th, when over 200 aircraft from 3, 4, 6 and 8 Groups attacked the Lille-Delivrance goods station and marshalling yards. 102 Squadron contributed sixteen aircraft, and a highly satisfactory outcome left installations and track severely damaged, with over 2,000 items of rolling stock destroyed. Sadly, 456 civilians were killed in adjacent residential districts, and this was to be a problem beyond solution. A second operation on this night involved similar numbers attacking the railway yards at Villeneuve-St-Georges in Paris, and while this also achieved moderate success, it too resulted in civilian deaths. Later on the 10th W/C Markland was installed as the new commanding officer of 78 Squadron in place of W/C Warner. W/C Markland had served with the squadron as a wireless operator during the Whitley period, and was the first of his trade to attain squadron commander status. Four railway yards were targeted in France on the 10/11th and one in Belgium, 4 Group and 102 Squadron assigned to Tergnier, where a successful outcome was achieved for the loss of ten Halifaxes. All sixteen from 102 Squadron came through more or less unscathed, however, and on the following night, nine were sent mining in the Kattegat, while a heavy and destructive raid was mounted by other elements of the Command against Aachen. 4 Group did not take part in a heavy and destructive area attack on Aachen on the 11/12th, but returned to Tergnier on the 18/19th with elements of 3 and 8 Groups and blocked fifty railway lines, but also hit nearby housing.

It was a week before the next major activity and during this period, on the 14th, the Command officially became subject to the dictates of SHAEF. This situation had existed in principle since the start of the Transportation Plan, but Harris would now have less room to manoeuvre, and would remain thus shackled until the Allied armies were sweeping towards the German frontier at the end of the summer. The next round of operations brought attacks on four French railway yards and a large mining effort in northern waters on the 18/19th, 102 Squadron supporting the latter with twelve aircraft. W/C Eayrs concluded his term of office as commanding officer of 640 Squadron on the 20th, and he was succeeded by W/C Carter who, it will be recalled, had been forced to relinquish his command of 10 Squadron through ill health in February 1943. 102 Squadron sent four gardeners to the St Malo area on the night of the 20/21st, and also twelve other aircraft to attack the marshalling yards at Ottignies as part of a force of almost 200. This was a busy night generally, on which 350 aircraft went to Cologne and caused massive damage, while the now independent 5 Group demonstrated the efficacy of its Mosquito low-level visual marking system at La Chapelle railway yards. On the 21/22nd 102 Squadron despatched ten aircraft to lay mines off Lorient, and twenty-four hours later sent fifteen back to the railway yards at Laon where a two-wave attack caused severe damage. While this was in progress, Düsseldorf was receiving a pounding from well over 500 aircraft, and Brunswick was escaping lightly at the hands of 5 Group. The night of the 23/24th was one of minor operations only, including mining at five locations in the Baltic. Thus far during the month 102 Squadron had operated without loss, but HX151 fell victim to a night fighter off Denmark and there were no survivors from the crew of F/O Hall. The squadron stayed at home on the 24/25th, while Karlsruhe sustained modest damage at the hands of 600 aircraft, and Munich succumbed to a sharp attack by 5 Group. It was during the latter that 102 Squadron's former son, W/C Leonard Cheshire, dived his Mosquito headlong into the murderous light flak of the Munich defences to mark the target, before screaming away across the rooftops to make his escape. This sortie probably sealed the award to Cheshire of the Victoria Cross at the conclusion of his operational career of 100 actions. Three operations were mounted on the 26/27th, against Essen, Schweinfurt and the railway yards at Villeneuve-St-Georges. 102 Squadron sent seventeen Halifaxes to the last mentioned which sustained moderate damage, and just one of the 217 participating aircraft was lost. There was similar fare for the Halifaxes of 4 and 6 Groups on the following night, this time at Aulnoye. A successful operation by over 200 aircraft cost a single Halifax, JN948 of 102 Squadron, which crashed in France, killing F/L Silverman and his crew. The month ended with seventeen mining sorties to various locations on the nights of the 29th and 30th.

May

May would see the departure from Pocklington of the Merlin Halifaxes, and no further operational losses would be sustained in the type although non-operational accidents accounted for two. JD304 was written off when a burst tyre caused the undercarriage to collapse at Marston Moor at the end of a ferry flight on the 2nd, and LW138 crash-landed with engine failure while training on the 6th. Happily, neither incident resulted in casualties among the crews of F/O Dodds and F/O Rank respectively. May began for the Group in general with an attack on railway yards and locomotive sheds at Mechelen in Belgium on the 1/2nd. Unfortunately, collateral damage to the town caused many casualties among the civilian population. Meanwhile on that night, eight 102 Squadron crews were sent mining at four locations off the French coast, and twelve similar sorties were carried out off Brest, Lorient and St Nazaire on the 4/5th, to be followed by six more to the same ports twenty-four hours later. During this period the Command had continued operations against railway targets, specific factories, airfields, ammunition dumps and a military camp. On the 7/8th, 6 Group mounted a small-scale raid on a coastal battery, a type of target destined to attract huge attention as the day of invasion drew ever nearer. In order to maintain the enemy belief that the invasion force would land in the Calais area, the closest point to England, elaborate deceptions were carried out. Among these was Bomber Command's concentration on coastal defences in the Pas-de-Calais, and only at the eleventh hour would targets in the genuine invasion area be attacked.

A busy month took elements of the Group to a railway target at Mantes-la-Jolie on the 6/7th, coastal batteries in the Pas-de-Calais on the 8/9th and 9/10th, railways again on the 10/11th, 11/12th and 12/13th before minor operations allowed a brief respite. Seven mining sorties over the 9/10th and 10/11th were the last to be undertaken by 102 Squadron in the Merlin Halifaxes, and the first examples of the Mk III arrived on the 11th. 102

Squadron was completely re-equipped with the Mk III by the 15th, allowing five aircraft to participate in a mining operation in the Heligoland Bight that night. One brought its mines back after problems with its H2s equipment, but the others all completed their assignments before returning safely. Earlier in the day 77 Squadron completed its final change of address with a move to Full Sutton. It left behind at Elvington its complement of Mk V Halifaxes, which became the property on the 16th of the newly-formed 346 Squadron, the first of two units to join 4 Group which were manned by members of Free French forces who had mostly served previously in North Africa. Lt Col Venot was installed as the first commanding officer, and he set about the task of bringing his charges up to operational status. A mining operation in the Kattegat was completed by 102 Squadron's participants without loss on the 21/22nd, the night on which 500 Lancasters returned to Duisburg for the first time in a year. Much damage was inflicted, but the loss of twenty-nine aircraft made it an expensive return and reaffirmed the hostility of 'Happy Valley'. On the following night, Dortmund was similarly honoured with its first raid for a year and this too was highly destructive, although at a cost of eighteen Lancasters. It is difficult to imagine the almost routine writing-off of forty-seven heavy bombers and 330 airmen, the equivalent of two three-flight squadrons, in the space of forty-eight hours. This night also brought 102 Squadron's first bombing operation in the new aircraft, which was against railway installations at Orleans. W/C Forsyth was posted from 466 Squadron on the 23rd and succeeded by W/C Connolly. 102 Squadron's next target was a heavy gun battery on the French coast at Colline Beaumont on the 24/25th, while other crews from the squadron went mining and over 400 aircraft pounded Aachen and its two main railway yards. On the 27/28th the military camp at Bourg Leopold in Belgium suffered severe damage at the hands of a predominantly Halifax force, but 102 Squadron registered its inevitable first loss of a Mk III Halifax. MZ649 was heading home over Belgium but failed to survive an encounter with a night fighter. F/O Huycke and four of his crew escaped by parachute before the crash, but two others were killed. The last night of the month took a 4 Group element to Trappes marshalling yards, where a successful operation ensued.

June

It is likely that the crews of 102 Squadron were buoyed by a new confidence in the vastly improved performance of the Mk III Halifax, but any illusions were shattered by a catastrophic time during June. 346 Squadron was declared operational at the start of the month and conducted its only operation on the Mk V on the night of the 1/2nd, when contributing twelve aircraft to a disappointing attack on a signals station at Ferme-d'Urvill. Thereafter the squadron began to receive Mk III Halifaxes. The run-up to D-Day involved 102 Squadron in an attack on a gun emplacement at Haringzelles in the Pas-de-Calais on the 2/3rd, as part of the invasion deception plan. Some 270 aircraft took part in attacks on four such sites for the loss of a single Lancaster. Meanwhile an attack on railway yards at Trappes by elements of 1 and 4

Groups became a disaster for the Halifax contingent. Of the 104 Halifaxes contributed by 4 Group squadrons, fifteen failed to return, a massive 14.5 per cent. Hardest hit was 158 Squadron which suffered the loss of six aircraft, five of them crashing on French soil while a sixth was written off at home after sustaining heavy damage during an attack by a night fighter. Three members of its crew were not on board when it crash-landed at Hurn, and although two of them survived and evaded capture, the body of the other was never found. 76 and 640 Squadrons each posted missing three crews from this operation, and 10 and 466 Squadrons two. Later on the 3rd 466 Squadron completed its move from Leconfield to Driffield, which would remain its home for the rest of the war. On the following day W/C Carter relinquished command of 640 Squadron in favour of W/C Maw, who had served previously as a flight commander with 10 Squadron. At 32 years of age W/C Maw was considerably older than most of his contemporaries. Over 1,000 aircraft were aloft on D-Day Eve, the night of the 5/6th, to bomb ten batteries on the Normandy coast. Although no direct reference was made at briefings to the invasion, crews were given strict flight levels and were instructed not to jettison bombs over the sea. Aircraft were taking off throughout the night, and those crews finding a gap in the cloud layer as they returned in dawn's early light were rewarded with a glimpse of the armada ploughing its way sedately across the Channel below. 102 Squadron despatched a personal record of twenty-six aircraft to its assigned target at Massy. That night another 1,000 aircraft concentrated their efforts against road and rail communications in or near nine towns on the approaches to the beachhead. W/C Calder completed his tour as commanding officer of 158 Squadron later on the 7th, and was posted to 1652 Conversion Unit as chief flying instructor. He would return to the operational scene in November when joining 617 Squadron as a flight commander having reverted to the rank of squadron leader. In the following March he would go down in history as the pilot of the first Lancaster to deliver a Barnes Wallis-designed 10-ton Grand Slam earthquake bomb in anger. His successor at 158 Squadron was W/C Dobson, who came in from 1663 Conversion Unit, and he was another graduate of the 76 Squadron school of excellence. The next two nights were devoted to road and rail communications targets behind enemy lines in the Normandy area, and returning from Alencon short of fuel on the 8/9th, 102 Squadron's MZ659 was successfully abandoned by P/O Sambell and his crew over Yorkshire. Less fortunate were their colleagues in LW140, which crashed in the county on return from a mining sortie on that same night and there were no survivors from the crew of W/O Jekyll. Elements of 1, 3, 4 and 8 Groups bombed railway targets at four locations on the 11/12th, among them Massy-Palaiseau, from which MZ651 failed to return having crashed in France with the loss of the entire crew of F/S Singleton.

A new oil campaign began at Gelsenkirchen on the 12/13th, where the Nordstern refinery was the objective. An outstandingly successful operation by elements of 1, 3 and 8 Groups caused severe damage to the plant, and halted all production of vital aviation and other fuels for a number of weeks. The first daylight operations since the departure of 2 Group from Bomber

Command a year earlier took place on the evening of the 14th. A two-phase assault was launched against the port of Le Havre to destroy the enemy fleet of E-boats and other fast light craft based there, which represented a threat to the Allied shipping serving the beachhead. The operation was entirely successful, and few if any craft survived. Later that night, 102 Squadron provided twenty-one aircraft to join an attack on a troop position at Evrecy near Caen, and this too was claimed as successful. Boulogne hosted an evening raid against its E-boat fleet on the 15th, and the results mirrored those at Le Havre. A second new campaign, this one against flying bomb launching and storage sites in the Pas-de-Calais, commenced on the 16/17th, a night on which 102 Squadron had its first taste of attacking a hotly-defended oil target. The Holten refinery at Sterkrade was cloud-covered, and while the ensuing bombing had little effect on production, the effect of the defences on the attackers was numbing. Thirty-one aircraft were hacked down, the majority of them by night fighters, and it was the Halifax brigade which was most sorely afflicted. 77 Squadron alone lost seven aircraft, while 102 Squadron posted missing five of its twenty-one participating crews. Night fighters accounted for LW192 and MZ642 over Holland, and there were no survivors from the crew of F/S Braddock in the former, and just two from the crew of Sgt Barr in the latter. MZ292 crashed into the sea off the Frisians, and took with it to their deaths the crew of F/S Kelso, B Flight commander S/L Fisher and his crew were lost without trace in MZ301, and finally, F/O Maxwell and his crew all died in MZ652.

Thereafter, bad weather brought a spate of scrubbed operations, and during this period 347 Squadron was formed at Elvington under the command of Lt Col Vigouroux. This was the second unit to be formed with Free French personnel and it inherited the Mk V Halifaxes previously owned by its sister unit 346 Squadron. Operations resumed for 102 Squadron on the night of the 22/23rd, when it was assigned to a railway target at Laon: 100 4 Group aircraft took part, of which fifteen were from 102 Squadron which also sent six aircraft mining off Brest. The squadron carried out its first daylight operation for two years when attacking a V-1 site at Noyelle-en-Chausse on the 24th under a fighter escort, and it was similar fare on the 25th when a site at Montorgueil was the target. MZ753 collided with a 77 Squadron Halifax in the target area, and the newly-appointed B Flight commander, S/L Treasure, died with his crew, along with those from the other aircraft. S/L Kercher overshot his landing on return, and although MZ752 was written off, the crew walked away. 347 Squadron went to war for the first time on the night of the 27/28th when participating in an attack on a V-Weapon site at Mont Candon, one of six similar targets for a total force of more than 700 aircraft. It was to be its only outing under Merlin power as the coming month would provide a fleet of new Mk III Halifaxes. On the 28/29th eighteen of 102 Squadron's twenty participating crews pressed on to bomb railway yards at Blainville and produced a scattered attack. Eleven 4 Group Halifaxes failed to return, and for the second time during the month, Pocklington registered the loss of five of its crews. All five crashed on French soil, LW159 and MZ646 definitely falling to night fighters, the former with just one survivor from the crew of

P/O Rogers, and the latter producing two survivors from the crew of Sgt Robinson, with both pilots among the dead. F/S Campbell and two of his crew were killed in LW143, but four men evaded capture after parachuting from MZ644, while their skipper, Sgt Jardine, and two others perished. There were evaders also from NA502, P/O Mulvaney and three others, but two of their colleagues were killed and the seventh man became a PoW. The loss of fifteen aircraft and thirteen crews made this the worst month in the squadron's history, but in contrast, the remainder of the year would bring an average loss per month of a more modest three aircraft.

July

July opened with a raid on a V-1 site at St-Martin-l'Hortier by daylight on the 1st, followed by another at Domlegger on the 4th. Earthworks at the site of the long-range V-3 'super gun' at Mimoyecques were attacked on the 6th, the occasion on which former 4 Group star W/C Cheshire, now of 617 Squadron, flew the one hundredth and final operation of his glittering career. On the 14th W/C Marchbanks concluded his long period in command, having seen the squadron through its toughest times, and he was replaced by W/C Wilson, a pre-war regular officer, who had served at that time with 40 Squadron. After concentrating on V-Weapon sites for most of the first half of the month, 102 Squadron provided four aircraft to an overall force of 900 for tactical operations around Caen on the 18th. The operations in support of the British Second Army's Operation *Goodwood* were mounted at first light under a fighter escort, and were deemed to be successful. The squadron's first loss of the month came during an operation against a V-1 construction site at Les Haut Boissons on the 23/24th when MZ298 crashed into the sea, it is believed, following a brush with a night fighter. P/O Donald and five of his crew were killed, while the sole survivor was rescued and returned home. Also on this night, Harris mounted the first raid for two months against a German urban target. Some 600 aircraft appeared suddenly and with complete surprise from behind an RCM screen provided by 100 Group and inflicted serious damage upon the town of Kiel and its port. On the 24/25th Harris embarked on a three-raid series against Stuttgart over a five-night period, at the conclusion of which its central districts lay in ruins. 102 Squadron participated in only this first raid, and lost LL552 to a crash in France with just one survivor from the crew of F/L Page. The last of the series took place in moonlight on the 28/29th, when night fighters fell upon the outbound Lancasters over France. Thirty-nine failed to return, while a further twenty-two were lost in a simultaneous raid on Hamburg. Support for American ground forces in Normandy was provided by almost 700 aircraft on the 30th, and on return in bad weather, 102 Squadron's NA503 crashed while trying to land at Morton-in-Marsh, killing F/S Hulme and his crew. It was on this morning that W/C Wilkerson carried out his final operation with 578 Squadron, bringing his career tally to forty-seven although he would remain in command for a further three weeks.

August

V-Weapon sites continued to dominate proceedings at the start of August, and there were also attacks on oil and fuel storage dumps and railway installations. Daylight operations were now a matter of course, and during the 3rd a total of 1,114 sorties were sent against three flying bomb storage sites. 102 Squadron was involved at two of these, Bois de Cassan and Forêt de Nieppe with fourteen and ten aircraft respectively, all of which returned safely. On the 11th MZ371 suffered engine failure and crashed on take-off when bound for railway yards at Somain, but without serious consequences for F/O Munroe and his crew. The thus far elusive target of Brunswick was selected to host an experimental raid on the 12/13th, to ascertain the ability of crews to locate and bomb a target on the strength of their own H2s returns without the presence of Pathfinders. The squadron contributed thirteen Halifaxes to this operation, which was not a success, and LW195 was shot up by a night fighter. The flight engineer was killed in the engagement before the previously mentioned F/O Sambell and the others were forced to bale out over France, and the navigator died when his parachute failed him. A simultaneous operation to bomb the Opel motor works at Rüsselsheim, for which 102 Squadron put up a further nine aircraft, ended in failure, and MZ647 did not return with the eight-man crew of F/L Young, all of whom were killed. 640 Squadron's commanding officer, W/C Maw, also failed to return from this operation, and it was later learned that he and three of his crew had lost their lives, while the four survivors were in enemy hands. He was succeeded on the 14th by W/C Viney, who had served in the previous year with 158 Squadron. W/C Iveson was posted to 1669 HCU from 76 Squadron also on the 14th, and he was succeeded by W/C Ralph Cassels. This day also brought a new squadron to 4 Group in the form of 462 Squadron RAAF, which took up residence at Driffield. Originally formed in Egypt in September 1942 as a Halifax unit under the command of W/C David Young, who, it will be recalled, had previously commanded 77 Squadron, 462 Squadron operated for the first time in January 1943 after moving to Cyrenaica. A three-month spell in Tunisia was followed by a return to Cyrenaica, where it remained until moving to Italy in February 1944 and being disbanded and reformed as 614 Squadron in March 1944. The Australian members of the squadron were sent to England and distributed around the other Australian units. 466 Squadron was already at Driffield, and a goodly number of its crews formed the nucleus of the new unit, while flight commander S/L D.E.S. Shannon was promoted to acting wing commander to take charge on the 18th. The first operation for the squadron came by daylight on the 25th, when the constructional works at Watten formed the target.

In preparation for his new night offensive against industrial Germany, Harris launched over 1,000 aircraft by daylight on the 15th to attack nine night-fighter airfields in Holland and Belgium. Briefed for Eindhoven, all fifteen crews from 102 Squadron carried out their assigned tasks and returned safely to Pocklington. Having hopefully hampered the night-fighter response, Harris sent a force each to Stettin and Kiel on the 16/17th, and lost a modest ten aircraft from the total of 800 despatched. One of these, however, was 102

Squadron's NA504, which went missing without trace from the latter with the crew of F/S Coghlan. The highly-respected and very popular W/C Wilkerson was posted out of 578 Squadron on the 23rd, and on the 28th he was assigned to 9 Course Empire Flying School at Hullavington in Wiltshire. This was a multi-national course for officer-ranking pilots with a minimum of 1,000 hours behind them, and was to equip them for senior posts in crew training. W/C James was appointed as his successor at 578 Squadron, and like Wilkerson, he would lead the squadron from the front. The second half of the month brought a number of attacks on oil targets, including on the 27th, the first daylight raid on Germany since 1941. 102 Squadron sent eighteen Halifaxes to Homberg as part of a force of over 200 aircraft targeting the Rhein-Preussen synthetic oil refinery at Meerbeck, and sixteen squadrons of Spitfires provided an escort for the approach and withdrawal stages. 76 Squadron put up twenty-one Halifaxes led for the first time by W/C Cassels, with W/C 'Tubby' Brooks of 635 Squadron acting as the Master Bomber. Flak was intense and the marking was conducted by Oboe in the face of five-eighths cloud cover. While the operation was not totally effective, some damage was achieved and no losses were incurred. The V-Weapon campaign concluded on the 28th with attacks on twelve sites, for which 102 Squadron's participation was not required.

September

September brought a concerted effort to capture the three French ports still in enemy hands, and no fewer than six operations were mounted against Le Havre between the 5th and the 11th. 102 Squadron was involved on the 9th and 10th without loss. 346 Squadron's commanding officer, Lt Col Venot, reached the target area on the latter occasion, but part of the bomb load failed to release. On landing at Elvington at 18.34 a 1,000lb bomb fell onto the tarmac and exploded, killing all on board with the exception of Venot, who sustained serious injury. Commandant Puget was promoted from within the squadron as his successor, and he would remain at the helm until after the war was over. By the end of the following day, the port of Le Havre had fallen to British forces. On the 12th over 100 Halifaxes of 4 Group attacked Münster, and left parts of its southern districts in flames. 102 Squadron's LL555 was damaged by flak, and was eventually crash-landed at the emergency strip at Woodbridge in Suffolk by F/S Fitt, and just one man sustained injuries. They were more fortunate than their colleagues in MZ699 which crashed in the target area, killing P/O Groves and one of his crew, and delivering the remainder into captivity. W/C Roncoroni departed 77 Squadron on the 15th and was succeeded by W/C Clark. Also on the 15th came the tragic news that W/C Wilkerson, late of 578 Squadron, had been killed in a flying accident. As part of his course he had flown with four fellow delegates to 61 OTU at Rednall in Shropshire in an American-built Martin Baltimore. One of the other officers took the pilot's seat for the return flight to Hullavington, but the aircraft crashed almost immediately after take-off, killing Wilkerson and one other.

On the 17th 102 Squadron's MZ289 headed out over the North Sea in the hands of Capt Thompson of the South African Air Force for a non-operational flight, and neither the Halifax nor the crew was seen again. This was the day on which German strongpoints around Boulogne received 3,000 tons of bombs from over 700 aircraft, and within a week the port was returned to Allied control. The first of six operations against enemy positions around Calais took place by daylight on the 20th, for which 102 Squadron put up thirteen aircraft without loss. There was no further offensive activity for the squadron during what remained of the month, but it was required to fulfil another important role. Between the 25th and 2 October, the squadron was one of a number from 4 Group to be employed to ferry fuel supplies to Melsbroek aerodrome at Brussels. Each aircraft could carry a consignment of 750 gallons in 165 cans, and 102 Squadron despatched in all 189 sorties during the period. During the course of the month, W/C Lawrence was posted out to Bomber Command HQ after completing his second tour with 78 Squadron and adding another thirteen operations to his tally. Until the appointment of his replacement, flight commander S/L Hurley filled the breach.

October

By the time October arrived, Calais had become the last major French port to return to Allied control. Having now discharged his primary obligation to SHAEF, Harris turned his attention fully towards industrial Germany, with a particular emphasis on oil production. 102 Squadron returned to its offensive role on the 6th when sending twenty-two aircraft to the oil refinery at Scholven-Buer, while another predominantly 4 Group force attacked a similar target at Sterkrade. It was to be a loss-free month for 102 Squadron, despite major operations of a strategic nature and in support of the ground forces. Elements of 3, 6 and 8 Groups began a new Ruhr offensive at Dortmund on the evening of the 6th, while 5 Group pounded Bremen with unbelievable fury. 4 Group sat out the evening having been active earlier in the day, but took off for the frontier town of Cleves in the late morning of the 7th to support ground forces. 102 Squadron put up twenty-four Halifaxes for this operation, and all returned safely. 4 and 6 Groups provided the main force for an attack on Bochum on the 9/10th as part of the new Ruhr campaign, and this time 102 Squadron contributed twenty aircraft without loss. Earlier in the day W/C U.Y. Shannon had been appointed as 10 Squadron's new commanding officer as successor to W/C Radford. At first light on the 14th, a massive force of over 1,000 aircraft took off for Duisburg, to carry out the first raid under Operation *Hurricane*. This was designed to demonstrate to the enemy the overwhelming superiority of Allied air power, and it therefore also involved the American 8th Air Force at a separate location. Almost 4,400 tons of bombs fell into the already shattered city, and similar numbers returned that night to press home the point about overwhelming superiority. 102 Squadron contributed twenty-five Halifaxes to the earlier raid and twenty-two to the later one, all returning safely. Much of the credit for despatching 2,018 aircraft in well under twenty-four hours should go to the ground crews and armourers, who must have toiled almost without break to turn round such a massive force. As an indication of the size and power of the forces available to Harris at this time, the Duisburg effort went ahead without 5 Group, which took advantage of the night-time activity over the Ruhr to deliver the first really devastating blow on Brunswick. Some 233 Lancasters completely destroyed 150 hectares of the city including the old town centre. Halifaxes made up half of the force of 500 aircraft sent to Wilhelmshaven on the night of the 15/16th, the night on which 10 Squadron's recently-appointed commanding officer, W/C Shannon, flew the first of his eleven operations with the squadron. 466 Squadron bade farewell to W/C Connolly on the 20th and welcomed W/C Wharton as his successor. Essen received its visit from the Hurricane force on the evening of the 23rd and again by daylight on the 25th, by which time it had lost its status as a major centre of war production. It was the turn of Cologne on the 28th, 30th and 31st, and like Essen it had by now largely ceased to function. The city's industries had been dispersed around the country and much of its population had been evacuated.

November

The Command's relatively light losses as the year drew to a close were indicative of the overwhelming numerical superiority of the Allied air forces, the advent of long-range escort fighters and the success of the oil campaign in drastically reducing the output of vital aviation fuel from the refineries. However, it would be wrong to assume that the enemy defences were incapable of occasionally inflicting painful reminders of the carnage of war. On the night of 2/3 November almost 1,000 aircraft raided Düsseldorf, and the Grim Reaper returned to 102 Squadron after a lengthy absence on duties elsewhere to claim a number of its personnel. MZ798 was hit by 'friendly fire' from another bomber, before being finished off by a night fighter over Belgium. Lt Begbie of the South African Air Force and two of his crew failed to survive, but their four colleagues landed in Allied-held territory and were soon returned to the squadron. LW141 came down on the German border with Belgium, and this time there was just one survivor from the crew of F/O Redmond. On the 4/5th Bochum was subjected to a heavy raid by 700 aircraft, and its central districts suffered severe damage to the tune of 4,000 buildings destroyed or severely damaged. The loss of twenty-eight aircraft, most of them Halifaxes, demonstrated the lingering lethal potential of the enemy defences, particularly around the Ruhr, and they claimed another 102 Squadron crew on this night. F/O Cameron and his crew were all killed when MZ772 crashed in Germany. Gelsenkirchen was pounded on the 6th, and this was followed by a period of relative inactivity for the 4 Group squadrons. On the 8th W/C Ling was posted out of 51 Squadron, and he was succeeded by W/C Holford who had served as a flight commander with 10 Squadron back in 1941. Support of American ground forces in the Rhine area on the 16th led to operations against the three towns of Düren, Heinsberg and Jülich during the afternoon. All were located in an arc from north to east of Aachen, and each was all but erased from the map, the last-mentioned at the hands of 4 and 6 Groups with Pathfinder markers. 102 Squadron contributed eighteen aircraft to a scattered attack on Münster on the 18th, and fifteen to a raid on the oil refinery at Sterkrade that failed to find the mark on the 21/22nd. Thereafter 4 Group underwent a week of frustrating scrubs because of the weather. Twenty-six 102 Squadron aircraft participated in a raid on Essen on the 28/29th and twenty-three took part in yet another assault on Duisburg by daylight on the 30th while in-between, a number of mining operations were undertaken. W/C Young became 78 Squadron's final wartime commanding officer during the course of the month.

December

It was becoming increasingly difficult to find worthwhile targets to attack in a country so laid to waste by continuous bombing, and a number of quite small and insignificant towns found themselves in the bombsights. Just two more 102 Squadron crews would be lost before the end of the year, although others were to be involved in a number of close calls. On the evening of 2 December twenty aircraft took off from Pocklington bound for Hagen in the Ruhr, and all returned after bombing the town through cloud on H2s. Railway installations were the principal objectives in the small town of Soest, just north of the now famous Möhne Dam on the 5/6th, but the town itself was also devastated by the accurate and concentrated bombing by over 400 aircraft. 102 Squadron's MZ450 was badly damaged, but made it home in the hands of F/L Carr and his crew, only to be declared beyond repair. Osnabrück was also bombed in difficult conditions on the following night as cloud swallowed up the markers. On the 9th 102 Squadron's MZ800 crash-landed at Pocklington at the end of a training flight, but S/L Ward and his crew walked away unhurt. Essen followed on the 12/13th, and Duisburg on the 17/18th with a series of scrubs in-between. 77 Squadron exchanged commanding officers for the final time during the war when W/C Forbes succeeded W/C Clark. Some scrubs actually came as preparations were in hand for take-off, as on the 21/22nd, when only five of fourteen 102 Squadron crews were allowed to go to Cologne, and only one of nine left for Bingen on the following night. The sting in the tail came during a raid on Mülheim airfield near Essen on the 24th, when flak brought down LW168, killing P/O Hislop and one of his crew while the five survivors were marched off into captivity. They were joined by four members of the crew of MZ871, which also crashed in Germany but their pilot, F/O Roberts and two others lost their lives. MZ827 crash-landed at Carnaby on return, but without injury to P/O Langham and his crew. Some elements of the Group took part in operations around St Vith on Boxing Day as the German break-out through the Ardennes faltered in what became known as the Battle of the Bulge. 462 Squadron departed 4 Group on the 29th to join 100 Group for bomber support duties out of Foulsham. By this time W/C D.E.S. Shannon had been sent home to Australia to work with Qantas Airways. It had been another uncompromising year for the crews of 102 Squadron, but the end was in sight as the scent of victory wafted in from the Continent. Nevertheless, much remained to be done before the proud and tenacious enemy forces finally laid down their arms.

1945

The New Year started with a bang, as the *Luftwaffe* launched its ill-conceived and ultimately ill-fated Operation *Bodenplatte* at first light on New Year's Morning. In an all-or-nothing attempt to destroy large numbers of Allied aircraft on the ground at the recently-liberated airfields in France, Holland and Belgium, the *Luftwaffe* committed almost its entire day-fighter strength to low-level bombing and strafing attacks. Those surviving the airfield flak had to run the gauntlet of Allied fighters as they tried to get home, and many failed. Around 250 BF109s and FW190s were shot down, and 150 or so pilots were killed, injured or taken prisoner, and this was a setback from which the *Luftwaffe* could never fully recover. The night-fighter force remained intact, however, and despite critical shortages in fuel and experienced manpower, it would still on occasions take a heavy toll of RAF bombers. 4 Group would negotiate the final months of the war without any major disasters, perhaps in a way balancing out the earlier war years when the Merlin-powered Halifaxes experienced a torrid time, both through design faults and enemy action. 10 Squadron would conduct the rest of its war under the command of W/C Dowden, who was appointed on 8 January. Just like W/Cs Lowe and Marchbanks, he was not a pilot but had spent his operational career as a bomb-aimer. His predecessor, W/C U.Y. Shannon, was promoted and installed as Station Commander at Full Sutton. 4 Group sent 100 Halifaxes to a benzol plant at Dortmund on New Year's Night, but scattered bombing left the target unscathed. While Nuremberg was undergoing a pounding at the hands of Lancasters on the 2/3rd, a large force of Halifaxes inflicted serious damage on two I.G. Farben chemicals factories at Ludwigshafen and nearby Oppau, and hit other industrial and railway buildings. The first major raid on Hanover since the series in the autumn of 1943 left almost 500 buildings in ruins on the 5/6th but cost thirty-one aircraft, the majority of them Halifaxes. On the following night, 1, 4 and 6 Groups targeted the railway district of Hanau and destroyed almost half of the town. During the remainder of January, 4 Group operated against railway yards at Saarbrücken on the 13/14th and a fuel storage depot at Dülmen on the 14/15th before conducting an area raid on Magdeburg on the 16/17th. This operation by over 350 aircraft cost seventeen Halifaxes, which represented a loss rate for the type of more than 5 per cent. By then W/C Barnard had assumed command of 102 Squadron on the 14th, and he would see it through almost to the end of the bombing war. W/C Badcoe became the last wartime commander of 640 Squadron on the 22nd on the departure of W/C Viney. W/C Badcoe had previously served with 10 and 77 Squadrons, and it was during his service with the latter that he had been awarded the DFC and Bar. While elements of 1, 3 and 8 Groups attacked Duisburg to good effect on the night of the 22/23rd, 4 and 5 Groups made up the main force for a relatively small-scale raid on Gelsenkirchen. On the 24th W/C Cassels was posted from the command of 76 Squadron to take up a new post at 42 Base. He was succeeded by W/C 'Chic' Whyte, who would remain in command until after the end of hostilities. 78 Squadron concluded consecutive loss-free months when coming through unscathed from a two-phase assault by more than 600 aircraft on Stuttgart on the night of the 28/29th.

February

The start of February brought 78 Squadron's first failure to return since early November, and ended that remarkable run of twelve weeks without having to post missing a crew. It negotiated the month's first outing, which was an ineffective attack on Mainz on the 1/2nd, without loss, and then joined 6 Group to bomb the oil refinery at Wanne-Eickel on the 2/3rd. The weather during the first week of February was not ideal for precision bombing, and cloud again prevented an accurate attack. NA167 did not return to Breighton with the rest of the 78 Squadron participants, and it was later learned that F/O Gutzewitz and three of his crew had perished, while three others were in enemy hands. The Command's generally poor performance during the period continued in 4 Group's case at Bonn and Gelsenkirchen on the 4/5th, when both built-up areas escaped fresh damage. As the British XXX Corps prepared to cross the German frontier near the Reichswald, Bomber Command was called upon to bomb the towns of Goch and Cleves, which the enemy had incorporated into its line of defence. 4 and 6 Groups acted as the main force at the former on the 7/8th, and much damage was inflicted before the target disappeared under smoke, and the Master Bomber was forced to call a halt. Very few locals remained in the town at this time, and the majority of the casualties were forced foreign workers who had been brought in to dig the defences. The 8/9th found 4 and 6 Groups returning to Wanne-Eickel for another shot at the oil refinery, but the raid was scattered and there was little fresh damage. A further attempt on the oil refinery at Wanne-Eickel on the 8/9th produced only very minor damage, and this was the final operation before the launching of the first of the Churchill-inspired series of attacks on Germany's eastern cities under Operation *Thunderclap*.

It was an all-Lancaster heavy force which vented its fury on the hapless inhabitants of Dresden on the 13/14th, in a two-phase attack that left a firestorm raging of unimaginable intensity. It took the lives of an estimated 35,000 people, and has since become the symbol of the horrors of area bombing, and has led to the unjustified vilification of Harris as the policy's architect. It will be recalled that the area-bombing directive had been issued while Harris was at sea on his way to take over the reins of Bomber Command in February 1942, and while he was a fierce advocate of the policy, he was not its creator. Harris's interest in Dresden as a worthwhile target was minimal, and he would have preferred to return to Berlin as the means to finally bring Germany to its knees. In the event, a higher political authority dictated otherwise, and then distanced itself from the legacy of Dresden when electoral votes at home in the coming peace became more important. The Halifaxes of Bomber Command sat out this operation, but returned to the fray on the following night when it was the turn of Chemnitz to experience its first major raid of the war at the hands of a *Thunderclap* force of over 700 Lancasters and Halifaxes from all but 5 Group. Many parts of the city were hit, but cloud cover affected the accuracy of the bombing, and much of it fell into open country. 78 Squadron's MZ791 suffered the failure of its navigational instruments while outbound and bombed an alternative target before landing at Manston. No injuries were reported among the crew of F/L Davidson, but the Halifax was eventually struck off charge as being beyond economical repair. One of the night's diversionary operations was a large mining effort in the Kadet Channel, from which 78 Squadron's MZ799 failed to return, and was eventually declared lost without trace with the crew of F/L Cumming. This was the only 78 Squadron crew to be posted missing from a mining operation. The town of Wesel was attacked four times between the 16th and the 19th, largely because it stood close to the area being fought over on the ground. 4 Group participated in the raid of the 17th, which was aborted by the Master Bomber because of cloud. W/C James vacated the hot seat at 578 Squadron on the 20th to be replaced by W/C Hancock. A successful 4 Group attack on the Rhenania-Ossag oil refinery at Düsseldorf on the 20/21st brought a complete halt to production, and an element from the Group joined forces with others to deliver the only attack of the war on the town of Worms on the 21/22nd, which laid waste to an estimated 39 per cent of its built-up area. A daylight attack on Essen by 4 and 6 Groups on the 23rd fell predominantly onto the Krupp complex, and probably ended all production there for the remainder of the war. The oil offensive continued at Kamen on the 24th, although most of the 4 and 6 Group bombs appear to have hit the town rather than the nearby refinery. Mainz was bombed by 4 and 6 Groups through cloud on the 27th, and the crews returned home without being able to assess the results of their efforts. In fact, in this last raid of the war on the town, over 5,600 buildings had been destroyed and its historic centre was all but wiped out.

March

March was to bring an unprecedented weight of bombs upon Germany's cities, and the month's account was opened at Mannheim and Ludwigshafen on the 1st. Only ninety Halifaxes took part, all from 6 Group, but 300 of the type took to the air around 0700 hours on the 2nd, and joined Lancasters and Mosquitos in an 850-strong force bound for a two-phase attack on Cologne. This operation would prove to be the last of the war on this once magnificent city, and it took place in clear conditions, inflicting massive damage right across the main part of the city on the west bank of the Rhine. Problems with the G-H station in England ruined the 3 Group second phase by 150 aircraft but this was academic, and the city fell to American forces four days later. On the night of the 3/4th, 4 Group carried out a successful attack on the oil refinery at Kamen, and eight of its Halifaxes were among the twenty bombers shot down by enemy intruders as they arrived home. The 4 Group losses were divided among six squadrons, but 78 Squadron was not affected. Having escaped serious damage on the night after Dresden, Chemnitz felt the weight of an accurate Bomber Command onslaught on the 5/6th, in which 4 Group played its part. W/C Dobson departed 158 Squadron on the 7th to be succeeded by W/C Read, who was promoted from B Flight commander, a post he had occupied since the autumn. His promotion to the command of the squadron was another example of a non-pilot being recognized as qualified for the task, he having served as a gunner. An attempt by a predominately Halifax force from 4 and 8 Groups to destroy the Deutsche Erdöl refinery at Hemmingstedt failed on the 7/8th, and this was followed on the next night by a raid by the same Groups on the shipyards in Hamburg. The new type XXI U-boats were being assembled here, but cloud compromised accuracy, and the shipyards were untouched. A new record was set on the 11th, when 1,079 aircraft took off in the late morning to raid Essen for the last time. The record lasted for a little over twenty-four hours and was surpassed in the early afternoon of the 12th, when 1,108 aircraft departed their stations to carry out the final raid of the war on Dortmund.

The Barmen half of Wuppertal wilted under a 4 and 6 Group assault on the 13th, and then the two Groups operated independently on the night of the 14/15th. Each was tasked with blocking the passage of enemy troops and supplies on their way to the front through the towns of Zweibrücken and Homberg, and little remained standing after the attacks. For 578 Squadron the war was now over and it was stood down from operations on the 15th. That same day other elements of 4 Group were assigned to a benzol plant at Bottrop, and 6 Group dealt with a similar target at Castrop-Rauxel, while that night they joined forces to devastate the centre and eastern districts of Hagen. Also on the 15th Lt Col Vigouroux stepped down as the commanding officer of 347 Squadron, and he was succeeded by Commandant Hoquetis, who would remain in post until after the war. An area raid by elements of 4, 6 and 8 Groups on Witten destroyed an estimated 60 per cent of the town's built-up area on the 18/19th, and then came daylight raids on Recklinghausen, Rheine, Dülmen and Sterkrade on the 20th, 21st, 22nd and 24th respectively. 78 Squadron's only incident of the month also occurred on the 24th, when NP998 collided with an obstacle while taxiing in the hands of F/O Hatherall during training and was written off. 4 Group operated in strength for the final time during the month on the 25th, when one element attacked Münster in company with 6 Group, and another went to Osnabrück with just Pathfinders for company. Both targets were effectively bombed, and this completed a loss-free month for 78 Squadron. W/C Hyland-Smith was posted out of 78 Squadron where he had been B Flight commander, and he succeeded W/C Barnard at 102 Squadron on the 27th. W/C Barnard would take over at 51 Squadron on 30 April, after the bombing war was over.

April

April would prove to be the final month of the bombing war for the heavy units, and 4 Group sat out the first few nights at home. W/C Hollings became 466 Squadron's final wartime commander on the 3rd on the departure of W/C Wharton. The new month's operations finally began for the Group on the night of the 4/5th. The target was the Rhenania oil refinery at Harburg, which was left severely damaged by a joint effort from 4 and 6 Groups. The single missing Halifax was from Breighton, and as events turned out, it was the last aircraft to fail to return from an operation on behalf of 78 Squadron. MZ460 exploded in the air with great force, scattering itself and the bodies of F/L Cox and his crew over a wide area of Germany. On the 8/9th 4 and 6 Groups attempted to rectify the recent failure to hit the U-boat yards in Hamburg, but the crews were unable to assess the effectiveness of their work. Certainly, much damage was caused within the city, but an American raid hours earlier made it impossible to credit destruction to a particular attack. On return 78 Squadron's MZ361 crashed into high ground in Yorkshire in poor visibility, and this was the very last aircraft written off by the squadron. F/L Jackson and three others survived with injuries, but the navigator, bomb-aimer and wireless operator became the last to have their names entered on the squadron Roll of Honour.

It was from this operation that 10 Squadron's LK753 failed to return and thereby produced that squadron's final air crew casualties. I am indebted to Norman Mackenzie of Wellington, New Zealand, the cousin of the pilot concerned, P/O Currie, for kindly providing me with the following account, which I reproduce verbatim:

> However, the sad truth of the matter is that whilst there was a severe engine vibration, and the port inner had to be shut down, this was not the real problem. On the way to the target area, the starboard outer engine had to be shut down, but worse, a parachute was lost when a crew member, unable to cope with the situation, baled out, but unfortunately in doing so, dislodged the navigator's parachute which fell out of the aircraft through the open hatch. With the plane losing height on two engines, and only five parachutes among six men, a shocked and no doubt traumatized crew decided that rather than leave one of their number without a parachute, they would all remain in the aircraft, in the belief that a safe crash-landing could be achieved. Fate was against them, and what was thought to be the River Rhine, turned out to be a wet street in the middle of Düsseldorf. In the darkness of the night, the reflection had led my cousin who was piloting the aircraft, and the navigator who was sitting alongside, into thinking that they were about to set down in the hoped-for softness of the Rhine River. The plane burst into flames on impact, and split in half at the bulkhead. The only survivor was the wireless operator, Sgt Sinnett, who staggered out of the aircraft with substantial burns to his legs, hands and the area of his face that had not been covered by his hands. In addition, a boot had been ripped off, and his leg was severely gashed. He spent two weeks in a German hospital before the area was captured by the Americans. He was then taken to an army hospital in Devon, where he spent the next eight weeks before being sent to Cosford to debriefing, prior to being sent home on sick leave.

On the 11th, 4 Group dealt effectively with railway yards at Nuremberg, and provided a strong contingent of Halifaxes for the massed bombing assault on the island of Heligoland on the 18th. This was 51 Squadron's final operation from Snaith, for which it contributed twenty Halifaxes to a force of over 900 aircraft, which left the island with the appearance of a cratered moonscape. On the 20th the squadron moved to Leconfield, from where just one operation would be mounted. 4 Group squadrons carried bombs for the very last time on the afternoon of the 25th, when again joining forces with 6 Group to attack the coastal batteries on the Frisian island of Wangerooge, which were barring the approaches to Bremen and Wilhelmshaven. 78 Squadron put up eighteen aircraft, all of which returned safely. The operation was ineffective, and tragically cost the lives of forty-one Canadian and British airmen in four Halifaxes and two Lancasters involved in collisions in the target area. Earlier in the day, over 300 Lancasters had carried out an almost symbolic raid on the SS barracks at Hitler's Eagle's Nest retreat at Berchtesgaden, and that night, 5 Group brought the heavy bombing war to a close with a raid on an oil refinery at Tonsberg in Norway. On the 30th, W/C Barnard was posted in as 51 Squadron's last wartime commanding officer, having relinquished his command of 102 Squadron a month earlier, and he would remain in the post until almost the end of the year.

There can be no question as to the importance of 4 Group's contribution to the success of Bomber Command. As the only Group capable on the outbreak of war of flying deep into enemy territory by night, it led the way. Not blessed initially with operating the most up-to-date, and until 1944 the most effective and reliable types, 4 Group's crews pressed on regardless, and some of the finest airmen in the entire Command graced 4 Group corridors. There are few who flew the Hercules Halifax who would not claim it to be a match for the Lancaster, and at the time of writing, at least, the spirit of 4 Group lives on in the likes of Jim Hopkins.

CHAPTER TWO

Quick Reference

Facts, Figures and General Information

AIR OFFICERS COMMANDING

Air Commodore	A. Coningham	3.7.39 to 28.7.41
Air Vice Marshal	C.R. Carr	28.7.41 to 12.2.45
Air Vice Marshal	J.R. Whitley	12.2.45 to 7.5.45

OPERATIONAL STATIONS

Breighton	Burn	Croft
Dalton	Dishforth	Driffield
East Moor	Elvington	Full Sutton
Holme-on-Spalding-Moor	Leconfield	Leeming
Linton-on-Ouse	Lissett	Melbourne
Middleton-St-George	Pocklington	Rufforth
Skipton-on-Swale	Snaith	Tholthorpe
Topcliffe		

4 GROUP STATIONS TRANSFERRED TO 6 GROUP ON 1.1.43

Croft	Dalton	Dishforth
East Moor	Leeming	Linton-on-Ouse
Middleton-St-George	Skipton-on-Swale	Tholthorpe
Topcliffe		

AIRCRAFT TYPES

Whitley	Wellington	Halifax

GROUP STRENGTH

As of September 1939
Operational squadrons
10, 51, 58, 77, 102
Non-operational squadrons
78

GROUP STRENGTH

As of April 1945
Operational squadrons
10, 51, 76, 77, 78, 102, 158, 346, 347, 466, 578, 640

QUICK REFERENCE STATION/SQUADRON

Breighton	78
Burn	431, 578
Croft	78, 419, 427, 431
Dalton	102, 428
Dishforth	10, 51, 78, 425
Driffield	77, 102, 104, 158, 405, 426, 462, 466
East Moor	158, 429
Elvington	77, 346, 347
Full Sutton	77
Holme-on-Spalding-Moor	76, 458
Leconfield	51, 196, 466, 640
Leeming	10, 35, 77, 102, 405, 408, 419, 420
Linton-on-Ouse	35, 51, 58, 76, 77, 78, 102
Lissett	158, 640
Melbourne	10
Middleton-St-George	78, 419, 420
Pocklington	102, 405
Rufforth	158
Skipton-on-Swale	420
Snaith	51, 578
Tholthorpe (satellite of Linton)	77
Topcliffe	77, 102, 405, 419, 424

QUICK REFERENCE STATION/SQUADRON DATES

Breighton	78	16.06.43 to 20.09.45
Burn	431	11.11.42 to 14.07.43
	578	06.02.44 to 15.04.45
Croft	78	20.10.41 to 10.06.42
	419	30.09.42 to 07.11.42
	419, 427	07.11.42 to 09.11.42
	427	09.11.42 to 04.05.43
Dalton	102	15.11.41 to 07.06.42
	428	07.11.42 to 01.06.43
Dishforth	10	25.01.37 to 15.09.39
	10, 78	15.09.39 to 15.10.39
	10	15.10.39 to 09.12.39
	10, 51	09.12.39 to 08.07.40
	51	08.07.40 to 15.07.40
	51, 78	15.07.40 to 07.04.41
	51	07.04.41 to 06.05.42
	425	25.06.42 to 15.10.42
	425, 426	15.10.42 to 15.05.43
Driffield	102	11.07.38 to 25.07.38
	77, 102	25.07.38 to 15.04.40
	102	15.04.40 to 04.05.40
	77, 102	04.05.40 to 25.08.40
	77	25.08.40 to 28.08.40
	104	01.04.41 to 23.04.41
	104, 405	23.04.41 to 20.06.41
	104	20.06.41 to 14.02.42
	158	14.02.42 to 06.06.42
	466	10.10.42 to 27.12.42
	462	14.08.44 to 29.12.44
East Moor	158	06.06.42 to 06.11.42
	429	07.11.42 to 08.43
Elvington	77	05.10.42 to 15.05.44
	346	16.05.44 to 20.06.44
	346, 347	20.06.44 to 10.45
Full Sutton	77	15.05.44 to 31.08.45
Holme-on-Spalding-Moor	458	25.08.41 to 02.42
	76	16.06.43 to 07.08.45
Leconfield	196	22.12.42 to 27.12.42
	196, 466	27.12.42 to 19.07.43
	466	19.07.43 to 07.01.44
	466, 640	07.01.44 to 03.06.44
	640	03.06.44 to 07.05.45
Leeming	10	08.07.40 to 25.08.40
	10, 102	25.08.40 to 01.09.40
	10	01.09.40 to 25.11.40

	10, 35	25.11.40 to 05.12.40
	10	05.12.40 to 05.09.41
	10, 77	05.09.41 to 06.05.42
	10	06.05.42 to 12.08.42
	10, 419	12.08.42 to 17.08.42
	10	17.08.42 to 19.08.42
	408	13.09.42 to 27.08.43
Linton-on-Ouse	51, 58	20.04.38 to 06.10.39
	51	06.10.39 to 15.10.39
	51, 78	15.10.39 to 09.12.39
	78	09.12.39 to 14.02.40
	58, 78	14.02.40 to 05.07.40
	58	05.07.40 to 28.08.40
	58, 77	28.08.40 to 05.10.40
	58	05.10.40 to 10.10.40
	58, 102	10.10.40 to 15.11.40
	58	15.11.40 to 05.12.40
	35, 58	05.12.40 to 12.04.41
	35, 58, 76	12.04.41 to 04.06.41
	35, 58	14.06.41 to 08.04.42
	35	08.04.42 to 15.08.42
	78	16.09.42 to 17.09.42
	76, 78	17.09.42 to 16.06.43
Lissett	158	28.02.43 to 17.08.45
Melbourne	10	19.08.42 to 06.08.45
Middleton-St-George	78	07.04.41 to 04.06.41
	76, 78	04.06.41 to 20.10.41
	76	20.10.41 to 10.06.42
	76, 78	10.06.42 to 16.09.42
	76	16.09.42 to 17.09.42
	420	10.42 to 09.11.42
	419, 420	09.11.42 to 15.05.43
Pocklington	405	20.06.41 to 07.08.42
	102	07.08.42 to 08.09.45
Rufforth	158	06.11.42 to 28.02.43
Skipton-on-Swale	420	06.08.42 to 10.42
Snaith	51	27.10.42 to 14.01.44
	51, 578	14.01.44 to 06.02.44
	51	06.02.44 to 20.04.45
Tholthorpe (satellite of Linton)	77	08.40 to 12.40
Topcliffe	77	05.10.40 to 15.11.40
	77, 102	15.11.40 to 05.09.41
	102	05.09.41 to 15.11.41
		07.06.42 to 07.08.42
	405	07.08.42 to 17.08.42
	405, 419	17.08.42 to 30.09.42
	405	30.09.42 to 15.10.42

405, 424	15.10.42 to 24.10.42
424	24.10.42 to 07.04.43

QUICK REFERENCE HALIFAX/SQUADRON

10 Squadron
HALIFAX
First received   12.41
First operation   18.12.41 German warships at Brest

35 Squadron
HALIFAX
First received   13.11.40
First operation   10/11.3.41 Le Havre

51 Squadron
HALIFAX
First received   11.42
First operation   8/9.01.43 Mining

76 Squadron
HALIFAX
First received   01.05.41
First operation   12/13.06.41 Hüls

77 Squadron
HALIFAX
First received   10.42
First operation   5/6.3.43 Mining

78 Squadron
HALIFAX
First received   03.42
First operation   29/30.04.42 Ostend

102 Squadron
HALIFAX
First received   12.41
First operation   14/15.04.42 Le Havre

158 Squadron
HALIFAX
First received   07.06.42
First operation   25/26.6.42 Bremen

346 Squadron
HALIFAX
First received   16.5.44
First operation   1/2.6.44 Ferme d'Urville Radar Station

347 Squadron

HALIFAX
First received   20.6.44
First operation   27/28.6.44 Mont Candon V-Weapon site

405 Squadron

HALIFAX
First received   23.04.42
First operation   30/31.05.42 Cologne

408 Squadron

HALIFAX
First received   11.10.42
No operations under 4 Group

419 Squadron

HALIFAX
First received   11.42
No operations under 4 Group

462 Squadron

HALIFAX
First received   08.44
First operation   27.08.44 Homberg

578 Squadron

HALIFAX
First received   16.01.44
First operation   20/21.01.44 Berlin

640 Squadron

HALIFAX
First received   07.01.44
First operation   20/21.01.44 Berlin

4 Group VCs

P/O C.J. Barton   578 Squadron   Nuremberg   30/31.03.44

Quick Reference Records

4 GROUP SORTIES AND LOSSES

Aircraft	Sorties	Losses
Whitley	9,169	288 (3.1%)
Wellington	2,901	97 (3.3%)
Halifax	45,337	1,124 (2.5%)
TOTAL	57,407	1,509 (2.6%)

Most operations overall   10 Squadron   609

Most bombing operations	10 Squadron	533
Most mining operations	102 Squadron	84
Most sorties	78 Squadron	6,237
Most aircraft lost	78/102 Squadrons	192
Highest % losses	102 Squadron	3.1%
Highest bomb tonnage	78 Squadron	16,900

Armstrong Whitworth Whitley

Most operations overall	77 Squadron	239
Most bombing raids	77 Squadron	223
Most sorties	51 Squadron	1,806
Highest operational losses	77 Squadron	56
Highest % losses	102 Squadron	3.8%

Vickers Wellington

Most operations overall	466 Squadron	89
Most bombing raids	405 Squadron	86
Most sorties	466 Squadron	844
Highest operational losses	466 Squadron	25
Highest % losses	158 Squadron	6.8%

Handley Page Halifax

Most operations overall	102 Squadron	407
Most bombing operations	76 Squadron	376
Most sorties	158 Squadron	5,161
Highest operational losses	78 Squadron	158
Highest % losses	78 Squadron	3.1%

SORTIES AND LOSSES BY YEAR

Year	Sorties	A/C Missing
1939	246	4
1940	3,862	47
1941	5,700	205
1942	4,957	223
1943	11,607	485
1944	25,464	402
1945	9,741	75
TOTAL	61,577	1,441

It will be noted that the totals above are at variance with those presented at the start of this section. STATISTICS. Who needs them !!!!!

CHAPTER THREE

The Squadrons

10 SQUADRON

Motto: Rem Acu Tangere   **Code: ZA**

Originally formed on 1 January 1915, 10 Squadron operated various training aircraft until posted to France in July of that year. It fulfilled an artillery observation and tactical reconnaissance role, with some light bombing activity until the end of hostilities, and returned to the UK in February 1919 for eventual disbandment in December. Reformation took place on 3 January 1928, and the squadron continued in existence from that point on. In March 1937 and while based at Dishforth, the squadron became the first to take delivery of the Whitley, with which, as a 4 Group squadron, it would enter the impending conflict. Known as 'Shiny Ten', 10 Squadron was one of five operational Whitley units in 4 Group at the outbreak of war. 4 Group crews alone had been trained to fly at night, and the first 10 Squadron crews went to war during the first week of hostilities to deliver leaflets to German cities. The squadron also conducted the first flights over Berlin at the start of October 1939. Apart from brief detachments to Coastal Command and the Middle East, 10 Squadron remained with 4 Group until war's end. The squadron converted to the Halifax in December 1941, and continued to operate the type throughout the remainder of its wartime career. Among its commanding officers was W/C Don Bennett, who later became the Air-Officer-Commanding the Pathfinder Force. 10 Squadron was always at the forefront of Bomber Command's campaigns, and ended the war with the highest number of operations in 4 Group and the second-highest number of sorties.

STATIONS

Dishforth	25.01.37 to 08.07.40
Leeming	08.07.40 to 19.08.42
Melbourne	19.08.42 to 06.08.45
Pocklington (temporary detachment)	28.08.42 to 23.10.42

COMMANDING OFFICERS

Wing Commander W.E. Staton DSO MC DFC	10.06.38 to 21.04.40
Wing Commander N.C. Singer	21.04.40 to 15.07.40
Wing Commander S.O. Bufton DFC	15.07.40 to 12.04.41
Wing Commander K.S. Ferguson (temp.)	to 13.11.40
Wing Commander V.B. Bennett DSO	12.04.41 to 08.09.41
Wing Commander J.A.H. Tuck DFC	08.09.41 to 15.04.42
Wing Commander D.C.T. Bennett DSO	15.04.42 to 03.05.42
Wing Commander J.B. Tait DSO DFC	04.05.42 to 04.06.42
Wing Commander D.C.T. Bennett DSO	04.06.42 to 04.07.42
Wing Commander Seymour-Price (Middle East Det.)	04.07.42
Wing Commander R.K. Wildey DFC	01.08.42 to 15.10.42
Wing Commander W. Carter	16.10.42 to 04.02.43
Wing Commander D.W. Edmonds DFC	04.02.43 to 08.10.43
Wing Commander J.F. Sutton DFC AFC	08.10.43 to 01.04.44
Wing Commander D.S. Radford DSO DFC AFC	01.04.44 to 09.10.44
Wing Commander U.Y. Shannon	09.10.44 to 08.01.45
Wing Commander A.C. Dowden	08.01.45 to 01.06.46

AIRCRAFT

Whitley IV	05.39 to 05.40
Whitley V	03.40 to 12.41
Halifax II	12.41 to 03.44
Halifax III	03.44 to 08.45

OPERATIONAL RECORD

Operations	Sorties	Aircraft Losses	% Losses
609	6,233	156	2.5

Category of Operations

Bombing	Mining	Other
533	61	15

Whitleys

Operations	Sorties	Aircraft Losses	% Losses
223	1,430	47	3.3

Category of Operations

Bombing	Mining	Other
208	0	15

Halifaxes

Operations	Sorties	Aircraft Losses	% Losses
386	4,803	109	2.3

Category of Operations

Bombing	Mining
325	61

TABLE OF STATISTICS
(Heavy squadrons)
11th highest number of overall operations in Bomber Command.
9th highest number of sorties in Bomber Command.
19th highest number of aircraft operational losses in Bomber Command.
9th highest number of bombing operations in Bomber Command.
15th highest number of mining operations in Bomber Command.

Out of 32 Halifax squadrons in Bomber Command
(Excluding SOE)
3rd highest number of overall Halifax operations in Bomber Command.
4th highest number of Halifax sorties in Bomber Command.
5th highest number of Halifax operational losses in Bomber Command.

Out of 25 operational squadrons in 4 Group
Highest number of overall operations in 4 Group.
2nd highest number of sorties in 4 Group.
5th highest number of aircraft operational losses in 4 Group.

Out of 6 Whitley squadrons in 4 Group
4th highest number of overall Whitley operations in 4 Group.
4th highest number of Whitley sorties in 4 Group.
5th highest number of Whitley operational losses in 4 Group.

Out of 15 operational Halifax squadrons in 4 Group
3rd highest number of overall Halifax operations in 4 Group.
4th highest number of Halifax sorties in 4 Group.
5th highest number of Halifax operational losses in 4 Group.

AIRCRAFT HISTORIES

Whitley	To December 1941.
K9017 ZA-A	To 78 Sqn.
K9018	FTR from leafleting sortie 1/2.10.39.
K9019	To 10 OTU.
K9020 ZA-L	To 78 Sqn.
K9021	To 51 Sqn.
K9022 ZA-M	Damaged beyond repair attempting to land at Dishforth while training 3.3.40.
K9023 ZA-E	To 10 OTU.
K9024	To 51 Sqn.
K9025	To 10 OTU.
K9026 ZA-O	To 78 Sqn.
K9027	To 19 OTU.
K9028 ZA-P	To 10 OTU.
K9029 ZA-D	To 10 OTU.
K9030	To 19 OTU.
K9031 ZA-G	To 10 OTU.

K9032	Crashed near Grimsby on return from reconnaissance sortie 7.4.40.
K9033	To 10 OTU.
K9034 ZA-S	To 78 Sqn.
K9035 ZA-H	To 10 OTU.
K9036 ZA-T	To 10 OTU.
K9037 ZA-J	To 10 OTU.
K9044 ZA-U	To 10 OTU.
N1354	From 77 Sqn. to 10 OTU.
N1482 ZA-K	To 10 OTU.
N1483 ZA-I	Ditched in the Irish Sea on return from Berlin 1.10.40.
N1484	To 10 OTU.
N1487	To 78 Sqn.
N1488	To 51 Sqn.
N1489	To 102 Sqn.
N1490	To 78 Sqn.
N1491	To 9 BGS.
N1492	To 19 OTU.
N1493	To 19 OTU.
N1494	To Hendon.
N1495	To 19 OTU.
N1496	FTR Kiel 8/9.7.40.
N1497 ZA-B	FTR Milan 15/16.8.40.
N1498	To Hendon.
P4935	FTR Berlin 6/7.9.40.
P4937	To 78 Sqn.
P4946 ZA-P	FTR Bremen 8/9.5.41.
P4952 ZA-H/R	Abandoned over Northumberland on return from Stettin 15.10.40.
P4953 ZA-F/X	To 10 OTU.
P4954 ZA-T	FTR French battle area 11/12.6.40.
P4955 ZA-G/A	Burnt out on the ground at Leeming 27.10.40.
P4956 ZA-O	To 10 OTU.
P4957 ZA-E	Crashed in Northumberland on return from Wilhelmshaven 29/30.10.40.
P4958 ZA-K	To 78 Sqn.
P4959 ZA-A	Destroyed by fire at Leeming 27.10.40.
P4960 ZA-S	Crashed on approach to Honington on return from Antwerp 20.6.40.
P4961 ZA-D	Abandoned over Suffolk on return from Berlin 21.12.40.
P4962 ZA-P	To 10 OTU.
P4963 ZA-B	Force-landed in Suffolk on return from Homberg 4.6.40.
P4965 ZA-H	Crashed off Kent coast on return from Turin 13/14.8.40.

P4966	Ditched off Yorkshire coast when bound for Antwerp 14.9.40.
P4967 ZA-J	Crash-landed in Yorkshire on return from Berlin 4.9.40.
P4990 ZA-T	FTR Milan 26/27.8.40.
P4993 ZA-V	Collided with balloon cable and crashed in Surrey on return from Le Havre 14.10.40.
P4994 ZA-U	Crashed on take-off from Leeming while training 22.12.40.
P5001 ZA-S	FTR Milan 5/6.11.40.
P5016 ZA-V	FTR Bremen 27/28.6.41.
P5018 ZA-Q	FTR Duisburg 30.6/1.7.41.
P5048 ZA-H	FTR Hamburg 10/11.5.41.
P5055 ZA-G	FTR Bremen 27/28.6.41.
P5094 ZA-B	Crash-landed at Leeming on return from Ostend 9.9.40.
P5109	FTR Warnemünde 11/12.9.41.
T4130	FTR Berlin 30.9/1.10.40.
T4143 ZA-J	Abandoned over Yorkshire on return from Stettin 15.10.40.
T4152 ZA-Z	FTR Stuttgart 21/22.10.40.
T4157 ZA-A	To 19 OTU.
T4176 ZA-N/R	To 58 Sqn.
T4179 ZA-U	From 10 OTU. FTR Bremen 27/28.6.41.
T4202 ZA-N	Abandoned over Yorkshire on return from Kiel 19.3.41.
T4220 ZA-S	FTR Wilhelmshaven 16/17.1.41.
T4230 ZA-R	FTR Merseburg 13/14.11.40.
T4231 ZA-A	FTR Hanover 25/26.7.41.
T4232 ZA-V/W	Crashed in Wales when bound for Lorient 13.11.40.
T4234 ZA-Z	Crashed in Westmoreland on return from Le Havre 23.8.41.
T4263 ZA-E	From 51 Sqn. To 19 OTU.
T4265 ZA-J	FTR Cologne 1/2.3.41.
Z6477 ZA-D	Abandoned over Lincolnshire on return from Düsseldorf 28.3.41.
Z6478 ZA-S	FTR Hüls 6/7.9.41.
Z6496 ZA-T	To A&AEE.
Z6557	FTR Bremen 16/17.4.41.
Z6559	From 51 Sqn. To 77 Sqn.
Z6561 ZA-J	From Leeming. FTR Bremen 27/28.6.41.
Z6564 ZA-Z	FTR Cologne 18/19.8.41.
Z6582	To 77 Sqn.
Z6584 ZA-N	Crashed in Norfolk on return from Duisburg following attack by intruder 1.7.41.
Z6586 ZA-F	From 102 Sqn. FTR Cologne 16/17.8.41.
Z6624 ZA-O	FTR Hanover 25/26.7.41.
Z6627 ZA-K	FTR Hamm 8/9.7.41.

Z6630	From 102 Sqn. To 77 Sqn.
Z6656 ZA-B	To 58 Sqn.
Z6669 ZA-B	To 1485 Flt.
Z6671	From 77 Sqn. FTR Bremen 18/19.6.41.
Z6672	FTR Cologne 18/19.8.41.
Z6721	Ditched when bound for Schwerte 12/13.6.41.
Z6793	FTR Münster 5/6.7.41.
Z6794	FTR Cologne 16/17.8.41.
Z6802 ZA-P	Ditched off Withernsea on return from Berlin 21.9.41.
Z6805	FTR Cologne 16/17.8.41.
Z6814	To 58 Sqn.
Z6815	FTR Kiel 8/9.8.41.
Z6816	FTR Osnabrück 7/8.7.41.
Z6817	To 78 Sqn.
Z6828 ZA-Q	To 102 Sqn.
Z6864	To 78 Sqn.
Z6867 ZA-Z	Ditched off Yorkshire coast on return from Warnemünde 12.9.41.
Z6932	Crashed on take-off from Acklington during air-test 6.9.41.
Z6941 ZA-O	Ditched off Milford Haven on return from Stuttgart 2.10.41.
Z6942	FTR Hüls 6/7.9.41.
Z6954	To 19 OTU.
Z6976 ZA-U	From 51 Sqn. To 10 OTU.
Z6979 ZA-Z	To 10 OTU.
Z6980	To 10 OTU.
Z9119 ZA-C	To 58 Sqn.
Z9143	To 77 Sqn.
Z9149 ZA-F	To 1481 Flt.
Z9156 ZA-A	To 19 OTU.
Z9160	To 161 Sqn.
Z9161 ZA-G/R	To 102 Sqn.
Z9162 ZA-Y	Crashed on approach to Leeming after early return from Dunkerque 7.12.41.
Z9163 ZA-H	To 77 Sqn.
Z9166 ZA-O	FTR Emden 30.11/1.12.41.
Z9188 ZA-V	Crashed in Yorkshire on return from Cologne 12.12.41.
Z9221 ZA-T	To 77 Sqn.
Z9225	To 77 Sqn.
Z9226 ZA-K	To 77 Sqn.
Z9227 ZA-W	To 58 Sqn.
Halifax	From December 1941.
L9524	From 35 Sqn. To 1659 CU.
L9569	From 35 Sqn. To 1658 CU.

L9614	Collided with V9981 during take-off at Leeming while training 29.12.41.
L9619 ZA-E	Abandoned over Yorkshire on return from St Nazaire 15/16.2.42.
L9621	To 78 CF.
L9622 ZA-G	Crashed in Yorkshire on return from Hamburg 15.1.42.
L9623 ZA-O	FTR Essen 1/2.6.42.
L9624	To 78 Sqn.
R9365	To 76 Sqn via 76 CF.
R9366 ZA-Y	To 76 Sqn via 76 CF.
R9367	To 35 Sqn via HCF.
R9368	To 78 Sqn via 1652 CU.
R9369	To 78C F.
R9370	To 35C F.
R9371 ZA-Z	Crashed on landing at Lossiemouth while in transit 9.3.42.
R9373	To 76 Sqn.
R9374 ZA-K	Ditched off Cornwall on return from Brest 30.12.41.
R9376 ZA-D	To 138 Sqn and back. To 10 CF and back. Force-landed near Melbourne 14.11.42.
R9382	To 76 CF.
R9383 ZA-A	From 102 Sqn. Abandoned over Yorkshire on return from Saarbrücken 20.9.42.
R9384	From 76 Sqn. To 1659 CU.
R9387	From A&AEE. To 1658 CU via 76 CF.
R9392 ZA-A	From 35 Sqn. To 1658 CU via 10 CF.
R9421	From 102 Sqn. To 10 CF. Belly-landed at Linton-on-Ouse 17.11.42.
R9428	From 35 Sqn. To 1661 CU via 10 CF.
R9430	Conversion Flt only. To 76 CF.
R9491	To 102 Sqn.
R9492 ZA-G	Crashed in Surrey on return from Dortmund 15.4.42.
R9493	To 35 CF.
R9495	To 102 Sqn.
R9497	To 102 Sqn.
R9498	To 102 Sqn.
R9528	To 102 Sqn.
R9529	To 102 Sqn.
V9980	From 76 Sqn. To 1658 CU via 10 CF.
V9981	Collided with L9614 on take-off from Leeming while training 29.12.41.
V9984	To 1659 CU.
V9985	To A&AEE.
V9986 ZA-M	FTR Kiel 26/27.2.42.
V9988	To 1658 CU via 10 CF.
W1003	To 158 CF.
W1006	Conversion Flt only. To 78 Sqn.

W1007	Conversion Flt only. To 78 Sqn.
W1010	To 10 CF and back. To 1658 CU.
W1013	To 78 Sqn.
W1037 ZA-U	FTR Aasenfjord (*Tirpitz*) 27/28.4.42.
W1038	To 158 Sqn.
W1039 ZA-O	Crashed near Melbourne during ferry flight 10.3.43.
W1040	To 158 Sqn.
W1041 ZA-W/B	FTR Aasenfjord (*Tirpitz*) 27/28.4.42.
W1042 ZA-T	FTR Cologne 30/31.5.42.
W1043 ZA-F	FTR Aasenfjord (*Tirpitz*) 30/31.3.42.
W1044 ZA-D	FTR Aasenfjord (*Tirpitz*) 30/31.3.42.
W1045 ZA-J	Ditched off South Devon on return from Dortmund 15.4.42.
W1052	To 102 Sqn.
W1054 ZA-H	From 102 Sqn. Crashed on landing at Leeming while in transit 30.4.42.
W1055	From Dishforth. To 102 Sqn.
W1056 ZA-N	From Dishforth. FTR Bremen 2/3.7.42.
W1057 ZA-X	FTR Mannheim 19/20.5.42.
W1058 ZA-S	From Dishforth. FTR Cologne 15/16.10.42.
W1098 ZA-W	FTR Essen 1/2.6.42.
W1106 ZA-A	To 76 Sqn.
W1116 ZA-P	FTR Krefeld 2/3.10.42.
W1146	To 35 Sqn and back. To 78 Sqn.
W1151 ZA-H	To Middle East.
W1155 ZA-U	Crashed at Leeming during air-test 25.6.42.
W1158 ZA-T	Crashed near Leeming when bound for Emden 19.6.42.
W1160	From 35 Sqn. Damaged February 1943 and SOC 16.3.43.
W1170 ZA-U	To Middle East.
W1171 ZA-X	To Middle East.
W1172 ZA-Q	To Middle East.
W1174 ZA-G	To Middle East.
W1176 ZA-Z	To Middle East.
W1178 ZA-T	To Middle East.
W1181	To 102 Sqn.
W1217 ZA-Z	From 158 Sqn. FTR Dortmund 23/24.5.43.
W1271	From 102 Sqn. To 419 Sqn.
W1276	From 10 CF. To 1652 CU.
W7659 ZA-F	To Middle East.
W7666 ZA-J	Crashed on approach to Leeming during air-test 24.5.42.
W7667 ZA-C	FTR Flensburg 1/2.10.42.
W7673	Crashed on landing at Leeming during air-test 8.5.42.
W7674 ZA-U	FTR Warnemünde 8/9.5.42.
W7678	From 78 Sqn. To 76 Sqn.
W7679 ZA-C	To Middle East.

W7695 ZA-D	To Middle East.
W7696 ZA-H	FTR Essen 5/6.6.42.
W7697 ZA-R	To Middle East.
W7716 ZA-I	To Middle East.
W7717 ZA-G/J	To Middle East.
W7718	To 405 Sqn.
W7756 ZA-L	To Middle East.
W7757 ZA-W	To Middle East.
W7758 ZA-Y	To Middle East.
W7767 ZA-O	FTR Duisburg 6/7.9.42.
W7772	From 51 Sqn. To 1654 CU.
W7852 ZA-K	FTR Flensburg 1/2.10.42.
W7855	Crashed on landing at Snaith while training 25.2.43.
W7865	From 158 Sqn. To 1658 CU.
W7867 ZA-F	Crashed on landing at Melbourne following early return from operation to Genoa 7.11.42.
W7869	To 419 Sqn.
W7870 ZA-G	FTR Kiel 13/14.10.42.
W7871 ZA-B/C	Crashed near Melbourne while training 30.11.42.
W7881	To 35 Sqn.
W7909 ZA-Z	From 102 Sqn. FTR Bochum 12/13.6.43.
BB192 ZA-B	Crashed on landing at Gt. Massingham on return from Bremen 14.9.42.
BB193	To 158 CF.
BB194 ZA-E	To 1658 CU via 10 CF.
BB201	FTR Emden 20/21.6.42.
BB207 ZA-M	From 158 Sqn. FTR Flensburg 1/2.10.42.
BB220 ZA-F	To 158 Sqn and back. To 1652 CU.
BB240	To 51 Sqn.
BB241	From 78 Sqn. To 51 Sqn.
BB243 ZA-G	From 102 Sqn via 102 CF. To 1661 CU.
BB248 ZA-J	From 77 Sqn. To 1658 CU.
BB249	To 158 Sqn.
BB252 ZA-X/Y	From 77 Sqn. FTR from mining sortie 9.1.43.
BB300 ZA-A	From 76 Sqn. To 1658 CU.
BB324 ZA-D/X	From 76 Sqn. FTR Mülheim 22/23.6.43.
BB427 ZA-X	From 77 Sqn. To 1658 CU.
DG222 ZA-Q	FTR Turin 11/12.12.42.
DG226 ZA-H	From 35 Sqn via 10 CF. To 158 Sqn.
DG230 ZA-V	To 1652 CU.
DT500 ZA-S	From 35 Sqn. To 419 Sqn.
DT520 ZA-J	FTR Flensburg 1/2.10.42.
DT541	From 76 Sqn. To 1658 CU.
DT549	To 1658 CU.
DT552	To 51 Sqn.
DT557 ZA-U	FTR from mining sortie 8/9.11.42.
DT561	To 51 Sqn.
DT566 ZA-X	To 1652 CU.

DT567	From 78 Sqn. To 51 Sqn.
DT572 ZA-M	FTR Stuttgart 22/23.11.42.
DT667	To 1652 CU.
DT720 ZA-L	From 158 Sqn. To 466 Sqn.
DT732 ZA-X	FTR Bochum 13/14.5.43.
DT746 ZA-S/Y	FTR Stuttgart 14/15.4.43.
DT776 ZA-T/R	To 466 Sqn.
DT778 ZA-N	FTR Essen 12/13.3.43.
DT783 ZA-Q	FTR Cologne 28/29.6.43.
DT784 ZA-M	FTR Cologne 3/4.7.43.
DT785 ZA-H	Crash-landed at Thornaby on return from Kiel 5.4.43.
DT786 ZA-X/P	To 1652 CU.
DT787 ZA-S	FTR Wuppertal 29/30.5.43.
DT788 ZA-E	FTR Cologne 14/15.2.43.
DT789 ZA-G/B	FTR Dortmund 23/24.5.43.
DT791 ZA-K	Crash-landed in Sussex on return from Pilsen 17.4.43.
DT792 ZA-F/D/O	Crash-landed at Melbourne on return from Hamburg 3.8.43.
HR691 ZA-K/W	To 1658 CU.
HR692 ZA-R	FTR Essen 12/13.3.43.
HR695 ZA-D	To 1658 CU.
HR696 ZA-G	FTR Dortmund 23/24.5.43.
HR697 ZA-F	FTR Cologne 28/29.6.43.
HR698 ZA-G/E	Crashed on take-off from Melbourne during training 1/2.8.43.
HR699 ZA-J	FTR Kiel 4/5.4.43.
HR757	To 158 Sqn.
HR805 ZA-H	From 405 Sqn. FTR Leipzig 19/20.2.44.
HR860 ZA-C	From 405 Sqn. To 1652 CU.
HR873 ZA-B	From 35 Sqn. To 102 Sqn.
HR879	From 35 Sqn. To 1663 CU.
HR920 ZA-L/C	FTR Montlucon 15/16.9.43.
HR921 ZA-D	Damaged beyond repair by night fighter during operation to Düsseldorf 3/4.11.43.
HR922 ZA-P	FTR Hanover 27/28.9.43.
HR924 ZA-N	From 102 Sqn. Abandoned over Yorkshire on return from Hanover 23.9.43.
HR952 ZA-T	From 51 Sqn. FTR Berlin 28/29.1.44.
HX156 ZA-N	From 102 Sqn. To 1652 CU.
HX159 ZA-L	FTR Hanover 27/28.9.43.
HX163 ZA-L	Damaged beyond repair during operation to Hanover 8/9.10.43.
HX164 ZA-K	FTR Frankfurt 20/21.12.43.
HX165 ZA-J	FTR Magdeburg 21/22.1.44.
HX170 ZA-O	To 1652 CU.
HX171 ZA-E	To 102 Sqn.
HX172 ZA-F	To 1652 CU.

HX174 ZA-H	FTR Kassel 22/23.10.43.
HX179 ZA-L	Crashed near Shipdham on return from Düsseldorf 3.11.43.
HX181 ZA-K	Crashed on landing at Tangmere on return from Leverkusen 19.11.43.
HX184	To 102 Sqn.
HX186 ZA-E	FTR Frankfurt 20/21.12.43.
HX190 ZA-E	FTR Mannheim 18/19.11.43.
HX191 ZA-J	FTR Leipzig 3/4.12.43.
HX232 ZA-E	From 35 Sqn. To 1658 CU.
HX281 ZA-R	Completed 100 operations.
HX286 ZA-R	From 35 Sqn. FTR Stade 9/10.4.45.
HX295 ZA-A	From 35 Sqn. FTR Essen 26/27.3.44.
HX323 ZA-C	From 35 Sqn. To 1658 CU.
HX326 ZA-N	From 35 Sqn. FTR Essen 26/27.4.44.
HX327	From 35 Sqn.
HX332 ZA-V	From 35 Sqn. Shot down by intruder over Yorkshire on return from Kamen 3/4.3.45.
HX343	From 415 Sqn. Crashed on take-off from Melbourne when bound for St Philibert Ferme 8.8.44.
HX347 ZA-Q	From 35 Sqn. FTR Mechelen 1/2.5.44.
HX357 ZA-J	From 35 Sqn.
JB899 ZA-M	From 405 Sqn. To 1662 CU.
JB910 ZA-T/J	To 1658 CU.
JB930 ZA-H	FTR Stettin 20/21.4.43.
JB958 ZA-W	FTR Essen 27/28.5.43.
JB960 ZA-N	FTR Essen 27/28.5.43.
JB961 ZA-R	FTR Montbeliard 15/16.7.43.
JB974 ZA-T	FTR Kassel 22/23.10.43.
JD105 ZA-K	Crashed in Yorkshire on return from Dortmund 5.5.43.
JD106	To 1666 CU.
JD109 ZA-Y	FTR Le Creusot 19/20.6.43.
JD119 ZA-C	Crashed in Leicestershire during cross-country exercise 20.8.43.
JD120 ZA-H	To 1658 CU.
JD146 ZA-B/V	FTR Berlin 22/23.11.43.
JD166 ZA-G	FTR Munich 6/7.9.43.
JD198 ZA-N	FTR Nuremberg 10/11.8.43.
JD199 ZA-W	To 1659 CU.
JD200 ZA-S	FTR Peenemünde 17/18.8.43.
JD202 ZA-Z	To 1658 CU.
JD207 ZA-V	FTR Essen 25/26.7.43.
JD211 ZA-Y	FTR Montbeliard 15/16.7.43.
JD255 ZA-R	From 158 Sqn. To 1658 CU.
JD272 ZA-F	FTR Hanover 27/28.9.43.
JD273 ZA-Y	FTR Berlin 28/29.1.44.
JD314 ZA-Q/X	FTR Berlin 29/30.12.43.

JD315 ZA-R	FTR Kassel 22/23.10.43.
JD322 ZA-V	FTR Mannheim 5/6.9.43.
JD364 ZA-T	FTR Munich 6/7.9.43.
JD367 ZA-O/Q-/Z	FTR Berlin 22/23.11.43.
JD368 ZA-A	FTR Nuremberg 27/28.8.43.
JD470 ZA-S	FTR Berlin 20/21.1.44.
JD473 ZA-X	Crashed on landing at Ford on return from Leverkusen 19.11.43.
JD474 ZA-R	FTR Frankfurt 20/21.12.43.
JN883 ZA-S	From 51 Sqn. FTR Berlin 15/16.2.44.
JN891 ZA-P	From 102 Sqn. FTR Berlin 28/29.1.44.
JN899 ZA-T	From 51 Sqn. FTR Berlin 20/21.1.44.
JN907	From 158 Sqn. To 1652 CU.
JN917 ZA-S	From 51 Sqn. To 1658 CU.
JN947 ZA-F	From 102 Sqn. FTR Düsseldorf 3/4.11.43.
JN948	To 102 Sqn.
JP118 ZA-D	SOC 15.11.46.
JP133 ZA-D	FTR Berlin 28/29.1.44.
LK753 ZA-S/Q/C/V	From 51 Sqn. FTR Hamburg 8/9.4.45.
LK812 ZA-Y	From 51 Sqn. To 1658 Sqn.
LK827 ZA-X/E/I	From 51 Sqn. FTR Osnabrück 6/7.12.44.
LL445	From 644 Sqn. To 1658 CU.
LL588	To 78 Sqn.
LL606 ZA-D-/B-	From 76 Sqn.
LV785 ZA-M/Q/C	From 35 Sqn. Crashed while trying to land at Melbourne on return from Dortmund 2.1.45.
LV818 ZA-W/K/F	From 35 Sqn. FTR Duisburg 17/18.12.44.
LV822	From 35 Sqn. To 51 Sqn.
LV825 ZA-G	From 35 Sqn. Crashed at Rawcliffe when bound for Domlegger 17.6.44.
LV832	From 35 Sqn. To 51 Sqn.
LV857	From 35 Sqn. To 51 Sqn.
LV858 ZA-J	From 35 Sqn. FTR Tergnier 10/11.4.44.
LV859 ZA-C	From 35 Sqn. FTR Essen 26/27.3.44.
LV860	From 35 Sqn. To 415 Sqn.
LV862	From 35 Sqn. To 51 Sqn.
LV863 ZA-O	From 35 Sqn. Crashed on take-off from Melbourne when bound for Aulnoye 28.4.44.
LV865	From 35 Sqn. To 51 Sqn.
LV866	From 35 Sqn. To 429 Sqn.
LV867 ZA-D	From 35 Sqn. FTR Düsseldorf 22/23.4.44.
LV870 ZA-H	From 35 Sqn. FTR Blainville-sur-l'Eau 28/29.6.44
LV878 ZA-V	From 35 Sqn. FTR Wilhelmshaven 15/16.10.44.
LV880	From 35 Sqn. To 51 Sqn.
LV881 ZA-V	From 35 Sqn. FTR Nuremberg 30/31.3.44.
LV882 ZA-D	From 35 Sqn. FTR Trappes 2/3.6.44.
LV906 ZA-F/Q	From 35 Sqn. FTR Aachen 24/25.5.44.

LV908 ZA-F/J	From 35 Sqn. Belly-landed at Melbourne on return from Wilhelmshaven 15.10.44.
LV909 ZA-A/P	From 35 Sqn. FTR Hanau 6/7.1.45.
LV912 ZA-A	From 35 Sqn. FTR Bottrop 20/21.7.44.
LW167 ZA-O	FTR Magdeburg 16/17.1.45.
LW234	From 77 Sqn. To 1663 CU.
LW289 ZA-Y	From 51 Sqn. To 1663 CU.
LW314 ZA-K	From 158 Sqn. To 1652 CU.
LW322 ZA-P	To 102 Sqn.
LW324 ZA-J	From 78 Sqn. FTR Leipzig 19/20.2.44.
LW332 ZA-G	To 102 Sqn.
LW336 ZA-L	To 102 Sqn.
LW371 ZA-B	From 35 Sqn. Crashed on landing at Melbourne on return from Laval airfield 9.6.44.
LW545 ZA-E/N/Z ZA-D/L	From 51 Sqn.
LW716 ZA-S/D/Y/Z	FTR Bochum 4/5.11.44.
LW717 ZA-W	FTR Blainville-sur-l'Eau 28/29.6.44.
LW718	To 158 Sqn.
LW719	To 158 Sqn.
LW720	To 158 Sqn.
MZ290 ZA-L/J/O	From 102 Sqn.
MZ300 ZA-I/K	From 102 Sqn.
MZ309 ZA-D/B	From 76 Sqn. Damaged beyond repair during an operation to Münster 13.9.44.
MZ312 ZA-E	FTR Bottrop 20/21.7.44.
MZ315 ZA-G	
MZ344	To 640 Sqn.
MZ345 ZA-G	To 640 Sqn.
MZ346 ZA-S/P	From 640 Sqn.
MZ354 ZA-M	From 76 Sqn.
MZ361	From BDU. To 78 Sqn.
MZ398	To 462 Sqn.
MZ403	To 462 Sqn.
MZ406	To 640 Sqn.
MZ409	To 640 Sqn.
MZ410	To EANS.
MZ411 ZA-M/A	To Leconfield.
MZ413 ZA-B	To 96 Sqn.
MZ417 ZA-E	From 78 Sqn.
MZ421 ZA-Z/X	From 76 Sqn.
MZ430 ZA-W	To Leconfield.
MZ433 ZA-X	Crashed on landing at Melbourne during transit from Carnaby after returning from Essen 11.3.45.
MZ464	From 433 Sqn. To 96 Sqn.
MZ532 ZA-Z	FTR Laval airfield 9/10.6.44.
MZ534 ZA-Z	To 1663 CU.
MZ574 ZA-V/W	FTR Neuss 23/24.9.44.

MZ576 ZA-T	Ditched off Lincolnshire coast on return from Cologne 28.10.44.
MZ584 ZA-V	FTR St-Martin-l'Hortier 2.7.44.
MZ630 ZA-S	FTR Trappes 2/3.6.44.
MZ684 ZA-B	FTR Laval airfield 9/10.6.44.
MZ732	To 76 Sqn.
MZ746 ZA-S	
MZ751 ZA-J	
MZ773 ZA-Y	FTR Brunswick 12/13.8.44.
MZ789 ZA-H	From 78 Sqn. Belly-landed in France on return from Essen 28/29.11.44.
MZ793 ZA-X	FTR from mining sortie 14/15.2.45.
MZ810	To 78 Sqn.
MZ826 ZA-M	FTR from mining sortie 15/16.10.44.
MZ844 ZA-D	FTR Watten 25.8.44.
MZ847 ZA-A	Belly-landed in Kent on return from operation to V2 rocket stores at Lumbres 1.9.44.
MZ902 ZA-R	From 76 Sqn.
MZ919 ZA-L	
MZ948 ZA-E	FTR Chemnitz 5/6.3.45.
NA114 ZA-K	From 76 Sqn. FTR Hanover 5/6.1.45.
NA149	To 76 Sqn.
NA162 ZA-W	To EANS.
NA195 ZA-F/R	
NA198 ZA-W	From 76 Sqn. To EANS.
NA228 ZA-D	
NA237 ZA-C	FTR Magdeburg 16/17.1.45.
NA275	To 78 Sqn.
NA506	To 346 Sqn.
NA627 ZA-Y	Crashed on landing at Melbourne on return from Bingen 22.12.44.
NP993 ZA-Q	From 78 Sqn. To Leconfield.
NP994 ZA-K	
NR130	To 78 Sqn.
NR131 ZA-N	FTR Chemnitz 5/6.3.45.
NR188 ZA-M	
NR189 ZA-Z	FTR Worms 21/22.2.45.
NR245 ZA-H	To 51 Sqn.
NR246 ZA-Y	FTR St Vith 26.12.44.
PN447 ZA-B	Damaged beyond repair during operation to Heligoland 18.4.45.
RG345 ZA-Y	
RG354 ZA-O	
RG422 ZA-C	From 96 Sqn.
RG423 ZA-P	From 96 Sqn.
RG424 ZA-T	From 96 Sqn. Undercarriage collapsed on landing at Melbourne on return from Hamburg 9.4.45.
RG425 ZA-Z	From 96 Sqn.

RG426 ZA-X	From 96 Sqn. FTR Worms 21/22.2.45.
RG427 ZA-N/V	From 96 Sqn.
RG428 ZA-F	From 96 Sqn.
RG429 ZA-H	From 96 Sqn.
RG431 ZA-Z	From 96 Sqn.
RG434 ZA-A	From 78 Sqn.
RG435 ZA-Y/G	From 77 Sqn.
RG438 ZA-S/N	Crashed on take-off from Melbourne while training 24.3.45.
RG439 ZA-Q/K	From 346 Sqn.
RG440 ZA-T/M	From 78 Sqn.
RG442 ZA-C/E	From 77 Sqn.
RG443 ZA-Q	From 77 Sqn. FTR Wanne-Eickel 2/3.2.45.
RG444	To 76 Sqn.

Heaviest Single Loss

27/28.06.41.	Bremen. 4 Whitleys.
01/02.10.42.	Flensburg. 4 Halifaxes.
28/29.01.44.	Berlin. 4 Halifaxes.

35 (Madras Presidency) Squadron

Motto: Uno Animo Agimus (We act with one accord)   **Code: TL**

35 Squadron was first formed as a corps reconnaissance unit on 1 February 1916, moving to France in January 1917 to carry out photographic and artillery observation duties. Ultimately becoming a general-purpose unit in 1918, the squadron received Bristol Fighters shortly before the war ended. Disbanded in June 1919, the squadron remained on the shelf for ten years until being reformed as a day-bomber unit. At the outbreak of WWII the squadron was employing Fairey Battles, but did not go to France with the other similarly-equipped units. It performed a training role until being absorbed into 17 OTU in April 1940. Reformed in 4 Group on 5 November 1940 to introduce the Halifax into operational service, 35 Squadron first operated on the night of 10/11 March 1941. Teething troubles restricted the serviceability of the type, and the need for constant modifications ensured slow progress. Nevertheless, 35 Squadron spearheaded 4 Group's contribution to the heavy bomber offensive and many leading lights served with it, among them James Tait, Leonard Cheshire and George Holden, all of whom would go on to command 617 Squadron, better known as the Dambusters. In August 1942 35 Squadron was selected to become a founder member of the Pathfinder Force, and departed 4 Group for good. Its link was not entirely broken, however, as it would be the responsibility of 4 Group to supply 35 Squadron with crews.

STATIONS

Boscombe Down	05.11.40 to 20.11.40
Leeming	20.11.40 to 05.12.40

| Linton-on-Ouse | 05.12.40 to 15.08.42 |
| Graveley | 15.08.42 to 10.09.46 |

COMMANDING OFFICERS

Wing Commander R.W.P. Collings AFC	05.11.40 to 03.07.41
Wing Commander B.V. Robinson DFC AFC	03.07.41 to 26.01.42
Wing Commander J.N.H. Whitworth DSO DFC	26.01.42 to 12.03.42
Wing Commander J.H. Marks DSO DFC	12.03.42 to 20.09.42
Wing Commander* B.V. Robinson DSO DFC AFC	20.09.42 to 01.05.43
Wing Commander D.F.E.C. Dean DFC	01.05.43 to 17.11.43
Wing Commander S.P. Daniels DSO DFC	17.11.43 to 25.07.44
Wing Commander** D.F.E.C. Dean DSO DFC	25.07.44 to 25.02.45
Wing Commander H.J. Le Good AFC	25.02.45 to 11.09.45

* Group Captain from 03.02.43
** Group Captain from 09.43

AIRCRAFT

| Halifax I | 12.40 to 02.42 |
| Halifax II | 01.42 to 03.44 |

OPERATIONAL RECORD

4 Group Halifaxes

Operations	Sorties	Aircraft Losses	% Losses
115	717	35	4.9

Category of Operations

Bombing	Leaflet
109	6

TABLE OF STATISTICS
(Heavy squadrons)
Out of 32 Halifax squadrons in Bomber Command
(Excluding SOE)

6th highest number of Halifax overall operations in Bomber Command.
11th highest number of Halifax sorties in Bomber Command.
7th highest number of Halifax operational losses in Bomber Command.

Out of 25 operational squadrons in 4 Group

14th highest number of overall operations in 4 Group.
15th highest number of sorties in 4 Group.
13th highest number of aircraft operational losses in 4 Group.

Out of 15 operational Halifax squadrons in 4 Group

12th highest number of Halifax overall operations in 4 Group.
13th highest number of Halifax sorties in 4 Group.
11th highest number of Halifax operational losses in 4 Group.

AIRCRAFT HISTORIES

Halifax	To March 1944.
L7244	From A&AEE. To AFEE.
L9486 TL-M/B	From A&AEE. To 28 CF.
L9487	Crashed near Dishforth during air-test 13.1.41.
L9488 TL-M	To 76 Sqn.
L9489 TL-F	Shot down by RAF fighter near Aldershot on return from Le Havre 10.3.41.
L9490 TL-L	Damaged beyond repair in ground accident 17.7.41.
L9491 TL-J	To 28 CF.
L9492 TL-K	To 76 Sqn.
L9493 TL-G	Crash-landed on approach to Linton-on-Ouse on return from Kiel 15/16.4.41.
L9494	To 76 Sqn.
L9495 TL-B	Belly-landed at Linton-on-Ouse while training 17.7.41.
L9496 TL-N	To 76 Sqn.
L9497 TL-K	Force-landed in Norfolk on return from Berlin 13.8.41.
L9498 TL-T	Crashed on landing at Linton-on-Ouse on return from Hüls 13.6.41.
L9499 TL-Q	FTR Kiel 30.6.41.
L9500 TL-H	FTR Magdeburg 14/15.8.41.
L9501 TL-Y	FTR Duisburg 28/29.8.41.
L9502 TL-R	FTR Frankfurt 7/8.7.41.
L9503 TL-P	FTR Hamburg 15/16.9.41.
L9504	To 102 CF.
L9506 TL-X	Crash-landed at Bircham Newton on return from Hanover 16.6.41.
L9507 TL-W	FTR Berlin 25/26.7.41.
L9508 TL-F/X	FTR Berlin 2/3.9.41.
L9509 TL-C	To 28 CF and back. To 28 CF.
L9510	To 76 Sqn.
L9511 TL-D/P	To 1652 CU.
L9512 TL-U	FTR La Pallice 24.7.41.
L9513	To 76 Sqn.
L9514	To 76 Sqn.
L9516	To 76 Sqn.
L9517	To 76 Sqn.
L9518	To 76 Sqn.
L9519	To 76 Sqn.
L9521 TL-Z	FTR Merseburg 8/9.7.41.
L9523	To 76 Sqn.
L9524 TL-V	To 10 Sqn.
L9525	To 28 CF.
L9526 TL-O	Force-landed in Norfolk on return from Turin 11.9.41.
L9527 TL-M	FTR La Pallice 24.7.41.

L9528	To 76 Sqn.
L9529	To 76 Sqn.
L9530	To 76 Sqn.
L9560 TL-F	FTR Berlin 2/3.9.41.
L9566 TL-R	FTR Turin 10/11.9.41.
L9568	Conversion Flt only. Struck by W1051 on ground at Linton-on-Ouse 7.5.42.
L9569	To 10 Sqn.
L9571	To 1652 CU.
L9572 TL-G	FTR Düsseldorf 24/25.8.41.
L9575	To 1652 CU.
L9579 TL-P	Crash-landed near Linton-on-Ouse on return from Nuremberg 13.10.41.
L9580	To 28 CF.
L9582 TL-T	FTR Hamburg 30.11/1.12.41.
L9584 TL-L	To 102 CF.
L9600 TL-U	FTR Cologne 11/12.12.41.
L9603 TL-P	FTR Essen 7/8.11.41.
L9605	To 1652 CU.
L9606	To 1652 CU.
L9607	To 1652 CU.
L9608	To 1652 CU.
L9610	To 1652 CU.
R9364 TL-M/N	To 76 Sqn.
R9367 TL-G	From HCF. To 1652 CU.
R9370	From 10 Sqn. Conversion Flt only. To 1658 CU.
R9372 TL-O	To 1652 CU.
R9377 TL-B	To 1652 CU.
R9381	From 1652 CU. Returned to 1652 CU.
R9386 TL-A	To 76 Sqn.
R9392	To 10 Sqn.
R9422	To 1652 CU and back. To 103 Sqn.
R9425	To 35 CF. Crashed in Yorkshire 16.4.42.
R9428	To 10 Sqn.
R9438 TL-H	FTR Aasenfjord (*Tirpitz*) 30/31.3.42.
R9439 TL-A	FTR Emden 6/7.6.42.
R9440	Crashed during landing at Linton-on-Ouse while training 13.3.42.
R9441 TL-S	To 102 Sqn.
R9442	To 102 Sqn.
R9444 TL-D	FTR Essen 2/3.6.42.
R9445 TL-T	Crash-landed at Oakington on return from Billancourt 3/4.3.42.
R9446	To 102 Sqn.
R9448	To 405 CF.
R9449	To 102 CF.
R9450 TL-K	FTR Essen 9/10.3.42.
R9483	To 405 CF.

R9488	To 102 Sqn.
R9489 TL-T	Crashed in Yorkshire during air-test 21.7.42.
R9493	From 10 Sqn. Conversion Flt only. To 1651 CU.
R9494	To 102 Sqn.
R9496 TL-H/L	FTR Aasenfjord (*Tirpitz*) 30/31.3.42.
V9978 TL-A	Ditched in the Channel on return from Brest 18.12.41.
V9979 TL-E	FTR Brest 30.12.41.
V9982	To 102 CF.
V9983	To 103 Sqn.
V9993	To 1652 CU.
V9994	To 1652 CU.
W1006	From 78 Sqn. Conversion Flt only. To 1635 CU.
W1015 TL-P	FTR Aasenfjord (*Tirpitz*) 30/31.3.42.
W1019	To 405 Sqn.
W1020 TL-K	FTR Aasenfjord (*Tirpitz*) 27/28.4.42.
W1021 TL-J	FTR Essen 8/9.6.42.
W1046 TL-N	To 161 Sqn.
W1047 TL-B	From 102 Sqn. FTR Aachen 5/6.10.42.
W1048 TL-S	From 102 Sqn. FTR Aasenfjord (*Tirpitz*) 27/28.4.42. Recovered 1973. On display at RAF Museum Hendon.
W1049 TL-V	From 102 Sqn. Ditched off Yarmouth on return from Essen 9.6.42.
W1050 TL-F	From 102 Sqn. FTR Stuttgart 6/7.5.42.
W1051 TL-C	From 102 Sqn. Crashed after landing at Linton-on-Ouse on return from Stuttgart 7.5.42.
W1053 TL-G	From 102 Sqn. FTR Aasenfjord (*Tirpitz*) 28/29.4.42.
W1100 TL-G	FTR Düsseldorf 31.7/1.8.42.
W1101 TL-S	FTR Mannheim 19/20.5.42.
W1102	To BDU.
W1105 TL-N	FTR Bremen 25/26.6.42.
W1117 TL-S	FTR Essen 16/17.6.42.
W1141	To 77 Sqn.
W1146	From 10 Sqn. Returned to 10 Sqn.
W1147 TL-J	FTR Duisburg 25/26.7.42.
W1154 TL-A	Abandoned over Kent on return from Duisburg 14.7.42.
W1159	Crashed on landing at Linton-on-Ouse during training 22.6.42.
W1160 TL-M	To 10 Sqn.
W1165	From 158 CF. To 1666 CU.
W1173	To 405 Sqn.
W1226 TL-J	FTR Flensburg 18/19.8.42. First Pathfinder loss.
W1231	From BDU. To NTU.
W1234	From 460 Sqn. To 1654 CU.
W1242 TL-G	FTR Le Havre 11/12.8.42.
W7656 TL-P	FTR Aasenfjord (*Tirpitz*) 28/29.4.42.

W7657 TL-L	FTR Saarbrücken 19/20.9.42.
W7658 TL-H	FTR Mannheim 19/20.5.42.
W7675	Crashed on landing at Linton-on-Ouse during air-test 8.5.42.
W7676 TL-P	FTR Nuremberg 28/29.8.42.
W7699 TL-F	FTR Essen 8/9.6.42.
W7700 TL-C	FTR Nuremberg 28/29.8.42.
W7701 TL-U	FTR Essen 8/9.6.42.
W7711	From BTU. To 1661 CU.
W7749	To 1659 CU.
W7760 TL-B	FTR Hamburg 26/27.7.42.
W7761 TL-N	Abandoned over Yorkshire on return from Duisburg 14.7.42.
W7765 TL-T	FTR Frankfurt 24/25.8.42.
W7778	To 1656 CU.
W7779 TL-R	To 1666 CU.
W7782	To 78 Sqn.
W7804	To 1666 CU.
W7806	Conversion Flt only. To 1652 CU.
W7808	From TFU. To NTU.
W7811	From BDU. To 1662 CU.
W7821	To 1658 CU.
W7823 TL-L	From TRE. To NTU.
W7825 TL-P	From BDU. FTR Düsseldorf 25/26.5.43.
W7851 TL-Y	From TFU. FTR Nuremberg 8/9.3.43.
W7866	To 1662 CU.
W7872	From TFU. To NTU.
W7873 TL-E/M	From TFU. FTR Pilsen 16/17.4.43.
W7874	From TFU. To NTU.
W7875	From TFU. To NTU.
W7876 TL-K	From TFU. FTR Wuppertal 29/30.5.43.
W7877 TL-O	From BDU. FTR Berlin 1/2.3.43.
W7878 TL-J	From TFU. FTR Krefeld 21/22.6.43.
W7881 TL-P	From 10 Sqn. To 78 Sqn.
W7885 TL-B	To 405 Sqn and back. FTR Lorient 13/14.2.43.
W7886 TL-C	FTR Berlin 17/18.1.43.
W7887 TL-E	Abandoned over Northamptonshire on return from Dortmund 5.5.43.
W7906 TL-Q	Crashed on landing at Harrowbeer on return from St Nazaire 28.2.43.
W7907 TL-M	FTR Berlin 27/28.3.43.
W7923 TL-D	Belly-landed at Graveley on return from Hamburg 4.2.43.
BB203	To 158 CF.
BB320	To 102 CF.
BB359	To 10 Sqn.
BB361 TL-V	FTR Krefeld 21/22.6.43.
BB366	To 1658 CU.

BB368 TL-H	Ditched off Norfolk coast on return from Krefeld 21/22.6.43.
BB370	To 102 Sqn.
BB372	From 405 Sqn. To 102 Sqn.
DG226	To 10 CF.
DG227	To 158 Sqn.
DT488 TL-S/Q	Crash-landed at Colerne on return from Turin 19.11.42. Following repair, FTR Dortmund 23/24.5.43.
DT489 TL-Y	Crashed in Huntingdonshire on return from Dortmund 5.5.43.
DT500	To 10 Sqn.
DT519	To 78 Sqn.
DT801 TL-A	FTR Duisburg 12/13.5.43.
DT803	To NTU.
DT804 TL-C	FTR Wuppertal 29/30.5.43.
DT805 TL-Y	FTR Münster 11/12.6.43.
DT806 TL-Z	FTR Frankfurt 10/11.4.43.

51 SQUADRON

Motto: Swift and Sure   **Code: MH LK C6**

The initial role for 51 Squadron after its formation on 15 May 1916 was air defence. Anti-Zeppelin patrols were conducted from airfields in East Anglia. The squadron was disbanded in June 1919, and it remained on the shelf until it was reformed at Driffield from B Flight of 58 Squadron on 5 March 1937. In February 1938 the squadron became the fourth in the Command to equip with Whitleys, and on 20 April it took up residence at Linton-on-Ouse. At the outbreak of war 51 Squadron was equipped with a mixture of Mk II and III Whitleys and was one of five operational units within 4 Group. Unlike many of the crews within the other Groups, those of 4 Group were trained to fly at night, and three from 51 Squadron carried out the Group's first operation on the opening night of the war, delivering propaganda leaflets to German cities. Apart from a six-month detachment to Coastal Command in 1942, 51 Squadron spent the entire war at the forefront of 4 Group's contribution to the bomber offensive. Among its more unusual operations were *Colossus*, the ultimately unsuccessful attempt to land a small special commando force to destroy an aqueduct in Italy, and the Bruneval raid, a highly successful similar operation which resulted in the capture of German radar technology and a German operator. The venerable old Whitley gave way to the Halifax in late 1942, and it was this type that saw the squadron through to the end of hostilities.

STATIONS

Linton-on-Ouse	20.04.38 to 09.12.39
Dishforth	09.12.39 to 06.05.42
Chivenor	06.05.42 to 27.10.42

Snaith   27.10.42 to 20.04.45
Leconfield   20.04.45 to 21.08.45

COMMANDING OFFICERS

Wing Commander J. Silvester	20.04.38 to 05.03.40
Wing Commander A.H. Owen	05.03.40 to 02.10.40
Wing Commander N.F. Brescon	02.10.40 to 16.12.40
Wing Commander J.B. Tait	16.12.40 to 13.01.41
Wing Commander R.C. Wilson	13.01.41 to 09.05.41
Wing Commander R.K. Burnett	09.05.41 to 15.11.41
Wing Commander P.C. Pickard DSO DFC	15.11.41 to 18.05.42
Wing Commander J.A.H. Tuck DSO	18.05.42 to 08.10.42
Wing Commander A.V. Sawyer DFC	08.10.42 to 28.04.43
Wing Commander A.D. Franks DSO DFC	28.04.43 to 14.11.43
Wing Commander D.S.S. Wilkerson DFC	14.11.43 to 14.01.44
Wing Commander R.C. Ayling	01.02.44 to 31.03.44
Wing Commander C.W.M. Ling	01.04.44 to 08.11.44
Wing Commander H.A.R. Holford	08.11.44 to 30.04.45
Wing Commander E.F.E. Barnard	30.04.45 to 03.12.45

AIRCRAFT

Whitley II	02.38 to 12.39
Whitley III	08.38 to 12.39
Whitley IV	11.39 to 05.40
Whitley V	05.40 to 11.42
Halifax II	11.42 to 01.44
Halifax III	01.44 to 06.45

OPERATIONAL RECORD

Operations	Sorties	Aircraft Losses	% Losses
497	5,959	158	2.7

Category of Operations

Bombing	Mining	Other
476	9	12

Whitleys

Operations	Sorties	Aircraft Losses	% Losses
233	1,806	50	2.8

Category of Operations

Bombing	Leaflet	Other
221	10	2

Halifaxes

Operations	Sorties	Aircraft Losses	% Losses
264	4,153	108	2.6

Category of Operations

Bombing	Mining
255	9

TABLE OF STATISTICS

Out of 32 Halifax squadrons in Bomber Command
(Excluding SOE)
7th highest number of overall Halifax operations in Bomber Command.
6th highest number of Halifax sorties in Bomber Command.
6th highest number of Halifax operational losses in Bomber Command.

Out of 25 operational squadrons in 4 Group
4th highest number of overall operations in 4 Group.
4th highest number of sorties in 4 Group.
4th highest number of aircraft operational losses in 4 Group.

Out of 6 Whitley squadrons in 4 Group
2nd highest number of overall Whitley operations in 4 Group.
Highest number of Whitley sorties in 4 Group.
3rd highest number of Whitley operational losses in 4 Group.

Out of 15 operational Halifax squadrons in 4 Group
6th highest number of Halifax overall operations in 4 Group.
6th highest number of Halifax sorties in 4 Group.
6th highest number of Halifax operational losses in 4 Group.

AIRCRAFT HISTORIES

Whitley	To November 1942.
K8937	To 7 BGS.
K8938	To 1Bat Flt.
K8939	Became ground-instruction machine 6.40.
K8940	To 166 Sqn.
K8941	To 19 OTU.
K8942	To 166 Sqn.
K8959	From 77 Sqn. To 10 OTU.
K8978	To 19 OTU.
K8979	To 58 Sqn.
K8980 MH-E	To 2BAT Flt.
K8981 MH-A	To 10 OTU.
K8982	To 19 OTU.

K8983	To 19 OTU.
K8984 MH-A/N	Abandoned over France after leafleting sortie 27/28.10.39.
K8988	Crash-landed in France on return from a leafleting sortie 27/28.10.39.
K8989 MH-M	To 19 OTU.
K9001	From 97 Sqn. Crashed soon after take-off from Linton-on-Ouse on ferry flight 19.9.39.
K9008 MH-J	From 97 Sqn. Crash-landed in France on return from leafleting sortie to Frankfurt 27/28.10.39.
K9021	From 10 Sqn. To 10 OTU.
K9024	From 10 Sqn. To 19 OTU.
K9038	From 1 AAS. To 10 OTU.
K9039	Crashed in Yorkshire during operation to Oslo 30.4/1.5.40.
K9040	FTR from training flight 5.4.40.
K9041	To 19 OTU.
K9042	To 10 OTU.
K9043 MH-G	FTR Aalborg 22/23.4.40.
K9045	To 19 OTU.
K9046	To 19 OTU.
K9047	To 10 OTU.
K9048 MH-P	FTR Aalborg 23/24.4.40.
N1390	To 77 Sqn.
N1394	To 78 Sqn.
N1405	FTR Hornum 19/20.3.40.
N1406	Abandoned over Yorkshire on return from Oslo 3.5.40.
N1407	To 78 Sqn.
N1408 MH-K	FTR Hanover 18/19.5.40.
N1414	Crash-landed in Norfolk on return from flare-dropping sortie off Belgian coast 8.9.40.
N1418	To 58 Sqn.
N1425	To 77 Sqn.
N1435	From AFEE. To AFEE.
N1443	To 78 Sqn.
N1464	SOC 24.2.44.
N1481	FTR Cologne 1/2.3.41.
N1485	To 78 Sqn.
N1486	To 78 Sqn.
N1488	From 10 Sqn. To 10 OTU.
N1504 MH-K	To 2BAT Flt.
N1525	To 78 Sqn.
N1526	To 10 OTU.
P4934 MH-A	Crashed off Durham coast on return from Cologne 27.2.41.
P4968	FTR Schornewitz 19/20.8.40.
P4969 MH-K	To 77 Sqn.

P4970	To PTS.
P4971	To 3 OTU.
P4972 MH-E	Crashed on landing at Dishforth on return from Merseburg 30.10.40.
P4973	FTR Berlin 4/5.9.40.
P4974	Abandoned over eastern England on return from Bremen 11/12.2.41.
P4980	FTR Jülich 21/22.5.40.
P4981	Abandoned over Yorkshire on return from Bremen 11/12.2.41.
P4982	Crashed in Buckinghamshire on return from Bordeaux 14/15.8.40.
P4983	FTR Gelsenkirchen 11/12.8.40.
P4984	Abandoned over Essex on return from Stettin 29.11.40.
P4985	To 77 Sqn.
P4986	FTR Bohlen 16/17.8.40.
P4987	To 24 OTU.
P4996	To 78 Sqn.
P5007	FTR Gelsenkirchen 19/20.7.40.
P5011 MH-K	Crashed on take-off from Dishforth while training 3.9.40.
P5013	Abandoned over Yorkshire on return from Bremen 11/12.2.41.
P5020	To 19 OTU.
P5021	Ditched in the North Sea on return from Berlin 10.9.40.
P5027 MH-H/L	SOC 20.2.44.
P5060	FTR Bremen 3/4.1.41.
P5095	Ditched near Liverpool on return from Milan 21.10.40.
P5105	To 78 Sqn.
P5106 MH-O	FTR Ludwigshaven 9/10.5.41.
P5108 MH-Q	FTR Cologne 1/2.3.41.
P5112	FTR Düsseldorf 7/8.12.40.
T4145	To 58 Sqn.
T4148 MH-R	From 10 Sqn. Crashed in Yorkshire after aborting operation to Cologne 26.2.41.
T4175	To 78 Sqn.
T4201	Ditched in The Wash on return from Stettin 29.11.40.
T4217 MH-H	Abandoned near Bircham Newton on return from Bremen 11/12.2.41.
T4218	Crashed on landing at Usworth on return from Gelsenkirchen 18.11.40.
T4224	To 19 OTU.
T4237 MH-E/A	Ditched off Yorkshire coast on return from Wilhelmshaven 23.6.41.
T4263	To 10 Sqn.

T4270 MH-M	Crashed on landing at Dishforth on return from Gelsenkirchen 10.1.41.
T4298 MH-K	FTR Kiel 7/8.4.41.
T4299 MH-B	Shot down by Hurricane over Dorset on return from Brest 3.4.41.
T4323 MH-N	To 10 OTU.
Z6469	To 58 Sqn.
Z6474 MH-H/A	Crashed soon after take-off from Dishforth bound for Stettin 29.9.41.
Z6479 MH-M	FTR Cologne 16/17.6.41.
Z6480 MH-L	To 81 OTU.
Z6481	To 10 OTU.
Z6482	FTR Kiel 24/25.4.41.
Z6487 MH-G	FTR Hanover 19/20.7.41.
Z6488 MH-W	FTR Frankfurt 6/7.8.41.
Z6505 MH-F	From 58 Sqn. FTR Düsseldorf 24/25.8.41.
Z6554	To 1485 Flt.
Z6555	To 78 Sqn.
Z6556 MH-Q	FTR Brest 3/4.4.41.
Z6559	To 10 Sqn.
Z6563 MH-T	FTR Düsseldorf 19/20.6.41.
Z6566 MH-Q	From 102 Sqn. FTR Cologne 18/19.8.41.
Z6567 MH-Z	FTR Essen 8/9.11.41.
Z6569 MH-S	FTR Cologne 18/19.8.41.
Z6579	To 24 OTU.
Z6657 MH-A	FTR Duisburg 11/12.6.41.
Z6662	To 19 OTU.
Z6663 MH-D	Crashed in Yorkshire on return from Dortmund 9.6.41.
Z6665	To 19 OTU.
Z6731 MH-A	Crashed in Suffolk on return from Cologne 19.8.41.
Z6738	To 81 OTU.
Z6741	FTR Brest 4/5.7.41.
Z6744	FTR Berlin 7/8.9.41.
Z6803 MH-J	FTR Frankfurt 5/6.8.41.
Z6808 MH-N	Abandoned near Swanton Morley on return from Frankfurt 7.8.41.
Z6811 MH-D	FTR Cologne 18/19.8.41.
Z6812 MH-A	From 102 Sqn. To 10 OTU.
Z6813 MH-K	To Armstrong Whitworth.
Z6819 MH-X	FTR Hanover 14/15.8.41.
Z6839 MH-O	FTR Berlin 7/8.11.41.
Z6840	To PTS.
Z6874	FTR Frankfurt 24/25.10.41.
Z6875	From 78 Sqn. To 1485 Flt.
Z6879 MH-B	To 10 OTU.
Z6933 MH-I	To 19 OTU.

Z6935	From 102 Sqn. Crashed in Dishforth circuit on return from Berlin 7.9.41.
Z6937	Crashed on approach to Dishforth on return from Berlin 8.9.41.
Z6938	FTR Berlin 7/8.9.41.
Z6957	FTR Hamburg 15/16.9.41.
Z6971	To 10 OTU.
Z6976	To 10 Sqn.
Z6978	From 78 Sqn. To 77 Sqn.
Z9119 MH-G	From 58 Sqn. FTR from patrol 3.8.42.
Z9130	FTR Berlin 7/8.11.41.
Z9131	To 161 Sqn.
Z9132	From 78 Sqn. To 81 OTU.
Z9133	To 1485 Flt and back. Crashed in Cornwall while on patrol 27.8.42.
Z9140	To 138 Sqn.
Z9141 MH-J	FTR Hamburg 31.10/1.11.41.
Z9144 MH-G	SOC 14.1.44.
Z9145 MH-K	Crashed in Yorkshire while training 22.10.41.
Z9146	To 138 Sqn.
Z9153	From 58 Sqn. FTR from patrol 16.10.42.
Z9164 MH-B/C	To 10 OTU.
Z9165	To 1484 Flt.
Z9201 MH-G	From 102 Sqn. Crashed at Dishforth 11.6.42.
Z9202 MH-P	FTR Emden 28/29.12.41.
Z9206 MH-A	To 1484 Flt.
Z9215 MH-C	From 78 Sqn. Ditched during shipping escort sortie 22.7.42.
Z9217 MH-F	From 102 Sqn. To 10 OTU.
Z9220 MH-A/V	FTR Hamburg 31.10/1.11.41.
Z9222 MH-C	From 102 Sqn. To PTS.
Z9228 MH-H	SOC 19.4.45.
Z9230	To 138 Sqn.
Z9274 MH-U	Crashed in Yorkshire on return from St Nazaire 28.3.42.
Z9296 MH-D	To 10 OTU.
Z9298 MH-B/D/F	To 138 Sqn and back. To 10 OTU.
Z9301 MH-N	FTR Emden 17/18.1.42.
Z9302	From 78 Sqn. To 10 OTU.
Z9304 MH-S	Ditched in Channel on return from St Nazaire 28.3.42.
Z9311 MH-J	FTR Emden 21/22.1.42.
Z9314 MH-L	To 297 Sqn and back. To 10 OTU.
Z9315 MH-V	FTR from leafleting sortie 26/27.1.42.
Z9322 MH-G	To 77 Sqn.
Z9323	Ditched off Cornwall during patrol 12.10.42.
Z9387 MH-M	FTR from patrol 7.9.42.
Z9421 MH-H	From 102 Sqn. To 10 OTU.

Z9423 MH-S	FTR Emden 26/27.1.42.
Z9424 MH-R	FTR Emden 15/16.1.42.
Z9425 MH-E	Crashed in Devon during patrol 24.9.42.
Z9465	FTR from patrol 30.9.42.
Z9481 MH-V	Crashed in Yorkshire on return from St Nazaire 28.3.42.
Z9511	FTR from patrol 12.7.42.
BD190 MH-J	Force-landed in Yorkshire on return from Rostock 24.4.42.
BD191	FTR from patrol 20.6.42.
BD192 MH-C	Ditched while on patrol 7.6.42.
BD258	FTR from patrol 30.9.42.
BD259	To 10 OTU.
BD260	To 138 Sqn.
BD359	To 10 OTU.

Halifax	From November 1942.
W1185 MH-V	From 103 Sqn. Crashed on landing at Burn after air-test 29.1.43.
W1212 MH-U	From 103 Sqn. To 1654 CU.
W1224 MH-E/A	From 103 Sqn. To 466 Sqn and back. To 1656 CU.
W7772 MH-S/O	From 103 Sqn. To 10 Sqn.
W7818 MH-T	From 103 Sqn. Crash-landed near Snaith during training 18.2.43.
W7855	From 10 Sqn. Crash-landed at Snaith during training 25.2.43.
W7860 MH-W	From 103 Sqn. To 1668 CU.
W7861 MH-B	From 103 Sqn. FTR Hamburg 3/4.3.43.
BB223 MH-C	From 103 Sqn. FTR Berlin 1/2.3.43.
BB240 MH-X	From 10 Sqn. To 1652 CU.
BB241 MH-S	From 10 Sqn. To 1652 CU.
BB244 MH-G/Q	From 78 Sqn. FTR Berlin 29/30.3.43.
BB253	To 1658 CU.
DT483 MH-F	From 103 Sqn. FTR from mining sortie 9/10.1.43.
DT506 MH-D	From 103 Sqn. Crash-landed at Pocklington on return from Lorient 15.1.43.
DT513 MH-H/N	From 103 Sqn. FTR Cologne 28/29.6.43.
DT526 MH-V	From 78 Sqn. FTR Bochum 13/14.5.43.
DT552	From 10 Sqn. To 1658 CU.
DT561 MH-K	From 10 Sqn. FTR Pilsen 16/17.4.43.
DT567 MH-F	From 10 Sqn. FTR from mining sortie 7/8.3.43.
DT568 MH-F	From 77 Sqn. FTR Bochum 12/13.6.43.
DT580 MH-Z	To 78 Sqn.
DT581 MH-Y	From 77 Sqn. Crashed in Yorkshire on return from mining sortie 21.1.43.
DT582 MH-X	From 77 Sqn. To 1666 CU.
DT584 MH-J	From 77 Sqn. To 1666 CU.
DT614 MH-H	To 1658 CU.

DT626	From 77 Sqn. To 1658 CU.
DT628 MH-B	From 77 Sqn. FTR Stettin 20/21.4.43.
DT637	From 158 Sqn. Force-landed near Riccall on return from Duisburg 13.5.43.
DT638 MH-C	To 158 Sqn.
DT645 MH-B	From 77 Sqn. FTR Duisburg 12/13.5.43.
DT648 MH-K	Crashed on landing at Snaith on return from St Nazaire 1.3.43.
DT649	From 77 Sqn. To 1658 CU.
DT666 MH-T	From 77 Sqn. Crashed near Snaith on return from Essen 4.4.43.
DT670 MH-C/M	From 77 Sqn. FTR Pilsen 16/17.4.43.
DT671 MH-S	From 158 Sqn. To 1652 CU.
DT685 MH-A	From 77 Sqn. FTR Duisburg 12/13.5.43.
DT686 MH-L/N	From 58 Sqn. FTR Kiel 4/5.4.43.
DT690 MH-A	FTR Pilsen 16/17.4.43.
DT693 MH-B/F	To 1661 CU.
DT705 MH-S	FTR Düsseldorf 27/28.1.43.
DT721 MH-J	FTR Düsseldorf 27/28.1.43.
DT722 MH-M	Destroyed by fire at Snaith 13.2.43.
DT724 MH-H	Destroyed by fire at Snaith 13.2.43.
DT729 MH-R	Crashed in Yorkshire while training 3.5.43.
DT730 MH-A	To 77 Sqn.
DT738 MH-D	FTR Essen 3/4.4.43.
DT742 MH-Y	Ditched off Norfolk coast on return from Düsseldorf 12.6.43.
HR711	To 102 Sqn.
HR716 MH-S	From 158 Sqn. To 102 Sqn.
HR726 MH-B/LK-B	FTR Berlin 22/23.11.43.
HR727 MH-V	From 102 Sqn. Crashed in Derbyshire on return from Frankfurt 5.10.43.
HR728 LK-D	FTR Kassel 3/4.10.43.
HR729 MH-R	FTR Pilsen 16/17.4.43.
HR730	To 102 Sqn.
HR731 MH-C	FTR Gelsenkirchen 25/26.6.43.
HR732 MH-Y	From 77 Sqn. FTR Leipzig 3/4.12.43.
HR733	FTR Essen 30.4/1.5.43.
HR747	Crashed on landing at Snaith on return from Düsseldorf 25/26.5.43.
HR749 MH-J	FTR Essen 25/26.7.43.
HR750 MH-W	FTR Essen 27/28.5.43.
HR755	From 158 Sqn. To 78 Sqn.
HR778	FTR Duisburg 26/27.4.43.
HR782 MH-A/R	FTR Leipzig 3/4.12.43.
HR783	Crashed in Yorkshire while training 6.8.43.
HR784	FTR Pilsen 16/17.4.43.
HR786 MH-J	FTR Duisburg 12/13.5.43.
HR787	FTR Duisburg 26/27.4.43.

HR788	FTR Düsseldorf 11/12.6.43.
HR789 MH-Z	FTR Essen 27/28.5.43.
HR790	FTR Bochum 13/14.5.43.
HR834 MH-V/Q	To 102 Sqn.
HR835	FTR Dortmund 23/24.5.43.
HR836	FTR Dortmund 23/24.5.43.
HR838 MH-Q	FTR Nuremberg 10/11.8.43.
HR839 LK-L	FTR Cologne 28/29.6.43.
HR842	FTR Dortmund 23/24.5.43.
HR843 MH-A	Crashed near Gatwick on return from Gelsenkirchen 10.7.43.
HR844	FTR Dortmund 23/24.5.43.
HR852 MH-D	FTR Düsseldorf 11/12.6.43.
HR853	FTR Düsseldorf 25/26.5.43.
HR858	From 158 Sqn. To 78 Sqn.
HR859	FTR Hamburg 2/3.8.43.
HR868 MH-B	To 1656 CU.
HR869 MH-Z	FTR Nuremberg 27/28.8.43.
HR870 MH-H	Crashed on take-off from Snaith when training 18.10.43.
HR930	To 1662 CU.
HR931 MH-F	FTR Berlin 31.8/1.9.43.
HR934	FTR Essen 25/26.7.43.
HR935 LK-J	To 77 Sqn.
HR936 MH-J	FTR Berlin 23/24.8.43.
HR939 MH-R	To 1652 CU.
HR940	FTR Hamburg 24/25.7.43.
HR946 MH-T	To 77 Sqn.
HR947 MH-K	To 102 Sqn.
HR948 MH-W	FTR Frankfurt 20/21.12.43.
HR949 MH-E	To 77 Sqn.
HR950 MH-X/S	FTR from operations 20.11.43.
HR951	Crashed on landing at Snaith while training 19.8.43.
HR952 MH-X	To 10 Sqn.
HR981 MH-D	From 158 Sqn. Crashed in Lincolnshire when bound for Nuremberg 10.8.43.
HX228	From RAE. To 1658 CU.
HX237	To 466 Sqn.
HX241 MH-J	To 78 Sqn.
HX321 MH-H	From 35 Sqn. Crashed on landing at Snaith on return from Caen 18.7.44.
HX330 MH-V	FTR Stuttgart 15/16.3.44.
HX350 MH-U/Y	FTR Tergnier 18/19.4.44.
HX355	To 78 Sqn.
JB792	Crashed on landing at Woolfox Lodge on return from Dortmund 24.5.43.
JB806 MH-J	FTR Duisburg 12/13.5.43.
JD118 LK-K	To 78 Sqn.

F/S Eric Warburton, the Canadian wireless operator/air gunner on board F/L Barsby's 51 Squadron Whitley Z9141, which was shot down into the Waddenzee by Ofw Paul Gildner of II/NJG 1 close to Texel on the way home from Hamburg on 31 October 1941. There were no survivors, and all lie in Den Burg Cemetery. (*Photo: Andreas Wachtel*)

P/O Stanley Steel from New Zealand, who was 2nd pilot to F/L Barsby. (*Photo: Andreas Wachtel*)

10 Squadron Whitley ZA-W on final approach to Leeming circa 1941. (*Photo: Yorkshire Air Museum*)

58 Squadron Whitley Z6498 GE-D at Linton-on-Ouse in 1941. This aircraft failed to return from Warnemünde on the night of 11/12.9.41. (*Photo: Yorkshire Air Museum*)

Whitley N1361 after being brought down by Flak Abteilung 292 over Belgium on the night of 23/24 May 1940. Records suggest this was a 58 Squadron aircraft, but the code EY-F clearly shows it as belonging to fellow Linton-on-Ouse residents 78 Squadron. At the time, however, 78 Squadron was not operational and the crew on this night was from 58 Squadron. Pilot F/L McLaren lost his life, but his four crew mates survived as PoWs. (*Photo: Yorkshire Air Museum*)

Len Cheshire (front row centre) at Linton-on-Ouse during his time at 35 Squadron in 1941. In the background stands the Mk I Halifax L9503, TL-P, the twenty-first production model of more than 6,000 built. (*Photo: Yorkshire Air Museum*)

W/C Arthur 'Lofty' Lowe was promoted to the command of 77 Squadron in December 1942. Having joined the RAF as a 'Halton Brat' in 1930, he learned the trade of wireless operator/air gunner. As such, his appointment to the command of a bomber squadron was not popular among the pilots, particularly his two flight commanders who considered themselves to have been overlooked. In time, his characteristic firmness, fairness and friendliness to all ranks would win over the detractors, and he became a popular and well-respected leader. (*Photo: Yorkshire Air Museum*)

In October 1943 W/C J. Roncoroni (back row left) succeeded W/C Lowe as commanding officer of 77 Squadron. Over the following eleven months he would guide the squadron through Bomber Command's toughest period, which encompassed the campaigns against Berlin, the French railway system, V-Weapon sites, oil and tactical support for the invasion forces after D-Day. (*Photo: Yorkshire Air Museum*)

A formation of 77 Squadron Whitleys over a wintry Yorkshire scene. Undercarriage down, they seem to be on approach to land. On the ground is a parachute with rigging lines stretched out. Whitleys were sometimes employed to drop troops, although any connection here is pure speculation. (*Photo: Yorkshire Air Museum*)

419 Squadron CO, W/C J. 'Moose' Fulton, introduces Queen Elizabeth to 'Pete' Peters RCAF and his crew at Croft, autumn 1942. (*Photo: Yorkshire Air Museum*)

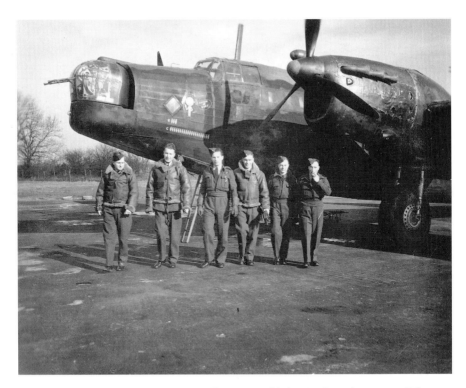

'Berlin or Bust', a Merlin-powered Wellington II with its 405 Squadron crew. (*Photo: Yorkshire Air Museum*)

158 Squadron's Halifax III, D-Dog, at Lissett. (*Photo: Yorkshire Air Museum*)

The famous 158 Squadron Halifax 'Friday the 13th', LV907, being prepared for a post-war exhibition on a bomb site in Oxford Street, London on 20 June 1945. LV907 completed 128 operations. (*Photo: Yorkshire Air Museum*)

October 1944. One of the 158 Squadron crews privileged to be associated with 'Friday'. Left to right: F/O Peters (bomb-aimer), Canada; F/S Murray (navigator), Canada; Sgt Hawthorn (flight engineer), England; F/O Gordon (pilot), Canada; F/S Hyde (mid-upper gunner), Canada; W/O Pye (rear gunner), Canada; F/S Little (wireless operator), USA. (*Photo: Yorkshire Air Museum*)

466 Squadron CO W/C Forsyth at debriefing with members of his crew. He later became station commander at Driffield. (*Photo: Yorkshire Air Museum*)

A Mk II Halifax of 102 Squadron stands ready for take-off on the threshold at Pocklington. (*Photo: Yorkshire Air Museum*)

Air-Commodore Gus Walker (seated centre), base commander, in the operations room at Pocklington in 1943. Standing behind him is W/C Carter. (*Photo: Yorkshire Air Museum*)

An early picture of Jimmy Marks (front row left) with his crew. One of the Command's stars, Jimmy's light shone bright as he progressed through the ranks to the command of 35 Squadron. During his six months at the helm, 35 Squadron was selected in August 1942 as a founder member of the Pathfinder Force. Barely a month later, on the night of 19/20 September, his Halifax W7657 TL-L fell victim to a night fighter over France during an operation to Saarbrücken. Marks and two of his crew were killed. (*Photo: Yorkshire Air Museum*)

Sgt William Foly was the bomb-aimer on board the 102 Squadron Halifax II JB918, DY-T. It was shot down into the sea north of Texel by Uffz Georg Kraft of IV/NJG 1out of Leeuwarden in the early hours of 27 April 1943. The Halifax was bound for Duisburg with an all-sergeant crew captained by Canadian Sgt Grainger, and there were no survivors. The bodies of Sgt Foly and his crew mate, mid-upper gunner Sgt Howard Beck, were washed ashore on Texel on the morning of the 28th, and buried with full military honours later that day. (*Photo: Yorkshire Air Museum*)

W/C David Wilkerson, the highly-esteemed first CO of 578 Squadron, who was tragically killed in a flying accident on 16 September 1944 at Rednal, Shropshire. (*Photo: Yorkshire Air Museum*)

W/C Hancock (third from right) and crew of 578 Squadron. Hancock was in command at the squadron's disbandment in March 1945. He spent the remainder of the war in command of 186 Squadron at Stradishall. (*Photo: Yorkshire Air Museum*)

W/C James (back row, second from right) with his crew after succeeding David Wilkerson as CO of 578 Squadron. (*Photo: Yorkshire Air Museum*)

78 Squadron CO, W/C Warner, with his crew by Halifax II W7930 EY-W at Breighton. This aircraft was shot down by flak over Holland during an operation to Mülheim on the night of 22/23 June 1943, when in the hands of an all NCO-crew. (*Photo: Yorkshire Air Museum*)

78 Squadron commanding officer, G/C Young, with his crew. (*Photo: Yorkshire Air Museum*)

F/L Wilkinson and five of his crew standing in front of a Wellington. This crew was lost in 10 Squadron Halifax JD974, ZA-T during an operation to Kassel on the night of 22/23 October 1943. (*Photo: Yorkshire Air Museum*)

Senior officers associated with 4 Group. Left to right: G/C Louis Greig; AVM Roddy Carr, AOC 4 Group; Sir Archibald Sinclair, Secretary of State for Air; W/C James Tait, CO of 78 Squadron and later 617 Squadron; G/C J.R. Whitely, station commander at Linton-on-Ouse; W/C Len Cheshire, CO of 76 Squadron and later 617 Squadron. (*Photo: Yorkshire Air Museum*)

'Bambi' of 640 Squadron at Leconfield. (*Photo: Yorkshire Air Museum*)

640 Squadron air and ground crew with Halifax III in June 1944. (*Photo: Yorkshire Air Museum*)

Halifax H7-O of 346 Squadron at Elvington on return from ops April 1945. (*Photo: Yorkshire Air Museum*)

578 Squadron's F/L Maxie Baer of Toronto buzzing the tower at Burn on the completion of his tour. (*Photo: Yorkshire Air Museum*)

French Halifaxes over Paris suburbs post-war. (*Photo: Yorkshire Air Museum*)

10 Squadron's RG442 ZA-E with Australian Dick Morris and his mixed-nationality crew at Melbourne in 1945. (*Photo: Yorkshire Air Museum*)

JD123 MH-S	From 77 Sqn. FTR Frankfurt 20/21.12.43.
JD125	To 77 Sqn.
JD153	To 1658 CU.
JD244 MH-K	FTR Krefeld 21/22.6.43.
JD245	To 502 Sqn.
JD248 MH-S	To 78 Sqn.
JD250 MH-R	FTR Wuppertal 24/25.6.43.
JD251 MH-X	FTR Mülheim 22/23.6.43.
JD252 MH-T	To 78 Sqn.
JD253 LK-A/E	FTR Hanover 8/9.10.43.
JD261 MH-J	FTR Gelsenkirchen 25/26.6.43.
JD262 MH-J	FTR Cologne 3/4.7.43.
JD263	FTR Mannheim/Ludwigshafen 5/6.9.43.
JD264 MH-U/LK-H	FTR Berlin 29/30.12.43.
JD266 LK-C	To 1659 CU.
JD299 LK-F	To 1663 CU.
JD300 MH-Y	From 158 Sqn. To 78 Sqn.
JD302	From 77 Sqn. To 102 Sqn.
JD308	To 1652 CU.
JD309	FTR Hamburg 29/30.7.43.
JD310	To 78 Sqn.
JD311 MH-L	To 102 Sqn.
JD461 LK-E	From 77 Sqn. To 102 Sqn.
JN883 LK-A	To 10 Sqn.
JN885 MH-A	FTR Hanover 8/9.10.43.
JN887	From 158 Sqn. To 78 Sqn.
JN891	To 102 Sqn.
JN899 LK-K	To 10 Sqn.
JN900	Crash-landed at Ridgewell following early return from Hanover 27/28.9.43.
JN901	FTR Hanover 22/23.9.43.
JN902 MH-H	FTR Berlin 31.8/1.9.43.
JN906 MH-D	To 78 Sqn.
JN917 MH-W	To 10 Sqn.
JN919 MH-B	From 158 Sqn. To 78 Sqn.
JN920 LK-L	FTR Kassel 22/23.10.43.
JN922 MH-Z	Crash-landed at Snaith following air-test 5.12.43.
JN923 MH-F	Damaged beyond repair during a bombing exercise 20.12.43.
JN924 MH-H/D	Damaged beyond repair by enemy action during mining sortie 2/3.10.43.
LK748	To 1658 CU.
LK750 MH-Y/Y2	FTR Frankfurt 18/19.3.44.
LK751	To 1663 CU.
LK753 MH-B	To 10 Sqn.
LK756 MH-J	To 578 Sqn.
LK812 MH-E	To 10 Sqn.
LK827	To 10 Sqn.

LK830	From 578 Sqn.
LK835 MH-U	Abandoned over Wales while training 22.5.44.
LK843	To 578 Sqn and back.
LK844 MH-M	Crashed in Yorkshire during training flight 14.11.44.
LK845	To 431 Sqn.
LK846	To 578 Sqn.
LK885 MH-Z	FTR Aachen 24/25.5.44.
LL270	To 644 Sqn.
LL328	To 644 Sqn.
LL331	To 644 Sqn.
LL548	From 578 Sqn.
LL612 MH-A/C6-A	Crashed on landing at Snaith on return from Essen 25.10.44.
LV774 MH-B	FTR Magdeburg 21/22.1.44.
LV775 MH-G	FTR Magdeburg 21/22.1.44.
LV777 MH-F/F2	FTR Nuremberg 30/31.3.44.
LV778 MH-T/C6-D C6-B	FTR Schweinfurt 24/25.2.44.
LV779 MH-L	FTR Magdeburg 21/22.1.44.
LV782 MH-T/E	From 35 Sqn. FTR Villers-Bocage 30.6.44.
LV783 MH-R/Z	FTR Montzen 27/28.4.44.
LV784 LK-K/MH-S	To 578 Sqn and back. FTR Aachen 24/25.5.44.
LV815	To 578 Sqn.
LV817	To 78 Sqn.
LV818	To 35 Sqn.
LV819 C6-F	From 78 Sqn. Damaged beyond repair during operation to Bochum 4/5.11.44.
LV820	To 578 Sqn.
LV822 MH-Z2	From 10 Sqn. FTR Nuremberg 30/31.3.44.
LV832 MH-P/X	From 10 Sqn.
LV857 MH-H2	From 10 Sqn. FTR Nuremberg 30/31.3.44.
LV862 MH-K/A	From 10 Sqn. Abandoned over UK on return from Croixdale 6.7.44.
LV865 MH-Y	From 10 Sqn. Crashed on take-off from Snaith when bound for Boulogne 17.9.44.
LV876	From 78 Sqn.
LV880 MH-E/C	From 10 Sqn. FTR Tergnier 10/11.4.44.
LV937 MH-E	From 578 Sqn. Completed over 100 operations.
LV952 MH-F	From 578 Sqn. FTR Hanover 5/6.1.45.
LW177 MH-N	FTR Bochum 4/5.11.44.
LW194	From 424 Sqn.
LW227	From 77 Sqn. To 102 Sqn.
LW286 LK-H	FTR Berlin 22/23.11.43.
LW287 MH-C	FTR from mining sortie 2/3.10.43.
LW289 MH-U/J	To 10 Sqn.
LW291	From 158 Sqn. To 78 Sqn.
LW299 MH-B	From 158 Sqn. To 102 Sqn.
LW348 LK-X	To 578 Sqn.

LW362 C6-C	To 578 Sqn and back. Crashed on landing at Snaith while training 25.8.44.
LW364 MH-K/B	Crashed in Yorkshire on return from Chateaudun 9.6.44.
LW442 MH-Q	To 187 Sqn.
LW445 MH-Z	To 1658 CU.
LW461 MH-D/Y	FTR Magdeburg 16/17.1.45.
LW465	From 78 Sqn. To 578 Sqn.
LW466 MH-H	FTR Berlin 28/29.1.44.
LW468	To 578 Sqn and back. FTR Magdeburg 21/22.1.44.
LW469 LK-A	To 578 Sqn.
LW470	To 158 Sqn.
LW471 MH-D	To 578 Sqn.
LW472 MH-H	To 578 Sqn.
LW473 MH-E	To 578 Sqn.
LW474 MH-B	To 578 Sqn.
LW475 MH-E	To 578 Sqn.
LW478	To 578 Sqn.
LW479 MH-E	FTR Montzen 27/28.4.44.
LW480 MH-A	To 347 Sqn.
LW481 MH-X	FTR Leipzig 19/20.2.44.
LW495 MH-C	To 578 Sqn.
LW496 MH-S/C6-A	To 578 Sqn.
LW497 MH-W	FTR Stuttgart 15/16.3.44.
LW498 C6-T MH-Z/T	FTR Aachen 24/25.5.44.
LW503	To 578 Sqn.
LW504 MH-Q C6-E/D	To 347 Sqn.
LW508 LK-Y	To 578 Sqn.
LW521	From 78 Sqn. To 466 Sqn.
LW522 MH-J	From 78 Sqn. FTR Tergnier 18/19.4.44.
LW537 MH-C2	FTR Nuremberg 30/31.3.44.
LW538 MH-T/N	To 578 Sqn and back. FTR Sterkrade 18/19.8.44.
LW539 MH-H/N/N2	To 578 Sqn and back. FTR Berlin 24/25.3.44.
LW540	To 578 Sqn.
LW541 MH-Y/C6-J	To 347 Sqn.
LW542	To 578 Sqn.
LW543 MH-R	To 578 Sqn.
LW544 MH-Q2	FTR Nuremberg 30/31.3.44.
LW545 MH-K/C6-D	To 10 Sqn.
LW546 C6-L/MH-R	FTR Hazebrouck 6.8.44.
LW553	To 578 Sqn.
LW556	From 578 Sqn. To 1665 CU.
LW557	To 578 Sqn.
LW578 C6-F	Crashed on landing at Snaith while training 22.4.44.
LW579 C6-E/MH-V	Crashed in Oxfordshire on return from Nuremberg 30/31.3.44.

LW588 MH-S/O	FTR Somain 11.8.44.
LW642 MH-L	To 347 Sqn.
LW671 MH-K	Crash-landed in Suffolk on return from Essen 27.3.44.
LW677 C6-B	To 158 Sqn.
LW679 MH-R	Crash-landed at Snaith while training 22.3.44.
LW689	From 429 Sqn. To 434 Sqn.
MZ319 MH-B	From 578 Sqn. FTR Gelsenkirchen 11.9.44.
MZ343 MH-T	FTR Sterkrade 6.10.44.
MZ348 MH-D	FTR Rheine 21.3.45.
MZ349 MH-U	FTR Brunswick 12/13.8.44.
MZ401	To 462 Sqn.
MZ402	To 462 Sqn.
MZ451 MH-F	From 424 Sqn. FTR Cologne 2.3.45.
MZ465 MH-Y	
MZ484	
MZ485	From 578 Sqn.
MZ487 MH-Z	FTR Wanne-Eickel 2/3.2.45.
MZ507 MH-P/P2	FTR Berlin 24/25.3.44.
MZ535	To 1658 CU.
MZ563	To 578 Sqn.
MZ565 MH-O	FTR Montzen 27/28.4.44.
MZ566 MH-Y	FTR Düsseldorf 22/23.4.44.
MZ571	To 347 Sqn.
MZ581 C6-C	Crashed on approach to Woodbridge on return from Bottrop 21.7.44.
MZ593 MH-Z	FTR Mechelen 1/2.5.44.
MZ624 MH-N	Damaged beyond repair during operation to Gelsenkirchen 11.9.44.
MZ634 MH-U	To 1659 CU.
MZ635	To 347 Sqn.
MZ643 MH-Z	Damaged beyond repair during operation to Amiens 12/13.6.44.
MZ689	To 77 Sqn.
MZ708	To 77 Sqn.
MZ743	To 77 Sqn.
MZ754 MH-U	From 424 Sqn.
MZ758 MH-V	Belly-landed near Strubby on return from Venlo airfield 3.9.44.
MZ765 MH-E	From 77 Sqn. Crashed in Sussex when bound for Wesel 17.2.45.
MZ766 MH-B/Z	
MZ767 MH-D	FTR Hanover 5/6.1.45.
MZ771	From 578 Sqn.
MZ790	From 578 Sqn.
MZ794 MH-T	From 578 Sqn. FTR Stuttgart 28/29.1.45.
MZ811 MH-X	FTR Hanau 6/7.1.45.
MZ820	

MZ821 MH-H	FTR Bottrop 20/21.7.44.
MZ851	
MZ868	
MZ870	Crashed on landing at Snaith while training 1.10.44.
MZ897	From 424 Sqn.
MZ916 MH-O	FTR Gelsenkirchen 11.9.44.
MZ917 MH-R	To 158 Sqn.
MZ918 MH-U	FTR Hanover 5/6.1.45.
MZ933 MH-W	FTR Bochum 4/5.11.44.
MZ934 MH-P	
MZ938	From 578 Sqn.
MZ972 MH-O	FTR Calais 24.9.44.
MZ974 MH-N	
MZ988	From 578 Sqn
NA123	From 578 Sqn.
NA150 MH-N	
NA196 MH-N	To EANS.
NA200	
NA493	To Handley Page.
NA496 MH-L	To 187 Sqn.
NA525	From 578 Sqn.
NA529	To 578 Sqn.
NA625	To 187 Sqn.
NA626	
NP932 MH-J	Crashed on approach to Snaith on return from Homberg 14.3.45.
NP933 MH-M	FTR Cleves 7.10.44.
NP934 MH-V	FTR Duisburg 17/18.12.44.
NP962 MH-V	
NP963 MH-R	
NP972	
NP974	To 1652 CU.
NR128 MH-S	Crashed on landing at Snaith while training 27.10.44.
NR129 MH-M	FTR Sterkrade 21/22.11.44.
NR142 MH-S	
NR202	
NR241 MH-A	Collided with MZ559 (578 Sqn) on approach to Snaith on return from Münster 18.11.44.
NR245	From 10 Sqn.
NR248 MH-A	FTR Duisburg 17/18.12.44.
NR254 MH-A	To Leconfield.
NR255 C6-H	From 578 Sqn.
PN184 MH-Q	To 640 Sqn.
RG445	
RG446 MH-U	

Heaviest Single Loss

30/31.3.44.	Nuremberg. 6 Halifaxes. 5 FTR, 1 Crashed.

58 SQUADRON

Motto: Alis Nocturnis (On the wings of the night)   **Code: GE**

First formed on 8 June 1916, 58 Squadron initially performed an advanced training role. It moved to France in January 1918 and carried out night operations against enemy bases and communications. In May 1919 the squadron began flying its aircraft to Egypt, where it was ultimately renumbered. Resurrected as a bomber unit in April 1924, the squadron operated a number of types before Whitleys began to arrive in October 1937. One of the mainstays of 4 Group in the early war years, a number of 58 Squadron's Whitleys were operational on the first night of hostilities to dispense propaganda leaflets over Germany. A month later the squadron was loaned to Coastal Command, but returned in February 1940 to produce an impressive record of service until its permanent posting to Coastal Command in April 1942.

STATIONS

Linton-on-Ouse	20.04.38 to 06.10.39
Boscombe Down	06.10.39 to 14.02.40
Linton-on-Ouse	14.02.40 to 08.04.42

COMMANDING OFFICERS

Wing Commander J. Potter	14.07.36 to 05.40
Wing Commander J.J.A. Sutton	05.40 to 07.11.40
Wing Commander K.B.F. Smith	07.11.40 to 15.06.41
Wing Commander R.W.M. Clark	15.06.41 to 01.08.42

AIRCRAFT

Whitley III	05.39 to 03.40
Whitley V	03.40 to 12.42

OPERATIONAL RECORD

Operations	Sorties	Aircraft Losses	% Losses
227	1,757	49	2.8

Category of Operations

Bombing	Leaflet
219	8

TABLE OF STATISTICS
Out of 25 operational squadrons in 4 Group

9th highest number of overall operations in 4 Group.
11th highest number of sorties in 4 Group.
9th highest number of aircraft operational losses in 4 Group.

Out of 6 Whitley squadrons in 4 Group

3rd highest number of overall Whitley operations in 4 Group.

2nd highest number of Whitley sorties in 4 Group.
4th highest number of Whitley operational losses in 4 Group.

AIRCRAFT HISTORIES

Whitley	To April 1942.
K8962	From 7 Sqn. To 10 OTU.
K8964 GE-R	From 7 Sqn. Damaged beyond repair. Operated on the first night of the war. SOC 23.1.40.
K8965	From 7 Sqn. Crashed on take-off from Reims-Champagne when bound for a leafleting sortie 11.9.39.
K8967 BW-D	From 7 Sqn. To 19 OTU.
K8969 GE-G	From 7 Sqn. Force-landed in France following leafleting sortie to the Ruhr on the first night of the war 4.9.39.
K8971	From 7 Sqn. To 10 BGS.
K8972	From 7 Sqn. To 10 OTU.
K8973 GE-K	From 7 Sqn. Operated on the first night of the war. To 10 OTU.
K8974	From 7 Sqn. To 19 OTU.
K8975	From 7 Sqn. To 10 OTU.
K8976	To 77 Sqn.
K8977	To 77 Sqn.
K8979 BW-H	From 51 Sqn. To 10 OTU.
K8990 GE-L	From 7 Sqn. Operated on the first night of the war. To 19 OTU.
K8999	From 97 Sqn. To 19 OTU.
K9000 GE-J	From 97 Sqn. To 19 OTU.
K9003	From 97 Sqn. To 166 Sqn.
K9004	From 97 Sqn. To 10 OTU.
K9005	From 97 Sqn. To 10 OTU.
K9006 BW-E	From 97 Sqn. Operated on the first night of the war. To 1 AAS.
K9007 BW-F	From 97 Sqn. To 10 OTU.
K9009 GE-M	From 97 Sqn. Operated on the first night of the war. To 10 BGS.
K9013 GE-W	From 97 Sqn. Operated on the first night of the war. To 166 Sqn.
N1361 GE-F	From 78 Sqn. FTR from communications target 23/24.5.40.
N1371 GE-L	To 102 Sqn.
N1389 GE-V	To 78 Sqn.
N1418	From 51 Sqn. To 19 OTU.
N1424 GE-P	FTR Leverkusen 11/12.7.40.
N1426 GE-O	To 19 OTU.
N1427 GE-K	Ditched off Margate on return from Genoa 3.9.40.
N1428 GE-B	To 10 BGS.

N1433 GE-D/E	To 102 Sqn.
N1434 GE-E	FTR Frankfurt-an-Oder 2/3.10.40.
N1435	To 77 Sqn.
N1436 GE-F	To 144 Sqn via 97 Sqn. Returned to 58 Sqn. To 10 OTU.
N1442 GE-N	FTR Essen 20/21.6.40.
N1444	To 10 OTU.
N1459 GE-A	Ditched off Harwich on return from Genoa 3.9.40.
N1460 GE-R	FTR Castrop-Rauxel 18/19.6.40.
N1461 GE-F	FTR Kiel (Scharnhorst) 1/2.7.40.
N1462 GE-V	FTR Cologne 17/18.6.41.
N1463 GE-L	FTR Gelsenkirchen 17/18.6.40.
N1465 GE-G	FTR Stavanger 30.4/1.5.40.
N1466	To 19 OTU.
N1469	To 1502 Flt.
N1470 GE-J	Crashed on take-off from Linton-on-Ouse when bound for Berlin 24.9.40.
N1472	FTR Paderborn 22/23.7.40.
N1521 GE-J	From 77 Sqn. FTR Wilhelmshaven 15/16.1.41.
N1527 GE-S	To 10 OTU.
P4941	To 78 Sqn.
P4943 GE-P	From BATDU. FTR Hamburg 6/7.11.40.
P4951	To 42 OTU.
P4988 GE-L	To 2 BAT Flt.
P4991 GE-N	FTR Düsseldorf 2/3.6.41.
P5002 GE-T	Abandoned over Yorkshire coast on return from Berlin 31.8.40.
P5003	To 19 OTU.
P5008 GE-M	FTR Hamm 18/19.9.40.
P5028	SOC post-war.
P5057	Lost after Squadron's posting to Coastal Command on 6.4.42.
P5058 GE-F	Ditched off Lincolnshire Coast on return from Pilsen 21.10.40.
P5076	To 19 OTU.
P5089 GE-D	Ditched off Norfolk coast on return from Pilsen 21.10.40.
P5097	To 102 Sqn.
P5098 GE-Q	Crashed on landing at Linton-on-Ouse following early return from Boulogne 23.12.40.
T4134 GE-T	From 77 Sqn. FTR Bremen 10/11.9.40.
T4137 GE-K	Crashed near Bircham Newton on return from Gelsenkirchen 7/8.10.40.
T4145 GE-P	From 51 Sqn. FTR Kiel 7/8.4.41.
T4146	To 102 Sqn.
T4150 GE-C	Crashed near Driffield on return from Stettin 15.10.40.
T4151	To 77 Sqn.

T4159 GE-J	FTR Mannheim 23/24.12.40.
T4170 GE-T	FTR Berlin 14/15.11.40.
T4171 GE-O	Shot down by intruder over Yorkshire on return from Pilsen 21.10.40.
T4174 GE-X	FTR Berlin 14/15.11.40.
T4176	From 10 Sqn. To 1481 Flt.
T4207 GE-D	Crashed in Yorkshire on return from Lorient 3.12.40.
T4210 GE-E	To 29 OTU.
T4211	SOC 31.12.40.
T4213 GE-K	Abandoned over Nottinghamshire on return from Bremen 12.2.41.
T4235 GE-O	To 102 Sqn.
T4236 GE-E	To 102 Sqn.
T4239 GE-M	FTR Berlin 14/15.11.40.
T4260	To 77 Sqn.
T4266 GE-O	Ditched in the North Sea on return from Berlin 18.4.41.
T4284	To 10 OTU.
T4285 GE-O	Crashed soon after take-off from Linton-on-Ouse when bound for Emden 24.7.41.
T4322 GE-R	Abandoned over Scotland on return from Bremen 12.2.41.
T4336 GE-E	From 102 Sqn. Crashed on landing at Church Fenton on return from Brest 5.5.41.
T4339	To 42 OTU.
Z6462 GE-D	FTR Wilhelmshaven 16/17.1.41.
Z6464	To 10 OTU.
Z6465 GE-U	Crashed in Shropshire on return from Brest 3.3.41.
Z6469 GE-L	From 51 Sqn. To 1481 Flt.
Z6485	To 102 Sqn.
Z6497	To 19 OTU.
Z6498 GE-D	FTR Warnemünde 11/12.9.41.
Z6499	To 10 OTU.
Z6504 GE-K	Ditched off Essex coast on return from Frankfurt 30.8.41.
Z6505	To 51 Sqn.
Z6506 GE-V	FTR Hamburg 30.11/1.12.41.
Z6507 GE-X	FTR Hamburg 30.11/1.12.41.
Z6575 GE-B	FTR Hamburg 30.11/1.12.41.
Z6580 GE-A	To 19 OTU.
Z6644 GE-O	FTR Osnabrück 7/8.7.41.
Z6656	From 10 Sqn. To 78 Sqn.
Z6659	To 10 OTU.
Z6660	To BOAC.
Z6666 GE-E	FTR Hamm 8/9.7.41.
Z6723	To 19 OTU.
Z6729 GE-T	FTR Cologne 16/17.8.41.
Z6739	To 3 OTU.

Z6814	From 10 Sqn. To 77 Sqn.
Z6818 GE-N	To 77 Sqn and back twice. FTR Essen 7/8.11.41.
Z6821	From 102 Sqn. To 1481 Flt.
Z6835 GE-Q	Crashed at Linton-on-Ouse on return from Frankfurt 7.8.41.
Z6836 GE-J	FTR Berlin 7/8.9.41.
Z6841 GE-F	FTR Düsseldorf 27/28.12.41.
Z6865 GE-V	Abandoned over Norfolk during operation to Ostend 20.9.41.
Z6869 GE-T	Crashed in Northumberland following recall when bound for Brest 3.9.41.
Z6931 GE-O	Abandoned over Yorkshire on return from Warnemünde 12.9.41.
Z6936 GE-Q	FTR Stettin 19/20.9.41.
Z6939 GE-E	Crashed while landing at Linton-on-Ouse on return from Stettin 30.9.41.
Z6944 GE-R	FTR Stettin 29/30.9.41.
Z6947	FTR Berlin 7/8.9.41.
Z6972 GE-P	FTR Berlin 7/8.11.41.
Z6977	From 78 Sqn. To 1481 Flt.
Z9119 GE-U	From 10 Sqn. To 51 Sqn.
Z9124	From 502 Sqn. To 77 Sqn.
Z9135	From 612 Sqn. To 3 OTU.
Z9142	To 77 Sqn.
Z9153	To 51 Sqn.
Z9154 GE-T	FTR Essen 10/11.10.41.
Z9155 GE-G	Crashed near Pocklington on return from Nuremberg 13.10.41.
Z9161	From 78 Sqn. Lost after Squadron's posting to Coastal Command on 6.4.42.
Z9195	To Coastal Command with 58 Sqn on 6.4.42.
Z9200	To 19 OTU.
Z9203 GE-O	To 10 OTU.
Z9204	Ditched off Skegness on return from Essen 11.10.41.
Z9205	FTR Berlin 7/8.11.41.
Z9208	To BOAC.
Z9209	To 77 Sqn.
Z9210 GE-J	FTR Düsseldorf 27/28.12.41.
Z9211 GE-Q	Ditched off Grimsby on return from Hamburg 30.11/1.12.41.
Z9227 GE-R	From 10 Sqn. FTR Emden 12/13.3.42.
Z9291	Lost after Squadron's posting to Coastal Command on 6.4.42.
Z9295	To 138 Sqn.
Z9305	From 78 Sqn. Shot down by friendly fire off Harwich when bound for Rotterdam 28.1.42.
Z9317 GE-L	To 77 Sqn.
Z9361	To 1485 Flt.

Z9374	To Coastal Command with 58 Sqn on 6.4.42.
Z9388	Lost after Squadron's posting to Coastal Command on 6.4.42.
Z9426	Lost after Squadron's posting to Coastal Command on 6.4.42.
Z9427	To 19 OTU.
Z9429 GE-E	To 77 Sqn.
Z9442	Lost after Squadron's posting to Coastal Command on 6.4.42.
Z9516	To Coastal Command with 58 Sqn on 6.4.42.
Z9517	Lost after Squadron's posting to Coastal Command on 6.4.42.
Z9518	Lost after Squadron's posting to Coastal Command on 6.4.42.
Z9521	Lost after Squadron's posting to Coastal Command on 6.4.42.
Z9522	Lost after Squadron's posting to Coastal Command on 6.4.42.
Z9524	Lost after Squadron's posting to Coastal Command on 6.4.42.
Z9525	Lost after Squadron's posting to Coastal Command on 6.4.42.
Z9526	To Coastal Command with 58 Sqn on 6.4.42.
Z9527	To Coastal Command with 58 Sqn on 6.4.42.
Z9528	To Coastal Command with 58 Sqn on 6.4.42.
AD711 GE-Z	To 77 Sqn.
BD189 GE-J	To 10 OTU.
BD207	To 19 OTU.
BD210	

76 SQUADRON

Motto: Resolute   **Code: MP**

Reformed on 1 May 1941, 76 Squadron became the second in Bomber Command to receive the Halifax. As an early recipient of the type, the squadron had large numbers of them pass through its hands. As many of the essential modifications could not be retro-fitted the process rendered previous variants obsolete, and they had to be replaced by fresh batches. Part of the squadron was posted to the Middle East in July 1942, while the home echelon was rebuilt to include a number of Norwegian crews. The first 8,000lb bomb was delivered by a 76 Squadron Halifax onto Essen in April 1942. Among its impressive list of commanding officers was Leonard Cheshire, who would go on to command 617 Squadron, better known as the Dambusters. At the conclusion of his operational career in July 1944, he would be awarded the Victoria Cross for his services to Bomber Command. Cheshire's brother Christopher was also a pilot with 76 Squadron until becoming a PoW in August 1941. 76 Squadron remained at the forefront of 4 Group operations until war's end and produced an impressive record of service.

STATIONS

Linton-on-Ouse	12.04.41 to 04.06.41
Middleton-St-George	04.06.41 to 17.09.42
Lossiemouth (detachment)	27.01.42 to 06.02.42
Tain, Ross and Cromarty (detachment)	27.03.42 to 08.04.42
	21.04.42 to 30.04.42
Linton-on-Ouse	17.09.42 to 16.06.43
Holme-on-Spalding-Moor	16.06.43 to 07.08.45

COMMANDING OFFICERS

Wing Commander S.O. Bufton DFC	12.04.41 to 28.05.41
Wing Commander G.T. Jarman DSO DFC	28.05.41 to 04.09.41
Wing Commander J.J.A. Sutton DFC	04.09.41 to 09.11.41
Squadron Leader J.T. Bouwens DFC (temp)	10.11.41 to 15.12.41
Wing Commander D.O. Young DFC AFC	15.12.41 to 14.07.42
Squadron Leader C.C. Calder DFC (temp)	14.07.42 to 05.08.42
Wing Commander G.L. Cheshire DSO DFC	05.08.42 to 07.04.43
Wing Commander D.C. Smith DFC	07.04.43 to 22.12.43
Wing Commander D. Iveson DSO DFC	22.12.43 to 14.08.44
Wing Commander R.K. Cassels DFC	14.08.44 to 24.01.45
Wing Commander L.G.A. Whyte	24.01.45 to 14.06.45

AIRCRAFT

Halifax I	04.41 to 12.42
Halifax II	10.41 to 09.43
Halifax V	02.43 to 07.44
Halifax III	01.44 to 05.45
Halifax VI	02.45 to 10.45

OPERATIONAL RECORD

Operations	Sorties	Aircraft Losses	% Losses
396	5,123	139	2.7

Category of Operations

Bombing	Mining	Other
376	17	3

TABLE OF STATISTICS
29th highest number of overall operations in Bomber Command.
24th highest number of sorties in Bomber Command.
25th highest number of aircraft operational losses in Bomber Command.
26th highest number of bombing operations in Bomber Command.

Out of 32 Halifax squadrons in Bomber Command
(Excluding SOE)
2nd highest number of overall Halifax operations in Bomber Command.
2nd highest number of Halifax sorties in Bomber Command.
4th highest number of Halifax operational losses in Bomber Command.

Out of 25 operational squadrons in 4 Group
6th highest number of overall operations in 4 Group.
7th highest number of sorties in 4 Group.
6th highest number of aircraft operational losses in 4 Group.

Out of 15 operational Halifax squadrons in 4 Group
2nd highest number of overall Halifax operations in 4 Group.
2nd highest number of Halifax sorties in 4 Group.
4th highest number of Halifax operational losses in 4 Group.

AIRCRAFT HISTORIES

Halifax	From May 1941.
L9488	From 35 Sqn. Crashed on take-off at Middleton-St-George 2.8.41.
L9492	From 35 Sqn. FTR Kiel 23/24.6.41.
L9494	From 35 Sqn. FTR La Pallice 24.7.41.
L9496	From 35 Sqn. To 28 Halifax CF 28.10.41.
L9510	From 35 Sqn. To 102 CF 2.7.42.
L9513	From 35 Sqn. To 28 Halifax CF 28.10.41.
L9514	From 35 Sqn. Crashed on landing at Middleton-St-George 15.6.41.
L9516	From 35 Sqn. FTR Karlsruhe 5/6.8.41.
L9517	From 35 Sqn. FTR La Pallice 24.7.41.
L9518	From 35 Sqn. Abandoned near Pocklington on return from Frankfurt 30.8.41.
L9519	From 35 Sqn. To 1652 CU on loan.
L9523 MP-Y	From 35 Sqn. To 78 CF 13.7.42.
L9528 MP-P	From 35 Sqn. To 1658 CU 31.12.42.
L9529	From 35 Sqn. FTR La Pallice 24.7.41.
L9530 MP-L	From 35 Sqn. FTR Berlin 12/13.8.41.
L9531 MP-R	FTR Berlin 12/13.8.41.
L9532	To 1652 CU 16.1.42.
L9533	Crashed on approach to Middleton-St-George while training 21.7.41.
L9534 MP-N/T	To 28 Halifax CF 2.11.41.
L9561 MP-H	FTR Bremen 12/13.10.41.
L9562	Crashed on approach to Middleton-St-George on return from Berlin 13.8.41.

L9563 MP-U	To 78 CF 17.6.42.
L9564 MP-A	From 12 MU. To 28 Halifax CF 18.11.41.
L9565 MP-B	To 28 Halifax CF 28.10.41.
L9567 MP-N	From 45 MU. Crashed near Bedford on return from Brest 14.9.41.
L9570 MP-E	From 8 MU. Crashed on landing at Tain, Scotland while training 6.2.42.
L9573 MP-D	To 1658 CU 31.12.42.
L9574 MP-R/C	To 76 CF 30.6.42.
L9577	To 1658 CU via 76 CF.
L9578 MP-C	From 12 MU. Crashed on landing at Middleton-St-George during training 15.1.42.
L9581 MP-Q	From 37 MU. Ditched off Aberdeen on return from Trondheim (*Tirpitz*) 30.1.42.
L9583 MP-M	From 45 MU. To 78 Sqn 20.2.42.
L9601 MP-F	From 8 MU. To 78 Sqn 20.2.42.
L9602 MP-N	From 45 MU. FTR Dunkerque 31.10/1.11.41.
L9604 MP-W	From 12 MU. Crashed on landing at Middleton-St-George on return from Hamburg 30.11/1.12.41.
L9608 MP-H	From 24 MU. To 1652 CU 14.2.42.
L9609 MP-V	From 37 MU. To 1652 CU 14.2.42.
L9611 MP-J	From 45 MU. Crashed on take-off from Middleton-St-George while training 17.1.42.
L9615 MP-X	From 24 MU. FTR Brest 30.12.41.
L9617 MP-A	From 37 MU. To 78 Sqn 27.2.42.
L9620 MP-O	To 78 Sqn via 76 CF & 1658 CU.
R9364	From 35 Sqn. To 78 Sqn 27.2.42.
R9365 MP-W/C	From 10 Sqn. FTR Essen 16/17.9.42.
R9366 MP-U	From 10 Sqn. Conversion Flt only. To 1658 CU.
R9373 MP-W	From 10 Sqn. To 78 Sqn 27.2.42.
R9375 MP-T	To 78 Sqn 27.2.42.
R9378 MP-K	From 78 Sqn. To 76 CF. Caught fire at Middleton-St-George while preparing for an operation to Bremen 25.6.42.
R9379 MP-L	From 12 MU. Crashed on landing 17.1.42.
R9382	From 10 Sqn. Conversion Flt only. To 408 CF 22.10.42.
R9384	From 12 MU. To 10 Sqn 3.9.42.
R9385	From Flight Refuelling Ltd. To RAE 8.10.42.
R9386 MP-J	From 35 Sqn. To 78 Sqn 27.2.42.
R9387 MP-Z	From 10 Sqn. To 1658 CU via 76 CF.
R9391 MP-K	From 102 Sqn. To 78 Sqn 22.2.42.
R9420 MP-G	To 78 Sqn 27.2.42.
R9427	To 78 Sqn 27.2.42.
R9430	From 10 CF. To 78 CF via 76 CF.
R9434	To 78 Sqn 27.2.42.
R9447 MP-R	To 78 Sqn 22.6.42.
R9451 MP-H	FTR Hamburg 3/4.5.42.

R9452 MP-L	Abandoned over Yorkshire after aborting sortie to Essen 13.4.42.
R9453 MP-L	FTR Aas Fjord (*Tirpitz*) 30/31.3.42.
R9454 MP-S	To 78 Sqn 24.6.42.
R9455 MP-C/O	To 78 Sqn 24.6.42.
R9456 MP-F	FTR Warnemünde 8/9.5.42.
R9457 MP-A	FTR Bremen 3/4.6.42.
R9482 MP-D	Crashed on take-off from Middleton-St-George on air-test 25.6.42.
R9484 MP-G	FTR Essen 10/11.4.42.
R9485 MP-P/H	To 76 CF. FTR Hamburg 26/27.7.42.
R9486 MP-Q	To 1652 CU and back. To 78 CF 25.8.42.
R9487 MP-M/X	FTR Essen 12/13.4.42.
V9980 MP-B	To 10 Sqn 27.2.42.
V9992 MP-M	From 1427 Flt. Crashed in Yorkshire while training 18.8.42.
W1006 EY-K	From 78 Sqn on loan retaining 78 Sqn codes.
W1013 EY-E	From 78 Sqn on loan retaining 78 Sqn codes.
W1014 EY-V	To 78 Sqn 27.2.42. From 78 Sqn on loan retaining 78 Sqn codes.
W1016 MP-B	FTR Osnabrück 9/10.8.42.
W1017 MP-T	FTR Dunkerque 27/28.4.42.
W1018 MP-M/EY-D	To 78 Sqn 22.6.42. From 78 Sqn on loan retaining 78 Sqn codes.
W1035 MP-U	Crashed on landing at Middleton-St-George on return from Bremen 4.6.42.
W1036 MP-Y/EY-K	To 78 Sqn 24.6.42. From 78 Sqn on loan retaining 78 Sqn codes.
W1063 EY-T	From 78 Sqn on loan retaining 78 Sqn codes.
W1064 MP-J	FTR Essen 1/2.6.42.
W1065 MP-G	FTR Gennevilliers 29/30.5.42.
W1093 EY-S	From 78 Sqn on loan retaining 78 Sqn codes.
W1104 MP-F	FTR Bremen 3/4.6.42.
W1106 MP-B	From 10 Sqn. FTR Osnabrück 9/10.8.42.
W1114 MP-F	From 8 MU. FTR Emden 20/21.6.42.
W1115	From 8 MU. To 78 Sqn 23.6.42.
W1144 MP-Q	To 78 Sqn and back. To Middle East 10.7.42.
W1148 MP-P	From 8 MU. To Middle East 16.7.42.
W1149 MP-R	From 78 Sqn. To Middle East 16.7.42.
W1150 MP-M	From 78 Sqn. Returned to 78 Sqn 1.8.42.
W1156 MP-Y	From 78 Sqn. To Middle East 10.7.42.
W1161 MP-O	From 78 Sqn. To Middle East 17.7.42.
W1168 MP-O	From 102 Sqn. To 1658 CU 8.2.43.
W1169 MP-S	From 45 MU. To Middle East 10.7.42.
W1177 MP-G	To Middle East 17.7.42.
W1180	From 77 Sqn. To 78 Sqn 29.6.42.
W1183 MP-M	From 77 Sqn. To Middle East 17.7.42.
W1184	To 78 Sqn 2.7.42.

W1228 MP-A	From 78 Sqn. Crashed in Yorkshire soon after take-off for Frankfurt 8/9.9.42.
W1236 MP-G	From 460 Sqn. FTR Duisburg 8/9.4.43.
W1244 MP-D	FTR Saarbrücken 1/2.9.42.
W7655 MP-L/C	To Middle East 10.7.42.
W7660 MP-L	FTR Mannheim 19/20.5.42.
W7661	From 78 Sqn. Collided with Oxford near Middleton-St-George while training 24.6.42.
W7664 MP-T	From RAE. To Middle East 17.7.42.
W7665 MP-N	Crashed while landing at Middleton-St-George during training 28.6.42.
W7670 MP-B	From 78 Sqn. Crashed in Yorkshire following early return from Vegesack 20.7.42.
W7671 MP-H	From 78 Sqn. To Middle East 17.7.42.
W7672 MP-E	From RAE. To Middle East 10.7.42.
W7678 MP-L	From 10 Sqn. FTR Hamburg 3/4.3.43.
W7702 MP-L	From 45 MU. To Middle East 16.7.42.
W7747 MP-G	To 78 Sqn and back. FTR Bremen 25/26.6.42.
W7754 MP-F	From 12 MU. To Middle East 10.7.42.
W7755 MP-A	From 12 MU. To Middle East 16.7.42.
W7762 MP-D	To Middle East 6.10.42.
W7781 MP-U	From 460 Sqn. To 1658 CU 2.2.43.
W7805 MP-L/M	FTR Essen 3/4.4.43.
W7812 MP-B	From 78 Sqn. FTR Flensburg 1/2.10.42.
W7813 MP-E	From 78 Sqn. To 77 Sqn 21.4.43.
W7820 MP-G/B	From 460 Sqn. To 102 Sqn 14.4.43.
W7856	From 78 Sqn. To 77 Sqn 21.12.43.
W7868 MP-R	To 1658 CU 2.2.43.
W7879	To 102 Sqn 31.10.42.
W7882	To 102 Sqn 31.10.42.
W7937	To 78 Sqn 10.2.43.
BB189 MP-H	From 8 MU. To 158 Sqn 15.10.42.
BB195 MP-B	From 12 MU. Abandoned over East Anglia on return from Düsseldorf 1.8.42.
BB196 MP-O	From 12 MU. Crash-landed at Catfoss during training 31.8.42.
BB199 MP-A	From 78 Sqn. Crashed near Middleton-St-George during air-test 16.6.42
BB221	From 103 Sqn. Returned to 103 Sqn 2.2.43.
BB222	Conversion Flt only.
BB237 MP-C	Crashed on landing at Benson on return from Genoa 24.10.42.
BB238 MP-J/P	To 77 Sqn 18.5.43.
BB239	To 78 Sqn 25.9.42.
BB242 MP-P	FTR Mannheim 6/7.12.42.
BB245 MP-V	From 158 Sqn. To 1658 CU and back. To 1658 CU.
BB246	To 1658 CU 2.2.43.
BB282 MP-R	From 1658 CU. FTR Essen 5/6.3.43.

BB284 MP-D	From 1658 CU. To 77 Sqn 14.4.43.
BB300 MP-A	From 1658 CU. To 10 Sqn 14.4.43.
BB324 MP-Q	To 10 Sqn 18.4.43.
BB365 MP-T	To 102 Sqn 1.5.43.
DG220 MP-F	From 78 Sqn. To 1658 CU via 76 CF.
DG234	From 1663 CU. Returned to 1663 CU.
DG353	From 8 MU. To 1663 CU 6.8.43.
DG394	From 1663 CU. Returned to 1663 CU 27.4.43.
DG420 MP-Q	From 1663 CU. Returned to 1663 CU 3.5.43.
DG421	From 1663 CU. Returned to 1663 CU 27.4.43.
DG422 MP-S	From 1663 CU. Returned to 1663 CU 3.5.43.
DG423 MP-H	From 1663 CU. FTR Duisburg 26/27.4.43.
DK128	To 1652 CU 8.3.43.
DK132 MP-V	From 1663 CU. Returned to 1663 CU 25.5.43.
DK134 MP-Y	From 45 MU. FTR Dortmund 4/5.5.43.
DK136 MP-U	From 8 MU. Crashed on landing on return from Nuremberg 10/11.8.43.
DK137 MP-R	From 8 MU. FTR Cologne 28.6.43.
DK138 MP-T/V/X	From 8 MU. To 1663 CU.
DK147 MP-A	From 8 MU. FTR Essen 27/28.5.43.
DK148 MP-J/G	From 8 MU. Crash-landed on return from Essen 25/26.7.43.
DK149 MP-A/B/D/G	To 1663 CU 26.9.43.
DK150 MP-E	FTR Cologne 28.6.43.
DK151 MP-K/T/M MP-Q	From 8 MU. To 1663 CU 10.11.43.
DK165 MP-E	FTR Pilsen 16/17.4.43.
DK166 MP-D	FTR Wuppertal 24.6.43.
DK167 MP-F/A	Completed 35 operations. Crashed on landing on return from Stuttgart 26/27.11.43.
DK168 MP-G/H/H	To 1663 CU 10.11.43.
DK169 MP-B/M	FTR Dortmund 23/24.5.43.
DK170 MP-C	FTR Düsseldorf 11/12.6.43.
DK171 MP-J	FTR Essen 30.4/1.5.43.
DK172 MP-L	FTR Dortmund 23/24.5.43.
DK173 MP-C/P	To 1663 CU 8.9.43.
DK174 MP-A/W	Crash-landed at Hartford Bridge on return from Cologne 3/4.7.43.
DK175 MP-O/T	Crashed on take-off when bound for Aachen 13/14.7.43.
DK176 MP-U	Crash-landed on return from Gelsenkirchen 9/10.7.43.
DK177 MP-H	FTR Bochum 12/13.6.43.
DK178 MP-Q/R/Y/U	To 1663 CU 23.6.44.
DK179 MP-S	To 1663 CU 31.12.43.
DK187 MP-Y/M	FTR Hamburg 24/25.7.43.
DK188 MP-V/J	Crash-landed at Shipdham on return from Hamburg 27/28.7.43.

DK193 MP-Y	From 48 MU. Crashed on take-off for Mönchengladbach 30/31.8.43.
DK194 MP-H/U/T	To 1663 CU 15.2.44.
DK195 MP-P	From 48 MU. Damaged by night fighter on operation to Mönchengladbach 30/31.8.43.
DK200 MP-L	FTR Düsseldorf 11/12.6.43.
DK201 MP-P/Q/P	FTR Kassel 3/4.10.43.
DK202 MP-Q	FTR Remscheid 30/31.7.43.
DK203 MP-A	Completed 33 operations. FTR Kassel 3/4.10.43.
DK204 MP-L	To 1663 CU 20.9.43.
DK205 MP-C/P	Damaged in accident 20.11.43. SOC March 45.
DK207 MP-X/S	FTR Mönchengladbach 30/31.8.43.
DK223 MP-W/N/N	FTR Mannheim 5/6.9.43.
DK224 MP-Q	FTR Mülheim 22/23.6.43.
DK231 MP-B	FTR Frankfurt 25/26.11.43.
DK236 MP-V	To 431 Sqn 6.3.44.
DK240 MP-G	FTR Milan 12/13.8.43.
DK241 MP-Q/Q	Crashed on landing on return from Berlin 23/24.8.43.
DK245 MP-H/G	Crashed on take-off for Berlin 28/29.1.44.
DK247 MP-W	FTR Kassel 3/4.10.43.
DK266 MP-O	FTR Hanover 27/28.9.43.
DK269 MP-J	FTR Nuremberg 27/28.8.43.
DT490 MP-F	To Conversion Flt and back. To 1658 CU 18.4.43.
DT492 MP-H	From 158 CF. Abandoned over English coast on return from Stuttgart 11/12.3.43.
DT496 MP-A	FTR Aachen 5/6.10.42.
DT508 MP-K	FTR Flensburg 23/24.9.42.
DT509	From 78 Sqn. Returned to 78 Sqn 31.10.42.
DT511 MP-B/O	FTR Duisburg 20/21.12.42.
DT515 MP-T	From 405 Sqn. FTR Genoa 7/8.11.42.
DT522 EY-R	From 78 Sqn on loan retaining 78 Sqn codes.
DT526 EY-L	From 78 Sqn on loan retaining 78 Sqn codes.
DT541 MP-S	Completed 31 operations. To 10 Sqn 21.4.43.
DT545 MP-Q	Crashed on take-off for Nuremberg 25/26.3.43.
DT550 MP-B	FTR from mining sortie 8/9.11.42.
DT554 MP-T	From 78 Sqn. To 1652 CU 20.7.43.
DT556 MP-A/U	From 78 Sqn. FTR Berlin 1/2.3.43.
DT563 MP-L/O	From 77 Sqn. FTR Berlin 29/30.3.43.
DT569 MP-C	From 158 Sqn. FTR Berlin 17/18.1.43.
DT570 MP-R	From 158 Sqn. FTR Duisburg 20/21.12.42.
DT571 MP-M	FTR Turin 20/21.11.42.
DT574	Crash-landed at Linton-on-Ouse on return from mining sortie 8.12.42.
DT575 MP-Y	FTR Pilsen 16/17.4.43.
DT621 MP-D	From 12 MU. FTR from mining sortie 21/22.1.43.
DT647 MP-P	From 12 MU. FTR Berlin 17/18.1.43.
DT698 MP-W	Damaged beyond repair Stuttgart 14/15.4.43.
DT744 MP-K	FTR Berlin 29/30.3.43.

DT751 MP-C	FTR Essen 12/13.3.43.
DT767 MP-J/V	FTR Berlin 1/2.3.43.
DT782 MP-J	Force-landed at base on return from Essen 12.3.43.
EB138	To 1663 CU 18.5.43.
EB204	Completed 32 operations. To 77 Sqn 10.3.44.
EB240 MP-P/P	Crashed on landing at Ford on return from Mannheim 5/6.9.43.
EB244 MP-X/X	FTR Hamburg 29/30.7.43.
EB245 MP-K	From 192 Sqn. To 1663 CU 5.2.44.
EB249 MP-E	FTR Hamburg 2/3.8.43.
EB250 MP-R	FTR Munich 6/7.9.43.
EB253 MP-Y/C	FTR Hanover 22/23.9.43.
HR727	To 102 Sqn 18.5.43.
HR748MP-R	To 78 Sqn 26.4.43.
JB800 MP-U	From 48 MU. FTR Pilsen 16/17.4.43.
JB870 MP-H	FTR Pilsen 16/17.4.43.
JB871 MP-V	FTR Frankfurt 10/11.4.43.
JB872 MP-C	To 78 Sqn 26.4.43.
JB873 MP-J	To 78 Sqn 26.4.43.
JB874 MP-L	To 78 Sqn 3.6.43.
JD145	To 78 Sqn 18.5.43.
LK630 MP-D	Abandoned soon after take-off when bound for Magdeburg 21/22.1.44.
LK631 MP-X/P	To 1663 CU 14.5.44.
LK645 MP-N/S	FTR Hanover 22/23.9.43.
LK646 MP-Q	To 1663 CU 15.2.44.
LK660 MP-S	To 77 Sqn 23.2.44.
LK664 MP-U	FTR Kassel 22/23.10.43.
LK667 MP-O	To 77 Sqn 18.2.44.
LK681 MP-A	Crashed in Yorkshire during an air-test 3.11.43.
LK687 MP-P	FTR Stuttgart 26/27.11.43.
LK732 MP-F	FTR Frankfurt 20/21.12.43.
LK733 MP-B	FTR Magdeburg 21/22.1.44.
LK737 MP-H	To 77 Sqn 19.3.44.
LK744 MP-Y	To 77 Sqn 17.2.44.
LK747 MP-B/J/Z/L	Completed 69 operations. To 1663 CU 6.12.44.
LK754 MP-W/M/I/S MP-Q/F/N	From 432 Sqn. Completed 44 operations. To 45 MU 25.4.45.
LK783 MP-C	FTR Trappes 2/3.6.44.
LK784 MP-D	FTR Trappes 2/3.6.44.
LK785 MP-T	Completed 56 operations. To 1658 CU 23.11.44.
LK788 MP-Q/B/O/Z MP-E/J/N	Completed 78 operations. To 29 MU 29.4.45.
LK789 MP-L	Shot down by intruder on return from Karlsruhe 24/25.4.44.
LK790 MP-K	FTR Berlin 24/25.3.44.
LK791 MP-H	FTR Frankfurt 18/19.3.44.

LK795 MP-P	FTR Nuremberg 30/31.3.44.
LK831 MP-N/H/A/B	Completed 83 operations. To 45 MU 16.4.45.
MP-C/E	
LK832 MP-H/V	Completed 82 operations. To 48 MU 10.5.45.
LK867 MP-P	Crashed on take-off for Trouville 11/12.5.44.
LK873 MP-S	FTR Acquet 18/19.7.44.
LK890 MP-T/J	To 1663 CU 15.2.44.
LK891 MP-X/X	FTR Hanover 27/28.9.43.
LK892 MP-C	FTR Mannheim 9/10.8.43.
LK902 MP-N/H	FTR Leipzig 3/4.12.43.
LK903 MP-G	FTR Frankfurt 25/26.11.43.
LK904 MP-T	FTR Kassel 3/4.10.43.
LK910 MP-P/J/H	To 1663 CU 15.2.44.
LK911 MP-Y	FTR Frankfurt 20/21.12.43.
LK912 MP-N	FTR Magdeburg 21/22.1.44.
LK921 MP-R	FTR Berlin 20/21.1.44.
LK922 MP-L	FTR Magdeburg 21/22.1.44.
LK926 MP-C	FTR Frankfurt 20/21.12.43.
LK929 MP-M	To 1663 CU 15.2.44.
LK932 MP-X	FTR Düsseldorf 3/4.11.43.
LK946 MP-F	FTR Stuttgart 26/27.11.43.
LK948 MP-T	FTR Düsseldorf 3/4.11.43.
LK949 MP-V	Damaged on operation to Düsseldorf 3/4.11.43 and SOC 16.11.43.
LK951 MP-Y/Y	To 1663 CU 15.2.44.
LK955 MP-W	To 77 Sqn 18.2.44.
LK957 MP-H	FTR Mannheim 18/19.11.43.
LK958 MP-Q/Q	FTR Berlin 20/21.1.44.
LK999 MP-V	FTR Berlin 20/21.1.44.
LL116 MP-X	FTR Berlin 20/21.1.44.
LL130 MP-P	To 77 Sqn 17.2.44.
LL140 MP-A	FTR Berlin 15/16.2.44.
LL184 MP-F	To 77 Sqn 17.2.44.
LL185 MP-G	FTR Magdeburg 21/22.1.44.
LL189 MP-C	Crashed on take-off for air-test 11.2.44.
LL215 MP-S	To 77 Sqn 17.2.44.
LL234 MP-E	To 77 Sqn.
LL235	To 77 Sqn 5.2.44.
LL237 MP-R/G	To 77 Sqn 17.2.44.
LL242 MP-L	To 77 Sqn 18.2.44.
LL244	To 77 Sqn 5.2.44.
LL246 MP-X	To 77 Sqn 19.2.44.
LL554 MP-X/H/Q	Completed 54 operations. To 29 MU 29.4.45.
MP-D/U/L/I/G-/S/G/A/B/Y	
LL577 MP-W/U/V/L	Completed 35 operations. FTR Bochum 4.11.44.
MP-M	
LL578 MP-Y/C/I/A	FTR Rüsselsheim 12/13.8.44.
MP-Q/M/H	

LL579 MP-G/W/Y/E Flew 46 operations. FTR Mainz 27/28.2.45.
    MP-L
LL598   To 462 Sqn 19.8.44.
LL599   To 462 Sqn 22.8.44.
LL606 MP-H/H/B/Z Flew 52 operations. To 10 Sqn 9.4.45.
    MP-N/E/D/U
LL607 MP-Y/X/J/O Flew 44 operations. To 78 Sqn 26.3.45.
LL608 MP-A/G/F/O Flew 44 operations. To 45 MU 20.4.45.
    MP-H/G/J/E/L
LV868   To 78 Sqn 26.2.44.
LV869 MP-P   To 78 Sqn 22.3.44.
LV872 MP-H   To 78 Sqn 24.2.44.
LV873 MP-U   To 78 Sqn 28.3.44.
LV874   To 78 Sqn 28.3.44.
LV876   To 78 Sqn 24.2.44.
LV877   To 78 Sqn 26.2.44.
LV901   To 78 Sqn 29.2.44.
LV915   To 78 Sqn 22.3.44.
LV916   To 78 Sqn 11.3.44.
LV947 MP-Z   From 433 Sqn. To 45 MU 13.4.45.
LV957   To 78 Sqn 31.3.44.
LV958   To 78 Sqn 31.3.44.
LW178   To 78 Sqn 24.5.44.
LW346 MP-G/A/D/Y From 578 Sqn. Became ground-instruction machine.
    MP-K
LW363 MP-F/Z/B   From 12 MU. Flew 40 operations. To 1658 CU
                  22.9.44.
LW573 MP-S   To 425 Sqn.
LW620 MP-G/G   Crashed at Hotham on return from Laon 22/23.6.44.
LW627 MP-Q/Q/J/Y Flew 84 operations. To 45 MU 13.4.45.
    MP-K/M/H-/O/H/W
LW628 MP-J   Damaged during operation to Nuremberg 30/31.3.44.
LW629 MP-M   FTR Stuttgart 1/2.3.44.
LW630 MP-S   To 347 Sqn 10.8.44.
LW631 MP-X/X/Z   Flew 76 operations. To 45 MU 13.4.45.
    MP-C/R/M/W/O/O/F/P/J/Y/Y
LW636 MP-X   Crashed soon after take-off for Stuttgart 1/2.3.44.
LW637 MP-R/C/B/S Flew 45 operations. To 1658 CU 21.11.44.
LW638 MP-Y/W   FTR Mont Fleury 6.6.44.
LW639 MP-G-/O/X   Flew 32 operations. To 1658 CU 25.11.44.
    MP-B/C
LW644 MP-O   FTR Amiens 12/13.6.44.
LW646 MP-E   From 78 Sqn. Flew 77 operations. To 1663 CU
                  5.12.44.
LW647 MP-W   FTR Nuremberg 30/31.3.44.
LW648 MP-A/Q   Flew 66 operations. FTR Bochum 4.11.44.
LW649 MP-B   Crashed Scunthorpe 3.3.44.
LW655 MP-V   From 78 Sqn. FTR Frankfurt 18/19.3.44.

LW656 MP-H/B	From 78 Sqn. Flew 33 operations. FTR Laon 22/23.6.44.
LW657 MP-G	From 78 Sqn. FTR Stuttgart 15/16.3.44.
LW681 MP-Y/Y	Crashed on landing on return from Amiens 12/13.6.44.
LW683 MP-D/Q/N	From 48 MU.
LW695 MP-I/M	Flew 35 operations. FTR Rüsselsheim 12.8.44.
LW696 MP-X	FTR Nuremberg 30/31.3.44.
MZ309	To 10 Sqn 8.6.44.
MZ310	To 78 Sqn 10.6.44.
MZ340	To 78 Sqn 27.6.44.
MZ346	From 640 Sqn on loan retaining 640 Sqn codes.
MZ353 MP-Z/D	From 77 Sqn. To 78 Sqn 10.4.45.
MZ354 MP-B/V	From 77 Sqn. To 10 Sqn 27.3.45.
MZ405 MP-Y/N	From 158 Sqn. To 45 MU 20.4.45.
MZ421 MP-K/M/B/Q	From 425 Sqn. To 10 Sqn 26.3.45.
MZ460 MP-Q	From 48 MU. Flew 33 operations. To 78 Sqn.
MZ516 MP-V	From 78 Sqn. Flew 77 operations. Abandoned over Norfolk on return from Mainz 1.2.45.
MZ524 MP-G/P	From 78 Sqn. Flew 35 operations. FTR Nucourt 15/16.7.44
MZ526 MP-N	From 45 MU. Crashed Eastrington when bound for Kiel 15/16.9.44.
MZ528 MP-K/J	From 78 Sqn. Flew 83 operations. To 45 MU 13.4.45.
MZ530 MP-U	From 78 Sqn. FTR Düsseldorf 22/23.4.44.
MZ531 MP-P/D	From 78 Sqn. FTR Juvisy 7/8.6.44.
MZ539 MP-X	From 78 Sqn. FTR Blainville 28/29.6.44.
MZ575 MP-W	FTR Hasselt 12/13.5.44.
MZ578 MP-I	FTR Düsseldorf 22/23.4.44.
MZ599 MP-U/U	Flew 51 operations. FTR Westkapelle 28.10.44.
MZ604 MP-W	FTR Trappes 2/3.6.44.
MZ622 MP-L	FTR Aachen 24/25.5.44.
MZ623 MP-P/P	FTR Aachen 24/25.5.44.
MZ679 MP-T/A/C	FTR Blainville 28/29.6.44.
MZ680 MP-Y/R	Flew 64 operations. Attacked by intruder on return from Kamen 3/4.3.45.
MZ691 MP-Q	Flew 53 operations. Crashed in Norfolk on return from Essen 23.10.44.
MZ693 MP-E/F/T	From 78 Sqn. Flew 77 operations. To 45 MU 4.5.45.
MZ732 MP-D	From 10 Sqn. Crashed at Carnaby on return from Croixdalle 6.7.44.
MZ736 MP-B	From 78 Sqn. FTR Blainville 28/29.6.44.
MZ740 MP-Y/R	Flew 55 operations. FTR St Vith 26.12.44.
MZ902 MP-H/W	From 102 Sqn.
MZ905 MP-H	From 433 Sqn. Collided with NA219 while taxiing out for Chemnitz operation 5/6.3.45.
MZ937 MP-R	From 102 Sqn. To 78 Sqn 9.4.45.

NA114	To 10 Sqn 17.10.44.
NA149 MP-C	From 10 Sqn. Flew 32 operations. To 45 MU 20.4.45.
NA163 MP-X/K	From 78 Sqn. Crashed on landing at Chedburgh on return from Bohlen 13/14.2.45.
NA164 MP-U	From 78 Sqn. Damaged on landing on return from Wesel 21.2.45.
NA170 MP-S	Belly-landed at Carnaby on return from Hanover 5.1.45.
NA171 MP-S/E	FTR Cologne 30.12.44.
NA172	To 78 Sqn 20.11.44.
NA198 MP-X	From 78 Sqn. Flew 33 operations. To 10 Sqn 1.4.45.
NA205 MP-J/C	To 192 Sqn 24.3.45.
NA218 MP-B	Damaged during operation to Hanover 5.1.45.
NA219 MP-D	Collided with MZ905 while taxiing out for Chemnitz operation 5/6.3.45.
NA220 MP-T	To 78 Sqn 23.3.45.
NA522	Crashed at Hotham during air-test 5.6.44.
NA530 MP-G/U/P/P MP-J	Flew 39 operations. To 1652 CU 25.11.44.
NA543 MP-J/X/Z/S	Flew 65 operations. To 45 MU 4.5.45.
NA548 MP-G	Flew 76 operations. Damaged during operation to Osnabrück 25.3.45.
NA553 MP-H/B/C/J MP-P	Flew 38 operations. To 1658 CU 5.12.44.
NA567 MP-W/A/S MP-Z/A/T/W	From 78 Sqn. Flew 31 operations. FTR Bochum 9.10.44.
NA570 MP-M/P	Flew 67 operations. To 45 MU 4.5.45.
NA571 MP-D/A/V	Flew 69 operations. To 29 MU 26.4.45.
NA575 MP-W/I/S/P MP-O/Y	To 45 MU 21.12.44.
NA584 MP-Z/X/T/B MP-Q/P/F/E	Flew 59 operations. Attacked by intruder on return from Kamen 3/4.3.45.
NA623 MP-A/H	Belly-landed at Middleton-on-the-Wolds on return from Essen 28/29.11.44.
NR121 MP-E	From 434 Sqn. FTR Worms 21/22.2.45.
NR200 MP-T/M	From 48 MU. Flew 38 operations. Damaged during raid on Osnabrück 25.3.45.
PP172 MP-Z	From 44 MU.
RG444 MP-U	From 10 Sqn. Crashed near Elloughton on return from Wesel 17.2.45.
RG493 MP-R	From 48 MU. To 158 Sqn 1.5.45.
RG496 MP-W	From 48 MU.
RG497 MP-S	From 29 MU.
RG506 MP-C	From 45 MU.
RG546 MP-J	From 45 MU.
RG551 MP-F	From 45 MU. To 158 Sqn 1.5.45.

RG553 MP-T	From 45 MU. FTR Wangerooge 25.4.45.
RG554 MP-E	From 45 MU. Damaged during operation to Hamburg 8/9.4.45.
RG555 MP-H	From 45 MU.
RG556 MP-D	From 45 MU.
RG558 MP-B	From 45 MU.
RG567 MP-K	
RG568 MP-U	From 45 MU.
RG583 MP-G	
RG591 MP-A	FTR Wangerooge 25.4.45.
RG597 MP-M	To 158 Sqn 1.5.45.
RG598 MP-N	
RG599 MP-L	
RG602 MP-O	
RG608 MP-P	
RG612 MP-X	
RG613 MP-Q	
RG618 MP-I	To 158 Sqn 1.5.45.
RG622 MP-I	Crashed on take-off for Heligoland 18.4.45.
RG623 MP-D	To 158 Sqn 1.5.45.
RG624	
RG656	
RG658	
TW790 MP-E	From 45 MU.
TW793 MP-F	From 48 MU. To 158 Sqn 1.5.45.
TW794 MP-V	From 29 MU. To 102 Sqn.
TW796 MP-Y	From 48 MU.

Heaviest Single Loss

03/04.10.43.	Kassel. 4 Halifaxes.
21/22.01.44.	Magdeburg. 4 Halifaxes.

77 SQUADRON

Motto: Esse Potius Quam Videri (To be rather than seem)   **Code: KN**

Originally formed as a home defence unit on 1 October 1916, 77 Squadron spent the remainder of the Great War protecting Edinburgh from Zeppelin raids. Disbandment followed in June 1919, and the number was not allotted again until 14 June 1937, when B Flight of 102 Squadron was designated as the new 77 Squadron. Whitleys were taken on charge in November 1938, by which time the squadron was resident at Driffield. Operational at the outbreak of war, 77 Squadron joined the other 4 Group Whitley units in dispensing propaganda leaflets over Germany. Bombing operations began for the squadron in March 1940. Among its commanding officers was W/C Don Bennett, who would later command the Pathfinder Force with distinction.

The squadron was detached to Coastal Command from May to October 1942, and on its return to 4 Group it began conversion to the Halifax. Always at the forefront of operations, 77 Squadron produced a fine record of service.

STATIONS

Driffield	25.07.38 to 15.04.40
Kinloss	15.04.40 to 04.05.40
Driffield	04.05.40 to 28.08.40
Linton-on-Ouse	28.08.40 to 05.10.40
Topcliffe	05.10.40 to 05.09.41
Leeming	05.09.41 to 06.05.42
Chivenor	06.05.42 to 05.10.42
Elvington	05.10.42 to 15.05.44
Full Sutton	15.05.44 to 31.08.45

COMMANDING OFFICERS

Wing Commander J. Bradbury DFC	20.02.39 to 01.11.39
Wing Commander C.H. Appleton	01.11.39 to 01.06.40
Wing Commander J.C. MacDonald DFC	01.06.40 to 14.08.40
Wing Commander G.T. Jarman DFC	14.08.40 to 21.05.41
Wing Commander D.P. Hanafin DFC	21.05.41 to 09.09.41
Wing Commander D.O. Young AFC	09.09.41 to 02.12.41
Wing Commander D.C.T. Bennett	02.12.41 to 14.04.42
Wing Commander J.R.A. Embling	14.04.42 to 03.12.42
Wing Commander A.E. Lowe MBE DFC	10.12.42 to 12.10.43
Wing Commander J.A. Roncoroni DFC	12.10.43 to 15.09.44
Wing Commander D.W.S. Clark DFC	15.09.44 to 21.12.44
Wing Commander J.D.R. Forbes DFC AFC	21.12.44 to 07.07.45

AIRCRAFT

Whitley III	11.38 to 10.39
Whitley V	09.39 to 10.42
Halifax II	10.42 to 11.42
Halifax V	11.42 to 12.42
Halifax II	12.42 to 05.44
Halifax III	05.44 to 03.45
Halifax VI	03.45 to 08.45

OPERATIONAL RECORD

Operations	Sorties	Aircraft Losses	% Losses
486	5,379	131	2.4

Category of Operations

Bombing	Mining	Other
443	27	16

Whitleys

Operations	Sorties	Aircraft Losses	% Losses
239	1,687	56	3.3

Category of Operations

Bombing	Leaflet	Reconnaissance
223	13	3

Halifaxes

Operations	Sorties	Aircraft Losses	% Losses
247	3,692	75	2.0

Category of Operations

Bombing	Mining
220	27

TABLE OF STATISTICS
(Heavy squadrons)
22nd highest number of overall operations in Bomber Command.
19th highest number of sorties in Bomber Command.
26th highest number of aircraft operational losses in Bomber Command.

Out of 32 Halifax squadrons in Bomber Command
(Excluding SOE)
8th highest number of Halifax overall operations in Bomber Command.
7th highest number of Halifax sorties in Bomber Command.
8th highest number of Halifax operational losses in Bomber Command.

Out of 25 operational squadrons in 4 Group
5th highest number of overall operations in 4 Group.
5th highest number of sorties in 4 Group.
7th highest number of aircraft operational losses in 4 Group.

Out of 6 Whitley squadrons in 4 Group
Highest number of Whitley overall operations in 4 Group.
3rd highest number of Whitley sorties in 4 Group.
Highest number of Whitley operational losses in 4 Group.

Out of 15 operational Halifax squadrons in 4 Group
7th highest number of Halifax overall operations in 4 Group.
7th highest number of Halifax sorties in 4 Group.
7th highest number of Halifax operational losses in 4 Group.

AIRCRAFT HISTORIES

Whitley	To October 1942.
K8947 KN-O	From 102 Sqn. FTR from leafleting sortie to Munich 15/16.10.39.
K8953	From 102 Sqn. To 2 BAT Flt.

K8959	To 51 Sqn.
K8960	To RAE.
K8961	Damaged beyond repair while taxiing at Buc in France on return from leafleting sortie to Essen 9.9.39.
K8976	From 58 Sqn. To 102 Sqn.
K8977 KN-P	From 58 Sqn. To 102 Sqn.
K8991	To 102 Sqn.
K8992	To 102 Sqn.
K8993	To 102 Sqn.
K8994	To 102 Sqn.
K8995	To 10 AGS.
K8996	To 102 Sqn.
K8997	To 102 Sqn.
K8998	To 102 Sqn.
K9014	From 97 Sqn. To 102 Sqn.
K9015 KN-R	To 102 Sqn.
N1347 KN-E	From 78 Sqn. Ditched on return from shipping sweep in the Kiel/Oslo area 11/12.4.40.
N1348 KN-G	From 78 Sqn twice. To RAE.
N1351	From 78 Sqn. FTR from reconnaissance sortie to the Ruhr 27/28.3.40.
N1352 KN-B	From 78 Sqn. Ditched on return from shipping raid to Trondheim 18.4.40.
N1353 KN-M	From 78 Sqn. Destroyed in air-raid on Driffield 15.8.40.
N1354 KN-L	From 78 Sqn. To 10 Sqn.
N1355 KN-X	From 78 Sqn. Crashed on landing at Cottam 20.8.40.
N1356 KN-D	From 78 Sqn. Crashed on landing in the Isle of Man while training 8.6.40.
N1357 KN-H	From 78 Sqn. Shot down and interned by Dutch during reconnaissance sortie 27/28.3.40.
N1358 KN-T	From 78 Sqn. FTR from leafleting sortie in the Wilhelmshaven and Hamburg area 24/25.10.39.
N1362	FTR Turin 11/12.6.40.
N1363	To 1 AAS.
N1364	FTR from leafleting sortie to Frankfurt 10/11.11.39.
N1365	To Topcliffe.
N1366	FTR Mönchengladbach 11/12.5.40.
N1367 KN-S	To 19 OTU.
N1368 KN-K	From 102 Sqn. Crashed on landing at Driffield while training 2.4.40.
N1371 KN-J/P	From 102 Sqn. To 19 OTU.
N1372 KN-J/O	From 102 Sqn. Crashed on approach to Abingdon following early return from operation to the French battle area 10.6.40.
N1373	From 102 Sqn. To 19 OTU.
N1379	From 102 Sqn. To 19 OTU.
N1384	FTR Cambrai 20/21.5.40.

N1387	Force-landed in Scotland on return from an operation to Norway 16/17.4.40.
N1388 KN-R	To 83 Sqn and back. Ditched in the North Sea during operation to Hanover 18.5.40.
N1390 KN-Q	From 51 Sqn. To 10 OTU.
N1410 KN-A	To 19 OTU.
N1415 KN-D	From 102 Sqn. To 19 OTU.
N1425 KN-E	From 51 Sqn. FTR Soest 18/19.9.40.
N1431 KN-D	Crashed on landing at Linton-on-Ouse while training 11.9.40.
N1432	FTR Hirson 28/29.5.40.
N1435 KN-O	From 58 Sqn. To RAE.
N1473	FTR Augsburg 24/25.8.40.
N1474	To 10 OTU.
N1476	From 97 Sqn. Ditched off Sussex coast on return from Wanne-Eickel 20.6.40.
N1493	From 19 OTU. FTR Hamburg 13/14.3.41.
N1501 KN-H	Destroyed in air-raid at Driffield 15.8.40.
N1506	Destroyed in air-raid at Driffield 15.8.40.
N1508 KN-B	Possibly burnt out at Finningley on return from Bapume 6/7.6.40. SOC 9.11.40.
N1521	From 97 Sqn. To 58 Sqn.
N1522 KN-G	From 97 Sqn. FTR Gelsenkirchen 4/5.6.40.
N1524 KN-G	From 102 Sqn. To 10 OTU.
P4938 KN-C/G	To 19 OTU.
P4942 KN-L	To 10 OTU.
P4947	Crashed on approach to Topcliffe on return from Brest 3.4.41.
P4948	FTR Frankfurt 29/30.6.40.
P4969 KN-H	From 51 Sqn. To 1502 BAT Flt.
P4985 KN-A	From 51 Sqn. To 19 OTU.
P4989 KN-V	To 102 Sqn.
P4992 KN-T	FTR Antwerp 18/19.9.40.
P5004 KN-J/U	To 10 OTU.
P5017	SOC 4.9.40.
P5023 KN-X	To 10 OTU.
P5042 KN-K	FTR Bremen 10/11.9.40.
P5044	Crashed in Hampshire on return from Bordeaux 14/15.8.40.
P5046 KN-O	From 102 Sqn. FTR Berlin 23/24.9.40.
P5049 KN-H	To 3 OTU.
P5056 KN-Y	Destroyed in air-raid at Driffield 15.8.40.
P5091 KN-Y	From 102 Sqn. Crashed in Yorkshire on return from Hanau 9.10.40.
P5111 KN-A	From Hendon. Crashed on landing at Abingdon on return from Bordeaux 28.12.40.
T4134	To 58 Sqn.

T4138 KN-M/H	Crashed in Yorkshire when returning from Berlin 15/16.12.40.
T4151 KN-M/N	From 58 Sqn. Ditched off Northumberland coast on return from Milan 6.11.40.
T4158 KN-B	To 78 Sqn.
T4160 KN-L	Ditched in the Channel on return from Turin 24.11.40.
T4164 KN-T	From Hendon. FTR Sterkrade 15/16.2.41.
T4169 KN-F	Crashed in Suffolk on return from Turin 24.11.40.
T4172 KN-R	Ditched off Yorkshire coast on return from Berlin 15.11.40.
T4200 KN-N	To 10 OTU.
T4205 KN-S	Crashed on landing at Topcliffe on return from Mannheim 4.12.40.
T4206 KN-A	Crashed on approach to Topcliffe on return from Stettin 15.10.40.
T4208 KN-O/T	FTR Wesseling 12/13.11.40.
T4212	Crashed on take-off from Topcliffe when bound for Boulogne 31.7.41.
T4226 KN-J	FTR Berlin 15/16.12.40.
T4238 KN-Y	FTR Berlin 14/15.11.40.
T4260 KN-D	From 58 Sqn. To 102 Sqn.
T4267 KN-R	Crashed and burnt out 25.12.40.
T4279 KN-F	FTR Schwerte 12/13.6.41.
T4292 KN-P	FTR Berlin 15/16.12.40.
T4293 KN-E	Damaged beyond repair in landing accident at Topcliffe on return from Bordeaux 28.12.40.
T4331 KN-Y	To 10 OTU.
T4332 KN-Q	Force-landed in Nottinghamshire while training 20.4.41.
T4333 KN-S	To 19 OTU.
T4335 KN-P	Force-landed in Glamorgan on return from Bordeaux 28.12.40.
T4336	To 102 Sqn.
T4337	To 10 OTU.
T4338 KN-L	FTR Berlin 17/18.4.41.
Z6461 KN-R	FTR Hamburg 2/3.5.41.
Z6463	Crashed in Yorkshire on return from Cologne 1/2.3.41.
Z6559	Crashed on landing at Topcliffe on return from Ludwigshaven 10.5.41.
Z6568 KN-B	Ditched in the North Sea on return from Bremen 27/28.6.41.
Z6570	FTR Berlin 9/10.4.41.
Z6578 KN-P	FTR Cologne 17/18.5.41.
Z6582	From 10 Sqn. Ditched in the North Sea following early return from Berlin 17/18.4.41.
Z6583	Crashed in Sussex on return from Brest 4.4.41.

Z6585	FTR Berlin 17/18.4.41.
Z6628 KN-M	To 19 OTU.
Z6629	To 161 Sqn.
Z6630	From 10 Sqn. FTR Bremen 27/28.6.41.
Z6640	From 1484 Flt. SOC 19.4.45.
Z6641	To 19 OTU.
Z6642	FTR Dortmund 6/7.7.41.
Z6643	Crashed in Wiltshire on return from La Pallice 24.7.41
Z6645 KN-N	To 10 OTU.
Z6647	FTR Bremen 27/28.6.41.
Z6648	Crash-landed at Derby on return from Frankfurt 3.9.41.
Z6654	Crash-landed on Cromer beach on return from Hüls 7.9.41.
Z6668	FTR Hüls 6/7.9.41.
Z6671	To 10 Sqn.
Z6740	Crashed in Warwickshire during training 6.8.41.
Z6743	FTR Aachen 9/10.7.41.
Z6751	To 502 Sqn.
Z6752 KN-F	FTR Dortmund 6/7.7.41.
Z6755	To 102 Sqn.
Z6799 KN-U	From 78 Sqn. FTR Osnabrück 7/8.7.41.
Z6800	To 102 Sqn.
Z6801	FTR Nuremberg 12/13.10.41.
Z6814	From 58 Sqn. To 161 Sqn.
Z6817	From 1484 Flt. To 10 OTU.
Z6818	From 58 Sqn. To 58 Sqn and back. Returned to 58 Sqn.
Z6822 KN-H	To 19 OTU.
Z6824	FTR Hüls 6/7.9.41.
Z6826	FTR Frankfurt 5/6.8.41.
Z6827	Ditched off Yorkshire coast on return from Berlin 21.9.41.
Z6863	To 102 Sqn.
Z6866	To 102 Sqn.
Z6873	From 78 Sqn. To 24 OTU.
Z6876	From 102 Sqn. Ditched in Bay of Biscay during patrol 7.7.42.
Z6878	To 44 Sqn.
Z6934	FTR Berlin 20/21.9.41.
Z6943 KN-A	FTR Wilhelmshaven 27/28.2.42.
Z6950	FTR Hamburg 31.10/1.11.41.
Z6952 KN-P	To 161 Sqn.
Z6953	FTR Hamburg 31.10/1.11.41.
Z6956 KN-B	FTR Düsseldorf 27/28.12.41.
Z6975 KN-V	Crashed on approach to Leeming on return from Boulogne 13.3.42.

Z6978 KN-P	From 51 Sqn. To 3 OTU.
Z9124	From 58 Sqn. To 502 Sqn.
Z9142	From 58 Sqn. SOC 12.3.44.
Z9143 KN-J	From 10 Sqn. To PTS.
Z9147	Crashed on landing at Leeming on return from Stettin 30.9.41.
Z9148 KN-W/L	To 138 Sqn and back. FTR Wilhelmshaven 27/28.2.42.
Z9150	FTR Stettin 29/30.9.41.
Z9163 KN-C	From 10 Sqn. To 502 Sqn.
Z9209 KN-G	From 58 Sqn. FTR from patrol 9.9.42.
Z9221	From 10 Sqn. Crashed in Yorkshire on return from an abortive operation to St Nazaire 28.3.42.
Z9225	From 10 Sqn. To 296 Sqn.
Z9226 KN-K	From 10 Sqn. FTR Düsseldorf 27/28.12.41.
Z9229 KN-M	From 102 Sqn. Crashed in Warwickshire on return from St Nazaire 16.2.42.
Z9231 KN-U	Crashed at Colerne airfield on return from St Nazaire 15/16.2.42.
Z9280 KN-Y/K	FTR Wilhelmshaven 27/28.2.42.
Z9290	From 78 Sqn. To 3 OTU.
Z9293 KN-G/D	From 102 Sqn. FTR Emden 12/13.3.42.
Z9294 KN-X	To 10 OTU.
Z9297	To 78 Sqn.
Z9299	FTR Emden 30.11/1.12.41.
Z9302	To 78 Sqn.
Z9306 KN-S	FTR Düsseldorf 27/28.12.41.
Z9309 KN-U/Y	From 78 Sqn. To 24 OTU.
Z9312 KN-S	From 78 Sqn. FTR Emden 12/13.3.42.
Z9317	From 58 Sqn. To 3 OTU.
Z9321	From 102 Sqn. To 10 OTU.
Z9322 KN-K	From 51 Sqn. To 81 OTU.
Z9363 KN-H	FTR Rostock 23/24.4.42.
Z9386 KN-W	From 78 Sqn. FTR Rostock 26/27.4.42.
Z9429	From 58 Sqn. To 10 OTU.
Z9438 KN-S	To 161 Sqn.
Z9440	To 10 OTU.
Z9461 KN-V	From 1485 Flt. Shot down over the North Sea during search for missing aircraft 13.8.42.
Z9462 KN-Y	SOC 1.1.44.
Z9477 KN-G	FTR from patrol 11.6.42.
Z9480	To 42 OTU.
Z9515 KN-H	FTR from shipping strike off Brittany 2.9.42.
AD695	From 24 OTU. To 53 Sqn.
AD698 KN-R	Crashed on Lundy during patrol 1.6.42
AD708	To 10 OTU.
AD711	From 58 Sqn. To 10 OTU.
BD195 KN-M	To 78 Sqn.

BD202	To 161 Sqn.
BD223	To 10 OTU.
BD228	To 161 Sqn.
BD252	To 1484 Flt.
BD253	To 1484 Flt.
Halifax	From October 1942.
W1141 KN-H	From 35 Sqn. Crashed on landing at Elvington while training 7.8.43.
W1157 KN-U	From 158 Sqn. FTR Krefeld 21/22.6.43.
W1180	To 76 Sqn.
W1183	To 78 Sqn.
W7813 KN-C	From 76 Sqn. FTR Düsseldorf 25/26.5.43.
W7856	From 78 Sqn. To 1658 CU.
BB238 KN-Y	From 76 Sqn. FTR Berlin 23/24.8.43.
BB244	To 78 Sqn.
BB247	To 78 Sqn.
BB248	To 10 Sqn.
BB252	To 10 Sqn.
BB284	From 76 Sqn. To 1668 Sqn.
BB366	From 158 Sqn. To 10 Sqn.
BB380	Crashed on take-off from Elvington while training 11.5.43.
BB427	To 10 Sqn.
DG250	To 518 Sqn.
DG251	To 518 Sqn.
DG270	To 1662 CU.
DG273	SOC 28.12.44.
DG274	To 518 Sqn.
DG275	To 1660 CU.
DG276	To 1663 CU.
DG278	To 1664 CU.
DG279	To 518 Sqn.
DJ980	To 1664 CU.
DJ981	To 518 Sqn.
DJ982	To 1664 CU.
DJ983	To 1663 CU.
DJ984	To Bircham Newton.
DJ985	To 518 Sqn.
DJ986	To Bircham Newton.
DT555	From 78 Sqn. Crashed on take-off from Elvington while training 4.1.43.
DT563	To 76 Sqn.
DT564	To 158 Sqn.
DT567	To 158 Sqn.
DT568	From TFU. To 51 Sqn.
DT578	From 78 Sqn. To 1658 CU.
DT579	To 158 Sqn.

DT581	To 51 Sqn.
DT582	To 51 Sqn.
DT583	To 158 Sqn.
DT584	To 51 Sqn.
DT585	To 158 Sqn.
DT588	To 102 Sqn.
DT612	To 1658 CU.
DT618	To 1658 CU.
DT625	Crashed in Yorkshire while training 20.12.42.
DT626	To 51 Sqn.
DT628	To 51 Sqn.
DT629	To 419 Sqn.
DT631 KN-E	Crashed while landing at Elvington during training 29.12.42.
DT632 KN-Z	FTR Duisburg 12/13.5.43.
DT637	To 158 Sqn.
DT643 KN-V	To 1654 CU.
DT645	To 51 Sqn.
DT649	To 51 Sqn.
DT666 KN-F	To 51 Sqn.
DT670	To 51 Sqn.
DT671	To 158 Sqn.
DT685	To 51 Sqn.
DT700 KN-U	From 158 Sqn. FTR Mülheim 22/23.6.43.
DT730 KN-B	From 51 Sqn. FTR Leipzig 3/4.12.43.
DT734 KN-J	FTR Munich 9/10.3.43.
DT736 KN-M	To 1652 CU.
DT751	To 76 Sqn.
DT793 KN-E	FTR Munich 6/7.9.43.
DT796 KN-D	FTR Duisburg 26/27.4.43.
DT807 KN-R	FTR Kassel 3/4.10.43.
EB204	From 76 Sqn. To 1663 CU.
HR714 KN-K	From 102 Sqn. FTR Stettin 20/21.4.43.
HR723	From 35 Sqn. To 1666 CU.
HR732	To 51 Sqn.
HR841 KN-T	From 35 Sqn. FTR Berlin 28/29.1.44.
HR932	From 78 Sqn. To 346 Sqn.
HR935 KN-Q	From 51 Sqn. To 346 Sqn.
HR946 KN-X	From 51 Sqn. FTR Berlin 20/21.1.44.
HR947	From 102 Sqn. To 1658 CU.
HR949 KN-H	From 51 Sqn. FTR Leipzig 19/20.2.44.
HX240	From 466 Sqn. To 102 Sqn.
JB781 KN-W	To 1652 CU.
JB783 KN-N	FTR Essen 30.4/1.5.43.
JB788	To 466 Sqn.
JB793	To 419 Sqn.
JB795 KN-H	FTR Munich 9/10.3.43.
JB803 KN-G	FTR Essen 30.4/1.5.43.

JB804 KN-Q	FTR Stettin 20/21.4.43.
JB837 KN-D	FTR Düsseldorf 25/26.5.43.
JB838 KN-U	FTR Essen 25/26.7.43.
JB839 KN-K	FTR Mannheim 5/6.9.43.
JB842 KN-E	FTR Berlin 29/30.3.43.
JB846 KN-L	FTR Essen 30.4/1.5.43.
JB847 KN-V	FTR Duisburg 8/9.4.43.
JB849	Crashed on landing at Elvington while training 18.3.43.
JB850 KN-V/E	FTR Hanover 22/23.9.43.
JB851 KN-J	FTR Berlin 31.8/1.9.43.
JB852 KN-G	FTR Krefeld 21/22.6.43.
JB853	To 1658 CU.
JB856 KN-T/G	FTR Kassel 22/23.10.43.
JB863 KN-V	Crashed in Yorkshire soon after take-off from Elvington when bound for Le Creusot 19.6.43.
JB865 KN-J	Crashed in Yorkshire on return from Duisburg 13.5.43.
JB892 KN-E	FTR Bochum 13/14.5.43.
JB908 KN-W	FTR Pilsen 16/17.4.43.
JB911 KN-X	To 1658 CU.
JB919	From 405 Sqn. To 1658 CU.
JB956 KN-O	FTR Hamburg 29/30.7.43.
JB963	From 405 Sqn. To 1674 CU.
JB970 KN-Q/U	FTR Mannheim 5/6.9.43.
JD110 KN-P	To 301 FTU.
JD121 KN-O	FTR Kassel 22/23.10.43.
JD123 KN-A	From 405 Sqn. To 51 Sqn.
JD125 KN-A	From 51 Sqn. FTR Milan 12/13.8.43.
JD126 KN-C	FTR Gelsenkirchen 9/10.7.43.
JD152 KN-Z	FTR Essen 27/28.5.43.
JD162 KN-H	Crash-landed at Elvington while training 24.9.43.
JD167 KN-Z	FTR Nuremberg 10/11.8.43.
JD168 KN-T	FTR Düsseldorf 11/12.6.43.
JD205 KN-Y	FTR Krefeld 21/22.6.43.
JD213 KN-V	FTR Mülheim 22/23.6.43.
JD247 KN-H	FTR Mannheim 18/19.11.43.
JD301 KN-L	FTR Mannheim 23/24.9.43.
JD302	To 51 Sqn.
JD313	To 1662 CU.
JD320 KN-C	Crashed at Elvington soon after take-off for Essen 25.7.43.
JD321 N-G	FTR Düsseldorf 3/4.11.43.
JD324 KN-U	FTR Peenemünde 17/18.8.43.
JD371 KN-O	To 429 Sqn and back. FTR Nuremberg 27/28.8.43.
JD378	To 102 Sqn.
JD379 KN-M	FTR Berlin 23/24.8.43.
JD383 KN-H	FTR Nuremberg 27/28.8.43.

JD385 KN-C	Damaged beyond repair during operation to Düsseldorf 3/4.11.43.
JD405 KN-Z	FTR Munich 6/7.9.43.
JD413 KN-G	FTR Berlin 31.8/1.9.43.
JD418 KN-A	FTR Berlin 31.8/1.9.43.
JD421	To 102 Sqn.
JD460 KN-D	FTR Mönchengladbach/Rheydt 30/31.8.43.
JD461	To 51 Sqn.
JD462	To 1658 CU.
JD465 KN-U	FTR Berlin 23/24.8.43.
JD471 KN-A	FTR Magdeburg 21/22.1.44.
JD472	To 1666 CU.
LK660	From 76 Sqn. To 346 Sqn.
LK667 KN-A	From 76 Sqn. FTR Amiens 15/16.3.44.
LK709 KN-R	From 434 Sqn. FTR Berlin 28/29.1.44.
LK710 KN-S	FTR Laon 22/23.4.44.
LK711 KN-V	FTR Berlin 28/29.1.44.
LK725	To 346 Sqn and back. To 1663 CU.
LK726 KN-O	FTR Berlin 15/16.2.44.
LK727	To 1663 CU.
LK728	To 346 Sqn.
LK729 KN-F	FTR Berlin 28/29.1.44.
LK730 KN-G	FTR Magdeburg 21/22.1.44.
LK731 KN-K	To 346 Sqn.
LK737	From 76 Sqn. To 346 Sqn.
LK744 KN-Y	From 76 Sqn. To 346 Sqn.
LK955	From 76 Sqn. To 346 Sqn.
LK999	From 76 Sqn. To 346 Sqn.
LL121 KN-G	FTR Frankfurt 20/21.12.43.
LL122 KN-Y	Crashed in Yorkshire while training 9.12.43.
LL124	To 346 Sqn.
LL125 KN-K	FTR Frankfurt 20/21.12.43.
LL126 KN-W	To 346 Sqn.
LL127 KN-H	To 1662 CU.
LL128 KN-C	Crashed on take-off from Elvington when bound for Berlin 20.1.44.
LL130 KN-T	From 76 Sqn. FTR Laon 23/24.3.44.
LL131	To 346 Sqn.
LL133	To 1663 CU.
LL138 KN-N	FTR Orleans 22/23.5.44.
LL143 KN-O	FTR Leipzig 19/20.2.44.
LL184 KN-K	From 76 Sqn. FTR Leipzig 19/20.2.44.
LL190 KN-N	FTR Magdeburg 21/22.1.44.
LL194	From 429 Sqn. To 1664 CU.
LL226	To 1667 CU.
LL227 KN-N	To 346 Sqn.
LL229 KN-Z	FTR Amiens 15/16.3.44.
LL234	From 76 Sqn. To ECFS.

LL235 KN-L	From 76 Sqn. FTR from mining sortie 23/24.4.44.
LL237	From 76 Sqn. To 346 Sqn.
LL238	To 346 Sqn.
LL239 KN-A	FTR Leipzig 19/20.2.44.
LL242	From 76 Sqn. To 346 Sqn.
LL244 KN-T	From 76 Sqn. FTR Berlin 15/16.2.44.
LL246	From 76 Sqn. To 346 Sqn.
LL253	To 346 Sqn.
LL395	To 346 Sqn.
LL396	To 346 Sqn.
LL397	To 346 Sqn.
LL398	To 346 Sqn.
LL454	From 1667 CU. Returned to 1667 CU.
LL544 KN-Y	To 1658 CU.
LL545	To 1663 CU.
LL549 KN-N	From 76 Sqn. FTR Montergueil 25.6.44.
LL552	To 102 Sqn.
LL555	To 102 Sqn.
LL556	To 102 Sqn.
LL557	To 102 Sqn.
LW179	To 102 Sqn.
LW191	To 102 Sqn.
LW192	To 102 Sqn.
LW195	To 102 Sqn.
LW224 KN-T	FTR Hanover 22/23.9.43.
LW227	To 51 Sqn.
LW228 KN-U	FTR Hanover 27/28.9.43.
LW233 KN-Z	FTR Magdeburg 21/22.1.44.
LW234	From 78 Sqn. To 10 Sqn.
LW237	From 78 Sqn. To 1658 CU.
LW241	To 102 Sqn and back. To 346 Sqn.
LW260	From 158 Sqn. To 1652 CU.
LW264 KN-K	Collided with Halifax LW333 (102 Sqn) near Pocklington on return from Berlin and crashed 22.11.43.
LW265 KN-Y	FTR Hanover 27/28.9.43.
LW267 KN-E	Damaged beyond repair during operation to Stuttgart 26/27.11.43.
LW269 KN-T	FTR Kassel 3/4.10.43.
LW270 KN-P	FTR from mining sortie 23/24.4.44.
LW290 KN-U	FTR Berlin 22/23.11.43.
LW291	To 158 Sqn.
LW292	To 158 Sqn.
LW295	From 102 Sqn. Crashed on take-off from Marston Moor 9.6.44.
LW341 KN-D	From Pocklington. FTR Berlin 15/16.2.44.
LW469	From 578 Sqn. To 1663 CU.
LW678	From 578 Sqn. To 347 Sqn.

MZ298	To 102 Sqn.
MZ300	To 102 Sqn.
MZ301	To 102 Sqn.
MZ321 KN-Q	Force-landed in Yorkshire when bound for Saarbrücken 13.1.45.
MZ334	
MZ335 KN-A/R	Crashed immediately after take-off from Full Sutton when bound for Ludwigshafen 2.1.45.
MZ336 KN-R	From 102 Sqn. Crashed on landing at Manston on return from Duisburg 18.12.44.
MZ346	From 102 Sqn. To 640 Sqn.
MZ347 KN-X/A	From 102 Sqn. FTR Brunswick 12/13.8.44.
MZ353	To 76 Sqn.
MZ354	To 76 Sqn.
MZ359 KN-G	
MZ360 KN-A	FTR Hanover 5/6.1.45.
MZ393	To 640 Sqn.
MZ396	To 462 Sqn.
MZ397	To 192 Sqn.
MZ428 KN-B	FTR Osnabrück 6/7.12.44.
MZ470 KN-F	Crash-landed at Full Sutton on return from Essen 12.12.44.
MZ486	To 346 Sqn.
MZ673	From 102 Sqn. To 297 Sqn.
MZ676	From 102 Sqn. To 1658 CU.
MZ678	From 640 Sqn. To 1658 CU.
MZ689 KN-Z	From 51 Sqn. FTR Goch 7/8.2.45.
MZ694	From 102 Sqn. Returned to 102 Sqn.
MZ695	From 102 Sqn.
MZ697 KN-L	To 347 Sqn.
MZ698 KN-J	FTR Sterkrade 16/17.6.44.
MZ699	To 102 Sqn.
MZ700	
MZ701	Crashed almost immediately after take-off from Full Sutton for training flight 8.6.44.
MZ702 KN-Q	Crashed in the English Channel on return from Laon 23.6.44.
MZ703	From 158 Sqn. Returned to 158 Sqn.
MZ704	To 1658 CU.
MZ705 KN-Q	FTR Sterkrade 16/17.6.44.
MZ708	From 51 Sqn.
MZ710 KN-E	From 102 Sqn. To 21 HGCU.
MZ711 KN-T	From 102 Sqn. FTR Sterkrade 16/17.6.44.
MZ715 KN-Z	FTR Sterkrade 16/17.6.44.
MZ735	To 466 Sqn.
MZ739	To 158 Sqn.
MZ743	From 51 Sqn. To 1658 CU.
MZ744	To 1663 CU.

MZ748 KN-A	FTR Blainville-sur-l'Eau 28/29.6.44.
MZ750 KN-J	Abandoned over Allied territory during operation to Jülich 16.11.44.
MZ765	To 51 Sqn.
MZ766	To 51 Sqn.
MZ767	To 51 Sqn.
MZ768 KN-Q	Crashed in Yorkshire while training 14.7.44.
MZ769	To 158 Sqn.
MZ801	From 102 Sqn. To 640 Sqn.
MZ803 KN-G	From 102 Sqn. FTR Böhlen 13/14.2.45.
MZ804	From 346 Sqn.
MZ809	From 102 Sqn. To 347 Sqn.
MZ812 KN-X	From 102 Sqn. FTR from mining sortie 12/13.1.45.
MZ827	To 102 Sqn.
MZ829 KN-X	FTR Düsseldorf 2/3.11.44.
MZ830	To 102 Sqn.
MZ923 KN-N	FTR Essen 28/29.11.44.
MZ924 KN-D	FTR from mining sortie 14/15.2.45.
MZ935 KN-Q	FTR Münster 12.9.44.
MZ936	To 347 Sqn.
NA109	
NA233	To 158 Sqn.
NA508 KN-A	From 102 Sqn. FTR Sterkrade 16/17.6.44.
NA511 KN-C	From 102 Sqn. Crash-landed at Full Sutton following early return from Maisy 6.6.44.
NA512	From 102 Sqn. To 347 Sqn.
NA515 KN-D	From 102 Sqn. To 347 Sqn.
NA520	To 347 Sqn.
NA524 KN-F	FTR Sterkrade 16/17.6.44.
NA525	To 578 Sqn.
NA531	To 1658 CU.
NA544	To 1663 CU.
NA545 KN-R	FTR Sterkrade 16/17.6.44.
NA572	To 102 Sqn.
NP763	From Pocklington. To 346 Sqn.
NP767	From Pocklington. To 347 Sqn.
NP860	From Pocklington. To 346 Sqn.
NP921	From Pocklington. To 347 Sqn.
NP947	From 424 Sqn. To 347 Sqn.
NP967 KN-N/Z	FTR Worms 21/22.2.45.
NR120	From 433 Sqn. To 640 Sqn.
NR210 KN-Z	From 102 Sqn. Crash-landed at Full Sutton after attack by intruder on return from Kamen 4.3.45.
NR229	To 346 Sqn.
PN175	To 347 Sqn.
PN379	To 158 Sqn.
PP208	To 347 Sqn.
RG346	To 466 Sqn.

RG348	To 640 Sqn.
RG435	To 10 Sqn.
RG442	To 10 Sqn.
RG443	To 10 Sqn.
RG480	
RG486	
RG487	
RG488	
RG490	From 102 Sqn. To 347 Sqn.
RG499	
RG500	To 347 Sqn.
RG501 KN-K	Undercarriage collapsed at Full Sutton while taxiing for take-off to Witten 19.3.45.
RG504	
RG507 KN-J	FTR Mathias Stinnes benzol plant at Bottrop 15.3.45.
RG508	
RG509	To 347 Sqn.
RG510	To 346 Sqn.
RG511	To 346 Sqn.
RG512	
RG513	To 346 Sqn.
RG527	
RG528	
RG529 KN-C	FTR Witten 18/19.3.45.
RG530	
RG531 KN-R	
RG532	To 102 Sqn.
RG533	
RG534	To 347 Sqn.
RG535	
RG536 KN-Y	
RG538	
RG539	
RG541 KN-W	Crashed on landing at Full Sutton during training 21.3.45.
RG542	
RG544	
RG584	
RG621	

Heaviest Single Loss

16/17.06.44.	Sterkrade. 7 Halifaxes FTR.

78 SQUADRON

Motto: Nemo Non Paratus (Nobody unprepared)   **Code: EY**

78 Squadron was formed on 1 November 1916 for home defence duties. Anti-Zeppelin patrols over the southern coast of England produced little return, and the squadron was eventually pulled back to defend the eastern approaches to London. From April 1918, the squadron was equipped with Sopwith Camels, and these were supplemented by Snipes around the time of the armistice. Like many units formed during the Great War, peace rendered it surplus to requirements and it was consigned to the shelf on the last day of 1919. 78 Squadron was resurrected at Boscombe Down on 1 November 1936 as a night-bomber unit, and was formed around 10 Squadron's B Flight. Equipped with Heyfords, the squadron moved to the newly-constructed station at Dishforth in April 1937, and began to convert to Whitleys in July. One of six Whitley squadrons in 4 Group at the outbreak of war, 78 Squadron was the only one not immediately declared operational. It performed a Group pool training role to feed new crews into the front-line units, until the formation of operational training units (OTUs) in July 1940 released it to enter the fray. From that moment the squadron remained at the forefront of the bomber offensive and made a massive contribution to its success. Halifaxes replaced the venerable Whitley in March 1942 and the type saw the squadron through to the end of hostilities. 78 Squadron set a number of operational performance records, but also sustained some of the heaviest aircraft losses in the Group and the Command.

STATIONS

Ternhill	01.09.39 to 15.09.39
Dishforth	15.09.39 to 15.10.39
Linton-on-Ouse	15.10.39 to 15.07.40
Dishforth	15.07.40 to 07.04.41
Middleton-St-George	07.04.41 to 20.10.41
Croft	20.10.41 to 10.06.42
Middleton-St-George	10.06.42 to 16.09.42
Linton-on-Ouse	16.09.42 to 16.06.43
Breighton	16.06.43 to 20.09.45

COMMANDING OFFICERS

Wing Commander R. Harrison	22.03.37 to 09.01.40
Wing Commander M. Wiblin	09.01.40 to 11.40
Wing Commander J.N.H. Whitworth	11.40 to 14.02.41
Wing Commander G.T. Toland	14.02.41 to 27.02.41
Wing Commander B.V. Robinson DFC	06.03.41 to 03.07.41
Wing Commander T. Sawyer DFC	03.07.41 to 01.01.42
Wing Commander E.J. Corbally	01.01.42 to 18.05.42
Wing Commander A.H.S. Lucas	18.05.42 to 10.07.42
Wing Commander J.B. Tait DSO DFC	10.07.42 to 01.11.42

Wing Commander G.B. Warner DFC AFC   01.11.42 to 01.08.43
Wing Commander G.K. Lawrence   01.08.43 to 10.04.44
Wing Commander A. Markland DSO DFC DFM   10.04.44 to 09.44
Squadron Leader F.A. Hurley   09.44 to 11.44
Wing Commander J.L. Young DFC   11.44 to 10.46

AIRCRAFT

Whitley I   07.37 to 10.39
Whitley IV   06.39 to 02.40
Whitley V   09.39 to 03.42
Halifax II   03.42 to 01.44
Halifax III   01.44 to 04.45
Halifax VI   04.45 to 07.45

OPERATIONAL RECORD

Operations	Sorties	Aircraft Losses	% Losses
525	6,237	192	3.1

Category of Operations

Bombing	Mining	Leaflet
486	32	7

Whitleys

Operations	Sorties	Aircraft Losses	% Losses
163	1,117	34	3.0

All bombing.

Halifaxes

Operations	Sorties	Aircraft Losses	% Losses
362	5,120	158	3.1

Category of Operations

Bombing	Mining	Leaflet
323	32	7

TABLE OF STATISTICS

19th highest number of overall operations in Bomber Command.
8th highest number of sorties in Bomber Command.
Equal 3rd highest (with 44 and 102 Sqns) number of aircraft losses in Bomber Command.
15th highest number of bombing operations in Bomber Command.
Highest Halifax percentage loss rate in Bomber Command.

Out of 32 Halifax squadrons in Bomber Command
(Excluding SOE)

4th highest number of overall Halifax operations in Bomber Command.
3rd highest number of Halifax sorties in Bomber Command.
Highest number of Halifax operational losses in Bomber Command.

Out of 25 operational squadrons in 4 Group

3rd highest number of overall operations in 4 Group.
Highest number of sorties in 4 Group.
Equal highest (with 102 Sqn) number of aircraft operational losses in 4 Group.

Out of 6 Whitley squadrons in 4 Group

Lowest number of Whitley overall operations in 4 Group.
Lowest number of Whitley sorties in 4 Group.
Lowest number of Whitley operational losses in 4 Group.

Out of 15 operational Halifax squadrons in 4 Group

4th highest number of Halifax overall operations in 4 Group.
3rd highest number of Halifax sorties in 4 Group.
Highest number of Halifax operational losses in 4 Group.

AIRCRAFT HISTORIES

Whitley	To March 1942.
K7262	To 51 Sqn.
K9017	From 10 Sqn. To 10 OTU.
K9020	From 10 Sqn. To 19 OTU.
K9026	From 10 Sqn. To 19 OTU.
K9034	From 10 Sqn. To 10 OTU.
K9049	To 19 OTU.
K9050	To CFS.
K9051	To 19 OTU.
K9052	To 19 OTU.
K9053	To 19 OTU.
K9054	To 19 OTU.
K9055	To 19 OTU.
N1347	To 77 Sqn.
N1348	To 77 Sqn and back. Returned to 77 Sqn.
N1350 EY-T	To 10 OTU.
N1351	To 77 Sqn.
N1352	To 77 Sqn.
N1353	To 77 Sqn.
N1354	To 77 Sqn.
N1355	To 77 Sqn.
N1356	To 77 Sqn.
N1357	To 77 Sqn.
N1358	To 77 Sqn.
N1359	To 10 OTU.
N1360	To 10 OTU.
N1361	To 58 Sqn.
N1389 EY-M	From 58 Sqn. To 19 OTU.
N1393 EY-N	To 19 OTU.
N1394	From 51 Sqn. To 10 OTU.
N1407	From 51 Sqn. To 10 OTU.

N1409 EY-P	To 19 OTU.
N1412 EY-Q	To 19 OTU.
N1416 EY-G	To 10 OTU.
N1437 EY-R	To 19 OTU.
N1443 EY-S	From 51 Sqn. To 19 OTU.
N1478 EY-J	FTR Vlissingen 14/15.9.40.
N1485 EY-A	From 51 Sqn. Abandoned over the Wash on return from Kiel 13/14.12.40.
N1486 EY-B	From 51 Sqn. To 19 OTU.
N1487	From 10 Sqn. FTR Soest 21/22.7.40.
N1490	From 10 Sqn. Crash-landed in Scotland during operation to Bremen 11/12.2.41.
N1525 EY-E	From 51 Sqn. FTR Cologne 1/2.3.41.
P4937	From 10 Sqn. Abandoned over Devon on return from Bremen 4.1.41.
P4941	From 58 Sqn. To 10 OTU.
P4950	FTR Lorient 28/29.12.40.
P4958	From 10 Sqn. Crashed on take-off from Linton-on-Ouse when bound for Lorient 2.12.40.
P4964	FTR Sterkrade 1/2.10.40.
P4996 EY-U	From 51 Sqn. Crashed in Scotland on return from Cologne 27.2.41.
P5005	From 102 Sqn. To 19 OTU.
P5026 EY-K	FTR Stettin 28/29.11.40.
P5105	From 51 Sqn. To 19 OTU.
T4131 EY-J/W	To 10 OTU.
T4147 EY-B/D	FTR Bremen 8/9.5.41.
T4156 EY-O/L	FTR Ruhland 19/20.11.40.
T4158	From 77 Sqn. Ditched near Dunkerque on return from Frankfurt 6/7.8.41.
T4165 EY-L	To 1419 Flt.
T4166	To 1419 Flt.
T4167 EY-S	FTR from Operation Colossus 10/11.2.41.
T4175	From 51 Sqn. To 10 OTU.
T4203	FTR Gelsenkirchen 9/10.1.41.
T4204	Abandoned over Yorkshire on return from Bremen 1.1.41.
T4209 EY-Q/W	Ditched in the North Sea on return from Hamm 9.7.41.
T4215 EY-J	To 24 OTU.
T4235	To 19 OTU.
T4236 EY-D/P/R	To 10 OTU.
Z6466 EY-A	FTR Düsseldorf 24/25.8.41.
Z6470 EY-G	FTR Düsseldorf 27/28.3.41.
Z6483	From 102 Sqn. Abandoned over Hertfordshire on return from Cologne 4.5.41.
Z6484	From 102 Sqn. FTR Kiel 28/29.5.41.
Z6490 EY-J	To 1484 Flt.

Z6491 EY-T	To 24 OTU.
Z6492 EY-K	FTR Cologne 16/17.6.41.
Z6493 EY-V	FTR Cologne 16/17.5.41.
Z6495 EY-S/U	From 102 Sqn. To 24 OTU.
Z6508	FTR Mannheim 27/28.8.41.
Z6555	From 51 Sqn. FTR Hamm 8/9.7.41.
Z6558 EY-H	FTR Cologne 2/3.7.41.
Z6560	FTR Bremen 18/19.6.41.
Z6571	Crashed in Yorkshire on return from Dortmund 9.6.41.
Z6577 EY-F/E	From 102 Sqn. FTR Cologne 16/17.8.41.
Z6625 EY-L	Crashed in Norfolk on return from Hamm 9.7.41.
Z6640 EY-R/Y	From A&AEE. To 1484 Flt.
Z6646 EY-G	Crashed in Middleton-St-George circuit while training 16.10.41.
Z6655 EY-E	Ditched in the North Sea on return from Kiel 9.8.41.
Z6656 EY-D	From 58 Sqn. Crashed in Yorkshire on return from St Nazaire 3.1.42.
Z6661	FTR Bremen 18/19.6.41.
Z6664	FTR Bremen 29/30.6.41.
Z6742	Abandoned over Essex on return from Düsseldorf 25.8.41.
Z6754	FTR Cologne 16/17.8.41.
Z6799	To 77 Sqn.
Z6817 EY-L	From 10 Sqn. To 1484 Flt.
Z6823 EY-B	FTR Cologne 16/17.8.41.
Z6825	Collided with Z9127 on flare path at Middleton-St-George when bound for Essen 10/11.10.41.
Z6838	Crashed soon after take-off from Middleton-St-George while training 29.7.41.
Z6864	From 10 Sqn. Crash-landed in Yorkshire on return from Hüls following attack by intruder 7.9.41.
Z6872	Crashed on landing at Middleton-St-George on return from Mannheim 28.8.41.
Z6873 EY-P	To 77 Sqn.
Z6875	From 102 Sqn. To 51 Sqn.
Z6880	To 19 OTU.
Z6881	FTR Hüls 6/7.9.41.
Z6948 EY-F	FTR Berlin 7/8.11.41.
Z6977 EY-N	To 58 Sqn.
Z6978	To 51 Sqn.
Z9126	FTR Stettin 29/30.9.41.
Z9127	Collided with Z6825 on flare path at Middleton-St-George when bound for Essen 10/11.10.41.
Z9129 EY-A	Ditched off Spithead during operation to Le Havre 17.12.41.
Z9132	To 51 Sqn.
Z9151	FTR Berlin 7/8.11.41.

Z9152 EY-W	FTR Kiel 1/2.11.41.
Z9157	To 19 OTU.
Z9161 EY-V	From 102 Sqn. To 58 Sqn.
Z9213	Abandoned over Kent on return from Nuremberg 15.10.41.
Z9214 EY-Q	FTR Boulogne 13/14.3.42.
Z9215	To 51 Sqn.
Z9224	To 161 Sqn.
Z9232	To 138 Sqn.
Z9275	To 138 Sqn.
Z9276 EY-B	Crash-landed near Driffield when bound for Düsseldorf 27.12.41.
Z9277 EY-S	Crashed in Yorkshire on return from Brest 18.12.41.
Z9290	To 77 Sqn.
Z9297	From 77 Sqn. To OADU.
Z9302	From 77 Sqn. To 51 Sqn.
Z9305 EY-W	Shot down off Essex coast by friendly AA fire when bound for Rotterdam 28.1.42.
Z9307	To 1502 BAT Flt.
Z9308 EY-M	Crash-landed in County Durham when bound for Brest 18.12.41.
Z9309 EY-W	To 77 Sqn.
Z9312	To 77 Sqn.
Z9320	Ditched in the Channel on return from Mannheim 15.2.42.
Z9386 EY-E	To 77 Sqn.
Z9389 EY-U	Crashed while landing at Croft on return from Boulogne 14.3.42.
BD195	From 77 Sqn. FTR from patrol 9.6.42.
Halifax	From March 1942.
L9563	From 76 Sqn. Conversion Flt only. To 1658 CU.
L9583 EY-W	From 76 Sqn. Conversion Flt only. Crashed on landing at Croft 8.5.42.
L9601	From 76 Sqn. Conversion Flt only. Crashed on landing at Middleton-St-George 23.8.42.
L9617	From 76 Sqn. To 1658 CU.
L9621	From 10 Sqn. Conversion Flt only. Crashed on landing at Croft 16.5.42.
L9624	From 10 Sqn. Belly-landed at Middleton-St-George 12.7.42.
R9363	To 405 CF.
R9364 EY-R	From 76 Sqn. FTR Essen 1/2.6.42.
R9368	From 10 Sqn via 1652 CU. To 405 CF.
R9369	From 10 Sqn. Conversion Flt only. To 405 CF.
R9373 EY-R	From 76 Sqn. To 1658 CU.
R9375	From 76 Sqn. To Handley Page.
R9378	From 102 Sqn. To 76 CF.

R9386	From 76 Sqn. To 405 CF.
R9391 EY-A	From 76 Sqn. FTR Hamburg 3/4.5.42.
R9420	From 76 Sqn. To 405 CF.
R9427	From 76 Sqn. Crashed on landing at Pocklington after ferry flight 23.4.42.
R9430	From 76 CF. Conversion Flt only. To 1658 CU.
R9434 EY-D	From 76 Sqn. To 158 CF via 1652 CU.
R9437	To 405 CF.
R9447	From 76 Sqn. FTR Flensburg 23/24.9.42.
R9454	From 76 Sqn. To 1658 CU via 78 CF.
R9455	From 76 Sqn. To 1658 CU via 78 CF.
R9486	From 76 Sqn. To 502 Sqn via 78 CF.
V9989 EY-P	To 1658 CU via 78 CF.
V9991 EY-P	Damaged in forced-landing on return from Cologne (W/C Lucas) 31.5.42. To 1658 CU.
W1006 EY-L/K	From 10 CF. To 35 CF.
W1007 EY-M/K	From 10 CF. To 138 Sqn.
W1013	From 10 Sqn. Crashed in Huntingdonshire after colliding with a 14 OTU Hampden on return from Cologne 31.5.42.
W1014	From 76 Sqn. To 158 CF.
W1016	FTR Osnabrück 9/10.8.42.
W1018	From 76 Sqn. FTR Genoa 23/24.10.42.
W1036	From 76 Sqn. FTR Flensburg 1/2.10.42.
W1059 EY-L	From RAE. Ditched in the Channel on return from Saarbrücken 29/30.7.42.
W1060 EY-M	To 502 Sqn.
W1061	FTR Mainz 11/12.8.42.
W1062	Crash-landed at Docking on return from Bremen 30.6.42.
W1063	FTR Genoa 7/8.11.42.
W1067	FTR Bremen 25/26.6.42.
W1090 EY-Q	Crashed on landing at Croft during air-test 27.5.42.
W1091	To 158 Sqn.
W1093 EY-S	To 1658 CU.
W1103	Crashed on approach to Croft while on air-test 20.5.42.
W1115	From 76 Sqn. FTR Mainz 11/12.8.42.
W1143 EY-F	FTR Essen 1/2.6.42 (10 Sqn crew).
W1144	From 76 Sqn. Returned to 76 Sqn.
W1146	From 10 Sqn. To 1659 CU.
W1149	To 76 Sqn.
W1150	To 76 Sqn and back. To 1659 CU.
W1156	To 76 Sqn.
W1161	To 76 Sqn.
W1180	From 76 Sqn. FTR Bochum 5/6.8.42.
W1184	From 76 Sqn. FTR Hamburg 26/27.7.42.
W1233	FTR Mainz 11/12.8.42.

W1237 EY-P	FTR Duisburg 6/7.8.42.
W1245 EY-B	FTR Mainz 11/12.8.42.
W1249	To 1659 CU.
W1250	To 1659 CU.
W1252	Abandoned over Northamptonshire on return from Frankfurt 8/9.9.42.
W1273	To 1659 CU.
W1275	FTR Krefeld 2/3.10.42.
W7661	To 76 Sqn.
W7662 EY-E	FTR Hamburg 3/4.5.42.
W7663 EY-F	FTR Ostend 29/30.4.42.
W7668	To 158 Sqn.
W7669 EY-H	Crashed during emergency landing soon after take-off from Croft when bound for Essen 5.6.42.
W7670	To 76 Sqn.
W7671	To 76 Sqn.
W7678	To 10 Sqn.
W7698	FTR Essen 1/2.6.42.
W7747	From 76 Sqn. Returned to 76 Sqn.
W7764	Ditched off Yorkshire coast when bound for Turin 11.12.42.
W7782 EY-C	From 35 Sqn. FTR Frankfurt 8/9.9.42.
W7784	To 158 Sqn.
W7809	FTR Saarbrücken 28/29.8.42.
W7812	To 76 Sqn.
W7813	To 76 Sqn.
W7822	From 76 CF. FTR Flensburg 26/27.9.42.
W7856	To 77 Sqn.
W7881	From 35 Sqn. To 1652 CU.
W7908	To 1658 CU.
W7922	To 102 Sqn.
W7926 EY-P	FTR Dortmund 23/24.5.43.
W7928	To 1652 CU.
W7929 EY-S	Crashed while landing at Docking on return from Essen 1.5.43.
W7930 EY-W	FTR Mülheim 22/23.6.43.
W7931 EY-J	FTR Duisburg 26/27.3.43.
W7932	FTR Düsseldorf 11/12.6.43.
W7937	From 76 Sqn. FTR Essen 3/4.4.43.
W7938 EY-U	FTR Hamburg 3/4.2.43.
W7939 EY-O	Abandoned over Yorkshire when bound for Berlin 29.3.43.
BB199	To 76 Sqn.
BB200	FTR Emden 19/20.6.42.
BB219	From 103 Sqn. To 158 Sqn.
BB236	FTR Flensburg 1/2.10.42.
BB239	From 76 Sqn. Crash-landed at Linton-on-Ouse following early return from Cologne 15.10.42.

BB241	To 10 Sqn.
BB244	From 77 Sqn. To 51 Sqn.
BB247	From 77 Sqn. To 1659 CU.
BB373 EY-K	From 405 Sqn. Collided with JB874 on approach to Leconfield on return from Berlin 24.8.43.
DG220 EY-B	To 76 Sqn.
DG221 EY-A	To A&AEE and back. To 1658 CU.
DT491	FTR Düsseldorf 10/11.9.42.
DT505	From 158 Sqn. Returned to 158 Sqn.
DT509	Ditched in the North Sea on return from Duisburg 20.12.42.
DT510	To 1658 CU.
DT516	Ditched in the North Sea on return from Genoa 8.11.42.
DT519	From 35 Sqn. To 1652 CU.
DT522 EY-B	Abandoned over Suffolk on return from Genoa 16.11.42.
DT525	Crashed in Yorkshire on return from mining sortie 5.11.42.
DT526	To 51 Sqn.
DT547	To 158 Sqn.
DT554	To 76 Sqn.
DT555	To 77 Sqn.
DT556	To 76 Sqn.
DT567	From 158 Sqn. To 10 Sqn.
DT577	Crashed on landing at Linton-on-Ouse during training 20.1.43.
DT578	To 77 Sqn.
DT580	From 51 Sqn. To 1658 CU.
DT768 EY-K/W	FTR Montbeliard 15/16.7.43.
DT770	Crashed on take-off from Linton-on-Ouse when bound for mining sortie 2.3.43.
DT771 EY-B/D	Crashed on take-off from Breighton when bound for Montbeliard 15.7.43.
DT773 EY-Q	FTR Pilsen 16/17.4.43.
DT774 EY-E	FTR Essen 12/13.3.43.
DT775 EY-F	FTR Frankfurt 10/11.4.43.
DT777	FTR Bochum 13/14.5.43.
DT780 EY-M	FTR Essen 3/4.4.p43.
HR657	From 408 Sqn. To 1667 CU.
HR659 EY-A	From 408 Sqn. FTR Pilsen 16/17.4.43.
HR664	From 408 Sqn. To 1652 CU.
HR684 EY-H	FTR Düsseldorf 11/12.6.43.
HR687	FTR Essen 5/6.3.43.
HR748	From 76 Sqn. To 1652 CU.
HR755	From 51 Sqn. To 1663 CU.
HR858	From 51 Sqn. To 1652 CU.
HR874 EY-B	FTR Mannheim 5/6.9.43.

HR932	From 158 Sqn. To 77 Sqn.
HR942	From 158 Sqn. To 102 Sqn.
HX241 EY-P	From 51 Sqn. FTR Nuremberg 30/31.3.44.
HX355 EY-D	From 51 Sqn. FTR Berlin 24/25.3.44.
JB784 EY-S	To 102 Sqn.
JB798 EY-P	From 405 Sqn. FTR Hamburg 29/30.7.43.
JB801 EY-G	FTR Aachen 13/14.7.43.
JB844	To 102 Sqn.
JB845	FTR Essen 3/4.4.43.
JB855 EY-H	From 138 Sqn. FTR Mülheim 22/23.6.43.
JB857	Crash-landed at Linton-on-Ouse following early return from Duisburg 8.4.43.
JB870	From 76 Sqn. FTR Pilsen 16/17.4.43.
JB872 EY-Q	From 76 Sqn. FTR Mannheim 5/6.9.43.
JB873 EY-J	From 76 Sqn. FTR Bochum 13/14.5.43.
JB874 EY-E	From 76 Sqn. Collided with BB373 on approach to Leconfield on return from Berlin 24.8.43.
JB875	From 405 Sqn. To 1658 CU.
JB903	FTR Dortmund 4/5.5.43.
JB907	From 405 Sqn. FTR Cologne 28/29.6.43.
JB915	FTR Dortmund 4/5.5.43.
JB924 EY-M	FTR Bochum 13/14.5.43.
JB926	To 1652 CU.
JB927	To 466 Sqn and back. To 1658 CU.
JB928 EY-S	FTR Gelsenkirchen 25/26.6.43.
JB962	FTR Wuppertal 24/25.6.43.
JB973	FTR Dortmund 4/5.5.43.
JD108 EY-U	FTR Aachen 13/14.7.43.
JD118 EY-U	From 51 Sqn. Crashed in Yorkshire on return from Leverkusen 19.11.43.
JD122 EY-A	FTR Dortmund 23/24.5.43.
JD145	From 76 Sqn. FTR Bochum 12/13.6.43.
JD148 EY-A	FTR Hamburg 27/28.7.43.
JD151 EY-M	Crashed on approach to Breighton on return from Nuremberg 11.8.43.
JD157 EY-T	Ditched off Essex coast on return from Gelsenkirchen 10.7.43.
JD160	FTR Dortmund 23/24.5.43.
JD161	Collided with 342 Sqn Boston on take-off from Hartford Bridge during training 16.10.43.
JD170	To 466 Sqn.
JD173 EY-V	To 1658 CU.
JD175 EY-F	FTR Aachen 13/14.7.43.
JD201 EY-Y	Crashed in Cambridgeshire when bound for Mönchengladbach 31.8.43.
JD203 EY-Z	Crash-landed in Surrey on return from Cologne 4.7.43.
JD248 EY-J	From 51 Sqn. FTR Berlin 23/24.8.43.

JD252 EY-W	From 51 Sqn. FTR Hamburg 29/30.7.43.
JD300	From 51 Sqn. To 1663 CU.
JD305 EY-C	Crashed in the North Sea on return from Berlin 23/24.8.43.
JD306 EY-X	Abandoned over Wales after being damaged by friendly AA fire during training 2/3.9.43.
JD310 EY-Z	From 51 Sqn. FTR Berlin 23/24.8.43.
JD328 EY-O	FTR Berlin 31.8/1.9.43.
JD329 EY-G	FTR Remscheid 30/31.7.43.
JD330 EY-F	FTR Essen 25/26.7.43.
JD370 EY-F	Crash-landed in Yorkshire soon after take-off for Peenemünde 17.8.43.
JD373	To 1652 CU.
JD375 EY-P	FTR Remscheid 30/31.7.43.
JD376	To 1663 CU.
JD377 EY-G	FTR Berlin 31.8/1.9.43.
JD406 EY-P	FTR Nuremberg 27/28.8.43.
JD409 EY-D	FTR Mönchengladbach 30/31.8.43.
JD414 EY-M	FTR Nuremberg 27/28.8.43.
JD416 EY-F	FTR Hanover 27/28.9.43.
JD417	To 1667 CU.
JD453 EY-C	FTR Mönchengladbach 30/31.8.43.
JD454 EY-E	FTR Munich 6/7.9.43.
JD455 EY-K	FTR Hanover 8/9.10.43.
JD475 EY-Z	FTR Mannheim 5/6.9.43.
JD476 EY-M	FTR Hanover 27/28.9.43.
JN887	From 51 Sqn. To 1663 CU.
JN906	From 51 Sqn. To 1663 CU.
JN919	From 51 Sqn. To 102 Sqn.
JN972	To 102 Sqn.
JN974 EY-M	FTR Frankfurt 20/21.12.43.
JP117 EY-Y	To 3 OAPU and back. Crashed in Yorkshire on return from Magdeburg 22.1.44.
JP118	To 102 Sqn.
JP120	To 102 Sqn.
JP126	To 102 Sqn.
JP129	To 1658 CU.
LK749 EY-J	FTR Essen 26/27.3.44.
LK750	To 51 Sqn.
LK762 EY-Z	FTR Nuremberg 30/31.3.44.
LK763 EY-K	FTR Schweinfurt 24/25.2.44.
LK829	To 1658 CU.
LK838 EY-E	FTR Bochum 4/5.11.44.
LK840 EY-J	FTR Laon 22/23.6.44.
LK847	
LK848	To 297 Sqn.
LK849	
LL546	To 1658 CU.

LL588 EY-O	From 10 Sqn. FTR Gelsenkirchen 6.10.44.
LL607	From 76 Sqn.
LL613	
LL614	
LV788	To 518 Sqn.
LV794 EY-O	FTR Augsburg 25/26.2.44.
LV795	Destroyed by fire on the ground at Breighton 8.5.44.
LV796 EY-K	FTR Cleves 7.10.44.
LV798 EY-A	Crashed in the North Sea on return from Berlin 15/16.2.44.
LV799 EY-C	Ditched in the North Sea when bound for Château Benapre 9.7.44.
LV813	Crashed while trying to land at Dunsfold on return from Stuttgart 21.2.44.
LV814 EY-C	FTR Stuttgart 20/21.2.44.
LV815	From 578 Sqn. To 1663 CU.
LV816 EY-N	FTR Leipzig 19/20.2.44.
LV817	From 51 Sqn. Crashed on take-off from Breighton when bound for mining sortie to Kiel Bay 3.2.44.
LV819	To 51 Sqn.
LV820 EY-F	From 578 Sqn. FTR Amiens 12/13.6.44.
LV868	From 76 Sqn. Crash-landed at West Malling on return from Juvisy 8.6.44.
LV869 EY-G	From 76 Sqn. FTR Kiel 15/16.9.44.
LV872	From 76 Sqn. Abandoned near Woodbridge on return from Essen 23.10.44.
LV873 EY-Q	From 76 Sqn. FTR Villeneuve-St-Georges 26/27.4.44.
LV874 EY-P	From 76 Sqn. FTR Douai 14/15.6.44.
LV876	From 76 Sqn. To 51 Sqn.
LV877 EY-S	FTR Tergnier 10/11.4.44.
LV899 EY-Q	FTR Nuremberg 30/31.3.44.
LV901	From 76 Sqn. Undercarriage collapsed while taxiing at Breighton on return from Bottrop 21.7.44.
LV903 EY-H	FTR Berlin 24/25.3.44.
LV905 EY-W	FTR Aachen 24/25.5.44.
LV915 EY-H	From 76 Sqn. FTR Amiens 12/13.6.44.
LV916	From 76 Sqn. Crashed in Yorkshire during training 23.4.44.
LV939	To 520 Sqn.
LV957 EY-X	FTR Brunswick 12/13.8.44.
LV958 EY-O	FTR Karlsruhe 24/25.4.44.
LW178	From 76 Sqn.
LW223 EY-P	Crashed while landing at Breighton on return from Leverkusen 19.11.43.
LW225 EY-C	FTR Bochum 29/30.9.43.
LW226	To 102 Sqn.
LW229 EY-Y	FTR Mannheim 5/6.9.43.

LW230 EY-G	FTR Hanover 27/28.9.43.
LW232 EY-O	FTR Hanover 22/23.9.43.
LW234	To 77 Sqn.
LW235 EY-B	To 102 Sqn.
LW236 EY-Q	FTR Hanover 8/9.10.43.
LW237	To 77 Sqn.
LW262 EY-Z	FTR Kassel 3/4.10.43.
LW263 EY-E	Crashed in Lincolnshire on return from Bochum 30.9.43.
LW266 EY-V	FTR Mannheim 23/24.9.43.
LW271 EY-S	FTR Frankfurt 20/21.12.43.
LW273 EY-L	FTR Mannheim 23/24.9.43.
LW277	From 158 Sqn. To 102 Sqn.
LW288	To 102 Sqn.
LW291 EY-M	From 51 Sqn. FTR Berlin 20/21.1.44.
LW293 EY-L	FTR Kassel 22/23.10.43.
LW294 EY-O	Crashed while landing at Breighton during training 20.10.43.
LW295	To 102 Sqn.
LW300 EY-H	Ditched in the North Sea on return from Magdeburg 22.1.44.
LW301 EY-C	FTR Kassel 22/23.10.43.
LW313 EY-U	FTR Leipzig 3/4.12.43.
LW315 EY-G	FTR Hanover 8/9.10.43.
LW316	From 158 Sqn. To 1663 CU.
LW318 EY-R	To 102 Sqn.
LW319 EY-U	Crashed while landing at Coltishall on return from Berlin 23.11.43.
LW320 EY-Z	FTR Frankfurt 20/21.12.43.
LW321 EY-T	FTR Cannes 11/12.11.43.
LW324	To 10 Sqn.
LW330 EY-O	From 102 Sqn. Crashed while waiting to land at Breighton on return from Frankfurt 21.12.43.
LW331	From 102 Sqn. Returned to 102 Sqn.
LW338 EY-Q	FTR Frankfurt 20/21.12.43.
LW342	To 102 Sqn.
LW367 EY-L	FTR Leipzig 19/20.2.44.
LW440	From 424 Sqn. To 462 Sqn.
LW465	To 51 Sqn.
LW501	To 466 Sqn.
LW507 EY-K	FTR Berlin 24/25.3.44.
LW509 EY-T	FTR Schweinfurt 24/25.2.44.
LW510	Crashed on approach to Cranfield on return from Berlin 24.3.44.
LW511 EY-Z	FTR Scholven-Buer 6.10.44.
LW512 EY-Q	FTR Frankfurt 22/23.3.44.
LW515 EY-A	FTR Karlsruhe 24/25.4.44.
LW516	To 466 Sqn.

LW517 EY-Y	FTR Le Mans 13/14.3.44.
LW518 EY-A	FTR Berlin 24/25.3.44.
LW519	Damaged beyond repair during operation to Bourg Leopold 27/28.5.44.
LW520	To 296 Sqn.
LW521	To 51 Sqn.
LW522	To 51 Sqn.
LW547	To 246 Sqn.
LW589 EY-G	FTR Berlin 24/25.3.44.
LW646	To 76 Sqn.
LW651	From 640 Sqn. To 22 HGCU.
LW655	To 76 Sqn.
LW656	To 76 Sqn.
LW657	To 76 Sqn.
MZ310 EY-U	From 76 Sqn. FTR Scholven-Buer 6.10.44.
MZ311	Crashed in Gloucestershire on return from mining sortie to La Rochelle 26.8.44.
MZ320	
MZ340 EY-X	From 76 Sqn. FTR Forêt de Nieppe 28.7.44.
MZ353	From 76 Sqn.
MZ361 EY-D	From 10 Sqn. Crashed in Yorkshire on return from Hamburg 9.4.45.
MZ391	
MZ392	
MZ412	SOC 2.5.45.
MZ414	
MZ415	
MZ417	From 425 Sqn. To 10 Sqn.
MZ426	From 102 Sqn.
MZ460 EY-R	From 76 Sqn. FTR Harburg 4/5.4.45.
MZ516	To 76 Sqn.
MZ524	To 76 Sqn.
MZ528	To 76 Sqn.
MZ530	To 76 Sqn.
MZ531	To 76 Sqn.
MZ539	To 76 Sqn.
MZ557	To 1652 CU.
MZ568 EY-M	FTR Juvisy 7/8.6.44.
MZ577 EY-O	FTR Juvisy 7/8.6.44.
MZ631 EY-Y	FTR Amiens 12/13.6.44.
MZ636 EY-T	FTR Juvisy 7/8.6.44.
MZ639	
MZ692 EY-P	FTR Laon 22/23.6.44.
MZ693	To 76 Sqn.
MZ736	To 76 Sqn.
MZ738	To 346 Sqn.
MZ761	
MZ762	From 346 Sqn.

MZ763 EY-S	From 346 Sqn. FTR Neuss 23/24.9.44.
MZ764	From 346 Sqn.
MZ774	To 1663 CU and back.
MZ787	From 346 Sqn. To 187 Sqn.
MZ788	From 346 Sqn.
MZ789	From 346 Sqn. To 10 Sqn.
MZ791 EY-T	Damaged beyond repair following early return from Chemnitz 14/15.2.45.
MZ799 EY-X	FTR from mining sortie 14/15.2.45.
MZ810 EY-F	From 10 Sqn. Crashed while waiting to land at Breighton on return from Sterkrade 21.11.44.
MZ848	
MZ849	Crash-landed at Carnaby on return from Münster 16.11.44.
MZ850	To EANS.
MZ937	From 76 Sqn.
NA163	To 76 Sqn.
NA167 EY-F	From 76 Sqn. FTR Wanne-Eickel 2/3.2.45.
NA172	From 76 Sqn.
NA176	
NA198	To 76 Sqn.
NA219	From 76 Sqn. To 199 Sqn.
NA220	From 76 Sqn.
NA275	From 10 Sqn. To 199 Sqn.
NA278	To 199 Sqn.
NA495	
NA513 EY-O	FTR Acquet 18/19.7.44.
NA546	To 346 Sqn.
NA547	To 346 Sqn.
NA549	To 346 Sqn.
NA551	To 346 Sqn.
NA567	To 76 Sqn.
NP930	
NP933	To 10 Sqn.
NP995	
NP998	Damaged beyond repair in taxiing accident at Breighton while training 24.3.45.
NR113	
NR130	From 10 Sqn.
NR155	
NR184	
NR247	
PP168	
PP176	
PP207	From 102 Sqn.
PP210	
RG354	To 10 Sqn.
RG434	To 10 Sqn.

RG440	To 10 Sqn.
RG648	From 347 Sqn.
RG649	From 347 Sqn.
RG650	
RG651	From 158 Sqn.
RG652	From 158 Sqn.
RG657	
RG659	
RG660	
RG662	
RG663	
RG664	
RG665	
RG666	
RG667	
TW775	

Heaviest Single Loss

24/25.3.44.   Berlin. 6 Halifaxes. 5 FTR. 1 crashed on return.

102 (CEYLON) SQUADRON

Motto: Tentate et Perficite (Attempt and achieve)   **Code: DY**

First formed in August 1917 as a night-bomber unit, 102 Squadron served in the Great War, operating from bases in France against targets behind enemy lines. Having returned to England in March 1919, the squadron was disbanded on 3 July of that year. It remained on the shelf until 1 October 1935, when it was resurrected from a detachment of 7 Squadron, and finally achieved independent squadron status on 13 March 1936. In October 1938 the squadron began conversion onto Whitleys, and it was with this type that it entered World War II, as one of 4 Group's five front-line units. 4 Group alone had the necessary experience to conduct night operations, the rest of the Command having been prepared for daylight activity, in line with the theory that the self-defending bomber formation would always get through to its target in sufficient numbers. The flaws in this theory would become manifest before the year was out, in a series of bitter lessons which were to cost 3 and 5 Groups dearly in crews. 102 Squadron was in action on just the second night of hostilities, dispensing propaganda leaflets over Germany. Apart from a number of short detachments to Coastal Command in 1939 and 1940, the squadron spent the entire war at the forefront of Bomber Command's and 4 Group's operations. The venerable Whitleys began to be exchanged for Halifaxes late in 1941, and successive variants of the type saw the squadron through to the end of the war. The squadron suffered the highest loss rate in 4 Group and equal 3rd highest operational losses in the whole of Bomber Command.

STATIONS

Driffield	11.07.38 to 25.08.40
Leeming	25.08.40 to 01.09.40

Prestwick   01.09.40 to 10.10.40
Linton-on-Ouse   10.10.40 to 15.11.40
Topcliffe   15.11.40 to 15.11.41
Dalton   15.11.41 to 07.06.42
Topcliffe   07.06.42 to 07.08.42
Pocklington   07.08.42 to 08.09.45

COMMANDING OFFICERS

Wing Commander C.F. Toogood   01.10.38 to 05.02.40
Wing Commander E. Burton   05.02.40 to 16.05.40
Wing Commander S.R. Groom   16.05.40 to 21.11.40
Wing Commander F.C. Cole   01.01.41 to 08.04.41
Wing Commander C.V. Howes   21.04.41 to 05.10.41
Wing Commander L. Howard   05.10.41 to 27.01.42
Wing Commander S.B. Bintley AFC   27.01.42 to 24.10.42
Wing Commander G.W. Holden DFC   26.10.42 to 20.04.43
Wing Commander H.R. Coventry   20.04.43 to 13.07.43
Wing Commander F.R.C. Fowle   15.07.43 to 17.09.43
Wing Commander S.J. Marchbank DFC   21.09.43 to 14.07.44
Wing Commander L.D. Wilson DFC AFC   14.07.44 to 14.01.45
Wing Commander E.F.E. Barnard   14.01.45 to 27.03.45
Wing Commander D.F. Hyland-Smith   27.03.45 to 28.02.46

AIRCRAFT

Whitley III   10.38 to 01.40
Whitley V   11.39 to 02.42
Halifax II   12.41 to 05.44
Halifax III   05.44 to 09.45

OPERATIONAL RECORD

Operations	Sorties	Aircraft Losses	% Losses
602	6,106	192	3.1

Category of Operations

Bombing	Mining	Other
491	84	27

Whitleys

Operations	Sorties	Aircraft Losses	% Losses
195	1,372	52	3.8

Category of Operations

Bombing	Mining	Other
181	0	14

Halifaxes

Operations	Sorties	Aircraft Losses	% Losses
407	4,734	140	3.0

Category of Operations

Bombing	Mining	Other
310	84	13

TABLE OF STATISTICS
(Heavy squadrons)

12th highest number of overall operations in Bomber Command.

10th highest number of sorties in Bomber Command.

3rd equal (with 44 & 78 Sqns) highest number of aircraft operational losses in Bomber Command.

14th highest number of bombing operations in Bomber Command.

Out of 32 operational Halifax squadrons
(Excluding SOE)

Highest number of Halifax overall operations in Bomber Command.

5th highest number of Halifax sorties in Bomber Command.

3rd highest number of Halifax operational losses in Bomber Command.

Out of 25 operational squadrons in 4 Group

2nd highest number of overall operations in 4 Group.

3rd highest number of sorties in 4 Group.

Highest equal (with 78 Sqn) number of aircraft operational losses in 4 Group.

Out of 6 Whitley squadrons in 4 Group

5th highest number of Whitley overall operations in 4 Group.

5th highest number of Whitley sorties in 4 Group.

2nd highest number of Whitley operational losses in 4 Group.

Highest Whitley percentage loss rate in 4 Group.

Out of 15 operational Halifax squadrons in 4 Group

Highest number of Halifax overall operations in 4 Group.

5th highest number of Halifax sorties in 4 Group.

3rd highest number of Halifax operational losses in 4 Group.

AIRCRAFT HISTORIES

Whitley	To February 1942.
K8943	Damaged beyond repair in landing accident at Aston Down during ferry flight 16.10.39.
K8944	To 19 OTU.
K8945 DY-V	To 19 OTU.
K8946	To 19 OTU.
K8947	To 77 Sqn.
K8948	To 10 OTU.
K8949	To 10 OTU.
K8950 DY-M	FTR from leafleting sortie 8/9.9.39.
K8951	To 19 OTU.

K8953	To 77 Sqn.
K8954	To 19 OTU.
K8955	Became ground-instruction machine May 1940.
K8956	To 10 OTU.
K8957 DY-D	To 166 Sqn.
K8958	Crashed near Driffield while training 15.10.39.
K8976 DY-E	From 77 Sqn. To 166 Sqn.
K8977	From 77 Sqn. To 166 Sqn.
K8985 DY-J	Forced to land in Belgium on leafleting sortie and interned 8/9.9.39.
K8986	To 166 Sqn.
K8987	To 166 Sqn.
K8991	From 77 Sqn. To 166 Sqn.
K8992	From 77 Sqn. To 166 Sqn.
K8993	From 77 Sqn. To 166 Sqn.
K8994	From 77 Sqn. To 10 OTU.
K8996	From 77 Sqn. Crashed on take-off from Catterick on ferry flight 18.10.39.
K8997	From 77 Sqn. To 19 OTU.
K8998	From 77 Sqn. To Shoeburyness 18.5.42.
K9012	From 97 Sqn. To 19 OTU.
K9014	From 77 Sqn. To 166 Sqn.
K9015 DY-B	From 77 Sqn. To 166 Sqn.
N1368 DY-K	To 77 Sqn.
N1369	To 19 OTU.
N1370 DY-F/J	To RAE.
N1371	To 77 Sqn.
N1372	To 77 Sqn.
N1373	To 77 Sqn.
N1375 DY-N	To RAE.
N1376 DY-O	FTR Gelsenkirchen 19/20.5.40.
N1377 DY-G/P/B	FTR Mannheim 26/27.7.40.
N1378 DY-B/Q	Destroyed in air-raid at Driffield 15.8.40.
N1379 DY-G/E	To 77 Sqn.
N1380 DY-R	FTR Oise Bridge at Ribemont 20/21.5.40.
N1381 DY-M	To 19 OTU.
N1382 DY-A	FTR Augsburg 16/17.8.40.
N1383 DY-H	FTR Aalborg Norway 25/26.4.40.
N1385 DY-G	To 19 OTU.
N1386 DY-P	To 19 OTU.
N1391 DY-H	To 19 OTU.
N1413 DY-K	Destroyed in air-raid at Driffield 15.8.40.
N1415 DY-D	To 77 Sqn.
N1417 DY-B	FTR Gelsenkirchen 19/20.5.40.
N1419 DY-J	To 19 OTU.
N1420 DY-L	Destroyed in air-raid at Driffield 15.8.40.
N1421 DY-C	FTR Fornebu Norway 29/30.4.40.
N1433	From 58 Sqn. To 19 OTU.

N1471 DY-R	To 2 BAT Flt.
N1475 DY-H	To 7 BGS.
N1489 DY-C	From 10 Sqn. Crashed in Yorkshire during cross-country exercise 29.8.40.
N1499 DY-M	FTR Sterkrade/Holten 18/19.6.40.
N1500	From SD Flt. Crashed in Scotland during a ferry flight 1.5.40.
N1502 DY-F/E	Ditched in the North Sea on return from Emden 13.7.40.
N1523 DY-B	From 97 Sqn. FTR Kiel 6/7.7.40.
N1524 DY-O	From 97 Sqn. To 77 Sqn.
N1528 DY-E	FTR Euskirchen 21/22.5.40.
P4933 DY-F	Abandoned over Yorkshire on return from Lunen 19.10.40.
P4936 DY-S/M	FTR Berlin 14/15.11.40.
P4945 DY-L	Destroyed in air-raid at Driffield 15.8.40.
P4989	From 77 Sqn. To 10 OTU.
P4995 DY-E	Ditched while on patrol 7.10.40.
P5005 DY-N	To 78 Sqn.
P5012 DY-G	FTR Berlin 15/16.12.40.
P5014 DY-J	From 19 OTU. FTR Essen 3/4.7.41.
P5015	From 19 OTU. To 10 OTU.
P5022	Destroyed in air-raid at Driffield 15.8.40.
P5046	To 77 Sqn.
P5072 DY-P	From 19 OTU. FTR Duisburg 20/21.11.40.
P5073 DY-C/D	Shot down by intruder over Yorkshire when bound for Berlin 24.10.40.
P5074 DY-O/Q	Abandoned over Sussex on return from Turin 24.11.40.
P5077 DY-B	FTR Le Havre 27/28.11.40.
P5082 DY-L	FTR Bremen 28/29.10.40.
P5091	To 77 Sqn.
P5092 DY-A	From 19 OTU. To 19 OTU.
P5097 DY-Q	From 58 Sqn. Crash-landed near King's Lynn on return from Berlin 14/15.11.40.
P5102 DY-C	To 3 OTU.
T4135 DY-K/S	Crashed on landing at Linton-on-Ouse following early return from Merseburg 6.11.40.
T4136 DY-H	Abandoned over Yorkshire on return from Stettin 26.10.40.
T4140 DY-H	Crashed while trying to land at Bircham Newton on return from Berlin 13.3.41.
T4146	From 58 Sqn. Crash-landed in Norfolk when bound for Ludwigshaven 9.5.41.
T4161	To 10 OTU.
T4214	To 1502 Flt.
T4216 DY-F	Ditched off Devon coast on return from Turin 24.11.40.

T4227 DY-R	FTR Bremen 2/3.1.41.
T4233 DY-K	FTR Duisburg 30.6/1.7.41.
T4260	From 77 Sqn. FTR Boulogne 15/16.4.41.
T4261 DY-S	Ditched off Norfolk coast on return from Cologne 1.3.41.
T4269	FTR Bremen 27/28.6.41.
T4273 DY-O/S	FTR Hamburg 13/14.3.41.
T4289	Ditched off Whitby on return from Berlin 16.12.40.
T4297	FTR Bremen 27/28.6.41.
T4326 DY-K	FTR Berlin 12/13.3.41.
T4330	Crashed in Norfolk during emergency landing on return from Essen 4.7.41.
T4334	FTR Berlin 17/18.4.41.
T4336	From 77 Sqn. To 58 Sqn.
Z6467	To 10 OTU.
Z6468	FTR Kiel 7/8.4.41.
Z6483	To 78 Sqn.
Z6484	To 78 Sqn.
Z6485	From 58 Sqn. To 10 OTU.
Z6489	FTR Schwerte 12/13.6.41.
Z6494	To 1485 Flt.
Z6495	To 78 Sqn.
Z6510	FTR Schwerte 13/14.6.41.
Z6562	To 19 OTU.
Z6565	Damaged beyond repair during operation to Schwerte 12/13.6.41.
Z6566	To 51 Sqn.
Z6572	FTR Bremen 27/28.6.41.
Z6573	FTR Essen 3/4.7.41.
Z6574 DY-B	FTR Hüls 6/7.9.41.
Z6576	FTR Hanover 25/26.7.41.
Z6577	To 78 Sqn.
Z6586	To 10 Sqn.
Z6630	To 10 Sqn.
Z6653	To 161 Sqn.
Z6746	Crashed on landing at Topcliffe on return from Hanover 15.8.41.
Z6747	To 161 Sqn.
Z6748 DY-A	To 19 OTU.
Z6749	FTR Kiel 1/2.11.41.
Z6755	From 77 Sqn. To 24 OTU.
Z6759	FTR Bremen 27/28.6.41.
Z6761	Crashed in Lincolnshire on return from Nuremberg 13.10.41.
Z6795	To 29 OTU.
Z6796	FTR Berlin 7/8.11.41.
Z6798	To 10 OTU.
Z6800	From 77 Sqn. FTR Hamburg 30.11/1.12.41.

Z6812	To 51 Sqn.
Z6820	FTR Berlin 7/8.11.41.
Z6821	To 58 Sqn.
Z6828	From 10 Sqn. To 161 Sqn.
Z6829	FTR Hanover 14/15.8.41.
Z6830	To 10 OTU.
Z6837	FTR Essen 31.8/1.9.41.
Z6842	FTR Hanover 14/15.8.41.
Z6862	Crashed soon after take-off from Topcliffe while training 21.8.41.
Z6863	From 77 Sqn. FTR Frankfurt 29/30.8.41.
Z6866	From 77 Sqn. FTR Hanover 25/26.7.41.
Z6868	Blew up on the ground during preparation for operation to Essen 31.8.41.
Z6870	Crashed at Topcliffe while training 11.9.41.
Z6871 DY-A	Crashed in Yorkshire on return from Stettin 30.9.41.
Z6875	To 78 Sqn.
Z6876	To 77 Sqn.
Z6877	FTR Hanover 14/15.8.41.
Z6935	To 51 Sqn.
Z6940	To 161 Sqn.
Z6945	To 10 OTU.
Z6946	Crashed in Suffolk on return from Frankfurt 3.9.41.
Z6949	Crashed while trying to land at Upper Heyford on return from Le Havre 30.9.41.
Z6951	Crashed in Norfolk on return from Frankfurt 30.8.41.
Z6958	Damaged beyond repair during operation to Duisburg 16/17.10.41.
Z6959	To 138 Sqn.
Z6970 DY-R	FTR Hüls 6/7.9.41.
Z6973	FTR Dunkerque 16/17.12.41.
Z6974	To 10 OTU.
Z9128	FTR Berlin 7/8.11.41.
Z9134	To 24 OTU.
Z9161	From 10 Sqn. To 78 Sqn.
Z9167	To 10 OTU.
Z9201	To 51 Sqn.
Z9212	FTR Essen 8/9.11.41.
Z9217	To 51 Sqn.
Z9219	To 10 OTU.
Z9222	To 51 Sqn.
Z9229	To 77 Sqn.
Z9281	Abandoned over Scotland on return from Hamburg 30.11/1.12.41.
Z9282	To 138 Sqn.
Z9283	FTR Emden 26/27.1.42.
Z9289	Crashed in Yorkshire on return from Brest 6.1.42.

Z9292	To 1485 Flt.
Z9293	To 77 Sqn.
Z9310	To 1485 Flt.
Z9321	To 77 Sqn.
Z9362	To 24 OTU.
Z9421 DY-L	To 51 Sqn.

Halifax	From December 1941.
L9504	From 35 Sqn. Conversion Flt only. To 1652 CU.
L9510	From 76 Sqn. Conversion Flt only. Crashed on landing at Pocklington 18.10.42.
L9532	From 1652 CU. To 408 CF.
L9565	From 28 CF. Conversion Flt only. Crashed on landing at Pocklington 2.11.42.
L9584	From 35 Sqn. Conversion Flt only. Crashed on landing at Pocklington 3.11.42.
R9378	To 78 Sqn.
R9380	To 103 CF.
R9383	To 10 Sqn.
R9384	To 76 Sqn.
R9388	To 158 CF.
R9389	To 1427 Flt.
R9390	To 103 CF via 460 CF.
R9391	To 76 Sqn.
R9418	To 1658 CU.
R9419	To 102 CF via 1427 Flt.
R9421	To 10 Sqn.
R9423	To 1652 CU via 102 CF.
R9424	To 1652 CU.
R9426	To 1652 CU via 102 CF.
R9429	Conversion Flt only. To 1658 CU via 460 Sqn.
R9441	From 35 Sqn. To 1652 CU.
R9442 DY-R	From 35 Sqn. FTR Saarbrücken 29/30.7.42.
R9446 DY-F	From 35 Sqn. FTR Bremen 25/26.6.42.
R9449 DY-T	From 35 Sqn. Damaged beyond repair along with W1239 (102 Sqn) in landing accident at Pocklington on return from Frankfurt 9.9.42.
R9484	From 35 Sqn. Crashed in Yorkshire during air-test 14.4.42.
R9488	From 35 Sqn. Crashed in Yorkshire during air-test 14.4.42.
R9491 DY-N	From 10 Sqn. FTR Essen 2/3.6.42.
R9494	From 35 Sqn. To 1652 CU.
R9495 DY-L	From 10 Sqn. FTR Bochum 5/6.8.42.
R9497	From 10 Sqn. To 1658 CU.
R9498	From 10 Sqn. To 1652 CU via 102 CF.
R9528	From 10 Sqn. FTR Dunkerque 27/28.4.42.
R9529 DY-H	From 10 Sqn. FTR Essen 1/2.6.42.

R9530 DY-J	FTR Essen 16/17.6.42.
R9531	To 1658 CU.
R9532 DY-D	Crashed on final approach to Dalton on return from Essen 2/3.6.42.
R9533	To 1652 CU via 102 CF.
V9982	From 35 Sqn. Conversion Flt only. Crash-landed in Yorkshire 11.5.42.
V9987 DY-U	To 102 CF and back. Returned to 102 CF. FTR Bremen 25/26.6.42.
W1004	To 460 CF.
W1005	To 1652 CU.
W1011	To 460 CF.
W1047	To 35 Sqn.
W1048	To 35 Sqn.
W1049	To 35 Sqn.
W1050	To 35 Sqn.
W1051	To 35 Sqn.
W1052	From 10 Sqn. To 1659 CU.
W1053	To 35 Sqn.
W1054	To 10 Sqn.
W1055 DY-F	From 10 Sqn. FTR Flensburg 23/24.9.42.
W1066 DY-H	FTR Flensburg 1/2.10.42.
W1099 DY-A	Crashed on emergency approach to Cottesmore during a leafleting sortie to France 20.5.42.
W1107	FTR Wilhelmshaven 8/9.7.42.
W1142	FTR Hamburg 26/27.7.42.
W1153	FTR Hamburg 26/27.7.42.
W1167 DY-J	Crashed on landing at Pocklington following early return from Kiel 13.10.42.
W1168	To 76 Sqn.
W1181 DY-D	From 10 Sqn. Collided with DT512 (102 Sqn) on landing at Holme-on-Spalding-Moor on return from Genoa 24.10.42.
W1238	Crashed in Wales during training 22.8.42.
W1239 DY-G	Struck on the ground at Pocklington by R9449 (102 Sqn) and damaged beyond repair 9.9.42.
W1247	To 1652 CU via 102 CF.
W1248 DY-O	Crash-landed in Yorkshire on return from Saarbrücken 2.9.42.
W1271	To 10 Sqn.
W7651 DY-M	FTR Essen 16/17.6.42.
W7652 DY-P	FTR Essen 16/17.6.42.
W7653 DY-A	FTR Cologne 27/28.4.42.
W7654 DY-Q	FTR Bremen 25/26.6.42.
W7677 DY-Q	FTR Frankfurt 8/9.9.42.
W7706 DY-O	Crash-landed at West Raynham on return from Bochum 6.8.42.

W7712 DY-S	Crash-landed at Honington on return from Saarbrücken 29.8.42.
W7746	FTR Aachen 5/6.10.42.
W7752 DY-R	FTR Düsseldorf 10/11.9.42.
W7759 DY-L	FTR Bremen 25/26.6.42.
W7783	From 158 Sqn. To 1658 CU.
W7807	Conversion Flt only. To 1652 CU.
W7820 DY-V	From 76 Sqn. Ditched in the North Sea on return from Dortmund 5.5.43.
W7821	From 35 Sqn via 1658 CU. FTR Hamburg 3/4.2.43.
W7824	FTR Aachen 5/6.10.42.
W7825	Conversion Flt only. To TFU.
W7857	To 419 Sqn.
W7858 DY-R	FTR Flensburg 1/2.10.42.
W7864 DY-F	FTR Hamburg 9/10.11.42.
W7879 DY-O	From 76 Sqn. Crashed near Dalton following early return from Wilhelmshaven 11.2.43.
W7880 DY-J	From 158 Sqn. FTR Cologne 14/15.2.43.
W7882 DY-P	From 76 Sqn. FTR Cologne 2/3.2.43.
W7883 DY-B/R	To 1658 CU and back. FTR Hamburg 29/30.7.43.
W7884 DY-H	From 158 Sqn. FTR Frankfurt 2/3.12.42.
W7909	To BDU and back. To 10 Sqn.
W7910	Crash-landed in Yorkshire while training 4.1.43.
W7911 DY-B	FTR Mannheim 6/7.12.42.
W7912	To 1658 CU.
W7913 DY-L/C	FTR Frankfurt 2/3.12.42.
W7914 DY-A	FTR Stuttgart 22/23.11.42.
W7915	Crash-landed at Bradwell Bay on return from Turin 11.12.42.
W7916 DY-L	FTR Frankfurt 2/3.12.42.
W7917	To A&AEE.
W7918 DY-T	FTR Düsseldorf 27/28.1.43.
W7919 DY-N	FTR Cologne 26/27.2.43.
W7920 DY-D	To 1658 CU.
W7921 DY-M	FTR Hamburg 3/4.2.43.
W7922	From 78 Sqn. Destroyed by fire at Pocklington 14.2.43.
W7924 DY-E	FTR Mannheim 6/7.12.42.
W7925 DY-S	FTR from mining sortie 8/9.12.42.
W7927	To 466 Sqn.
W7933	Crashed in Yorkshire on return from Turin 12.12.42.
W7934 DY-R/J	FTR Wuppertal 29/30.5.43.
W7935 DY-F/Y	Ditched off Yarmouth on return from Bochum 14.5.43.
W7936	To 1653 CU.
BB197	To 102 CF. Crashed on landing at Marston Moor 18.8.42.
BB211 DY-A	FTR Osnabrück 9/10.8.42.

BB243	To 10 Sqn via 102 CF.
BB245	To 158 Sqn.
BB249 DY-Z	From 158 Sqn FTR Gelsenkirchen 9/10.7.43.
BB320	From 35 Sqn. To 1662 CU.
BB365	From 76 Sqn. To 1668 CU.
BB370	From 35 Sqn. Crashed on landing at Pocklington while training 20.10.43.
BB372	From 35 Sqn. To 1652 CU.
BB383	To 1654 CU.
BB428 DY-Q	FTR Cologne 3/4.7.43.
DT485	From 158 Sqn. To 1668 CU.
DT512 DY-Q	Struck by W1181 (102 Sqn) on the ground at Holme-on-Spalding-Moor on return from Genoa 24.10.42.
DT517 DY-G	FTR Flensburg 23/24.9.42.
DT518	Crashed soon after take-off from Pocklington for ferry flight 30.10.42.
DT539 DY-A	FTR Hamburg 9/10.11.42.
DT540	To 419 Sqn.
DT548	To 419 Sqn.
DT559	To 158 Sqn.
DT588	From 77 Sqn. To 1652 CU.
DT702 DY-K	From 158 Sqn. Crashed on landing at Pocklington on return from air-test 29.8.43.
DT703	From 158 Sqn. To 1654 CU.
DT739 DY-P	FTR Essen 12/13.3.43.
DT743	To 1658 CU.
DT747 DY-P	FTR Stettin 20/21.4.43.
DT779	Crashed on take-off from Pocklington when bound for mining sortie 26.2.43.
DT799 DY-L	FTR Essen 12/13.3.43.
DT800 DY-P	Crashed at Colchester when bound for Nuremberg 25.2.43.
DT808	To 405 Sqn.
HR663 DY-Q/T	FTR Pilsen 16/17.4.43.
HR667 DY-H/U/O	FTR Dortmund 4/5.5.43.
HR668 DY-S	To 1662 CU.
HR669 DY-E	FTR Cologne 26/27.2.43.
HR711 DY-J/C	From 51 Sqn. FTR Hamburg 29/30.7.43.
HR712 DY-M	FTR Stettin 20/21.4.43.
HR714	To 77 Sqn.
HR716 DY-P	From 51 Sqn. Crash-landed near Driffield on return from Berlin 21.1.44.
HR727	From 76 Sqn. To 51 Sqn.
HR730	From 51 Sqn. To 1659 CU.
HR754	To 158 Sqn.
HR755	To 158 Sqn.
HR804 DY-T	From 35 Sqn. Crashed in Yorkshire following early return from Frankfurt 26.11.43.

HR811 DY-C	From 35 Sqn. FTR Frankfurt 25/26.11.43.
HR834	From 51 Sqn. To 1659 CU.
HR867 DY-A	From 405 Sqn. FTR Berlin 29/30.12.43.
HR873	From 10 Sqn. To 1663 CU.
HR911 DY-L	FTR Kassel 22/23.10.43.
HR919 DY-O	Crashed in Yorkshire on return from Modane 17.9.43.
HR924	To 10 Sqn.
HR927 DY-N	To 1667 CU.
HR942	From 78 Sqn. To 1663 CU.
HR947	From 51 Sqn. To 77 Sqn.
HR978 DY-V	From 158 Sqn. FTR Laon 23/24.3.44.
HX149 DY-J	FTR Magdeburg 21/22.1.44.
HX150 DY-M	FTR Magdeburg 21/22.1.44.
HX151 DY-M	FTR from mining sortie 24.4.44.
HX153	To 1663 CU.
HX154 DY-K	FTR Hanover 22/23.9.43.
HX155 DY-Q	FTR Berlin 15/16.2.44.
HX156	To 10 Sqn.
HX158 DY-O	FTR from mining sortie 11/12.11.43.
HX171	From 10 Sqn. To 1662 CU.
HX173 DY-N	FTR Hanover 8/9.10.43.
HX180 DY-E	Crashed on landing at Elvington while training 1.10.43.
HX182	To 1663 CU.
HX184	From 10 Sqn. To 1652 CU.
HX185 DY-B	FTR Leipzig 19/20.2.44.
HX187 DY-H/X	FTR Berlin 20/21.1.44.
HX188	Force-landed near Carnaby on return from Münster 12.9.44.
HX240	From 77 Sqn. To 1658 CU.
JB782 DY-W	FTR Mannheim 9/10.8.43.
JB784	From 78 Sqn. To 1658 CU.
JB794 DY-G	Crashed on approach to Pocklington following early return from Nuremberg 10.8.43.
JB799 DY-E	FTR Duisburg 12/13.5.43.
JB834 DY-C	FTR Wuppertal 24/25.6.43.
JB835 DY-X	FTR Nuremberg 27/28.8.43.
JB836 DY-T	FTR Essen 12/13.3.43.
JB840 DY-N	FTR Nuremberg 8/9.3.43.
JB843 DY-F	FTR Gelsenkirchen 25/26.6.43.
JB844	From 78 Sqn. To 1663 CU.
JB848 DY-G	Crashed soon after take-off from Pocklington when bound for Berlin 29.3.43.
JB864 DY-B	FTR Hamburg 27/28.7.43.
JB867	Crashed on take-off from Pocklington during training 5.5.43.
JB868 DY-T	FTR Bochum 12/13.6.43.
JB869 DY-H	FTR Dortmund 4/5.5.43.

JB894 DY-X	FTR Aachen 13/14.7.43.
JB918 DY-T	FTR Duisburg 26/27.4.43.
JB921 DY-B	FTR Munich 6/7.9.43.
JB964 DY-G	FTR Bochum 13/14.5.43.
JD111 DY-P	Crash-landed at Pocklington on return from Mönchengladbach 31.8.43.
JD112 DY-H	FTR Dortmund 23/24.5.43.
JD127 DY-U	Crashed on take-off from Pocklington when bound for Berlin 23.8.43.
JD128 DY-M	FTR Mönchengladbach 30/31.8.43.
JD144 DY-U/Q	FTR Wuppertal 24/25.6.43.
JD149 DY-H	FTR Essen 27/28.5.43.
JD150 DY-A	FTR Hamburg 27/28.7.43.
JD165 DY-S	Ditched off Montrose during operation to Berlin 28/29.1.44.
JD169 DY-J	FTR Essen 25/26.7.43.
JD206 DY-T	Ditched off Dutch coast on return from Krefeld 21/22.6.43.
JD276 DY-Z	Crashed near Pocklington while training 3.10.43.
JD296 DY-B	Crashed while landing at Ashbourne on return from Peenemünde 18.8.43.
JD297 DY-Q	FTR Aachen 13/14.7.43.
JD302 DY-O	From 51 Sqn. Crashed near Norwich on return from Berlin 20/21.1.44.
JD303 DY-S	FTR Leipzig 3/4.12.43.
JD304 DY-Y	From A&AEE. Crashed on landing at Marston Moor during ferry flight 2.5.44.
JD307	To 1667 CU.
JD311	From 51 Sqn. To 1662 CU.
JD316 DY-X	FTR Hamburg 24/25.7.43.
JD366 DY-V	FTR Frankfurt 25/26.11.43.
JD369 DY-A	FTR Nuremberg 10/11.8.43.
JD378 DY-C	From 77 Sqn. FTR Leverkusen 22/23.8.43.
JD407 DY-R	FTR Berlin 23/24.8.43.
JD408 DY-R	FTR Mannheim 9/10.8.43.
JD412 DY-X	From 408 Sqn. FTR Berlin 29/30.12.43.
JD415	To 1662 CU.
JD421	From 77 Sqn. To 1658 CU.
JD461 DY-Y	From 51 Sqn. FTR Berlin 20/21.1.44.
JD467 DY-R	FTR Frankfurt 20/21.12.43.
JD469	To 1662 CU.
JN891	From 51 Sqn. To 10 Sqn.
JN908 DY-Z	FTR Kassel 22/23.10.43.
JN909 DY-B	FTR Berlin 31.8/1.9.43.
JN919	From 78 Sqn. Abandoned over Yorkshire while training 6.5.44.
JN947	To 10 Sqn.
JN948 DY-N	From 10 Sqn. FTR Aulnoye 27/28.4.44.

JN949 DY-D	Crashed on landing at Pocklington while training 22.12.43.
JN950	To 1663 CU.
JN951 DY-N	FTR Berlin 20/21.1.44.
JN952 DY-L	FTR Magdeburg 21/22.1.44.
JN972 DY-H	From 78 Sqn. FTR Leipzig 19/20.2.44.
JP118	From 78 Sqn. To 1662 CU.
JP120	From 78 Sqn. To 1662 CU.
JP126	From 78 Sqn. To 1663 CU.
LL552 DY-X	From 77 Sqn. FTR Stuttgart 24/25.7.44.
LL555 DY-W	From 77 Sqn. Crash-landed at Woodbridge on return from Münster 12.9.44.
LL556	From 77 Sqn. To 347 Sqn.
LL557	From 77 Sqn. To 346 Sqn.
LL581	To 346 Sqn.
LL590	To 347 Sqn.
LL597 DY-X	From 347 Sqn. FTR Hanover 5/6.1.45.
LW134	To 520 Sqn.
LW138	Crash-landed near Pocklington while training 7.5.44.
LW140 DY-Q/M	Crashed in Yorkshire on return from mining sortie 8/9.6.44.
LW141 DY-U	FTR Düsseldorf 2/3.11.44.
LW142 DY-N	FTR Goch 7/8.2.45.
LW143 DY-O	FTR Blainville-Sur-l'Eau 28/29.6.44.
LW158 DY-P	Undershot landing at Pocklington on return from Dortmund 1.1.45.
LW159 DY-Q	FTR Blainville-Sur-l'Eau 28/29.6.44.
LW160	To 1652 CU.
LW168 DY-O	FTR Mülheim airfield 24.12.44.
LW179 DY-Y	From 77 Sqn. FTR Magdeburg 16/17.1.45.
LW191	From 77 Sqn.
LW192 DY-R/H	From 77 Sqn. FTR Sterkrade/Holten 16/17.6.44.
LW195 DY-J/H	From 77 Sqn. FTR Brunswick 12/13.8.44.
LW226	From 78 Sqn. To 1662 CU.
LW227 DY-X	From 51 Sqn. FTR Berlin 20/21.1.44.
LW235	From 78 Sqn. To 1666 CU.
LW241	From 77 Sqn. Returned to 77 Sqn.
LW274 DY-R	From 158 Sqn. FTR Magdeburg 21/22.1.44.
LW277 DY-Y	From 78 Sqn. FTR Berlin 28/29.1.44.
LW288	From 78 Sqn. To 1652 CU.
LW295	From 78 Sqn. To 77 Sqn.
LW299	From 51 Sqn. To 1663 CU.
LW318	From 78 Sqn. To 1658 CU.
LW322	From 10 Sqn. To 1663 CU.
LW329	To 1652 CU.
LW330	To 78 Sqn.
LW331 DY-D	To 78 Sqn and back. Ditched on return from mining sortie 26.2.44.

LW332	From 10 Sqn. To 1652 CU.
LW333 DY-K	Collided with LW264 (77 Sqn) near Pocklington on return from Berlin 22.11.43.
LW335	To 1652 CU.
LW336	From 10 Sqn. To 1662 CU.
LW337 DY-F	FTR Berlin 20/21.1.44.
LW339 DY-F	FTR Berlin 15/16.2.44.
LW342	From 78 Sqn. To 1662 CU.
MZ289 DY-J	FTR from training flight over the North Sea 17.9.44.
MZ290	To 1659 CU and back. To 10 Sqn.
MZ292 DY-C	FTR Sterkrade/Holten 16/17.6.44.
MZ298 DY-F	From 77 Sqn. FTR Les Hauts Boissons 24.7.44.
MZ300	From 77 Sqn. To 10 Sqn.
MZ301 DY-M	From 77 Sqn. FTR Sterkrade/Holten 16/17.6.44.
MZ336	To 77 Sqn.
MZ346	To 77 Sqn.
MZ347	To 77 Sqn.
MZ371 DY-G	Crashed on take-off from Pocklington when bound for Somain marshalling yards 11.8.44.
MZ426	To 78 Sqn.
MZ450 DY-B	Damaged beyond repair while approaching Pocklington on return from Soest 5/6.12.44.
MZ642 DY-O/U	FTR Sterkrade/Holten 16/17.6.44.
MZ644 DY-V	FTR Blainville-Sur-l'Eau 28/29.6.44.
MZ646 DY-W	FTR Blainville-Sur-l'Eau 28/29.6.44.
MZ647 DY-R	FTR Rüsselsheim 12/13.8.44.
MZ648	To 1663 CU.
MZ649 DY-Y	FTR Bourg Leopold 27/28.5.44.
MZ651 DY-Z	FTR Massy Palaiseau 11/12.6.44.
MZ652 DY-Z	FTR Sterkrade/Holten 16/17.6.44.
MZ659 DY-T	Abandoned near Carnaby on return from Alencon 9.6.44.
MZ673	To 77 Sqn.
MZ676	To 77 Sqn.
MZ694	To 77 Sqn and back. To 1665 CU.
MZ695	To 77 Sqn.
MZ699 DY-T	From 77 Sqn. FTR Münster 12.9.44.
MZ710	To 77 Sqn.
MZ711	To 77 Sqn.
MZ745	To 297 Sqn.
MZ752 DY-K	Crashed on landing at Pocklington on return from Montorgueil 25.6.44.
MZ753 DY-M	FTR Montorgueil 25.6.44.
MZ770	To 640 Sqn.
MZ771	To 578 Sqn.
MZ772 DY-Q	FTR Bochum 4/5.11.44.
MZ790	From 346 Sqn. To 578 Sqn.
MZ796 DY-M	FTR Hanover 5/6.1.45.

MZ797	To 640 Sqn.
MZ798 DY-M	FTR Düsseldorf 2/3.11.44.
MZ800	Crashed on landing at Carnaby on return from Münster 18.11.44.
MZ801	To 77 Sqn.
MZ803	To 77 Sqn.
MZ809	To 77 Sqn.
MZ812	To 77 Sqn.
MZ827	From 77 Sqn. Damaged beyond repair during operation to Mülheim airfield 24.12.44.
MZ830	From 77 Sqn. Crashed in Yorkshire on return from Amiens marshalling yards 15/16.3.44.
MZ871 DY-G	FTR Mülheim 23/24.12.44.
MZ902	From 424 Sqn. To 76 Sqn.
MZ937	To 76 Sqn.
MZ938	To 578 Sqn.
NA165	To 519 Sqn.
NA173	To 578 Sqn.
NA175 DY-Q	FTR Goch 7/8.2.45.
NA502 DY-S	FTR Blainville 28/29.6.44.
NA503 DY-U	Crashed in Gloucestershire on return from Normandy battle area 30.7.44.
NA504 DY-Y	FTR Kiel 16/17.8.44.
NA508	To 77 Sqn.
NA509	To 420 Sqn.
NA511	To 77 Sqn.
NA512	To 77 Sqn.
NA515	To 77 Sqn.
NA559	To 1665 CU.
NA564	To 346 Sqn.
NA565	To 1665 CU.
NA572	From 77 Sqn. To 347 Sqn.
NA599	
NA602 DY-Y	FTR Hanover 5/6.1.45.
NA615	From 346 Sqn.
NA619	To 462 Sqn.
NA681	To 347 Sqn.
NP950 DY-Q	Crashed on landing at Pocklington on return from Düsseldorf 20/21.2.45.
NP966	
NP988	To 347 Sqn.
NR186 DY-U	Crashed on landing at Pocklington on return from Ludwigshafen 2.1.45.
NR187	To 111 OTU.
NR210	From 424 Sqn. To 77 Sqn.
NR211	To 78 Sqn.
NR225	To 158 Sqn.
NR242	To 346 Sqn.

PN176	
PN395	From 96 Sqn. To 346 Sqn.
PP171 DY-H	
PP177	
PP179 DY-A	FTR Witten 18/19.3.45.
PP182	
PP186/PP187	
PP203/PP204	
PP206	
PP207	To 78 Sqn.
PP208	From 347 Sqn.
PP209	
PP211	
RG481	
RG482	
RG483	
RG484	
RG485	
RG489	
RG490	To 77 Sqn.
RG498 DY-N	Crashed on landing at Manston on return from Bottrop/Castrop-Rauxel 15.3.45.
RG502 DY-Q	FTR Chemnitz 5/6.3.45.
RG503/RG505	
RG532	From 77 Sqn.
RG550	
RG555	From 76 Sqn.
RG556	From 76 Sqn.
RG558	From 76 Sqn.
RG585	
RG610	To 640 Sqn.
RG668	From 347 Sqn.
TW789	
TW794	From 76 Sqn.

Heaviest Single Loss

20/21.01.44.   Berlin. 7 Halifaxes. 5 FTR. 2 crashed on return.

104 SQUADRON

Motto: Strike Hard   **Code: EP**

104 Squadron was first formed as a light bomber unit in September 1917. It moved to France in May 1918 to undertake strategic operations against Germany. Disbanded at the end of June 1919, the squadron remained on the shelf until being reformed from C Flight of 40 Squadron in January 1936. Ultimately designated a training squadron, it was eventually assimilated into the OTU system. Re-formed again as a Wellington unit in 4 Group at the start of April 1941, 104 Squadron went to war for the first time on 9 May. Equipped

with the Merlin-powered Mk II variant of the type, the squadron was able to carry the 4,000lb 'Cookie' blockbuster bomb. In October, fifteen of the squadron's aircraft and crews were posted to the Middle East on what was intended to be a temporary move. The home echelon rebuilt while the coveted squadron number was fought over. It had been intended that the home unit would retain the number, and that the overseas element would be re-designated. However, the decision was made to renumber the home echelon, and on 14 February 1942 it was reconstituted as 158 Squadron.

STATIONS
Driffield   01.04.41 to 14.02.42

COMMANDING OFFICERS
Squadron Leader D.B.G. Tomlinson   01.04.41 to 23.04.41
Squadron Leader P.R. Beare   23.04.41 to 11.05.41
Wing Commander W.S.G. Simonds   11.05.41 to 20.07.41
Wing Commander P.R. Beare   20.07.41 to 08.05.42
Squadron Leader W.M. Protheroe (home echelon)   16.10.41 to 14.02.42

AIRCRAFT
Wellington II   01.04.41 to 07.43

OPERATIONAL RECORD

Operations	Sorties	Aircraft Losses	% Losses
60	373	13	3.5
All bombing			

TABLE OF STATISTICS
Out of 25 operational squadrons in 4 Group
16th highest number of overall operations in 4 Group.
18th highest number of sorties in 4 Group.
17th highest number of aircraft operational losses in 4 Group.

Out of 12 operational Wellington squadrons in 4 Group
4th highest number of Wellington overall operations in 4 Group.
4th highest number of Wellington sorties in 4 Group.
5th highest number of Wellington operational losses in 4 Group.

AIRCRAFT HISTORIES

Wellington	From April 1941 to February 1942.
W5362 EP-J	FTR Berlin 7/8.9.41.
W5366	From 1443 Flt. SOC 31.10.41.
W5392	To 158 Sqn.
W5394	To 12 Sqn.
W5398	To Malta.
W5415	To 158 Sqn.

W5416	FTR Kiel 19/20.8.41.
W5417 EP-F	FTR Emden 15/16.1.42.
W5425	To 158 Sqn.
W5426	SOC 12.3.44.
W5429	Damaged beyond repair 29.12.41.
W5431	To 158 Sqn.
W5432 EP-H	Crashed in Devon during air-test 27.9.41.
W5435 EP-F	Crashed in Yorkshire during operation to Frankfurt 2.9.41.
W5437	To 158 Sqn.
W5438 EP-E	FTR Brest 24.7.41.
W5441	Crashed in Yorkshire while training 12.9.41.
W5443 EP-T	FTR Berlin 12/13.8.41.
W5453	To 305 Sqn.
W5461 EP-R	FTR Berlin 12/13.8.41.
W5477	Crashed on landing at Driffield on transit flight 23.8.41.
W5479	To 158 Sqn.
W5482	To 158 Sqn.
W5485 EP-J	FTR Karlsruhe 5/6.8.41.
W5486 EP-H	FTR Hanover 14/15.8.41.
W5491	From 405 Sqn. Crashed on take-off from Driffield during training 9.1.42.
W5493 EP-D	From 405 Sqn. Crashed in Yorkshire on return from Emden 16.1.42.
W5498	To 405 Sqn.
W5500	
W5513 EP-P	FTR Hanover 14/15.7.41.
W5517	Crash-landed at Horsham-St-Faith on return from Saarbrücken 6.8.41.
W5523	From 12 Sqn. Returned to 12 Sqn.
W5531	To 158 Sqn.
W5532 EP-M	Crashed in Lincolnshire when bound for Cologne 17.8.41.
W5554	To Malta.
W5561	To 405 Sqn.
W5576 EP-N	FTR Turin 10/11.9.41.
W5580 EP-K	FTR Berlin 2/3.8.41.
W5583	To OADU and back. To Malta.
W5589	To 405 Sqn.
W5595 EP-E	From 405 Sqn. FTR Duisburg 28/29.8.41.
W5611	From 12 Sqn. Returned to 12 Sqn.
Z8345 EP-S	
Z8358	To 405 Sqn.
Z8374	To Malta.
Z8400	To 158 Sqn.
Z8404	To Malta.
Z8405	To 158 Sqn.

Z8408	To 158 Sqn.
Z8411	From 214 Sqn. To Malta.
Z8413	To 158 Sqn.
Z8414	To Malta.
Z8415	
Z8419	To 405 Sqn.
Z8426 EP-E	FTR Dunkerque 7/8.12.41.

158 SQUADRON

Motto: Strength in Unity   **Code: NP**

First formed in September 1918, 158 Squadron did not become operational before the Great War ended. It was re-formed in 4 Group on 14 February 1942 from the remnant of 104 Squadron, and inherited Wellington Mk II aircraft. These were exchanged for Halifaxes in June 1942, and operations on the type began before the month was out. Short detachments to Coastal Command at the end of the year were followed by a return to 4 Group and a position at the forefront of 4 Group operations for the remainder of the war. 158 Squadron was the proud guardian of Halifax III LV907, Friday the Thirteenth, which completed 128 operations, a Halifax record, and survived the war.

STATIONS

Driffield	14.02.42 to 06.06.42
Pocklington (detachment)	14.02.42 to 05.03.42
East Moor	06.06.42 to 06.11.42
Beaulieu (detachment)	25.10.42 to 05.12.42
Rufforth	06.11.42 to 28.02.43
Manston (detachment)	07.11.42 to 25.11.42
Lissett	28.02.43 to 17.08.45

COMMANDING OFFICERS

Wing Commander P. Stevens DFC	14.02.42 to 07.10.42
Wing Commander C.G.S.R. Robinson DFC	07.10.42 to 10.03.43
Wing Commander T.R. Hope DFC	10.03.43 to 10.08.43
Wing Commander C.C. Calder DSO DFC MiD	11.08.43 to 07.06.44
Wing Commander P. Dobson DSO DFC AFC	07.06.44 to 07.03.45
Wing Commander G.B. Read DFC	07.03.45 to 12.06.45

AIRCRAFT

Wellington II	02.42 to 06.42
Halifax II	06.42 to 01.44
Halifax III	01.44 to 06.45
Halifax VI	04.45 to 07.45

OPERATIONAL RECORD

Operations	Sorties	Aircraft Losses	% Losses
356	5,368	159	3.0

Wellingtons

Operations	Sorties	Aircraft Losses	% Losses
81	207	14	6.8

Category of Operations

Bombing	Mining
78	3

Halifaxes

Operations	Sorties	Aircraft Losses	% Losses
275	5,161	145	2.8

Category of Operations

Bombing	Mining
267	8

TABLE OF STATISTICS

31st highest number of overall operations in Bomber Command.
20th highest number of sorties in Bomber Command.
17th highest number of aircraft operational losses in Bomber Command.

Out of 25 operational squadrons in 4 Group

7th highest number of overall operations in 4 Group.
6th highest number of sorties in 4 Group.
3rd highest number of aircraft operational losses in 4 Group.

Out of 12 operational Wellington squadrons in 4 Group

3rd highest number of overall Wellington operations in 4 Group.
6th highest number of Wellington sorties in 4 Group.
4th highest number of Wellington operational losses in 4 Group.

Out of 15 operational Halifax squadrons in 4 Group

5th highest number of overall Halifax operations in 4 Group.
Highest number of Halifax sorties in 4 Group.
2nd highest number of Halifax operational losses in 4 Group.

AIRCRAFT HISTORIES

Wellington	From January 1942 to June 1942.
W5357	To Defford.
W5358 NP-T	From 12 Sqn. FTR Essen 12/13.4.42.
W5387 NP-V	From 12 Sqn. FTR Warnemünde 8/9.5.42.
W5392 NP-L	From 104 Sqn. FTR Cologne 30/31.5.42.
W5415	From 104 Sqn. SOC 15.1.42.
W5424 NP-G	To 12 Sqn 11.6.42.
W5425	From 104 Sqn. To 1446 Flt.

W5431 NP-W	From 104 Sqn. Crashed at Driffield on return from Essen 10.3.42.
W5437	From 104 Sqn. To 12 Sqn 4.6.42.
W5479	From 104 Sqn. To 311 FTU.
W5482 NP-X	From 104 Sqn. FTR Lille 10/11.4.42.
W5525 NP-V	From 405 Sqn. FTR Essen 12/13.4.42.
W5531	From 104 Sqn. To 405 Sqn.
W5562 NP-Z/H	To 405 Sqn and back. FTR Warnemünde 8/9.5.42.
W5564 NP-P	From 405 Sqn. To 1443 Flt.
W5575 NP-R	From 12 Sqn. FTR Hamburg 17/18.4.42.
Z8375 NP-B	From 405 Sqn. To 12 Sqn 11.6.42.
Z8400 NP-A	From 104 Sqn. To 12 Sqn 4.6.42.
Z8405 NP-B	From 104 Sqn. To 1446 Flt.
Z8408	From 104 Sqn. SOC 15.1.42.
Z8412 NP-M	From 405 Sqn. To 12 Sqn 4.6.42.
Z8413	From 104 Sqn. SOC 15.1.42.
Z8420 NP-P	From 405 Sqn. To 12 Sqn 23.5.42.
Z8429 NP-J	From 75 Sqn. To 12 Sqn.
Z8439 NP-R	FTR Warnemünde 8/9.5.42.
Z8441 NP-K	From 75 Sqn. Crashed on approach to Pocklington on return from Billancourt 3.3.42.
Z8490 NP-N	From 214 Sqn. FTR Dortmund 14/15.4.42.
Z8511 NP-Z	FTR Hamburg 8/9.4.42.
Z8521 NP-N	From 405 Sqn. FTR Kiel 28/29.4.42.
Z8523 NP-K	To 305 Sqn 16.6.42.
Z8525 NP-H	FTR Ostende 29/30.4.42.
Z8526 NP-Y	To 12 Sqn 23.5.42.
Z8528 NP-E	To 305 Sqn 23.5.42.
Z8532 NP-F	To 12 Sqn 23.5.42.
Z8534 NP-R	To 1443 Flt.
Z8536 NP-S	Crashed on take-off from Pocklington when bound for Kiel 26.2.42.
Z8577 NP-T	From 405 Sqn. FTR Cologne 30/31.5.42.
Z8585 NP-Z	From 405 Sqn. To 12 Sqn 4.6.42.
Z8595 NP-Q	To 305 Sqn 26.5.42.
Z8597 NP-X	From 405 Sqn. To 305 Sqn 23.5.42.
Z8600 NP-B	FTR Warnemünde 8/9.5.42.
Halifax	From June 1942.
R9367	To 1652 CU 17.8.43.
R9373 NP-W	To 1658 CU 4.2.43.
R9388 NP-Y	From 102 Sqn. Conversion Flt only. To 1658 CU 31.10.42.
R9434	From 78 Sqn via 1652 CU. Conversion Flt only. To 1674 CU.
W1003	From 10 Sqn. Conversion Flt only. To 1658 CU 9.9.42.
W1014 NP-X	From 78 Sqn. Conversion Flt only. To 1656 CU.

W1038 NP-N	From 10 Sqn. Crash-landed in Yorkshire during training 16.10.42.
W1040 NP-G	From 10 Sqn. FTR Duisburg 21/22.7.42.
W1091 NP-W	From 78 Sqn. To 1652 CU 5.4.43.
W1108 NP-E	FTR Cologne 15/16.10.42.
W1157 NP-A/E	To 77 Sqn 11.4.43.
W1162 NP-D	FTR Vegesack 19/20.7.42.
W1164 NP-B	FTR Hamburg 26/27.7.42.
W1165	Conversion Flt only. To 35 Sqn.
W1166 NP-L/U/M	To 1652 CU 12.4.43.
W1179 NP-S	FTR Vegesack 19/20.7.42.
W1182 NP-L	From 103 Sqn. Collided with Wellington BK460 when bound for Lorient 13/14.2.43.
W1190 NP-T	FTR Düsseldorf 31.7/1.8.42.
W1211 NP-J	FTR Duisburg 25/26.7.42.
W1214 NP-D	FTR Bremen 4/5.9.42.
W1215 NP-C	FTR Bochum 5/6.8.42.
W1217 NP-S/L	From 103 Sqn. To 10 Sqn 23.4.43.
W1221 NP-R/B/M/H	To 1654 CU 14.9.43.
W1222 NP-S	FTR Essen 16/17.9.42.
W1246 NP-C	To 1656 CU.
W1251 NP-T	From 103 Sqn. To 1659 CU.
W1253 NP-M	Crashed in the Humber on return from Genoa 8.11.42.
W7668 NP-N	From 78 Sqn. To 1666 CU.
W7745 NP-K	FTR Düsseldorf 10/11.9.42.
W7750 NP-M	FTR Duisburg 6/7.8.42.
W7751 NP-F	FTR from mining sortie 9/10.1.43.
W7753 NP-P	FTR Duisburg 13/14.7.42.
W7766 NP-H	Crashed at East Moor on return from Kiel 14.10.42.
W7777 NP-V/O	FTR Saarbrücken 19/20.9.42.
W7783 NP-J/O	To 102 Sqn 12.4.43.
W7784 NP-Q	From 78 Sqn. Crashed in Yorkshire when bound for Duisburg 20.12.42.
W7859 NP-K/T	Crashed in Sussex on return from Genoa 16.11.42.
W7862 NP-D	FTR Genoa 23/24.10.42.
W7863 NP-V	FTR Nancy/Strasbourg 17/18.11.42.
W7865 NP-A/G	To 10 Sqn 10.4.43.
W7880 NP-E	To 102 Sqn 25.1.43.
W7884	To 102 Sqn 29.10.42.
BB189	From 76 Sqn. To 1658 CU.
BB193	Conversion Flt only.
BB203	Conversion Flt only. Crashed in Yorkshire while training 16.7.42.
BB205 NP-B	FTR Bremen 14.9.42.
BB207	To 10 Sqn 19.7.42.
BB208 NP-V/P	To 1659 CU 7.12.42.

BB209 NP-G	Crashed in Lincolnshire on return from Turin 19.11.42.
BB213	To 1658 CU 9.8.42.
BB219	From 78 Sqn. To 1659 CU 5.12.42.
BB220NP-B	From 10 Sqn. Returned to 10 Sqn 29.4.43.
BB245	From 102 Sqn. To 76 Sqn.
BB249	From 10 Sqn. To 102 Sqn 20.4.43.
DG223 NP-Q	Crashed in Yorkshire when bound for Mannheim 6.12.42.
DG225 NP-N	Ditched off Scarborough on return from Bremen 26.6.42.
DG226	From 10 Sqn. To 1658 CU 6.4.43.
DG227 NP-Q	From 35 Sqn. FTR Duisburg 13/14.7.42.
DT485 NP-K/C	From 103 Sqn. To 102 Sqn 23.4.43.
DT492	Conversion Flt only. To 76 Sqn 14.10.42.
DT505 NP-H	From 103 Sqn. To 78 Sqn and back. Damaged in accident 5.3.43.
DT521 NP-O	To 1652 CU.
DT524	From 460 Sqn. To 1658 CU 31.12.42.
DT544 NP-R	Crashed in Buckinghamshire on return from Mannheim 7.12.42.
DT547	From 78 Sqn. To 1652 CU.
DT558 NP-H	Abandoned over Somerset on return from Genoa 16.11.42.
DT559 NP-D	From 102 Sqn. To 466 Sqn 29.9.43.
DT564 NP-B	From 77 Sqn. SOC 22.1.43.
DT567	From 77 Sqn. To 78 Sqn.
DT569	To 76 Sqn.
DT570	To 76 Sqn.
DT579 NP-V	From 77 Sqn. FTR Turin 11/12.12.42.
DT583 NP-O	From 77 Sqn. FTR from mining sortie 20/21.1.43.
DT585 NP-L/A	From 77 Sqn. To 1658 CU.
DT622 NP-P	Force-landed in Yorkshire when bound for a mining sortie 9.1.43.
DT635 NP-F	FTR Essen 3/4.4.43.
DT637 NP-C	From 77 Sqn. To 51 Sqn.
DT638	From 51 Sqn. SOC 30.4.43.
DT640 NP-X	Damaged in taxiing accident at Rufforth 18.2.43.
DT644 NP-Y	FTR from mining sortie 18/19.2.43.
DT668 NP-R	FTR Nuremberg 25/26.2.43.
DT671 NP-R	From 77 Sqn. To 51 Sqn.
DT681 NP-J	FTR Lorient 29/30.1.43.
DT694 NP-N	FTR Cologne 14/15.2.43.
DT696 NP-Q	Crashed in Yorkshire on return from Cologne 14.2.43.
DT697 NP-B	To 1658 CU.
DT700 NP-S	To 77 Sqn.
DT701 NP-T	FTR Lorient 7/8.2.43.

DT702 NP-U	To 102 Sqn.
DT703 NP-V	To 102 Sqn.
DT720 NP-P/Y	To 10 Sqn.
DT731 NP-K	To 419 Sqn.
DT740 NP-Z/P	To 1658 CU.
DT747 NP-P/Z	Lost 21.4.43. Details uncertain.
DT748 NP-J	FTR Stuttgart 11/12.3.43.
DT795 NP-N	FTR Essen 3/4.4.43.
HR715 NP-A/E	FTR Bochum 29/30.9.43.
HR716 NP-R/F	To 51 Sqn 24.12.43.
HR717 NP-E	FTR Wuppertal 29/30.5.43.
HR718 NP-H/A	FTR Berlin 23/24.8.43.
HR719 NP-M	FTR Düsseldorf 11/12.6.43.
HR720 NP-B	FTR Aachen 13/14.7.43.
HR721 NP-S/J	Abandoned over Selsey Bill on return from Nuremberg 11.8.43.
HR722 NP-C	FTR Stettin 20/21.4.43.
HR724 NP-W	FTR Bochum 12/13.6.43.
HR725 NP-C	FTR Berlin 23/24.8.43.
HR734 NP-P	FTR Cologne 3/4.7.43.
HR735 NP-N	FTR Krefeld 21/22.6.43.
HR737 NP-U	FTR Duisburg 26/27.4.43.
HR738 NP-Z/P	FTR Berlin 31.8/1.9.43.
HR739 NP-Y/C/U	FTR Mönchengladbach 30/31.8.43.
HR740 NP-K	FTR Bochum 12/13.6.43.
HR751 NP-J	FTR Hamburg 2/3.8.43.
HR752 NP-T	FTR Montbeliard 15/16.7.43.
HR753 NP-B	FTR Berlin 27/28.3.43.
HR754 NP-K	From 102 Sqn. Crashed in Yorkshire on return from Essen 4.4.43.
HR755 NP-X	From 102 Sqn. To 51 Sqn.
HR757 NP-M	From 10 Sqn. FTR Berlin 29/30.3.43.
HR758 NP-Y	FTR Pilsen 16/17.4.43.
HR773 NP-A	FTR from mining sortie 28/29.4.43.
HR775 NP-V	FTR Essen 27/28.5.43.
HR776 NP-O/S	FTR Hanover 22/23.9.43.
HR779 NP-Z	FTR Mannheim 16/17.4.43.
HR780 NP-D	To 419 Sqn.
HR781 NP-F	To 1658 CU and back. FTR Dortmund 23/24.5.43.
HR785 NP-G	Crashed in Lincoln on return from Krefeld 22.6.43.
HR791 NP-L/V/H	FTR Cannes 11/12.11.43.
HR837 NP-F	To 1656 CU 12.4.44.
HR840 NP-R	FTR Wuppertal 29/30.5.43.
HR858 NP-O	To 51 Sqn 24.12.43.
HR932 NP-K/T	To 78 Sqn 24.12.43.
HR933 NP-P	FTR Gelsenkirchen 9/10.7.43.
HR937 NP-L/D/P	FTR Berlin 31.8/1.9.43.
HR938 NP-L	FTR Nuremberg 10/11.8.43.

HR941 NP-A	FTR Hamburg 24/25.7.43.
HR942 NP-V	To 78 Sqn 24.12.43.
HR943 NP-I/Z/F	FTR Munich 6/7.9.43.
HR944 NP-K	FTR Berlin 23/24.8.43.
HR945 NP-Y	FTR Hanover 8/9.9.43.
HR977 NP-E/D	FTR Berlin 22/23.11.43.
HR978 NP-J/Y	To 102 Sqn.
HR979 NP-L	FTR Berlin 23/24.8.43.
HR980 NP-E	FTR Berlin 23/24.8.43.
HR981	To 51 Sqn.
HR987 NP-P	From 35 Sqn. Returned to 35 Sqn.
HX320 NP-A/J	FTR Aachen 24/25.5.44.
HX322 NP-B	FTR Nuremberg 30/31.3.44.
HX329 NP-K/Y	FTR Gelsenkirchen 12.9.44.
HX331 NP-L	Crashed on take-off from Lissett when bound for Berlin 29.1.44.
HX333 NP-J	FTR Berlin 28/29.1.44.
HX334 NP-C	FTR Hasselt 12/13.5.44.
HX335 NP-P	FTR Magdeburg 21/22.1.44.
HX338 NP-D/W	Crashed in Wales during training 14.7.44.
HX340 NP-N/Q/A	To 1652 CU.
HX342 NP-F	FTR Frankfurt 22/23.3.44.
HX344 NP-E/C/U/B NP-K	To 517 Sqn.
HX346 NP-M	To 620 Sqn.
HX348 NP-O	FTR Berlin 15/16.2.44.
HX349 NP-G	FTR Nuremberg 30/31.3.44.
HX351 NP-F/S	Crashed near Catfoss when bound for Leipzig 20.2.44.
HX356 NP-J/G	To 640 Sqn and back. Crashed soon after take-off from Lissett 8.11.44.
JB789 NP-X/V/Z	To 1658 CU.
JD115 NP-A/D	FTR Frankfurt 20/21.12.43.
JD116 NP-G/A	FTR Aachen 13/14.7.43.
JD117 NP-U	FTR Düsseldorf 11/12.6.43.
JD208 NP-H	Crashed near Driffield on return from Essen 26.7.43.
JD246 NP-R	FTR Berlin 31.8/1.9.43.
JD249 NP-U	FTR Nuremberg 10/11.8.43.
JD255 NP-M	To 10 Sqn.
JD259 NP-R	FTR Mülheim 22/23.6.43.
JD260 NP-S	FTR Peenemünde 17/18.8.43.
JD265 NP-W/G	FTR Stuttgart 26/27.11.43.
JD267 NP-K/C	To 1662 CU.
JD277	FTR Hamburg 29/30.7.43.
JD298 NP-N	FTR Nuremberg 27/28.8.43.
JD300 NP-Y/X/G	To 51 Sqn.
JN884 NP-F	FTR Essen 25/26.7.43.
JN886 NP-B	To 1666 CU.

JN887 NP-T/E	To 51 Sqn.
JN903 NP-H/C	FTR Berlin 31.8/1.9.43.
JN904 NP-K	FTR Modane 16/17.9.43.
JN905 NP-L	FTR Hanover 27/28.9.43.
JN907 NP-N	To 10 Sqn.
JN919 NP-B	To 51 Sqn.
LK760 NP-H/W/E	Crashed on take-off from Lissett en route for Versailles 8.6.44.
LK786 NP-J	To 640 Sqn.
LK787 NP-A/S/U	FTR Frankfurt 18/19.3.44.
LK808 NP-V	To 1652 CU.
LK826 NP-Y	FTR Tergnier 10/11.4.44.
LK839 NP-S	Crashed in Yorkshire on approach to Lissett 17.8.44.
LK841 NP-X	FTR Trappes 3.6.44.
LK850 NP-K/P/B/G NP-H	Crashed on take-off from Lissett when bound for Duisburg 15.10.44.
LK863 NP-Y/C	FTR Versailles 8.6.44.
LK864 NP-Z/V/Z2	To 1658 CU.
LK875 NP-Q	FTR Trappes 2/3.6.44.
LK876 NP-O/Z2	To 1652 CU.
LK877 NP-A	FTR Trappes 2/3.6.44.
LL604	To 462 Sqn.
LL615 NP-I	From 466 Sqn. To AFEE.
LV771 NP-R/N/D/Y	FTR Bochum 4/5.11.44.
LV772 NP-H	FTR Berlin 15/16.2.44.
LV773 NP-R	FTR Berlin 20/21.1.44.
LV786 NP-P	FTR Leipzig 19/20.2.44.
LV790 NP-L	FTR Amiens 12/13.6.44.
LV792 NP-E	Damaged beyond repair Trappes 2/3.6.44.
LV835 NP-K	Crashed on landing at Friston on return from Stuttgart 2.3.44.
LV907 NP-F	From Leconfield. Friday the 13th.
LV917 NP-T/H/C	SOC 18.5.45.
LV918 NP-O	FTR Aachen 24/25.5.44.
LV920 NP-D	FTR Düsseldorf (Reisholz) 20/21.2.45.
LV921 NP-B	FTR Trappes 2/3.6.44.
LV940 NP-J	Damaged in collision at Lissett 8.11.44.
LV946 NP-K	From 640 Sqn. FTR Tergnier 18/19.4.44.
LV948 NP-R	From 640 Sqn. Crashed on take-off from Lissett when bound for Hasselt 12.5.44.
LV954 NP-Q	FTR Tergnier 18/19.4.44.
LW118 NP-X	FTR Aachen 24/25.5.44.
LW244 NP-U	To 1656 CU.
LW245 NP-P	FTR Frankfurt 20/21.12.43.
LW246 NP-Z	Crashed in Yorkshire during fighter affiliation 14.9.43.
LW259 NP-F	FTR Kassel 22/23.10.43.
LW260 NP-C/H	To 77 Sqn.

LW261 NP-V	FTR Hanover 22/23.9.43.
LW268 NP-J/P	Crashed on take-off from Lissett when bound for Kassel 22.10.43.
LW274 NP-Z	To 102 Sqn.
LW277 NP-S	To 78 Sqn.
LW278 NP-K	Crashed in Yorkshire during bombing exercise 3.10.43.
LW283 NP-V	Crashed in Lincolnshire on return from Mannheim 24.9.43.
LW291 NP-J	From 77 Sqn. To 51 Sqn.
LW292 NP-V	From 77 Sqn. FTR Kassel 3/4.10.43.
LW296 NP-B	FTR Kassel 3/4.10.43.
LW297 NP-E	FTR Kassel 22/23.10.43.
LW298 NP-L	FTR Düsseldorf 3/4.11.43.
LW299 NP-C	To 51 Sqn.
LW314 NP-O/L	To 10 Sqn.
LW316 NP-U	To 78 Sqn.
LW317 NP-P	FTR Hanover 8/9.10.43.
LW369	To 640 Sqn 16.1.44.
LW422	To 640 Sqn 21.1.44.
LW430	To 640 Sqn 16.1.44..
LW434	To 640 Sqn 16.1.44.
LW439	To 640 Sqn 16.1.44.
LW441	To 640 Sqn 16.1.44.
LW443	To 640 Sqn 16.1.44.
LW446	To 640 Sqn 16.1.44.
LW459	To 640 Sqn 16.1.44.
LW463	To 640 Sqn 16.1.44.
LW464	To 640 Sqn 16.1.44.
LW470 NP-L/M/Z	From 51 Sqn. To 1658 CU.
LW477	To 640 Sqn 16.1.44.
LW499	To 640 Sqn 16.1.44.
LW500	To 640 Sqn 16.1.44.
LW501 NP-M	From 466 Sqn. FTR Leipzig 19/20.2.44.
LW502	To 640 Sqn 16.1.44.
LW505	To 640 Sqn 16.1.44.
LW506	To 640 Sqn 16.1.44.
LW513	To 640 Sqn 16.1.44.
LW514	To 640 Sqn 16.1.44.
LW554	To 640 Sqn 28.1.44.
LW555	To 640 Sqn 1.2.44.
LW556	To 640 Sqn 28.1.44.
LW580 NP-S/O	FTR Frankfurt 22/23.3.44.
LW581	Crashed on take-off from Lissett 8.6.44.
LW617 NP-I/A	From 432 Sqn. Crashed on landing at Lissett 24.10.44.
LW634 NP-P	FTR Nuremberg 30/31.3.44.
LW635 NP-M	FTR Trappes 2/3.6.44.

LW653 NP-K/T	FTR Aachen 24/25.5.44.
LW658 NP-R/U	To 1658 CU.
LW677 NP-Z/Z2/N	From 51 Sqn. To 1663 CU.
LW718 NP-T	From 10 Sqn. Crashed in Norfolk on return from Berlin 24.3.44.
LW719 NP-V/Q/P NP-J/I/K	From 10 Sqn.
LW720 NP-W	From 10 Sqn. FTR Aachen 24/25.5.44.
LW721 NP-U/S	FTR Berlin 24/25.3.44.
LW722 NP-T/U	To 460 Sqn.
LW723 NP-X	FTR Tergnier 10/11.4.44.
LW724 NP-S	FTR Nuremberg 30/31.3.44.
MZ286 NP-Y/X	Crashed off Bridlington soon after take-off when bound for Caen 18.7.44.
MZ337 NP-C/F/A	From 346 Sqn. FTR Gelsenkirchen/Nordstern 13.9.44.
MZ338 NP-E/Z/S/U	From 346 Sqn. To 520 Sqn.
MZ339 NP-E/C	From 346 Sqn.
MZ350 NP-P/R	FTR Chemnitz 14/15.2.45.
MZ351 NP-I/X	FTR Worms 21/22.2.45.
MZ352 NP-K	FTR Ardouval 20/21.7.44.
MZ356 NP-M	From 415 Sqn.
MZ366 NP-M	Crashed while landing at Lissett on return from Hanau 6.1.45.
MZ367 NP-C/A/I	FTR Brunswick 12/13.8.44.
MZ368	To 466 Sqn.
MZ373 NP-K/L/O	
MZ374 NP-Y/B	SOC 7.5.45.
MZ395 NP-C	From 466 Sqn. FTR Hanover 5/6.1.45.
MZ399 NP-Z	From 466 Sqn.
MZ403	From 466 Sqn. Damaged while landing at Lissett on return from Wanne-Eickel 3.2.45.
MZ405	From 434 Sqn. To 76 Sqn.
MZ408	To 640 Sqn.
MZ432 NP-Q	FTR Hanover 5/6.1.45.
MZ468 NP-E/F/I	From 462 Sqn.
MZ480 NP-K	
MZ492 NP-O	To 640 Sqn.
MZ533 NP-G	FTR Tergnier 10/11.4.44.
MZ542 NP-Z	FTR Tergnier 10/11.4.44.
MZ567 NP-Q/B	FTR Amiens 12/13.6.44.
MZ580 NP-M	To 21 HGCU.
MZ582 NP-T/Z2	To 1665 CU.
MZ703 NP-K	To 77 Sqn and back. FTR Caen 18.6.44.
MZ730 NP-Q	FTR Caen 18.7.44.
MZ734 NP-I/L/Q/U	FTR Essen 25.10.44.
MZ737 NP-C	To 346 Sqn.
MZ739 NP-N	From 77 Sqn.

MZ741 NP-E	To 346 Sqn.
MZ742	To 346 Sqn.
MZ759 NP-W/M/K NP-Q	FTR Gladbeck 24.3.45.
MZ760 NP-N	FTR Brunswick 12/13.8.44.
MZ769 NP-A/H/D	From 77 Sqn.
MZ775 NP-U/P/O/J NP-S	From 466 Sqn.
MZ797 NP-Q	From 640 Sqn.
MZ813 NP-Y	From 424 Sqn. Crashed in Suffolk on return from Worms 21.2.45.
MZ815 NP-I	To 640 Sqn.
MZ818	From 433 Sqn. To 640 Sqn.
MZ846 NP-U/D/Y/A NP-T	From 434 Sqn.
MZ854 NP-O	Written off at Lissett on return from Watten 25.8.44.
MZ855	To 640 Sqn.
MZ862 NP-Z/K	Damaged beyond repair by bomb blast at Lissett 15.10.44.
MZ881 NP-P/A/G NP-C/E/Y	From 434 Sqn.
MZ911	To 640 Sqn.
MZ912	To 640 Sqn.
MZ917 NP-R	From 51 Sqn.
MZ921 NP-P/M/Q	From 434 Sqn.
MZ926 NP-S	From 640 Sqn. To 462 Sqn.
MZ927 NP-E/Y	FTR Magdeburg 16/17.1.45.
MZ928 NP-Z2	
MZ930	To 640 Sqn.
MZ931	SOC 21.2.45.
MZ945 NP-W	From 466 Sqn. FTR Essen 25.10.44.
NA181 NP-E	From 425 Sqn.
NA194 NP-Q/G/O/H	
NA221 NP-A/Z	From 640 Sqn.
NA233 NP-F/T	From 77 Sqn.
NA519 NP-A	To 347 Sqn 14.7.44.
NA523 NP-E	To 297 Sqn.
NA566 NP-A/A2/S NP-H/Y/K	To 1652 CU 29.11.44.
NP876	
NP973 NP-P/Q	FTR Goch 7/8.2.45.
NP991 NP-G/A	
NP996	From 640 Sqn.
NR133 NP-J	
NR170 NP-U	
NR174 NP-L	
NR176 NP-V	
NR177 NP-W	

NR179	To 466 Sqn 25.10.44.
NR183	To 466 Sqn 25.10.44.
NR185	To 466 Sqn 25.10.44.
NR190 NP-F/T	Crash-landed at Woodbridge on return from Hanover 5/6.1.45.
NR195 NP-G/C/I	FTR Hanau 6/7.1.45.
NR225 NP-W	From 102 Sqn.
NR233 NP-J	FTR Duisburg 17/18.12.44.
NR240 NP-N/I	From 640 Sqn.
NR251 NP-D/G/B	FTR Hanover 5/6.1.45.
PN192 NP-N	To 462 Sqn.
PN379 NP-R	From 77 Sqn.
PN380 NP-M	FTR Essen 23.2.45.
PN437 NP-X	Crashed in Yorkshire on return from Kamen 3/4.3.45.
PN438 NP-X	To 171 Sqn.
PN444 NP-S	
PP166	
PP167 NP-S	
PP169	
PP175 NP-T	
RG436 NP-M	FTR Reisholz 20/21.2.45.
RG437 NP-D	From 466 Sqn.
RG493	From 76 Sqn.
RG593 NP-K	
RG597	From 76 Sqn.
RG618	From 76 Sqn.
RG623	From 76 Sqn.
RG639 NP-J	
RG640 NP-E	
RG641 NP-X	
RG643 NP-H	
RG644 NP-R	
RG651	To 78 Sqn.
RG652	To 78 Sqn.
RG672	
RG673	
TW782	
TW793	From 76 Sqn.

Heaviest Single Loss

23/24.08.43.	Berlin. 5 Halifaxes.
24/25.05.44.	Aachen. 5 Halifaxes.
02/03.06.44.	Trappes. 5 Halifaxes.

196 SQUADRON

Motto: Sic Fidem Servamus (Thus we keep the faith)   **Code: ZO**

Formed at Driffield in Yorkshire in November 1942, 196 Squadron joined the ranks of 4 Group as a standard bomber unit equipped with Wellingtons. It went to war for the first time in February 1943 and took part in fifty-six operations, launching more than 500 sorties. In July 1943 it was posted to 3 Group, where it converted to Stirlings and resumed operations at the end of August. In November 1943 the squadron was posted from Bomber Command to take up airborne support duties carrying paratroopers and towing gliders.

STATIONS

Driffield	07.11.42 to 22.12.42
Leconfield	22.12.42 to 19.07.43

COMMANDING OFFICERS

Wing Commander R.H. Waterhouse	07.11.42 to 31.03.43
Wing Commander A.G. Duguid	31.03.43 to 26.06.43
Wing Commander N. Alexander	26.06.43 to 08.44

AIRCRAFT

Wellington X	01.12.42 to 07.43

OPERATIONAL RECORD

Operations	Sorties	Aircraft Losses	% Losses
56	517	13	2.5

Category of Operations

Bombing	Mining
33	23

TABLE OF STATISTICS
Out of 42 Wellington squadrons in Bomber Command

34th highest number of Wellington overall operations in Bomber Command.
28th highest number of Wellington sorties in Bomber Command.
34th equal (with 104 Sqn) highest number of Wellington operational losses in Bomber Command.

Out of 25 operational squadrons in 4 Group

18th highest number of overall operations in 4 Group.
18th highest number of sorties in 4 Group.
17th equal (with 104 Sqn) highest number of operational losses in 4 Group.

Out of 12 Wellington squadrons in 4 Group

5th highest number of Wellington overall operations in 4 Group.
3rd highest number of Wellington sorties in 4 Group.
5th equal (with 104 Sqn) highest number of Wellington losses in 4 Group.

AIRCRAFT HISTORIES

Wellington	From December 1942 to July 1943.
X3357	From 419 Sqn. To 429 Sqn.
X3704	From 156 Sqn. To 429 Sqn.
Z1670	To 429 Sqn.
BJ715	From 101 Sqn. To 429 Sqn.
BK499	To 429 Sqn.
HE161	From 429 Sqn. Crashed in Yorkshire during air-test 26.2.43.
HE162	From 429 Sqn. FTR Dortmund 4/5.5.43.
HE163	From 429 Sqn. Crash-landed in Yorkshire when bound for mining sortie 1.6.43.
HE165	From 429 Sqn. To 25 OTU.
HE166	From 429 Sqn. Crashed soon after take-off from Tangmere on transit flight 15.4.43.
HE167 ZO-A	From 429 Sqn. FTR from mining sortie 23/24.3.43.
HE168 ZO-X	From 429 Sqn. FTR Duisburg 26/27.4.43.
HE169	From 429 Sqn. FTR Cologne 14/15.2.43.
HE170	From 429 Sqn. FTR from mining sortie 28/29.4.43.
HE171	From 429 Sqn. Crash-landed at Grove airfield, Buckinghamshire during training 7.5.43.
HE178	To 27 OTU.
HE179	To 27 OTU.
HE180	To 27 OTU.
HE181 ZO-H	Crashed on take-off from Leconfield during training 21.3.43.
HE220	FTR from mining sortie 28/29.4.43.
HE351	To 466 Sqn.
HE385	FTR Bochum 29/30.3.43.
HE387 ZO-Z	FTR Mannheim 16/17.4.43.
HE392	To 431 Sqn.
HE394	To 431 Sqn.
HE395	FTR from mining sortie 28/29.4.43.
HE398	FTR Duisburg 12/13.5.43.
HE412	FTR Gelsenkirchen 25/26.6.43.
HE469	Abandoned over Surrey on return from Mannheim 17.4.43.
HE470	To 199 Sqn.
HE548	FTR Bochum 29/30.3.43.
HE685	To 23 OTU.
HE901	From 425 Sqn. To 166 Sqn.
HE980	FTR Cologne 3/4.7.43.
HE987	To 1483 Flt.
HE988	To 166 Sqn.
HE989	To 199 Sqn.
HF464	To 27 OTU.
HF465	To 83 OTU.
HF484	To 26 OTU.

HF513	To 466 Sqn.
HF516	To 466 Sqn.
HF545	To 466 Sqn.
HZ362	To 17 OTU.
HZ478	FTR Cologne 3/4.7.43.
HZ532	To 28 OTU.
HZ533	To 28 OTU.
HZ580	To 466 Sqn.
LN293	To 466 Sqn.
LN432	To 27 OTU.
MS486	Crashed in Norfolk on return from Düsseldorf 12.6.43.
MS488	From 429 Sqn. To 27 OTU.
MS490	To 27 OTU.
MS491	Crash-landed in Lincolnshire on return from Duisburg 27.4.43.

Posted to 38 Group 19.7.43.

346 (GUYENNE) SQUADRON

(No motto)   **Code: H7**

346 Squadron was the first of two Free French heavy bomber units to be formed in 4 Group and manned largely by French air and ground crews who had served previously in North Africa. Formed at Elvington on 16 May and initially equipped with Mk V Halifaxes, the squadron soon converted to Mk III and later Mk VI versions, and made a major contribution to 4 Group operations. During the final week of September 1944 the squadron joined others of the Group to deliver much-needed petrol supplies to Brussels in support of the 2nd Army. Following VE Day the squadron remained at Elvington until relocating to France in October 1945.

STATIONS
Elvington	16.05.44 to 10.45

COMMANDING OFFICERS
Lt Colonel G. Venot	16.05.44 to 10.09.44
Commandant G.E. Puget	11.09.44 to 10.45

AIRCRAFT
Halifax V	05.44 to 06.44
Halifax III	06.44 to 04.45
Halifax VI	03.45 to 11.45

OPERATIONAL RECORD
Operations	Sorties	Aircraft Losses	% Losses
121	1,479	15	1.1

Category of Operations

Bombing	Fuel Delivery
1,371	108

TABLE OF STATISTICS
Out of 32 Halifax squadrons in Bomber Command
(Excluding SOE)

24th highest number of Halifax overall operations in Bomber Command.

27th highest number of Halifax sorties in Bomber Command.

26th equal (with 347 Sqn) highest number of Halifax operational losses in Bomber Command.

Out of 25 operational squadrons in 4 Group

13th highest number of overall operations in 4 Group.

12th highest number of sorties in 4 Group.

15th equal (with 347 Sqn) highest number of aircraft operational losses in 4 Group.

Out of 15 operational Halifax squadrons in 4 Group

11th highest number of Halifax overall operations in 4 Group.

11th highest number of Halifax sorties in 4 Group.

13th equal (with 347 Sqn) highest number of Halifax operational losses in 4 Group.

AIRCRAFT HISTORIES

Halifax	From May 1944.
HR932	From 77 Sqn. To 1663 CU.
HR935	From 77 Sqn. To 1658 CU.
LK660	From 77 Sqn. To 1663 CU.
LK725	From 77 Sqn. Returned to 77 Sqn.
LK728	From 77 Sqn. To 347 Sqn.
LK731	From 77 Sqn. To 347 Sqn.
LK737	From 77 Sqn. To 347 Sqn.
LK744	From 77 Sqn. To 347 Sqn.
LK955	From 77 Sqn. Damaged beyond repair during operation to Amiens 13.6.44.
LK999	From 77 Sqn. To 347 Sqn.
LL124	From 77 Sqn. To 347 Sqn.
LL126	From 77 Sqn. To 347 Sqn.
LL131	From 77 Sqn. To 347 Sqn.
LL227 H7-K	From 77 Sqn. To 347 Sqn.
LL237	From 77 Sqn. To 347 Sqn.
LL238	From 77 Sqn. To 347 Sqn.
LL242	From 77 Sqn. To 347 Sqn.
LL246	From 77 Sqn. To 347 Sqn.
LL253	From 77 Sqn. To 347 Sqn.
LL395	From 77 Sqn. To 347 Sqn.

LL396	From 77 Sqn. To 347 Sqn.
LL397	From 77 Sqn. To 347 Sqn.
LL398	From 77 Sqn. To 347Sqn.
LL462	To 347 Sqn.
LL463	To 347 Sqn.
LL551	
LL553	
LL557	To 347 Sqn.
LL573	To 347 Sqn.
LL581	From 102 Sqn. To 347 Sqn.
LL583	
LL586	
LW241	From 77 Sqn. To 1663 CU.
LW438 H7-K	From 424 Sqn. Crashed on take-off from Elvington when bound for Gelsenkirchen 22.1.45.
LW443 H7-E	From 640 Sqn. FTR Düsseldorf 2/3.11.44.
MZ337	To 158 Sqn.
MZ338	To 158 Sqn.
MZ339	To 158 Sqn.
MZ365	From BDU.
MZ472	To Farnborough.
MZ477	
MZ486	From 77 Sqn.
MZ490	
MZ709	
MZ737	From 158 Sqn.
MZ738 H7-H	From 78 Sqn. FTR Chemnitz 5/6.3.45.
MZ741 H7-A	From 158 Sqn. FTR Witten 18/19.3.45.
MZ742 H7-A	From 158 Sqn. FTR Essen 23.10.44.
MZ762	To 78 Sqn.
MZ763	To 78 Sqn.
MZ764	To 78 Sqn.
MZ787	To 78 Sqn.
MZ788	To 78 Sqn.
MZ789	To 78 Sqn.
MZ790	To 102 Sqn.
MZ804	To 77 Sqn.
MZ830 H7-V	Crashed in Yorkshire on return from Hagen 15.3.45.
NA121 H7-D	FTR Bochum 4/5.11.44.
NA166 H7-G	FTR Hagen 15/16.3.45.
NA506	From 10 Sqn. To 1663 CU.
NA546 H7-F/G	From 78 Sqn. FTR Bochum 4/5.11.44.
NA547 H7-V	From 78 Sqn. FTR Worms 21/22.2.45.
NA549 H7-N	From 78 Sqn. FTR Bochum 4/5.11.44.
NA551 H7-E	From 78 Sqn. Collided with NA546 (346 Sqn) over Yorkshire on return from V1 site at Hauts-Buissons 13.7.44.
NA554	

NA555 H7-L	FTR Scholven-Buer 6.10.44.
NA556	
NA557 H7-L	FTR Sterkrade 21/22.11.44.
NA558 H7-N	FTR Bochum 4/5.11.44.
NA561	
NA562	To 1663 CU.
NA564	From 102 Sqn.
NA576	To 347 Sqn.
NA577	To 347 Sqn.
NA585 H7-M	Destroyed at Elvington when hung-up bomb fell out and exploded on return from Le Havre 10.9.44.
NA615	To 102 Sqn.
NA620	
NP763	From 77 Sqn.
NP860	From 77 Sqn.
NR181 H7-J	FTR Bochum 4/5.11.44.
NR229 H7-D	From 77 Sqn. Crashed in County Durham after being attacked by an intruder on return from Kamen 3.3.45.
NR232	
NR242	From 102 Sqn.
PN170	
PN179 H7-M	FTR Worms 21/22.2.45.
PN365	
PN395	From 102 Sqn. Damaged beyond repair in landing accident at Orly, Paris after transit flight 13.4.45.
RG439	To 10 Sqn.
RG491	
RG495	
RG510	From 77 Sqn.
RG511	From 77 Sqn.
RG513	From 77 Sqn.
RG540	
RG543	To 347 Sqn.
RG545	To 347 Sqn.
RG547	To 347 Sqn.
RG548	To 347 Sqn.
RG560	
RG561	To 347 Sqn.
RG562	
RG563	
RG564	To 640 Sqn.
RG567	From 76 Sqn.
RG568	To 347 Sqn.
RG587	
RG592 H7-P	Crashed on landing at Elvington while training 7.4.45.
RG594	

RG595	To 347 Sqn.
RG605	To 347 Sqn.
RG606	To 347 Sqn.
RG607	
RG609	
RG619	From 347 Sqn.
RG620	From 347 Sqn.
RG646	From 347 Sqn.
RG647	From 347 Sqn.
RG653	From 347 Sqn.
RG654	Crashed on landing at Elvington while training 3.5.45.
RG655	From 466 Sqn.

Heaviest Single Loss

4/5.11.44.   Bochum. 5 Halifaxes FTR.

347 (TUNISIE) SQUADRON

(No motto)   **Code: L8**

Formed at Elvington on 20 June 1944, 347 Squadron was the second heavy bomber unit to join 4 Group with personnel drawn largely from Free French forces serving previously in North Africa. Initially equipped with MK V Halifaxes donated by its sister squadron, 347 soon took on Mk IIIs and became a regular contributor to 4 Group operations. During the final week of September 1944 the squadron delivered more than 84,000 gallons of petrol in 113 sorties to Brussels to support the 2nd Army. In October 1945 the squadron relocated to France.

STATIONS

Elvington   20.06.44 to 10.45

COMMANDING OFFICERS

Lt Colonel M. Vigouroux   01.08.44 to 15.03.45
Commandant F-X. Hoquetis   15.03.45 to 10.45

AIRCRAFT

Halifax V   20.06.44 to 07.44
Halifax III   07.44 to 04.45
Halifax VI   03.45 to 11.45

OPERATIONAL RECORD

Operations	Sorties	Aircraft Losses	% Losses
110	1,355	15	1.1

Category of Operations

Bombing	Fuel Delivery
1,242	113

TABLE OF STATISTICS
Out of 32 Halifax squadrons in Bomber Command
(Excluding SOE)

26th highest number of Halifax overall operations in Bomber Command.

28th highest number of Halifax sorties in Bomber Command.

26th equal (with 346 Sqn) highest number of Halifax operational losses in Bomber Command.

Out of 25 operational squadrons in 4 Group

15th highest number of overall operations in 4 Group.

13th highest number of sorties in 4 Group.

15th equal (with 346 Sqn) highest number of aircraft operational losses in 4 Group.

Out of 15 operational Halifax squadrons in 4 Group

13th highest number of Halifax overall operations in 4 Group.

12th highest number of Halifax sorties in 4 Group.

13th equal (with 346 Sqn) highest number of aircraft operational losses in 4 Group.

AIRCRAFT HISTORIES

Halifax	From June 1944.
LK728 L8-D	From 346 Sqn. Crashed in Yorkshire on return from Mimoyecques 6.7.44.
LK731	From 346 Sqn. To 1663 CU.
LK737	From 346 Sqn. To 1652 CU.
LK744	From 346 Sqn. To 1652 CU.
LK793	From 466 Sqn. To 1663 CU.
LK999	From 346 Sqn. To 1659 CU.
LL124	From 346 Sqn. To 1662 CU.
LL126	From 346 Sqn. To 1662 CU.
LL131	From 346 Sqn. To 1659 CU.
LL227	From 346 Sqn. To 1658 CU.
LL237	From 346 Sqn. To 1658 CU.
LL238	From 346 Sqn. To 1658 CU.
LL242	From 346 Sqn. To 1662 CU.
LL246	From 346 Sqn. To 1662 CU.
LL253	From 346 Sqn. To 1658 CU.
LL395	From 346 Sqn. To 1652 CU.
LL396	From 346 Sqn. To 1663 CU.
LL397	From 346 Sqn. To 1663 CU.
LL398	From 346 Sqn. To 1658 CU.
LL462	From 346 Sqn. To 1658 CU.

LL463	From 346 Sqn. To 1659 CU.
LL507	To 1658 CU.
LL556	From 102 Sqn. Crashed on take-off from Elvington when bound for Heligoland 18.4.45.
LL557 L8-U	From 346 Sqn. FTR Hanover 5/6.1.45.
LL573 L8-B	From 346 Sqn. Crash-landed at Carnaby on return from Wesel 17.2.45.
LL581	From 346 Sqn.
LL587	Crashed in Northamptonshire on return from Gelsenkirchen 23.1.45.
LL590 L8-L	From 102 Sqn. FTR Saarbrücken 13/14.1.45.
LL597	To 102 Sqn.
LL602	
LL603	
LW480	From 51 Sqn. To 1658 CU.
LW504	From 51 Sqn. To 1658 CU.
LW541	From 51 Sqn.
LW630	From 76 Sqn.
LW642	From 51 Sqn. To 1663 CU.
LW678	From 77 Sqn.
MZ489 L8-L	FTR Mülheim airfield Essen 24.12.44.
MZ571	From 51 Sqn. To 1658 CU.
MZ635	From 51 Sqn. To 1652 CU.
MZ697	From 77 Sqn. To 1658 CU.
MZ809	From 77 Sqn.
MZ909 L8-A	From 433 Sqn. FTR Homburg 14/15.3.45.
MZ936	From 77 Sqn.
MZ984 L8-G	FTR Ludwigshaven as the result of US anti-aircraft fire 2/3.1.45.
MZ985	
MZ986 L8-B	FTR Magdeburg 16/17.1.45.
NA174	Blew up at Elvington while being prepared for an operation to Mönchengladbach 28.12.44.
NA182	To Conversion to Mk VI.
NA197 L8-H	FTR Goch 7/8.2.45.
NA232	From 96 Sqn.
NA260 L8-G	FTR Goch 7/8.2.45.
NA263	To 171 Sqn.
NA512	From 77 Sqn. Landed at Melsbroek with multiple engine problems during operation to Cologne 28.10.44 and abandoned.
NA515	From 77 Sqn.
NA519	From 158 Sqn. Ditched in the North Sea when bound for Cologne 28.10.44.
NA520	From 77 Sqn.
NA529	From 578 Sqn. FTR Fromental 7/8.8.44.
NA572 L8-L	From 102 Sqn. FTR Magdeburg 16/17.1.45.
NA576	From 346 Sqn. To 21 HGCU.

NA577	From 346 Sqn.
NA606	FTR Gelsenkirchen 11.9.44.
NA616	FTR Venlo 3.9.44.
NA678	
NA680 L8-H	Shot down by intruder over Lincolnshire on return from Kamen 4.3.45.
NA681 L8-G	From 102 Sqn. FTR Homburg 14/15.3.45.
NP767	From 77 Sqn.
NP921 L8-E	From 77 Sqn. FTR Wangerooge 25.4.45.
NP947	From 77 Sqn.
NP988	From 102 Sqn.
NR151	
NR153 L8-D	FTR Osnabrück 6/7.12.44.
NR226 L8-P	Crashed on landing at Friston, Sussex on return from Chemnitz 6.3.45.
NR235 L8-O	Shot down by intruder over Yorkshire on return from Kamen 4.3.45.
NR287 L8-C	Crashed in Yorkshire on return from Hagen 15.3.45.
PN167	
PN175	From 77 Sqn.
PP165	
PP208	From 77 Sqn. To 102 Sqn.
RG490	From 77 Sqn.
RG492	
RG500	From 77 Sqn.
RG509	From 77 Sqn.
RG534	From 77 Sqn.
RG543	From 346 Sqn.
RG545	From 346 Sqn.
RG547	From 346 Sqn.
RG548	From 346 Sqn.
RG561	From 346 Sqn.
RG583	From 76 Sqn.
RG586	From 346 Sqn.
RG595	From 346 Sqn.
RG605	From 346 Sqn.
RG606	From 346 Sqn.
RG619	To 346 Sqn.
RG620	To 346 Sqn.
RG625	
RG645	
RG646	To 346 Sqn.
RG647	To 346 Sqn.
RG648	To 78 Sqn.
RG649	To 78 Sqn.
RG653	To 346 Sqn.
RG661	From 466 Sqn.

RG668   To 102 Sqn.
RG669
RG670

405 (VANCOUVER) SQUADRON (RCAF)

Motto: Ducimus (We lead)   **Code: LQ**

405 Squadron was the first Canadian unit to form in Bomber Command, and this it did on 23 April 1941 on the 4 Group station at Driffield in Yorkshire. It became the second squadron in the Command to fully equip with the Merlin-powered Wellington II, and operated these until they were replaced by Halifaxes in April 1942. In late October the squadron departed Bomber Command for a five-month tour of duty with Coastal Command. In February 1943, shortly before the completion of this maritime interlude, the squadron was officially adopted by the city of Vancouver and proudly carried its name into battle for the remainder of the war. It was in March 1943 that the squadron departed 4 Group to join the Canadian 6 Group, but shortly afterwards it was posted again to become the only Canadian squadron to join the Pathfinder Force. Among its commanding officers was W/C Johnny Fauquier who served two terms at the helm, and saw out the last four months of the bombing war as the commanding officer of 617 Squadron, better known as the Dambusters.

STATIONS

Driffield	23.04.41 to 20.06.41
Pocklington	20.06.41 to 07.08.42
Topcliffe	07.08.42 to 24.10.42

COMMANDING OFFICERS

Squadron Leader D.G. Tomlinson	08.05.41 to 20.05.41
Wing Commander P.A. Gilchrist DFC	20.05.41 to 24.07.41
Squadron Leader W.B. Keddy (temp)	25.07.41 to 16.08.41
Wing Commander R.M. Fenwick-Wilson	17.08.41 to 16.02.42
Wing Commander G.D. MacAllister	16.02.42 to 27.02.42
Wing Commander J.E. Fauquier DFC	27.02.42 to 06.08.42
Wing Commander L.D.G. Fraser DFC	07.08.42 to 19.11.42

AIRCRAFT

Wellington II	06.05.41 to 04.42
Halifax II	04.42 to 09.43

OPERATIONAL RECORD

Operations	Sorties	Aircraft Losses	% Losses
122	918	46	5.0

Category of Operations

Bombing	Leaflet
120	2

Wellingtons

Operations	Sorties	Aircraft Losses	% Losses
86	522	20	3.8
All bombing			

Halifaxes

Operations	Sorties	Aircraft Losses	% Losses
36	396	26	6.6

Category of Operations

Bombing	Leaflet
34	2

TABLE OF STATISTICS

27th highest number of overall operations in Bomber Command.
34th highest number of sorties in Bomber Command.
21st highest number of bombing operations in Bomber Command.
32nd equal highest (with 214 Sqn) number of aircraft operational losses in Bomber Command.

Out of 32 Halifax squadrons in Bomber Command
(Excluding SOE)

29th highest number of Halifax overall operations in Bomber Command.
29th highest number of Halifax sorties in Bomber Command.
15th highest Halifax operational losses in Bomber Command.

Out of 42 Wellington squadrons in Bomber Command

24th highest number of Wellington overall operations in Bomber Command.
27th highest number of Wellington sorties in Bomber Command.
24th highest number of Wellington operational losses in Bomber Command.

Out of 25 operational squadrons in 4 Group

12th highest number of overall operations in 4 Group.
14th highest number of sorties in 4 Group.
10th highest number of aircraft operational losses in 4 Group.

Out of 12 operational Wellington squadrons in 4 Group

2nd highest number of Wellington overall operations in 4 Group.
Highest number of Wellington bombing operations in 4 Group.
2nd highest number of Wellington sorties in 4 Group.
2nd highest number of Wellington operational losses in 4 Group.

Out of 15 operational Halifax squadrons in 4 Group

Lowest number of Halifax overall operations in 4 Group.
Lowest number of Halifax sorties in 4 Group.
12th highest number of Halifax operational losses in 4 Group.

AIRCRAFT HISTORIES

Wellington	From April 1941 to April 1942.
W5368 LQ-K	From 142 Sqn. To 12 Sqn.
W5390 LQ-X	From 21 OTU. FTR Dortmund 14/15.4.42.
W5421 LQ-T	To 12 Sqn.
W5427 LQ-N	From 12 Sqn. FTR Dortmund 14/15.4.42.
W5476 LQ-H	FTR Hamburg 30.11/1.12.41.
W5483 LQ-J	FTR Berlin 2/3.8.41.
W5484 LQ-G	To 12 Sqn.
W5487	Destroyed by fire in enemy air-raid at Driffield 4.6.41.
W5488 LQ-D/B	FTR Duisburg 28/29.8.41.
W5489 LQ-A	Destroyed by fire at Pocklington on return from Frankfurt 25.10.41.
W5490 LQ-D	Crashed on approach to Pocklington on return from Dortmund 7.7.41.
W5491	To 104 Sqn.
W5492 LQ-K	Crashed near Pocklington during air-test 18.9.41.
W5493	To 104 Sqn.
W5495 LQ-W	To 12 Sqn.
W5496 LQ-M	FTR Hanover 14/15.8.41.
W5497 LQ-M	Crashed during landing at Pocklington on return from training 18.3.42.
W5498	From 104 Sqn. To 1448 Flt.
W5515 LQ-R/Y	To 305 Sqn.
W5516 LQ-D	FTR Kiel 26/27.2.42.
W5518	To 15 OTU.
W5521 LQ-P	FTR Berlin 7/8.9.41.
W5522 LQ-Q	FTR Cologne 16/17.6.41.
W5525	To 158 Sqn.
W5527 LQ-F	FTR Hamburg 2/3.8.41.
W5530 LQ-L	To 1443 Flt.
W5531 LQ-U	From 158 Sqn. Crashed in Suffolk on return from Essen 13.4.42.
W5534 LQ-N	FTR Hanover 14/15.7.41.
W5535	Crashed near Pocklington while training 1.9.41.
W5537 LQ-Q/O	FTR Brest 24.7.41.
W5550	To 305 Sqn.
W5551 LQ-U	FTR Brest 24.7.41.
W5553 LQ-D	FTR Berlin 7/8.11.41.
W5560 LQ-M	Crash-landed at Lindholme following early return from Wilhelmshaven 22.12.41.
W5561 LQ-J	From 104 Sqn. FTR Emden 28/29.12.41.
W5562	From 158 Sqn. Returned to 158 Sqn.
W5564 LQ-Q	To 158 Sqn.
W5565	To 1443 Flt.
W5572	To 1443 Flt.
W5581 LQ-V	Ditched off Cornwall on return from Brest 24.7.41.

W5589 LQ-F	From 104 Sqn. Crashed while trying to force-land in Yorkshire during air-test 5.1.42.
W5595	To 104 Sqn.
Z8329 LQ-L	Ditched in the North Sea following early return from Bremen 17.1.42.
Z8344 LQ-F	FTR Stettin 19/20.9.41.
Z8358 LQ-B	From 104 Sqn. FTR Hamburg 8/9.4.42.
Z8375	From 218 Sqn. To 158 Sqn.
Z8412 LQ-P	To 158 Sqn.
Z8414 LQ-U	To 104 Sqn.
Z8418	To 1443 Flt.
Z8419 LQ-V	From 104 Sqn. FTR Le Havre 22/23.10.41.
Z8420	To 158 Sqn.
Z8421 LQ-T	To 15 OTU.
Z8428 LQ-N	FTR Essen 10/11.3.42.
Z8431 LQ-J	From 218 Sqn. To 12 Sqn.
Z8437	From 218 Sqn. To 12 Sqn.
Z8439	From 21 OTU. To 158 Sqn.
Z8493	To 12 Sqn.
Z8521	To 158 Sqn.
Z8527 LQ-L	FTR Poissy 1/2.4.42.
Z8530 LQ-A	Abandoned over Hampshire on return from Dortmund 15.4.42.
Z8577	To 158 Sqn.
Z8585	To 158 Sqn.
Z8596	To 305 Sqn.
Z8597	To 158 Sqn.
Halifax	From April 1942 to September 1943.
R9363 LQ-Q	From 78 Sqn. Conversion Flt only. To 408 CF.
R9368	From 78 Sqn. Conversion Flt only. To 1659 CU.
R9369	From 78 CF. Conversion Flt only. To 1659 CU.
R9386	From 78 Sqn. Conversion Flt only. To 1659 CU.
R9420	From 78 Sqn. Conversion Flt only. To 1659 CU.
R9437	From 78 Sqn. Conversion Flt only. To 1659 CU.
R9448	From 35 Sqn. Conversion Flt only. To 1659 CU.
R9483	From 35 Sqn. Conversion Flt only. To 1659 CU.
W1019	From 35 Sqn. To 419 Sqn.
W1092 LQ-A	To 1659 CU.
W1094 LQ-B/F	Crashed on approach to St Eval on return from anti-submarine patrol 26.11.42 (Coastal Command).
W1095 LQ-N	To 1659 CU.
W1096 LQ-O	Crashed in Essex 17.11.42 (Coastal Command).
W1097 LQ-P	Crash-landed at Aberporth while training 12.7.42.
W1109 LQ-S	FTR Düsseldorf 31.7/1.8.42.
W1110 LQ-C	FTR Bremen 27/28.6.42.
W1111 LQ-D	FTR Essen 8/9.6.42.
W1112 LQ-E	To 1659 CU.

W1113 LQ-G	FTR Bremen 29/30.6.42.
W1145 LQ-S	Abandoned by crew near Binbrook following return from Emden 7.6.42.
W1152	To Middle East.
W1173	From 35 Sqn. To 1659 CU.
W1175 LQ-Q	FTR Bremen 27/28.6.42.
W1186 LQ-P	FTR Hamburg 26/27.7.42.
W1230 LQ-L	FTR Hamburg 26/27.7.42.
W1274 LQ-R	FTR Flensburg 23/24.9.42.
W7703 LQ-Q	Crashed while trying to land at West Malling on return from Aachen 6.10.42.
W7704 LQ-M	To 1659 CU via 405 CF.
W7707 LQ-K	FTR Cologne 30/31.5.42.
W7708 LQ-H	FTR Essen 8/9.6.42.
W7709 LQ-J	FTR Osnabrück 9/10.8.42.
W7710 LQ-R	FTR Flensburg 1/2.10.42.
W7713 LQ-T	FTR Essen 1/2.6.42.
W7714 LQ-K	FTR Bremen 29/30.6.42.
W7715 LQ-H	FTR Bremen 29/30.6.42.
W7718 LQ-T	From 10 Sqn. FTR Düsseldorf 31.7/1.8.42.
W7748 LQ-D	FTR Mainz 11/12.8.42.
W7763 LQ-C	FTR Osnabrück 6/7.10.42.
W7768	Crashed on the Isle of Wight on return from Coastal Command patrol 20.12.42.
W7769 LQ-Q/K	Crashed on approach to Pocklington on return from Duisburg 24.7.42.
W7770 LQ-E	FTR Essen 16/17.9.42.
W7780 LQ-Q	FTR Flensburg 1/2.10.42.
W7802 LQ-T	FTR Flensburg 1/2.10.42.
W7803 LQ-B	FTR Stuttgart 11/12.3.43.
W7810	To 1659 CU.
W7853	To 1659 CU.
W7885	From 35 Sqn. Returned to 35 Sqn.
BB210	To 1659 CU.
BB212 LQ-P/U	FTR Stuttgart 11/12.3.43.
DT507	To 1659 CU.
DT515	To 76 Sqn.
DT551	To 1659 CU.
DT553	To 1659 CU.
DT560	To 1666 CU.
DT565	To 1659 CU.
DT573	To 1659 CU.
DT695	To 1652 CU.
DT699 LQ-G	FTR from mining sortie 6/7.4.43.
DT704 LQ-H	FTR Kiel 4/5.4.43.
DT723 LQ-F	FTR Essen 3/4.4.43.
DT741 LQ-P	FTR Essen 30.4/1.5.43.
DT745 LQ-V	FTR Stuttgart 11/12.3.43.

DT772	To 408 Sqn.
DT802	To 1659 CU.
DT808 LQ-V	From 102 Sqn. FTR Essen 3/4.4.43.

Posted to Coastal Command 24.10.42.

408 (GOOSE) SQUADRON (RCAF)
(Non-operational)
Motto: For Freedom   **Code: EQ**

Formed in 5 Group in June 1941 as the second Canadian unit in Bomber Command, 408 Squadron was equipped with Hampdens and briefly Manchesters. It conducted more than 190 operations before being posted to 4 Group, where it converted to Halifaxes. No operations were carried out until after the squadron was posted as a founder member to the Canadian 6 Group on New Year's Day 1943.

STATIONS
Leeming   17.09.42 to 27.08.43

COMMANDING OFFICERS
Wing Commander W.D.S. Ferris DFC   01.09.42 to 26.10.43

AIRCRAFT
Halifax V   10.42 to 12.42

AIRCRAFT HISTORIES
Halifax II   From October 1942 to August 1943.
L9524   From 1659 CU. Conversion Flt only. Became ground-instruction machine.
L9532   From 102 Sqn. Conversion Flt only. To 1659 CU.
R9363   From 405 CF. Conversion Flt only. To 1659 CU.
R9382   From 76 CF. Conversion Flt only. To 1659 CU.
DG231   To 1663 CU.
DG233   To 1659 CU and back. To 518 Sqn.
DG234   To 1659 CU.
DG235   To 1659 CU and back. To Rolls Royce.
DG236   To 1663 CU.
DG237   To 518 Sqn.
DG238   Crashed near Croft during fighter affiliation exercise 9.11.42.
DG239   To 1659 CU.
DG240   To 518 Sqn.
DG241   To 1668 CU.
DG242   SOC 28.4.45.
DG243   To 1668 CU.

DG246	To 1663 CU.
DG247	To 1664 CU.
DG248	To 1663 CU.
DG249	To Rotol.
DG253	To 138 Sqn.
DG277	To 1663 CU.
DT546	From 10 Sqn. To 1659 CU.
DT673 EQ-G/A	Crash-landed at Leeming on return from Essen 4.4.43.
DT674 EQ-A	FTR Essen 27/28.5.43.
DT675	To 1656 CU.
DT676	To 1659 CU.
DT677	To 1659 CU.
DT678 EQ-C	Crash-landed in Nottinghamshire on return from Lorient 23.1.43.
DT679 EQ-Q	FTR Berlin 29/30.3.43.
DT680 EQ-D	FTR Hamburg 3/4.2.43.
DT682 EQ-F	Crashed in Nottinghamshire soon after take-off during transit 2.2.43.
DT749 EQ-O	FTR Hamburg 27/28.7.43.
DT750 EQ-U	Crashed in Yorkshire on return from Cologne 14.2.43.
DT752 EQ-W	FTR Pilsen 16/17.4.43.
DT769 EQ-J	FTR Aachen 13/14.7.43.
DT772 EQ-F/E	From 405 Sqn. FTR Krefeld 21/22.6.43.
DT781 EQ-D	To 1668 CU.
DT790 EQ-S	Crashed near Leeming on return from Essen 13.3.43.
DT797 EQ-H	FTR Berlin 1/2.3.43.

Posted to 6 Group 1.1.43.

419 (MOOSE) SQUADRON (RCAF)

Motto: Moosa Aswiyita   **Code: VR**

Formed in 3 Group under the BACTP agreement on 15 December 1941, 419 Squadron was the third Canadian unit to be formed in Bomber Command and operated Wellingtons. Its inspirational first Commanding Officer, W/C 'Moose' Fulton was lost on operations in 1942, but his nickname lived on in the squadron title. The squadron was posted to 4 Group in August 1942 and continued to carry out operations on Wellingtons until being posted to Middleton-St-George, where conversion began onto Halifaxes. No operations were conducted on the new type until the squadron's transfer as a founder member of the Canadian 6 Group on 1 January 1943.

STATIONS

Leeming	12.08.42 to 18.08.42
Topcliffe	18.08.42 to 30.09.42

Croft	30.09.42 to 09.11.42
Middleton-St-George	09.11.42 to 01.06.45

COMMANDING OFFICERS

Wing Commander A.P. Walsh DFC AFC	05.08.42 to 03.09.42
Squadron Leader J.D. Pattison (temp)	03.09.42 to 08.09.42
Wing Commander M.M. Fleming DSO DFC	08.09.42 to 08.10.43

AIRCRAFT

Wellington IC	01.42 to 11.42
Wellington III	02.42 to 11.42
Halifax II	11.42 to 04.44

OPERATIONAL RECORD
Wellingtons

Operations	Sorties	Aircraft Losses	% Losses
11	65 approx	9	5.8

TABLE OF STATISTICS
Out of 25 operational squadrons in 4 Group

23rd highest number of overall operations in 4 Group.
23rd highest number of sorties in 4 Group.
19th highest number of aircraft operational losses in 4 Group.

Out of 12 operational Wellington squadrons in 4 Group

10th highest number of Wellington overall operations in 4 Group.
10th highest number of Wellington sorties in 4 Group.
7th highest number of Wellington operational losses in 4 Group.

AIRCRAFT HISTORIES

Wellington	From January 1942 to November 1942.
X3308 VR-O	Ditched off Suffolk coast on return from Bremen 14.9.42.
X3357 VR-T	To 196 Sqn.
X3390	From 75 Sqn. To 214 Sqn and back. To 57 Sqn and back. To 427 Sqn.
X3562	To 427 Sqn.
X3563 VR-T	To 427 Sqn.
X3659 VR-B	To 427 Sqn.
X3699 VR-V	To 426 Sqn.
X3711 VR-R	FTR Karlsruhe 2/3.9.42.
X3752	To 427 Sqn.
X3796 VR-C	Crashed in Lincolnshire during air-test 15.9.42.
X3873	To 427 Sqn.
Z1572 VR-Q	From 75 Sqn. To 427 Sqn.

Z1599	To 426 Sqn.
Z1604	To 427 Sqn.
Z1623 VR-V	FTR Aachen 5/6.10.42.
Z1626 VR-G	To 427 Sqn.
Z1676	To 427 Sqn.
Z1680	From 29 OTU. To 426 Sqn.
BJ602 VR-J	FTR Bremen 4/5.9.42.
BJ604 VR-A	To 427 Sqn.
BJ668 VR-X	To 427 Sqn.
BJ729 VR-R	FTR Aachen 5/6.10.42.
BJ778	To 427 Sqn.
BJ886	To 427 Sqn.
BJ887 VR-H	Destroyed at Topcliffe when struck by 405 Sqn Halifax BB212 returning from Düsseldorf 11.9.42.
BJ919	To 426 Sqn.
BK268	To 427 Sqn.
BK269 VR-C	FTR Krefeld 2/3.10.42.
BK270	FTR Cologne 15/16.10.42.
BK276	To 427 Sqn.
BK335 VR-Y	Crashed on approach to Croft while training 10.10.42.
BK343	To 427 Sqn.
BK364	To 427 Sqn.
BK389	To 427 Sqn.
DF664 VR-E	FTR Kiel 13/14.10.42.
DF665 VR-Q	FTR Saarbrücken 28/29.8.42.

Posted to 6 Group 1.1.43.

420 (SNOWY OWL) SQUADRON (RCAF)

Motto: Pugnames Finitum (We fight to the end)   **Code: PT**

The second Canadian squadron to be formed as a Hampden unit in 5 Group after 408, 420 Squadron came into existence in December 1941. Ninety operations were carried out before the squadron was posted to 4 Group in August 1942 to convert to Wellingtons. It carried out a further twenty-four operations before being posted as a founder member to the Canadian 6 Group on New Year's Day 1943.

STATIONS

Skipton-on-Swale	06.08.42 to 14.10.42
Operations mounted from Leeming	05.10.42 to 14.10.42
Middleton-St-George	14.10.42 to 15.05.43

COMMANDING OFFICERS

Wing Commander D.A.R. Bradshaw	19.12.41 to 11.04.43

AIRCRAFT
Wellington III/X   08.42 to 11.43

OPERATIONAL RECORD

Operations	Sorties	Aircraft Losses	% Losses
24	142	7	4.9

Category of Operations

Bombing	Mining	Other
13	10	1

TABLE OF STATISTICS
Out of 25 operational squadrons in 4 Group
20th equal (with 425 Sqn) highest number of overall operations in 4 Group.
22nd highest number of sorties in 4 Group.
23rd highest number of operational losses in 4 Group.

Out of 12 operational Wellington squadrons in 4 Group
6th equal (with 425 Sqn) highest number of Wellington overall operations in
    4 Group.
8th highest number of Wellington sorties in 4 Group.
11th highest number of Wellington operational losses in 4 Group.

AIRCRAFT HISTORIES

Wellington	From July 1942 to January 1944.
X3335	To 18 OTU.
X3392	From 115 Sqn. To 22 OTU.
X3553	From 425 Sqn. To 427 Sqn.
X3800	To 18 OTU.
X3808 PT-B	FTR Cologne 15/16.10.42.
X3809 PT-O	To 26 OTU.
X3814 PT-P	FTR Bochum 29/30.3.43.
X3926	To 26 OTU.
X3963 PT-D	Crashed in Norfolk on return from Kiel 13/14.10.42.
Z1679 PT-B	FTR Hamburg 9/10.11.42.
Z1724 PT-X/C	Crashed in Yorkshire following structural failure while training 1.3.43.
BJ644	To 1485 Flt.
BJ717	To 26 OTU.
BJ915	To 18 OTU.
BJ917	To 26 OTU.
BJ966 PT-R	FTR from mining sortie 21/22.1.43.
BK235 PT-T	To 1485 Flt.
BK295	To 23 OTU.
BK296 PT-J	FTR from mining sortie 13/14.3.43.
BK297	To 29 OTU.
BK330 PT-K	FTR Lorient 13/14.2.43.

BK331	To 18 OTU.
BK365	To 18 OTU.
BK457	To 26 OTU.
BK468 PT-R	From 427 Sqn. FTR Cologne 26/27.2.43.
DF615 PT-S	FTR Lorient 29/30.1.43.
DF626 PT-Y	To 156 Sqn and back. Crashed at Exeter on return from Lorient 29/30.1.43.
DF636 PT-S	Crashed while trying to land at Leeming on return from Kiel 13/14.10.42.
DF637 PT-F	To 16 OTU.

Posted to 6 Group 1.1.43.

424 (TIGER) SQUADRON (RCAF)
(Non-operational)

Motto: Castigandos Castigamos   **Code: QB**

(We chastise those who deserve to be chastised)

Formed as a Wellington unit in 4 Group in October 1942, 424 Squadron carried out no operations before being posted to the Canadian 6 Group as a founder member on New Year's Day 1943.

STATIONS

Topcliffe	15.10.42 to 07.04.43

COMMANDING OFFICERS

Wing Commander H.M. Carscallen	15.10.42 to 16.04.43

AIRCRAFT

Wellington III/X	10.42 to 01.44

AIRCRAFT HISTORIES

Wellington	From October 1942 to January 1944.
X3284	From 57 Sqn. To 426 Sqn.
X3401	To 18 OTU.
X3409	From 466 Sqn. To 82 OTU.
X3426	To 18 OTU.
X3460	From 57 Sqn. To 426 Sqn.
X3789	To 1485 Flt.
X3790	From 466 Sqn. To 26 OTU.
Z1674 QB-G	To 21 OTU.
Z1691 QB-R	To 1485 Flt.
Z1692	From 466 Sqn. To 26 OTU.
BJ658 QB-Q	FTR from mining sortie 6/7.2.43.
BJ712	To 18 OTU.
BJ714 QB-F	FTR Lorient 26/27.1.43.
BK144 QB-V	To 18 OTU.

BK348 QB-J	FTR Essen 12/13.3.43.
BK398 QB-W	To 26 OTU.
BK435 QB-U	From 466 Sqn. FTR from a mining sortie 20/21.2.43.
BK436 QB-P	Abandoned over Wiltshire on return from Lorient 29.1.43.
BK490	To 26 OTU.
BK560	To 12 OTU.
DF613	To 12 OTU.
DF618	From 22 OTU. To 30 OTU.
DF621	To 12 OTU.
DF671	To 18 OTU.

Posted to 6 Group 1.1.43.

425 (ALOUETTE) SQUADRON (RCAF)

Motto: I shall pluck you   **Code: KW**

Formed as a Wellington unit in 4 Group in June 1942, 425 Squadron was manned predominantly by French Canadians. It conducted twenty-four operations before being transferred as a founder member to 6 Group on New Year's Day 1943.

STATIONS

Dishforth   25.06.42 to 15.05.43

COMMANDING OFFICERS

Wing Commander J.W.M. St Pierre   25.06.42 to 30.09.43

AIRCRAFT

Wellington III   25.06.42 to 12.43

OPERATIONAL RECORD

Operations	Sorties	Aircraft Losses	% Losses
24	135	3	2.2

Category of Operations

Bombing	Mining	Other
13	10	1

TABLE OF STATISTICS
Out of 25 operational squadrons in 4 Group

20th equal (with 420 Sqn) highest number of overall operations in 4 Group.
23rd highest number of sorties in 4 Group.
21st equal (with 458 Sqn) highest number of operational losses in 4 Group.

Out of 12 Wellington squadrons in 4 Group

6th equal (with 425 Sqn) highest number of Wellington overall operations in 4 Group.

8th highest number of Wellington sorties in 4 Group.

11th highest number of Wellington operational losses in 4 Group.

AIRCRAFT HISTORIES

Wellington	From June 1942 to January 1944.
X3361	Crashed soon after take-off from Kingscliffe for ferry flight 1.2.43.
X3364	From 115 Sqn. To 426 Sqn.
X3393	From 115 Sqn. Returned to 115 Sqn.
X3551	To 23 OTU.
X3553 KW-H	From 12 Sqn. To 420 Sqn.
X3648 KW-R	From 101 Sqn. To 18 OTU.
X3763 KW-L	FTR Stuttgart 14/15.4.43.
X3803	To 20 OTU.
X3872 KW-A	To 29 OTU.
X3876	To 12 OTU.
X3943 KW-G	Crashed in Essex on return from Aachen 5/6.10.42.
Z1603 KW-C	To 26 OTU.
Z1729 KW-T	FTR Duisburg 20/21.12.42.
Z1742 KW-C	FTR from mining sortie 6/7.2.43.
BJ605	To 27 OTU.
BJ644 KW-Q	From 1485 Flt. To 27 OTU.
BJ652 KW-E	To 27 OTU.
BJ655	To 156 Sqn via 1483 Flt.
BJ656	To 1483 Flt.
BJ657 KW-G	FTR Mannheim 6/7.12.42.
BJ669	From 156 Sqn. To 26 OTU.
BJ695	Crashed in Yorkshire during fighter affiliation exercise 22.9.42.
BJ699	To RAE.
BJ700	To 1483 Flt.
BJ755	To 429 Sqn.
BJ764	Crashed at Swanton Morley on return from Hamburg 9/10.11.42.
BJ783 KW-F	Force-landed in Yorkshire on return from Kiel 13/14.10.42.
BJ846	Crashed in Yorkshire on return from a mining sortie 11/12.11.42.
BJ892	To 26 OTU.
BJ894 KW-K	Crashed in Essex while training 16.11.42.
BJ918 KW-F	Crashed on take-off from Dishforth when bound for St Nazaire 28.2.43.
BJ958 KW-N	Crashed in Yorkshire soon after take-off from Elsham Wolds on transit flight to Dishforth 23.10.42.

BK153 KW-P	To 23 OTU.
BK308	To 18 OTU.
BK332 KW-O	To 1485 Flt.
BK333	To 17 OTU.
BK334 KW-B	FTR Hamburg 3/4.3.43.
BK337	To 428 Sqn.
BK340 KW-T	FTR Essen 12/13.3.43.
BK344	FTR Hamburg 3/4.3.43.
BK401	To 426 Sqn.
BK465	To 426 Sqn via 16 OTU.
BK496	To 17 OTU.
BK539 KW-S	To 16 OTU.
BK557 KW-S	FTR Hamburg 9/10.11.42.
DF617	To 426 Sqn.
HE260	To Middle East.
HE261	To Middle East.
HE268	From 304 Sqn. To 6 OTU.
HE269	To 311 FTU.
HE324	To 17 OTU.
HE329	From 420 Sqn. To Middle East.
HE423 KW-A	To 429 Sqn.
HE475 KW-E	FTR Mannheim 16/17.4.43.
HE486	To 30 OTU.
HE491 KW-B	FTR from mining sortie 11/12.4.43.
HE500	To 26 OTU.
HE514	From 420 Sqn. To 432 Sqn.
HE516	To 3 ADU.
HE521	To Middle East.
HE522	To Middle East.
HE551	To Middle East.
HE568	From 420 Sqn. To 1 OADU.
HE592 KW-Q	FTR Duisburg 8/9.4.43.
HE595	To 429 Sqn.
HE655	To 166 Sqn.
HE733 KW-S	FTR Stuttgart 14/15.4.43.
HE865	To 429 Sqn.
HE900	To Middle East.
HE901	To 196 Sqn.
HE903	To 3 OTU.
HE930	To Middle East.
HE931	To Middle East.
HE970	To Middle East.
HE976	To Middle East.
HE977	To Middle East.
HE978	To 29 OTU.
HE979	To Middle East.
HZ277	To 199 Sqn.
HZ355	To 429 Sqn.

HZ468	From 420 Sqn.
HZ471	To 429 Sqn.
LN409	To 431 Sqn.
LN436	To Middle East.
LN440	To Middle East.
MS492	To Middle East.
MS493	To 166 Sqn.

Posted to 6 Group 1.1.43.

426 (THUNDERBIRD) SQUADRON (RCAF)
(Non-operational)

Motto: On wings of fire   **Code: OW**

Formed in mid-October 1942 as a Wellington squadron in 4 Group, 426 did not conduct any operations until after being posted as a founder member of the Canadian 6 Group on New Year's Day 1943.

STATIONS
Dishforth   15.10.42 to 17.06.43

COMMANDING OFFICERS
Wing Commander S.S. Blanchard   15.10.42 to 14.02.43

AIRCRAFT
Wellington III   15.10.42 to 06.43

AIRCRAFT HISTORIES

Wellington	From October 1942 to July 1943.
X3284 OW-X	From 424 Sqn. FTR from mining sortie 9/10.3.43.
X3348	From 466 Sqn. To 427 Sqn.
X3364	From 425 Sqn. Crashed on take-off from Dishforth for mining sortie 27.2.43.
X3420 OW-H	From 419 Sqn. FTR Cologne 14/15.2.43.
X3458	From 1418 Flt. To 16 OTU.
X3460	From 424 Sqn. To 17 OTU.
X3461	From 466 Sqn. To 12 OTU.
X3600	From 57 Sqn. To 12 OTU.
X3696 OW-T	From 57 Sqn. FTR Duisburg 26/27.3.43.
X3699	From 419 Sqn. FTR Kiel 4/5.4.43.
Z1599 OW-B/M	From 419 Sqn. FTR Cologne 26/27.2.43.
Z1680 OW-R	From 419 Sqn. FTR from intruder sortie to Oldenburg 30.1.43.
BJ762 OW-O	FTR Bochum 29/30.3.43.
BJ888	To 20 OTU.
BJ919 OW-P	From 419 Sqn. FTR Wilhelmshaven 19/20.2.43.
BK140	To 26 OTU.

BK142 OW-A	To 30 OTU.
BK165 OW-F	From 427 Sqn. FTR Lorient 14/15.1.43.
BK401 OW-M	From 425 Sqn. FTR Essen 5/6.3.43.
BK431	To 29 OTU.
BK440 OW-V	To 26 OTU.
BK452	To 29 OTU.
BK456 OW-C	To 26 OTU.
BK465	From 425 Sqn via 16 OTU. To 29 OTU.
BK471 OW-W	From 466 Sqn. To 18 OTU.
BK505	To 18 OTU.
BK542	To 12 OTU.
DF617	To 425 Sqn.
DF619	To 20 OTU.
DF620	Crash-landed at Topcliffe while training 7.2.43.

Posted to 6 Group 1.1.43.

427 (LION) SQUADRON (RCAF)

Motto: Ferte Manus Certe   **Code: ZL**

One of three Canadian Wellington squadrons to be formed in 4 Group on 7 November 1942, 427 Squadron was declared operational remarkably quickly on 1 December. It was not until mid-month, however, that it launched its first sorties, and that proved to be the only operation carried out by the Lions as a 4 Group unit. On New Year's Day 1943, 427 Squadron became a founder member of the Canadian 6 Group.

STATIONS
Croft   07.11.42 to 04.05.43

COMMANDING OFFICERS
Wing Commander D.H. Burnside   07.11.42 to 05.09.43

AIRCRAFT
Wellington III/X   11.42 to 05.43

OPERATIONAL RECORD
Operations	Sorties	Aircraft Losses	% Losses
1	3	0	0.0

Category of Operations
Bombing	Mining
0	1

TABLE OF STATISTICS
Out of 25 operational squadrons in 4 Group
Lowest number of overall operations, sorties and losses.

Out of 12 operational Wellington squadrons in 4 Group
Lowest number of overall operations, sorties and losses.

AIRCRAFT HISTORIES

Wellington	From November 1942 to May 1943.
X3348 ZL-Z	From 426 Sqn. Crash-landed in Derbyshire on return from Lorient 26/27.1.43.
X3390 ZL-W	From 419 Sqn. FTR from mining sortie 2/3.3.43.
X3553 ZL-Y	From 420 Sqn. To 29 OTU.
X3562 ZL-H	From 419 Sqn. To 29 OTU.
X3563 ZL-T	From 419 Sqn. Abandoned over Eire on return from St Nazaire 28.2/1.3.43.
X3659	From 419 Sqn. To 1485 Flt.
X3752 ZL-P	From 419 Sqn. To 23 OTU.
X3873 ZL-W/R	From 419 Sqn. FTR from mining sortie 21/22.1.43.
Z1572 ZL-Q	From 419 Sqn. To 16 OTU.
Z1604 ZL-U/P	From 419 Sqn. To 29 OTU.
Z1626 ZL-V/G	From 419 Sqn. To 16 OTU.
Z1676 ZL-S	From 419 Sqn. Crash-landed in Eire on return from Lorient 16/17.2.43.
Z1719 ZL-P/J	To 18 OTU.
BJ604 ZL-A	From 419 Sqn. Crashed on landing at Middleton-St-George while in transit 8.1.43.
BJ668 ZL-X	From 419 Sqn. FTR Lorient 4/5.2.43.
BJ778 ZL-D	From 419 Sqn. Crashed in Yorkshire on return from a mining sortie 12.2.43.
BJ886 ZL-F	From 419 Sqn. FTR Cologne 26/27.2.43.
BK137 ZL-A	To 12 OTU.
BK143	To 311 FTU.
BK164 ZL-E	To 16 OTU.
BK165	To 426 Sqn.
BK268 ZL-C	From 419 Sqn. Crashed in Rutland on return from Cologne 26/27.2.43.
BK276 ZL-O	From 419 Sqn. Crashed on take-off from Croft while training 15.11.42.
BK337	From 428 Sqn. To 29 OTU.
BK343 ZL-V	From 419 Sqn. FTR St Nazaire 28.2/1.3.43.
BK364 ZL-G	From 419 Sqn. FTR Lorient 15/16.1.43.
BK389 ZL-L	From 419 Sqn. FTR Oldenburg 30.1.43.
BK437 ZL-K	To 29 OTU.
BK438 ZL-R	To 29 OTU.
BK468	To 420 Sqn.
BK558 ZL-Z	To 12 OTU.

Posted to 6 Group 1943.

428 (GHOST) SQUADRON (RCAF)

(Non-operational)

Motto: Usque ad Finem (To the very end)   **Code: NA**

Formed as a Wellington squadron in 4 Group in November 1942, 428 Squadron conducted no operations with the Group before becoming a founder member of the Canadian 6 Group on New Year's Day 1943.

STATIONS
Dalton   07.11.42 to 01.06.43

COMMANDING OFFICERS
Wing Commander A. Earle   07.11.42 to 20.02.43

AIRCRAFT
Wellington III/X   07.11.42 to 06.43

AIRCRAFT HISTORIES

Wellington	From November 1942 to June 1943.
X3541 NA-N	To 29 OTU.
X3543	To 29 OTU.
X3545	From 466 Sqn. To CGS.
X3546	From 466 Sqn. To CGS.
X3550 NA-J	To 17 OTU.
Z1718	To 18 OTU.
Z1719 NA-P	To 18 OTU.
Z1722	To 17 OTU.
Z1727 NA-K	From 156 Sqn. To 1485 Flt.
BK154	To 16 OTU.
BK155	To 1485 Flt.
BK156	To 18 OTU.
BK337	From 425 Sqn. To 427 Sqn.
BK562	To 30 OTU.
BK563 NA-R	To 29 OTU.
BK564 NA-R	FTR Bochum 29/30.3.43.
DF635 NA-I	From 156 Sqn. FTR Duisburg 8/9.4.43.
DF668	From 156 Sqn. To 16 OTU.

Posted to 6 Group 1.1.43.

429 (BISON) SQUADRON (RCAF)

Motto: Fortunae Nihil (Nothing to chance)   **Code: AL**

Formed as a Wellington unit in 4 Group in November 1942, 429 Squadron operated for the first time on 21 January 1943. Most Canadian squadrons joined 6 Group on its formation on New Year's Day 1943, but it was a further three months before 429 Squadron eventually made the move.

STATIONS
East Moor   07.11.42 to 12.08.43

COMMANDING OFFICERS
Wing Commander J.A.P. Owen   07.11.42 to 31.05.43

AIRCRAFT
Wellington X   07.11.42 to 09.43

OPERATIONAL RECORD

Operations	Sorties	Aircraft Losses	% Losses
19	158	7	4.4

Category of Operations

Bombing	Mining
11	8

TABLE OF STATISTICS
Out of 25 operational squadrons in 4 Group
22nd highest number of overall operations in 4 Group.
21st highest number of sorties in 4 Group.
19th highest number of aircraft operational losses in 4 Group.

Out of 12 operational Wellington squadrons in 4 Group
9th highest number of overall Wellington operations in 4 Group.
7th highest number of Wellington sorties in 4 Group.
8th highest number of Wellington operational losses in 4 Group.

AIRCRAFT HISTORIES
Wellington	From November 1942 to September 1943.
X3357	From 196 Sqn. To 18 OTU.
X3399	To 26 OTU.
X3480	From 75 Sqn. To 419 Sqn.
X3704	From 196 Sqn. To 23 OTU.
Z1670	From 196 Sqn. Crashed in Yorkshire during air-test 3.4.43.
Z1696	To 18 OTU.
BJ715	From 196 Sqn. To 30 OTU.

BJ755 AL-Z	From 425 Sqn. Crashed soon after take-off from East Moor when bound for Essen 5.3.43.
BJ798	From 466 Sqn. Crashed on landing at Henley while training 24.2.43.
BJ799	To 30 OTU.
BJ908	From 466 Sqn. To 23 OTU.
BJ920 AL-E	FTR Bochum 29/30.3.43.
BK146	To 30 OTU.
BK162 AL-B	FTR Mannheim 16/17.4.43.
BK163 AL-H	FTR Lorient 26/27.1.43.
BK429 AL-Q	FTR from mining sortie 9/10.3.43.
BK430	From 196 Sqn. To 20 OTU.
BK432 AL-S	FTR from mining sortie 21/22.1.43.
BK499	From 196 Sqn. To 86 OTU.
BK540 AL-C	FTR Bochum 29/30.3.43.
DF624	From 156 Sqn. Abandoned over Yorkshire during training 21.12.42.
DF625	From 466 Sqn. To 26 OTU.

Posted to 6 Group 1.4.43.

431 (IROQUOIS) SQUADRON (RCAF)

Motto: Warriors of the air　　　　　　　　**Code: SE**

Formed as a Wellington unit in 4 Group in November 1942, 431 Squadron had to wait until the start of March 1943 before launching its first operation. Unlike the majority of other Canadian squadrons, 431 did not transfer immediately to 6 Group on its formation at the start of 1943, but continued to operate with 4 Group until finally making the move in July.

STATIONS
Burn　　　　　　　　　11.11.42 to 14.07.43

COMMANDING OFFICERS
Wing Commander J. Coverdale　　　01.12.42 to 22.06.43
Wing Commander W.D.M. Newson　　26.06.43 to 10.05.44

AIRCRAFT
Wellington X　　　　　　11.42 to 07.43

OPERATIONAL RECORD

Operations	Sorties	Aircraft Losses	% Losses
49	321	18	5.6

Category of Operations

Bombing	Mining
25	24

TABLE OF STATISTICS
Out of 24 squadrons in 4 Group
18th highest number of overall operations in 4 Group.
19th highest number of sorties in 4 Group.
14th highest number of aircraft operational losses in 4 Group.

Out of 12 Wellington squadrons in 4 Group
2nd highest number of overall Wellington operations in 4 Group.
5th highest number of Wellington sorties in 4 Group.
6th highest number of Wellington operational losses in 4 Group.

AIRCRAFT HISTORIES

Wellington	From November 1942 to July 1943.
HE182 SE-A	FTR Bochum 29/30.3.43.
HE183 SE-J	FTR Bochum 13/14.5.43.
HE184 SE-M	FTR Düsseldorf 11/12.6.43.
HE197	To 17 OTU.
HE198 SE-D	To 17 OTU.
HE199	To 82 OTU.
HE200 SE-P	FTR from mining sortie 21/22.5.43.
HE201 SE-T	To 82 OTU.
HE202 SE-Z	FTR from mining sortie 7/8.3.43.
HE203 SE-B	FTR Wuppertal 29/30.5.43.
HE204	To 17 OTU.
HE205 SE-X	To 18 OTU.
HE213 SE-F	FTR Frankfurt 10/11.4.43.
HE265	To 82 OTU.
HE374 SE-X	FTR Stuttgart 14/15.4.43.
HE379 SE-H	FTR Mannheim 16/17.4.43.
HE392 SE-L	From 196 Sqn. FTR Düsseldorf 11/12.6.43.
HE394 SE-V	From 196 Sqn. FTR Mülheim 22/23.6.43.
HE396	To 6 OTU.
HE440 SE-Y	FTR Duisburg 12/13.5.43.
HE443 SE-O	FTR Cologne 28/29.6.43.
HE476 SE-Z	Crash-landed in Yorkshire on return from Duisburg 27.4.43.
HE502	To 17 OTU.
HE503 SE-S	FTR Duisburg 26/27.3.43.
HE518	From 30 OTU. Returned to 30 OTU.
HE748	To 82 OTU.
HE983	To 18 OTU.
HE990 SE-Z	FTR Düsseldorf 25/26.5.43.
HF518 SE-J	FTR Krefeld 21/22.6.43.
HF543 SE-P	Damaged beyond repair in collision with Halifax DK192 (427 Sqn) on the ground at Oulton on return from Düsseldorf 12.6.43.
HF603	To 166 Sqn.

HF604	To 15 OTU.
HZ357 SE-S	FTR Stuttgart 14/15.4.43.
HZ484	To 466 Sqn.
LN282	To 82 OTU.
LN283	To 82 OTU.
LN284 SE-Q	FTR Cologne 3/4.7.43.
LN290	To 82 OTU.
LN291	To 82 OTU.
LN295	To 27 OTU.
LN403	To 17 OTU.
LN405	To 17 OTU.
LN409	From 425 Sqn. To 17 OTU.
MS475	To 27 OTU.
MS489	From 429 Sqn. To 17 OTU.

Posted to 6 Group 14.7.43.

458 SQUADRON (RAAF)

(No motto)   **Code: FU**
Formed in New South Wales, Australia in July 1941, 458 Squadron was the
second Australian unit to arrive in Bomber Command. It eventually found its
way to 4 Group, where it began to operate on Wellingtons in October of that
year. Its time with Bomber Command was cut short by a posting to the Middle
East in February 1942.

STATIONS
Holme-on-Spalding-Moor   25.08.41 to 22.02.42

COMMANDING OFFICERS
Wing Commander N.G. Mulholland   25.08.41 to 22.02.42

AIRCRAFT
Wellington   25.08.41 to 06.45

OPERATIONAL RECORD

Operations	Sorties	Aircraft Losses	% Losses
10	65	3	4.6
All bombing			

TABLE OF STATISTICS
Out of 25 operational squadrons in 4 Group
24th highest number of overall operations in 4 Group.
24th highest number of sorties in 4 Group.
23rd highest number of aircraft operational losses in 4 Group.

Out of 12 operational Wellington squadrons in 4 Group
11th highest number of overall Wellington operations in 4 Group.
11th highest number of Wellington sorties in 4 Group.
10th highest number of Wellington operational losses in 4 Group.

AIRCRAFT HISTORIES

Wellington	From October 1941 to February 1942.
R1490	To 301 Sqn.
R1695	To 460 Sqn.
R1765	Abandoned over Hampshire on return from Le Havre 22/23.10.41.
R1775	FTR Emden 15/16.11.41.
R1785	FTR Cherbourg 9.1.42.
R1795	To 300 Sqn.
Z1161	From 99 Sqn. To 21 OTU.
Z1174	To 1446 Flt.
Z1182 FU-G	Crashed soon after take-off from Holme-on-Spalding-Moor when bound for Brest 6.1.42.
Z1183	To 300 Sqn.
Z1204	To 301 Sqn.
Z1205	To 142 Sqn.
Z1212	To 460 Sqn.
Z1214	To 142 Sqn.
Z1215	From 301 Sqn. To 300 Sqn.
Z1218 FU-D	FTR Antwerp 20/21.10.41.
Z1219	To 301 Sqn.
Z1246	Destroyed by fire on the ground at Holme-on-Spalding-Moor 24.11.41.
Z1254	To 460 Sqn.
Z1261	From De Havilland. To 142 Sqn.
Z1272	To 301 Sqn.
Z1273	To 301 Sqn.
Z1274	To 142 Sqn.
Z1279	To 300 Sqn.
Z1280	To 301 Sqn.
Z1286	To 142 Sqn.
Z1290	To 460 Sqn.
Z1291	To 300 Sqn.
Z1312	Crashed in Dorset following early return from Cherbourg 9.1.42.
Z1320	To 300 Sqn.
Z1324	To 142 Sqn.
Z1333	To 301 Sqn.
Z1338	To 142 Sqn.
Z1377	To 301 Sqn.
DV501	To 26 OTU.
DV502	To Middle East.

DV521	To Middle East.
DV522	To 1443 Flt.
DV539	To Middle East.
DV541	To Middle East.
DV550	To 15 OTU.
DV555	To Middle East.

Posted to Middle East February 1942.

462 SQUADRON (RAAF)

(No motto)   **Code: Z5**

Re-formed in 4 Group on 12 August 1944, 462 Squadron performed a standard heavy bomber role with Halifaxes until its transfer to 100 Group in December 1944 to assume Radio Counter Measures duties.

STATIONS

Driffield   14.08.44 to 29.12.44

COMMANDING OFFICERS

Wing Commander D.E.S. Shannon   18.08.44 to 30.12.44

AIRCRAFT

Halifax III   08.44 to 09.45

OPERATIONAL RECORD

Operations	Sorties	Aircraft Losses	% Losses
45	544	6	1.1
All bombing			

TABLE OF STATISTICS
Out of 25 operational squadrons in 4 Group
19th highest number of overall operations in 4 Group.
16th highest number of sorties in 4 Group.
21st highest number of aircraft operational losses in 4 Group.

Out of 15 operational Halifax squadrons in 4 Group
14th highest number of overall Halifax operations in 4 Group.
14th highest number of Halifax sorties in 4 Group.
Lowest number of Halifax operational losses in 4 Group.

AIRCRAFT HISTORIES

Halifax	From August 1944.
HX244	From 466 Sqn. To 640 Sqn.
LK786	From 640 Sqn. To 1658 CU.
LL598 Z5-A	From 76 Sqn.

LL599 Z5-E	From 76 Sqn. Collided with Lancaster LM691 of 625 Sqn over Germany during an operation to Essen 23.10.44.
LL600 Z5-C	From 578 Sqn. Crash-landed in Suffolk out of fuel on return from Neuss 23.9.44.
LL601	From 578 Sqn. To 1658 CU.
LL604 Z5-D	From 158 Sqn. FTR Bochum 9/10.10.44.
LL609	
LL610 Z5-U	FTR Düsseldorf 2/3.11.44.
LL611	To 1658 CU.
LV955	From 466 Sqn. To 192 Sqn.
LV993	From 429 Sqn via 1664 CU.
LW440	From 78 Sqn. To 1663 CU.
MZ296 Z5-N	From 466 Sqn. FTR Duisburg 15.10.44.
MZ306	From 466 Sqn.
MZ308	From 466 Sqn.
MZ341	From 466 Sqn.
MZ342	From 466 Sqn. To 192 Sqn.
MZ370 Z5-L	From 466 Sqn.
MZ396	From 77 Sqn.
MZ398	From 10 Sqn. To 466 Sqn and back.
MZ400 Z5-J	From 466 Sqn. FTR Bochum 9/10.10.44.
MZ401 Z5-D	From 51 Sqn. To 466 Sqn and back. FTR Düsseldorf 2/3.11.44.
MZ402 Z5-V	From 51 Sqn. To 466 Sqn and back.
MZ403	From 10 Sqn. To 466 Sqn.
MZ429	From 466 Sqn.
MZ431	From 466 Sqn.
MZ447 Z5-A	From 434 Sqn.
MZ448	
MZ457	
MZ461 Z5-G	
MZ467 Z5-C	
MZ469 Z5-N	
MZ479 Z5-B	
MZ648	To 158 Sqn.
MZ792	From 466 Sqn. Returned to 466 Sqn.
MZ913 Z5-N	From 434 Sqn.
MZ926	From 158 Sqn. To BDU.
NA147	
NA148	
NA240 Z5-V	
NA521	From 102 Sqn. To 1663 CU.
NA621	To 1658 CU.
NA622	To 1658 CU.
NP989	To 466 Sqn.
NP990	To 192 Sqn.
NR119	

NR127	From 466 Sqn. Returned to 466 Sqn.
NR132	To 466 Sqn.
NR152	To 466 Sqn.
PN168	
PN180	To 192 Sqn.
PN192	From 158 Sqn.
PN423	
PN426	
PN427	
PN429 Z5-E	
PN430	
PN432	From 640 Sqn.
PN433	
PN442	
PN445	From 640 Sqn.

Posted to 100 Group 29.12.44.

466 SQUADRON (RAAF)

(No motto)   **Code: HD**

Formed as a Wellington unit in 4 Group in October 1942, 466 Squadron performed a standard heavy bomber role for the remainder of the war. Halifaxes replaced the Wellingtons in September 1943 and saw the squadron through to the end of hostilities.

STATIONS

Driffield	10.10.42 to 27.12.42
Leconfield	27.12.42 to 03.06.44
Driffield	03.06.44 to 26.10.45

COMMANDING OFFICERS

Wing Commander R.E. Bailey	10.10.42 to 29.09.43
Wing Commander D.T. Forsyth	29.09.43 to 23.05.44
Wing Commander H.W. Connolly	23.05.44 to 20.10.44
Wing Commander A. Wharton	20.10.44 to 03.04.45
Wing Commander A. Hollings	03.04.45 to 26.10.45

AIRCRAFT

Wellington X	10.42 to 09.43
Halifax II (non-op)	09.43 to 10.43
Halifax III	10.43 to 05.45

OPERATIONAL RECORD

Operations	Sorties	Aircraft Losses	% Losses
264	3,328	65	1.9

Category of Operations

Bombing	Mining
214	50

Wellingtons

Operations	Sorties	Aircraft Losses	% Losses
89	844	25	3.0

Category of Operations

Bombing	Mining
46	43

Halifaxes

Operations	Sorties	Aircraft Losses	% Losses
175	2,484	40	1.6

Category of Operations

Bombing	Mining
168	7

TABLE OF STATISTICS
Out of 25 operational squadrons in 4 Group
8th highest number of overall operations in 4 Group.
8th highest number of sorties in 4 Group.
8th highest number of aircraft operational losses in 4 Group.

Out of 12 operational Wellington squadrons in 4 Group
Highest number of overall Wellington operations in 4 Group.
Highest number of Wellington sorties in 4 Group.
Highest number of Wellington operational losses in 4 Group.

Out of 15 operational Halifax squadrons in 4 Group
8th highest number of overall Halifax operations in 4 Group.
9th highest number of Halifax sorties in 4 Group.
8th equal (with 578 & 640 Sqns) highest number of Halifax operational losses in 4 Group.

AIRCRAFT HISTORIES

Wellington	From October 1942 to September 1943.
X3348	From 9 Sqn. To 426 Sqn.
X3409	To 424 Sqn.
X3461	From 75 Sqn. To 426 Sqn.
X3545	To 428 Sqn.
X3546	To 428 Sqn.
X3790	To 424 Sqn.
Z1692	To 424 Sqn.
BJ798	To 429 Sqn.
BJ908	To 429 Sqn.

BK435	To 424 Sqn.
BK471	To 426 Sqn.
DF625	To 429 Sqn.
HE149 HD-J	Crashed in Yorkshire during training 31.12.42.
HE150	FTR Düsseldorf 11/12.6.43.
HE151	To 26 OTU.
HE152 HD-L	FTR from mining sortie 14/15.1.43.
HE153	Crashed on approach to Leconfield on return from Cologne 15.2.43.
HE154	FTR Düsseldorf 11/12.6.43.
HE155 HD-H	FTR Duisburg 8/9.4.43.
HE156	To 20 OTU.
HE164	From 429 Sqn. FTR Cologne 14/15.2.43.
HE212	FTR Wuppertal 29/30.5.43.
HE326	FTR Mülheim 22/23.6.43.
HE351	From 196 Sqn. To 26 OTU.
HE366	To 23 OTU.
HE368	Crashed in Nottinghamshire on return from Lorient 26.1.43.
HE376 HD-R	FTR from mining sortie 1/2.3.43.
HE383 HD-W	Crashed in Leconfield circuit while training 31.12.42.
HE386 HD-Z	FTR from mining sortie 16/17.5.43.
HE389	To 23 OTU.
HE391 HD-Y	Crashed into the North Sea during a cross-country exercise 22.12.42.
HE393	Crashed on landing at Leconfield on return from mining sortie 6.2.43.
HE397	FTR Emden 30.1.43.
HE410 HD-T	FTR from mining sortie 21/22.1.43.
HE411	To 23 OTU.
HE434	To 20 OTU.
HE471	FTR Emden 30.1.43.
HE473	From BDU. To 12 OTU.
HE501 HD-J	FTR Mannheim 16/17.4.43.
HE506 HD-N	FTR Frankfurt 10/11.4.43.
HE529	To 30 OTU.
HE530	FTR Dortmund 4/5.5.43.
HE531	Crash-landed at Kirmington on return from Wilhelmshaven 19/20.2.43.
HE549	To 18 OTU.
HE570	To 26 OTU.
HE872	To 26 OTU.
HE984	To 83 OTU.
HE989	From 199 Sqn. To 12 OTU.
HF471	To 30 OTU.
HF473	To 12 OTU.
HF481	FTR from mining sortie 28/29.6.43.
HF485	To 82 OTU.

HF513	From 196 Sqn. To 83 OTU.
HF516	From 196 Sqn. To 30 OTU.
HF517	To 83 OTU.
HF519	To 26 OTU.
HF544	FTR Gelsenkirchen 25/26.6.43.
HF545	From 196 Sqn. To 30 OTU.
HF569	FTR Cologne 3/4.7.43.
HF601	FTR from mining sortie 5/6.7.43.
HF602	To 82 OTU.
HZ256	To 17 OTU.
HZ257	FTR from mining sortie 21/22.5.43.
HZ269	FTR Wuppertal 29/30.5.43.
HZ270 HD-Q	FTR Essen 5/6.3.43.
HZ271	Partially abandoned over Yorkshire on return from Bochum 14.5.43.
HZ279	To 11 OTU.
HZ472	To 16 OTU.
HZ477	To 82 OTU.
HZ479	To 82 OTU.
HZ484	From 431 Sqn. To 300 Sqn.
HZ486	To 300 Sqn.
HZ518	To 432 Sqn.
HZ530	Crashed in Yorkshire on return from Duisburg 13.5.43.
HZ531	Collided with LN292 (466 Sqn) over Yorkshire when bound for Mönchengladbach 31.8.43.
HZ580 HD-C	From 196 Sqn. FTR Essen 25/26.7.43.
LN286	To 83 OTU.
LN287	To 12 OTU.
LN288	FTR Aachen 13/14.7.43.
LN289	To 12 OTU.
LN292	Collided with HZ531 (466 Sqn) over Yorkshire when bound for Mönchengladbach 31.8.43.
LN293	From 196 Sqn. To 12 OTU.
LN392	To 83 OTU.
LN400	To 16 OTU.
LN401	To 12 OTU.
LN404	Crash-landed near Leconfield during training 11.3.43.
LN428	To 16 OTU.
LN442	FTR from mining sortie 11/12.8.43.
LN443	To 82 OTU.
LN453	To 82 OTU.
MS473 HD-Q	FTR Bochum 13/14.5.43.
MS483	To 26 OTU.
MS494	FTR Wuppertal 29/30.5.43.

Halifax	From September 1943.
W1224	From 51 Sqn. Returned to 51 Sqn.
W7927	From 102 Sqn. To 1658 CU.
DT554 HD-J	From 158 Sqn. Crashed off Yorkshire coast during training 3.11.43.
DT720	From 10 Sqn. To 1658 CU.
DT776	From 10 Sqn. To 1658 CU.
HX231 HD-B	FTR Frankfurt 18/19.3.44.
HX233 HD-C	FTR Berlin 28/29.1.44.
HX235 HD-D	Crashed on landing at Catfoss following early return from a mining sortie 1.12.43.
HX236 HD-J	FTR Frankfurt 20/21.12.43.
HX237 HD-A	From 51 Sqn. Crashed on take-off from Leconfield during training 25.11.43.
HX239 HD-G	Force-landed in Norfolk on return from Berlin 29.1.44.
HX240	To 77 Sqn.
HX242 HD-L	FTR Trappes 2/3.6.44.
HX243 HD-D	FTR Stuttgart 24/25.7.44.
HX244	To 462 Sqn.
HX247	Crashed on landing at Leconfield on return from Magdeburg 22.1.44.
HX266	To 1658 CU.
HX267 HD-U	FTR Bourg Leopold 27/28.5.44.
HX271 HD-V	FTR Trappes 2/3.6.44.
HX273 HD-W	FTR Frankfurt 20/21.12.43.
HX274 HD-X	FTR Tergnier 10/11.4.44.
HX276 HD-Y	Undercarriage collapsed while stationary at Leconfield 9.12.43.
HX278 HD-Z	FTR Berlin 20/21.1.44.
HX293 HD-F	FTR Berlin 15/16.2.44.
HX294 HD-A	FTR Berlin 28/29.1.44.
HX296	Crashed in Yorkshire while attempting an emergency landing at a decoy site 16.12.43.
HX312 HD-K	FTR Magdeburg 21/22.1.44.
HX336 HD-M	FTR Berlin 15/16.2.44.
HX337 HD-W	FTR Düsseldorf 22/23.4.44.
HX341 HD-D	FTR Stuttgart 15/16.3.44.
HX343	To 415 Sqn.
HX345 HD-Y	FTR Berlin 28/29.1.44.
HX354 HD-J	Crashed on landing at Leconfield during training 10.1.44.
JB788	From 77 Sqn. To 1652 CU.
JB927	From 78 Sqn. Returned to 78 Sqn.
JD170	From 78 Sqn. To 1652 CU.
LK793	From 640 Sqn. To 347 Sqn.
LL615	To 158 Sqn.
LV781 HD-H	FTR Leipzig 19/20.2.44.

LV791	Abandoned over UK on return from Acheres 1.5.44.
LV823	To 640 Sqn.
LV824	Crash-landed at Leconfield during training 27.5.44.
LV826 HD-J	FTR Hasselt 12/13.5.44.
LV827	FTR Frankfurt 18/19.3.44.
LV833 HD-P	FTR Stuttgart 24/25.7.44.
LV837	To 520 Sqn.
LV875 HD-F	FTR Tergnier 10/11.4.44.
LV900 HD-H	FTR Berlin 24/25.3.44.
LV904	To 1658 CU.
LV919 HD-O	FTR Hasselt 12/13.5.44.
LV936 HD-D	FTR Bochum 4/5.11.44.
LV943 HD-G	FTR Mantes la Jolie 6/7.5.44.
LV946	To 640 Sqn.
LV948	To 640 Sqn.
LV949	Crashed on landing at Carnaby during training 9.3.45.
LV955	To 462 Sqn.
LV956 HD-R	FTR Tergnier 18/19.4.44.
LW116 HD-X	FTR Siracourt 22.6.44.
LW172 HD-F	Crashed on approach to Driffield on return from Hamburg 9.4.45.
LW369 HD-F	From 640 Sqn. FTR Frankfurt 18/19.3.44.
LW372 HD-C	FTR Sterkrade 6.10.44.
LW501	From 78 Sqn. To 158 Sqn.
LW502	From 640 Sqn. Returned to 640 Sqn.
LW506	From 640 Sqn. Returned to 640 Sqn.
LW516	From 78 Sqn. To 640 Sqn.
LW521	From 51 Sqn. Ditched off Dorset coast on return from Stuttgart 15/16.3.44.
MZ283 HD-F	FTR Juvisy 7/8.6.44.
MZ287	To 517 Sqn.
MZ294	To 1652 CU.
MZ296	To 462 Sqn.
MZ299 HD-H	FTR Wilhelmshaven 15/16.10.44.
MZ305	Crashed in Kent during a cross-country exercise 14.6.44.
MZ306	To 462 Sqn.
MZ307	Crashed on take-off from Driffield when bound for Boulogne 17.9.44.
MZ308	To 462 Sqn.
MZ313	Abandoned over Kent on return from Vaires 18.7.44.
MZ341	To 462 Sqn.
MZ342	To 462 Sqn.
MZ368 HD-X	From 158 Sqn. FTR Coquereaux 9.8.44.
MZ370	To 462 Sqn.
MZ395	To 158 Sqn.
MZ398	From 462 Sqn. Returned to 462 Sqn.

MZ399	To 158 Sqn.
MZ400	To 462 Sqn.
MZ401	From 462 Sqn. Returned to 462 Sqn.
MZ402	From 462 Sqn. Returned to 462 Sqn.
MZ403	From 462 Sqn. To 158 Sqn.
MZ404	To 640 Sqn.
MZ407	To 640 Sqn.
MZ429	To 462 Sqn.
MZ431	To 462 Sqn.
MZ494	To 640 Sqn.
MZ735	To 640 Sqn.
MZ775	To 158 Sqn.
MZ792	To 462 Sqn and back.
MZ877 HD-P	Crashed on take-off from Driffield during training 12.11.44.
MZ914	Damaged beyond repair during operation to Chemnitz 5/6.3.45. SOC 7.3.45.
MZ915 HD-T	FTR Kiel 15/16.9.44.
MZ939	To 640 Sqn.
MZ945	To 158 Sqn.
NA199	
NP923	From 640 Sqn. To Pocklington.
NP931	To 640 Sqn.
NP968	From 432 Sqn. FTR Hamburg 8/9.4.45.
NP969 HD-Q	FTR Magdeburg 16/17.1.45.
NP971	From 432 Sqn.
NP975 HD-H	FTR Bingen 22/23.12.44.
NP976	
NP989	From 462 Sqn.
NR125	From 426 Sqn.
NR127	To 462 Sqn and back.
NR132 HD-Z	From 462 Sqn. FTR Bochum 4/5.11.44.
NR152	From 462 Sqn.
NR154	
NR169	
NR179 HD-C	From 158 Sqn. Shot down by intruder near Driffield on return from Kamen 3/4.3.45.
NR183	From 158 Sqn.
NR185	From 158 Sqn.
NR201	
NR234	
NR238	
NR250 HD-N	From 640 Sqn. Shot down by intruder near Driffield on return from Kamen 3/4.3.45.
NR286	From 640 Sqn.
PN181	
PN182	From 640 Sqn.
PN184	From 640 Sqn.

RG346	From 77 Sqn.
RG437	To 158 Sqn.
RG494	From 640 Sqn.
RG549	From 640 Sqn.
RG557	From 640 Sqn.
RG559	From 640 Sqn. To 346 Sqn.
RG565	From 640 Sqn.
RG566	From 640 Sqn.
RG588	From 640 Sqn.
RG589	From 640 Sqn.
RG590	From 640 Sqn. To 346 Sqn.
RG596	From 640 Sqn.
RG600	From 640 Sqn. To 346 Sqn.
RG603	From 640 Sqn.
RG604	From 640 Sqn.
RG614	From 640 Sqn.
RG615	From 640 Sqn.
RG616	From 640 Sqn.
RG655	From 640 Sqn. To 346 Sqn.
RG661	From 640 Sqn. To 347 Sqn.

Heaviest Single Loss

28/29.1.44.   Berlin. 5 Halifaxes. 3 FTR. 2 crashed on return.

578 SQUADRON

Motto: Accuracy   **Code: LK**

Formed on 14 January 1944 from C Flight of 51 Sqn, 578 Squadron began operations six nights later as a standard 4 Group squadron of the line. The war's only Halifax VC was awarded posthumously to the squadron's P/O Cy Barton following the ill-fated Nuremberg operation at the end of March 1944. The squadron's final operation came earlier than for most on 13 March 1945, and it was stood down two days later.

STATIONS

Snaith	14.01.44 to 06.02.44
Burn	06.02.44 to 15.03.45

COMMANDING OFFICERS

Wing Commander D.S.S. Wilkerson DFC	14.01.44 to 23.08.44
Wing Commander A.G.T. James OBE	23.08.44 to 20.02.45
Wing Commander E.L. Hancock	20.02.45 to 15.03.45

AIRCRAFT

Halifax III	01.44 to 03.45

OPERATIONAL RECORD

Operations	Sorties	Aircraft Losses	% Losses
155	2,721	40	1.5
All bombing			

TABLE OF STATISTICS
Out of 32 Halifax squadrons in Bomber Command
(Excluding SOE)

19th highest number of overall Halifax operations in Bomber Command.

9th highest number of Halifax sorties in Bomber Command.

17th equal (with 466 & 640 Sqns) highest number of Halifax operational losses in Bomber Command.

Out of 25 operational squadrons in 4 Group

11th highest number of overall operations in 4 Group.

9th highest number of sorties in 4 Group.

11th equal (with 640 Sqn) highest number of aircraft operational losses in 4 Group.

Out of 15 operational Halifax squadrons in 4 Group

10th highest number of Halifax overall operations in 4 Group.

8th highest number of Halifax sorties in 4 Group.

8th equal (with 466 and 640 Sqns) highest number of aircraft operational losses in 4 Group.

AIRCRAFT HISTORIES

Halifax	From January 1944.
LK756 LK-J	From 51 Sqn. Crashed on approach to Burn on return from Le Mans 14.3.44.
LK794 LK-Q	Crashed in Berkshire when bound for Caen 18.7.44.
LK797 LK-E	Crash-landed at Ryehope Colliery, Sunderland on return from Nuremberg 31.3.44. P/O Cyril Barton awarded a posthumous VC.
LK809 LK-H	To 1652 CU.
LK830 LK-N/O	To 51 Sqn.
LK834 LK-E	Crashed in Yorkshire following a collision with MZ696 (578 Sqn) on return from Bottrop 21.7.44.
LK843 LK-E	From 51 Sqn. Returned to 51 Sqn.
LK846 LK-R	From 51 Sqn. Abandoned over Suffolk when bound for Nieppe 3.8.44.
LL548 LK-C	To 51 Sqn.
LL558 LK-R	FTR Hemmingstedt 7/8.3.45.
LL559 LK-U	Crashed on landing at Bovingdon and collided with NA173 (578 Sqn) on return from Chemnitz 6.3.45.
LL584 LK-E	FTR Gelsenkirchen 11.9.44.
LL585 LK-B	To 1652 CU.
LL600	To 462 Sqn.

LL601	To 462 Sqn.
LV784	From 51 Sqn. Returned to 51 Sqn.
LV815	From 51 Sqn. To 78 Sqn.
LV820	From 51 Sqn. To 78 Sqn.
LV937	To 51 Sqn.
LV952	To 51 Sqn.
LW346 LK-Z	To 76 Sqn.
LW347	From 424 Sqn. Returned to 424 Sqn.
LW348 LK-X	From 51 Sqn. Crashed near Biggin Hill on return from Stuttgart 16.3.44.
LW362	From 51 Sqn. Returned to 51 Sqn.
LW383 LK-K	From 420 Sqn. FTR Rüsselsheim 12/13.8.44.
LW465	From 51 Sqn. To 1652 CU.
LW468 LK-J	From 51 Sqn. FTR Magdeburg 21/22.1.44.
LW469 LK-A	From 51 Sqn. To 77 Sqn.
LW471	From 51 Sqn. To 171 Sqn.
LW472 LK-H	From 51 Sqn. FTR Berlin 24/25.3.44.
LW473 LK-F/B	From 51 Sqn.
LW474 LK-B/Z	From 51 Sqn. To 1663 CU.
LW475 LK-E	From 51 Sqn. To 1652 CU.
LW478 LK-S	From 51 Sqn. Crashed on approach to Silverstone on return from Nuremberg 31.3.44.
LW495 LK-C	From 51 Sqn. Crashed in Yorkshire on return from Stuttgart 16.3.44.
LW496 LK-O	From 51 Sqn. To 1663 CU.
LW503 LK-Z	From 51 Sqn. FTR Schweinfurt 24/25.2.44.
LW508 LK-Y	From 51 Sqn. FTR Berlin 24/25.3.44.
LW538	From 51 Sqn. Returned to 51 Sqn.
LW539	From 51 Sqn. Returned to 51 Sqn.
LW540 LK-R	From 51 Sqn. FTR Frankfurt 22/23.3.44.
LW542 LK-S	From 51 Sqn. FTR Stuttgart 15/16.3.44.
LW543	From 51 Sqn.
LW553 LK-U	From 51 Sqn. FTR Frankfurt 18/19.3.44.
LW556	From 640 Sqn. To 51 Sqn.
LW557 LK-Q	From 51 Sqn. FTR Berlin 15/16.2.44.
LW586 LK-P	FTR Schweinfurt 24/25.2.44.
LW587 LK-V/A	Completed 104 operations.
LW675 LK-B	FTR Amiens 12/13.6.44.
LW678 LK-L	To 77 Sqn.
MZ319	To 51 Sqn.
MZ485	To 51 Sqn.
MZ508 LK-N	FTR Nuremberg 30/31.3.44.
MZ511 LK-M	FTR Bottrop 20/21.7.44.
MZ512 LK-C	FTR Berlin 24/25.3.44.
MZ513 LK-K	FTR Mont Fleury 5/6.6.44.
MZ515 LK-T	
MZ518 LK-O	FTR Düsseldorf 22/23.4.44.

MZ519 LK-U	Crashed in Nottinghamshire on return from Croixdalle 6.7.44.
MZ527 LK-W/D	Completed 105 operations. SOC 22.4.45.
MZ543	
MZ556 LK-P	FTR Bottrop 20/21.7.44.
MZ558	To 190 Sqn.
MZ559 LK-K	Crashed in Yorkshire following a collision with NR241 (51 Sqn) on return from Münster 18.11.44.
MZ560 LK-J	
MZ563 LK-Y	From 51 Sqn. FTR Düsseldorf 22/23.4.44.
MZ572 LK-C	FTR Bottrop 20/21.7.44.
MZ583 LK-Y/S	FTR Dülmen 14/15.1.45.
MZ592 LK-G	FTR Amiens 12/13.6.44.
MZ617 LK-D	FTR Bottrop 20/21.7.44.
MZ619 LK-H	FTR Chateaudun 6/7.6.44.
MZ696 LK-K	Crashed in Yorkshire following a collision with LK834 (578 Sqn) on return from Bottrop 21.7.44.
MZ771	From 102 Sqn. To 51 Sqn.
MZ790	From 102 Sqn. To 51 Sqn.
MZ794	To 51 Sqn.
MZ938	From 102 Sqn. To 51 Sqn.
MZ987 LK-M	Crashed on landing at Wormingford airfield in Essex on return from Essen 12.12.44.
MZ988	To 51 Sqn.
MZ989	To 298 Sqn.
NA123	To 51 Sqn.
NA173 LK-K	From 102 Sqn. Destroyed in collision with LL559 (578 Sqn) on the ground at Bovingdon airfield on return from Chemnitz 6.3.45.
NA501 LK-X	FTR Bingen 22/23.12.44.
NA525	From 77 Sqn. To 51 Sqn.
NA529	From 51 Sqn. To 347 Sqn.
NA568 LK-Q	FTR Gelsenkirchen 11.9.44.
NA569 LK-U	Crashed on landing at Burn on return from Essen 23.10.44.
NA574 LK-D	Crashed in Yorkshire during a fighter affiliation exercise 26.1.45.
NA586	
NA601 LK-M	Crashed on take-off from Marston Moor for transit flight 25.9.44.
NA603 LK-T	FTR Magdeburg 16/17.1.45.
NA604 LK-T	FTR Rüsselsheim 12/13.8.44.
NA605 LK-R	Crashed on take-off from Burn when bound for Bochum 9.10.44.
NA617	To 1652 CU.
NA618 LK-N	FTR Reisholz (Düsseldorf) 20/21.2.45.
NA624 LK-A	
NA670 LK-L	FTR Worms 21/22.2.45.

NA671
NR150 LK-P   FTR Hemmingstedt 8.3.45.
NR191 LK-K   From 192 Sqn. FTR Reisholz ((Düsseldorf)
                  20/21.2.45.
NR193 LK-V   FTR Duisburg 30.11/1.12.44.
NR255   To 51 Sqn.
RG353 LK-E   FTR Worms 21/22.2.45.
RG367 LK-O   FTR Hanover 5/6.1.45.

Heaviest Single Loss

20/21.7.44.   Bottrop. 4 Halifaxes FTR. 2 Halifaxes crashed on
                  return.

640 SQUADRON

(No motto)   **Code: C8**

Formed on 7 January 1944 from C Flight of 158 Squadron, 640 Squadron
operated as a standard heavy bomber unit within 4 Group until war's end.
Operating Hercules-powered Halifaxes throughout, the squadron set a record
by winning the Group bombing trophy five times.

STATIONS

Leconfield   07.01.44 to 07.05.45

COMMANDING OFFICERS

Wing Commander D.J. Eayrs   07.01.44 to 20.04.44
Wing Commander W. Carter DFC   20.04.44 to 04.06.44
Wing Commander M.T. Maw   04.06.44 to 13.08.44
Wing Commander J.M. Viney DFC   14.08.44 to 22.01.45
Wing Commander E.C. Badcoe DFC   22.01.45 to 07.05.45

AIRCRAFT

Halifax III   07.01.44 to 03.45
Halifax VI   03.45 to 07.05.45

OPERATIONAL RECORD

Operations	Sorties	Aircraft Losses	% Losses
170	2,423	40	1.7
All bombing			

TABLE OF STATISTICS
Out of 25 operational squadrons in 4 Group

10th highest number of overall operations in 4 Group.
10th highest number of sorties in 4 Group.
11th equal (with 578 Sqn) highest number of aircraft operational losses in 4
    Group.

Out of 15 operational Halifax squadrons in 4 Group
9th highest number of overall Halifax operations in 4 Group.
10th highest number of Halifax sorties in 4 Group.
8th equal (with 466 & 578 Sqns) highest number of Halifax operational losses
in 4 Group.

AIRCRAFT HISTORIES

Halifax	From January 1944.
HX244 C8-G	From 462 Sqn. Crashed on landing at Leconfield following early return from Gelsenkirchen 13.9.44.
HX356	From 158 Sqn. Returned to 158 Sqn.
LK757 C8-M	Crashed while trying to land at Boscombe Down on return from a tactical support operation in the Caen battle zone.
LK786	From 158 Sqn. To 462 Sqn.
LK793	To 466 Sqn.
LK865 C8-Q	FTR Bourg Leopold 27/28.5.44.
LK866 C8-L	FTR Versailles/Matelot 7/8.6.44.
LL543	To 296 Sqn.
LV823	From 466 Sqn. To 1663 CU.
LV946	From 466 Sqn. To 158 Sqn.
LV948	From 466 Sqn. To 158 Sqn.
LW369	From 158 Sqn. To 466 Sqn.
LW422 C8-R	From 158 Sqn. FTR Leipzig 19/20.2.44.
LW430 C8-T	From 158 Sqn. FTR Berlin 24/25.3.44.
LW434 C8-H	From 158 Sqn. FTR Trappes 2/3.6.44.
LW439 C8-V	Abandoned over Yorkshire on return from Berlin 16.2.44.
LW441 C8-T	From 158 Sqn. FTR Tergnier 10/11.4.44.
LW443	From 158 Sqn. To 346 Sqn.
LW446	From 158 Sqn. To 296 Sqn.
LW459 C8-W	From 158 Sqn. FTR Magdeburg 21/22.1.44.
LW463 C8-A	From 158 Sqn. FTR Sterkrade 16/17.6.44.
LW464 C8-F	From 158 Sqn. FTR Stuttgart 24/25.7.44.
LW477	From 158 Sqn. To 426 Sqn.
LW499 C8-G	From 158 Sqn. FTR Hasselt 12/13.5.44.
LW500 C8-Z	From 158 Sqn. To 466 Sqn and back. FTR Nuremberg 30/31.3.44.
LW502 C8-Y	From 158 Sqn. To 466 Sqn and back. Crashed on take-off from Leconfield when bound for Mimoyecques 27.6.44.
LW505 C8-J	From 158 Sqn. FTR Stuttgart 20/21.2.44.
LW506 C8-X	From 158 Sqn. To 466 Sqn and back. FTR Montzen 27/28.4.44.
LW513 C8-W	From 158 Sqn. Crashed on approach to Leconfield following early return from Berlin 30.1.44.
LW514	From 158 Sqn. To BTU.

LW516	From 466 Sqn.
LW549	
LW550 C8-U	FTR Leipzig 19/20.2.44.
LW554 C8-D	From 158 Sqn. To 1665 CU.
LW555 C8-L	From 158 Sqn. FTR Nuremberg 30/31.3.44.
LW556	From 158 Sqn. Returned to 158 Sqn.
LW585 C8-H	Crashed in Yorkshire on return from Berlin 16.2.44.
LW640 C8-J	FTR Düsseldorf 22/23.4.44.
LW641	To 1658 CU.
LW650 C8-S	Damaged beyond repair during operation to Frankfurt 22/23.3.44.
LW651	To 78 Sqn.
LW652	To 1658 CU.
LW654 C8-D	FTR Dijon 10/11.8.44.
LW673	Crashed on take-off from Leconfield when bound for Gelsenkirchen 13.9.44.
LW722 C8-S	From 466 Sqn. FTR Tergnier 18/19.4.44.
MZ344 C8-H	From 10 Sqn.
MZ345 C8-G	From 10 Sqn. FTR Rüsselsheim 12/13.8.44.
MZ346	From 77 Sqn. To 10 Sqn.
MZ393	From 77 Sqn.
MZ394	
MZ404 C8-G	From 466 Sqn.
MZ406 C8-Q	From 10 Sqn. FTR Scholven-Buer 12.9.44.
MZ407	From 466 Sqn.
MZ408 C8-L	From 158 Sqn. Crashed while trying to land at Leconfield on return from Julich 16.11.44.
MZ409 C8-C	From 10 Sqn. FTR Bochum 4/5.11.44.
MZ492 C8-X	From 158 Sqn. Crashed soon after take-off from Leconfield when bound for Wanne-Eickel 2.2.45.
MZ494 C8-B	From 466 Sqn. FTR Witten 18/19.3.45.
MZ500	To 1658 CU.
MZ510 C8-Q	FTR Berlin 24/25.3.44.
MZ541 C8-U	FTR Trappes 2/3.6.44.
MZ544 C8-Z	To 1658 CU.
MZ561 C8-B	To 1652 CU.
MZ562 C8-A	FTR Hasselt 12/13.5.44.
MZ579 C8-T	FTR Aachen 24/25.5.44.
MZ640 C8-N	Crashed on take-off from Leconfield for training sortie 23.9.44.
MZ675 C8-V	FTR Aachen 24/25.5.44.
MZ677 C8-G	FTR Trappes 2/3.6.44.
MZ678 C8-P	To 77 Sqn.
MZ707	To 1658 CU.
MZ731	To 1658 CU.
MZ733 C8-H	Crashed in Kent on return from Wizernes 28.6.44.
MZ735	From 466 Sqn.
MZ770	From 102 Sqn.

MZ797	From 102 Sqn. To 158 Sqn.
MZ801	From 77 Sqn. SOC 19.4.45.
MZ818	From 158 Sqn.
MZ855 C8-F	From 158 Sqn. FTR Rüsselsheim 12/13.8.44.
MZ856 C8-S	FTR Chemnitz 14/15.2.45.
MZ911	From 158 Sqn.
MZ912 C8-Y	From 158 Sqn. FTR Gelsenkirchen 13.9.44.
MZ925 C8-F	FTR Sterkrade 6.10.44.
MZ926	To 158 Sqn.
MZ930 C8-K	From 158 Sqn. FTR Bochum 4/5.11.44.
MZ939 C8-M	From 466 Sqn. FTR Osnabrück 6/7.12.44.
NA221	To 158 Sqn.
NA222 C8-O	
NA492 C8-X	Crashed while trying to land at Woodbridge on return from Hasselt 13.5.44.
NA521	To 462 Sqn.
NA560 C8-A	FTR Les Landes 9.8.44.
NA563 C8-Y	FTR Dijon 10/11.8.44.
NA573 C8 H	To 1658 CU.
NA578	FTR Watten 25.8.44.
NP923	To 466 Sqn.
NP931 C8-J	From 466 Sqn. Crashed while trying to land at Woodbridge on return from Kamen, possibly as the result of an intruder attack 4.3.45.
NP953 C8-G	FTR Chemnitz 14/15.2.45.
NP958	
NP965 C8-Y	FTR Cologne 2.3.45.
NP996	To 158 Sqn.
NP997	
NR120 C8-M	From 77 Sqn. Ran out of fuel over France on return from Chemnitz and was safely abandoned by its crew 5/6.3.45.
NR204 C8-C	FTR Magdeburg 16/17.1.45.
NR236	
NR237	
NR240	To 158 Sqn.
NR250	To 466 Sqn.
NR286	To 466 Sqn.
NR289	
PN182	To 466 Sqn.
PN184	From 51 Sqn. To 466 Sqn.
PN432	To 462 Sqn.
PN445	To 462 Sqn.
RG348	From 77 Sqn.
RG494	To 466 Sqn.
RG549	To 466 Sqn.
RG552 C8-B	Damaged beyond repair following heavy landing at Leconfield on return from Hamburg 9.4.45.

RG557   To 466 Sqn.
RG559   To 466 Sqn.
RG564 C8-P   From 346 Sqn. FTR Heligoland 18.4.45.
RG565   To 466 Sqn.
RG566   To 466 Sqn.

Abbreviations

A&AEE	Aeroplane and Armaments Experimental Establishment
AA	Anti-Aircraft fire
AACU	Anti-Aircraft Cooperation Unit
AAS	Air Armament School
AASF	Advance Air Striking Force
AAU	Aircraft Assembly Unit
ACM	Air Chief Marshal
ACSEA	Air Command South-East Asia
AFDU	Air Fighting Development Unit
AFEE	Airborne Forces Experimental Establishment
AFTDU	Airborne Forces Tactical Development Unit
AGS	Air Gunners School
AMDP	Air Members for Development and Production
AOC	Air Officer Commanding
AOS	Air Observers School
ASRTU	Air-Sea Rescue Training Unit
ATTDU	Air Transport Tactical Development Unit
AVM	Air Vice-Marshal
BAT	Beam Approach Training
BCBS	Bomber Command Bombing School
BCDU	Bomber Command Development Unit
BCFU	Bomber Command Film Unit
BCIS	Bomber Command Instructors School
BDU	Bombing Development Unit
BSTU	Bomber Support Training Unit
CF	Conversion Flight
CFS	Central Flying School
CGS	Central Gunnery School
C-in-C	Commander-in-Chief
CNS	Central Navigation School
CO	Commanding Officer
CRD	Controller of Research and Development
CU	Conversion Unit
DGRD	Director General for Research and Development
EAAS	Empire Air Armament School

285

EANS	Empire Air Navigation School
ECDU	Electronic Countermeasures Development Unit
ECFS	Empire Central Flying School
ETPS	Empire Test Pilots School
F/L	Flight Lieutenant
Flt	Flight
F/O	Flying Officer
FPP	Ferry Pilots School
F/S	Flight Sergeant
FTR	Failed to Return
FTU	Ferry Training Unit
G/C	Group Captain
Gp	Group
HCU	Heavy Conversion Unit
HGCU	Heavy Glider Conversion Unit
LFS	Lancaster Finishing School
MAC	Mediterranean Air Command
MTU	Mosquito Training Unit
MU	Maintenance Unit
NTU	Navigation Training Unit
OADU	Overseas Aircraft Delivery Unit
OAPU	Overseas Aircraft Preparation Unit
OTU	Operational Training Unit
P/O	Pilot Officer
PTS	Parachute Training School
RAE	Royal Aircraft Establishment
SGR	School of General Reconnaissance
Sgt	Sergeant
SHAEF	Supreme Headquarters Allied Expeditionary Force
SIU	Signals Intelligence Unit
S/L	Squadron Leader
SOC	Struck off Charge
SOE	Special Operations Executive
Sqn	Squadron
TF	Training Flight
TFU	Telecommunications Flying Unit
W/C	Wing Commander
Wg	Wing
WIDU	Wireless Intelligence Development Unit
W/O	Warrant Officer

Bibliography

Air War Over France. Robert Jackson. Ian Allan
Als Deutschlands Dämme Brachen. Helmut Euler. Motor Buch Verlag
At First Sight. Alan B. Webb
Avenging in the Shadows. Ron James. Abington Books
Avro Lancaster. The definitive record. Harry Holmes. Airlife
Avro Manchester. Robert Kirby. Midland Counties Publications
Battle Under the Moon. Jack Currie. Air Data
Battle-Axe Blenheims. Stuart R. Scott. Budding Books
Beam Bombers. Michael Cumming. Sutton Publishing
Beware of the Dog at War. John Ward
Black Swan. Sid Finn. Newton
Bomber Command. Max Hastings. Pan
Bomber Command War Diaries. Martin Middlebrook/Chris Everitt. Viking
Bomber Group at War. Chaz Bowyer. Book Club Associates
Bomber Harris. Charles Messenger. Arms and Armour Press
Bomber Harris. Dudley Saward. Cassel
Bomber Intelligence. W.E. Jones. Midland Counties Publications
Bomber Squadron at War. Andrew Brookes. Ian Allan
Bomber Squadrons at War. Geoff D. Copeman. Sutton Publishing
Bombers Over Berlin. Alan W. Cooper. Patrick Stephens Ltd
Bombing Colours 1937–1973. Michael J.F. Bowyer. Patrick Stephens Ltd
Confounding the Reich. Martin W. Bowman/Tom Cushing. Pen and Sword
    Aviation
De Havilland Mosquito Crash Log. David J. Smith. Midland Counties
    Publications
Despite the Elements. 115 Squadron History. Private
Diary of RAF Pocklington. M. Usherwood. Compaid Graphics
Each Tenacious. A.G. Edgerley. Square One Publications
Feuersturm über Hamburg. Hans Brunswig. Motor Buch Verlag
Forever Strong. Norman Franks. Random Century
From Hull, Hell and Halifax. Chris Blanchett. Midland Counties Publications
Gordon's Tour with Shiny 10. J. Gordon Shirt. Compaid Graphics
Great Raids. Vols 1 and 2. Air Commodore John Searby DSO DFC. Nutshell
    Press
Halifax at War. Brian J. Rapier. Ian Allan
Hamish. The story of a Pathfinder. Group Captain T.G. Mahaddie. Ian Allan

Heavenly Days. Group Captain James Pelly-Fry DSO. Crecy Books
In Brave Company. W.R. Chorley. P.A. Chorley
Joe: The Autobiography of a Trenchard Brat. Wing Commander J. Northrop DSO DFC AFC. Square One Publications
Lancaster at War, Vols 1, 2 & 3. Mike Garbett/Brian Goulding. Ian Allan
Lancaster: The Story of a Famous Bomber. Bruce Robertson. Harleyford Publications Ltd
Lancaster to Berlin. Walter Thompson DFC*. Goodall Publications
Low Attack. John de Lacy Wooldridge DSO DFC and Bar, DFM. Crecy
Massacre Over the Marne. Oliver Clutton-Brock. Patrick Stephens Ltd
Master Airman. Alan Bramson. Airlife
Melbourne Ten. Brian J. Rapier. Air Museum Publications (York) Ltd
Mission Completed. Sir Basil Embry. Four Square Books
Mosquito. C. Martin Sharp/Michael J.F. Bowyer. Crecy
Night Fighter. C.F. Rawnsley/Robert Wright. Collins
Night Flyer. Squadron Leader Lewis Brandon DSO DFC. Goodall Publications
Night Intruder. Jeremy Howard-Williams. Purnell Book Services
No Moon Tonight. Don Charlwood. Goodall Publications
On The Wings Of The Morning. RAF Bottesford 1941–45. Vincent Holyoak. Privately published
On Wings of War. A history of 166 Squadron. Jim Wright. 166 Squadron Association
Only Owls and Bloody Fools Fly At Night. Group Captain Tom Sawyer DFC. Goodall Publications
Pathfinder. AVM D.C.T. Bennett. Goodall Publications
Pathfinder Force. Gordon Musgrove. MacDonald and Janes
Reap the Whirlwind. Dunmore and Carter. Crecy
Royal Air Force Aircraft Serial Numbers. All volumes. Air-Britain
Royal Air Force Bomber Command Losses. Vols 1, 2, 3, 4, 5 and 6. W.R. Chorley. Midland Counties Publications
Silksheen. Geoff D. Copeman. Midland Counties Publications
Snaith Days. K.S. Ford. Compaid Graphics
Start im Morgengrauen. Werner Girbig. Motor Buch Verlag
Stirling Wings. Jonathon Falconer. Alan Sutton Publications
Strike Hard. A bomber airfield at war. John B. Hilling. Alan Sutton Publishing
Sweeping the Skies. David Gunby. Pentland Press
The Avro Lancaster. Francis K. Mason. Aston Publications
The Berlin Raids. Martin Middlebrook. Viking Press
The Dambusters Raid. John Sweetman. Arms and Armour Press
The Halifax File. Air-Britain
The Hampden File. Harry Moyle. Air-Britain
The Handley Page Halifax. K.A. Merrick. Aston Press
The Hornets' Nest. History of 100 Squadron RAF 1917–1994. Arthur White. Square One Publications
The Lancaster File. J.J. Halley. Air-Britain.

The Other Battle. Peter Hinchliffe. Airlife
The Pendulum and the Scythe. Ken Marshall. Air Research Publications
The Squadrons of the Royal Air Force. James J. Halley. Air-Britain
The Starkey Sacrifice. Michael Cumming. Sutton Publishing Ltd
The Stirling Bomber. Michael J.F. Bowyer. Faber
The Stirling File. Bryce Gomersall. Air-Britain
The Wellington Bomber. Chaz Bowyer. William Kimber
The Whitley File. R.N. Roberts. Air-Britain
They Led the Way. Michael P. Wadsworth. Highgate
To See The Dawn Breaking. W.R. Chorley. Compaid Graphics
Valiant Wings. Norman Franks. Crecy
Wellington: The Geodetic Giant. Martin Bowman. Airlife
White Rose Base. Brian J. Rapier. Aero Litho Company (Lincoln) Ltd
Wings of Night. Alexander Hamilton. Crecy
2 Group RAF: A Complete History. Michael J.F. Bowyer. Crecy
101 Squadron. Special Operations. Richard Alexander
207 Squadron RAF Langar 1942–43. Barry Goodwin/Raymond Glynne-
    Owen. Quacks Books
408 Squadron History. The Hangar Bookshelf. Canada

Most of the figures used in the statistics section of this work have been drawn from the *Bomber Command War Diaries* by Martin Middlebrook and Chris Everitt, and I am indebted to Martin Middlebrook for allowing me to use them.

Other Titles
by Chris Ward

Dambusters, The Definitive History. Red Kite, 2003

3 Group Bomber Command. Pen & Sword, 2008

5 Group Bomber Command. Pen & Sword, 2007

6 Group Bomber Command. Pen & Sword, 2009

Dambuster Crash Sites. Pen & Sword, 2008

Dambusters. The Forging of a Legend. Pen & Sword, 2009

Images of War. 617 Dambuster Squadron at War. Pen & Sword, 2009